THE FUTURE OF HEGEL

'. . . nothing will ever absolve us from following step by step, page by page, the extraordinary trajectory of *The Future of Hegel* . . . I once again urge all to read this book.' *Jacques Derrida*

The Future of Hegel is one of the most important recent books on Georg Wilhelm Friedrich Hegel, a philosopher who has had a crucial impact on the shape of Continental philosophy. Published here in English for the first time, it includes a substantial preface by Jacques Derrida in which he explores the themes and conclusions of Malabou's book.

The Future of Hegel: Plasticity, Temporality and Dialectic restores Hegel's rich and complex concepts of time and temporality to contemporary philosophy. It examines Hegel's concept of time, relating it to perennial topics in philosophy such as substance, accident and the identity of the subject. Catherine Malabou also contrasts her account of Hegelian temporality with the interpretation given by Heidegger in *Being and Time*, arguing that it is the concept of 'plasticity' that best describes Hegel's theory of temporality.

The Future of Hegel also develops Hegel's preoccupation with the history of Greek thought and Christianity and explores the role of theology in Hegel's thought.

Essential reading for those interested in Hegel and contemporary Continental philosophy, *The Future of Hegel* will also be fascinating to those interested in the ideas of Heidegger and Derrida.

Catherine Malabou is Professor of Philosophy at the University of Paris X, Nanterre.

Translated by Lisabeth During.

THE FUTURE OF HEGEL

Plasticity, Temporality and Dialectic

Catherine Malabou

Translated by Lisabeth During

Translation funded by Éditions Leo Scheer

LONDON AND NEW YORK

First published in French as *L'Avenir de Hegel*

First published in English 2005
by Routledge
2 Park Square, Milton Park, Abingdon,
Oxfordshire, OX14 4RN

Simultaneously published in the USA and Canada
by Routledge
270 Madison Ave, New York, NY 10016

Routledge is an imprint of the Taylor & Francis Group

Reprinted 2009

Preface by Jacques Derrida, first published in French as 'Le temps des adieux: Heidegger (lu par) Hegel (lu par) Malabou' in *Revue Philosophique* © PUF 1998; this translation © Routledge 2005

Typeset in Times by
Florence Production Ltd, Stoodleigh, Devon

British Library Cataloguing in Publication Data
A catalogue record for this book is available
from the British Library

Library of Congress Cataloging in Publication Data
Malabou, Catherine.
[Avenir de Hegel. English]
The future of Hegel : plasticity, temporality, and dialectic /
Catherine Malabou ; translated by Lisabeth During.
p. cm.
1. Hegel, Georg Wilhelm Friedrich, 1770–1831 – Criticism and interpretation. 2. Hegel, Georg Wilhelm Friedrich, 1770–1831. – Contributions in the concept of time. 3. Hegel, Georg Wilhelm Friedrich, 1770–1831. – Contributions in the concept of dialectic. I. Title.
B2948.M26313 2004
193–dc22 200400094

ISBN 0–415–28720–0 (hbk)
ISBN 0–415–28721–9 (pbk)

ISBN 978–0–415–28720–3 (hbk)
ISBN 978–0–415–28721–0 (pbk)

CONTENTS

PREFACE BY JACQUES DERRIDA

A time for farewells: Heidegger (read by) Hegel (read by) Malabou[1]

The future, tell me, the future would then have a history.

Yes, if we are to believe *The Future of Hegel*. And also time, time itself would have a history. And history then, history would also have a history, a singular history setting the stage for the protagonists of a philosophical gigantomachia already engaged over questions like: 'What *is* history?', 'What *is* time', 'What *is* the future?', 'What is the authority of 'What *is* . . .' in all of these questions?', 'And how may we reflect on the *being* of this 'is' or on the present tense working here?', etc.

The Future of Hegel! There is, to begin with, the art of the title. This would be the first entitlement to our admiration. If the art of the title is a grand art, that is because it is double: it is at once a conceptual and a plastic art, an art which gives one form and one form only, the most economical, while at the same time, in order to *cease* itself, grasps and receives, in two nouns and four words, *The Future of Hegel*, the immensity of *three questions*. Nothing less, in fact, than the heart of three redoubtable questions. The very economy of plasticity can only *give* a form to the title if *at the same time* (and I purposefully say *at the same time*, for this expression shall henceforth never leave us) it grasps its form, and can only grasp it if *at the same time* it receives it from a final or destinal unity. For what will be shown is that these three questions, in the end, only shape and arrange themselves into one.

I understand. First question, then: Does Hegel have a future? Or again, does he remain, as so many current philosophers commonly believe, yes, too commonly, in their classes, courses where they 'go through' the history of philosophy, a thinker of the past or a simple passé thinker?

Certainly, but at once, a second question emerges from the fold of the first. A question already implied in the first and which displaces its accent from the *future* to what *is to be had*: Does Hegel, the philosopher, *have* a future, in the sense of: 'has he (*thought*) the future? Will he have had a *concept* of the future?' Is there a future, or a place for the future according to his vision and in his philosophy? Will he have thought the future *as such*?

We must listen to and contest those who believed this could be doubted: currently and commonly, this suspicion is in the air, and it rests upon a certain trend of the day, a certain current or movement of time. For the answer to these two initial questions will turn an entire current of recent thought backwards. Yes, Hegel is a thinker of the future. Yes, he has a future for he has also, contrarily to what we may believe, thought the future, its being, the possibility and the necessity of what we suppose may be recognized under this noun, the future, a noun which also bears in French a certain verbal form, that which is *to come*. Hence, inevitable but still astonishing, precisely where we see it coming without ever seeing it come, the third question, which we still may consider as the same question, is at the same time the most grave and difficult. It hauls and pulls us away from what could seem to resemble a debate on a towering ancestor between philosophers or historians of philosophy: in what way does the possibility of the *future in general* depend on the future of *Hegel*, on the future *promised to* this thinker as well as on the future *thought by* this thinker? Such is the scope of this book, such is what is at stake in this book, and its most troubling risk: will there and can there be a future after the supposed end of history, beyond this *scene* or '*topos*' called 'absolute knowledge'? Beyond a certain interpretation or presentation of time in general? And what may it be? Can the future, what is to come, be thought, be conceived or be announced by the question 'what is . . .' or even, more generally, by what is called and what we may call a 'question'? And in what way would all of these phrases here formed belong to the tradition, in what way do they come from the tradition, and furthermore, do they belong to the future of Hegel's name? Or to the interpretation associated to his heritage?

To salute a great book, should or would we speak henceforth of an event?

Yes, in reading *The Future of Hegel*, it would be tempting to do so, it would be a strong temptation to salute this work while endlessly urging it to help us think what it means to *salute* and what is meant by this strange word '*salutation*' (greeting, acknowledgment, welcome, but also, salvation, redemption, deliverance, liberation . . .). It remains extremely difficult to understand exactly what is meant and what we mean to say when we utter 'salutations' to another, for example when the moment comes to say 'goodbye' or 'farewell', but also, sometimes, in the Midi, when the other appears in the middle of the day ('hello!', 'good day!', 'greetings and salutations!' or 'farewell and adieu!'[2]). Is it a word, this word 'salutation', like this other word 'farewell' or even 'adieu'? Are these words or are they something like the withholding of a phrase, a wish or a prayer ('be well!', farewell!', 'be saved!', 'may your salvation, health or redemption be secured and maintained!', 'be with God', etc.), the time of a calling, something like an appeal, henceforth suspended amid more than one simple meaning, at the very moment of an encounter or of a separation? However, a certain reserve or distance holds us back from saluting or hailing a book too loudly or too soon: but also, whether this is warranted or not, there is the belief that only the future will have decided, what *will have been* this book and if it *will have sealed* such an event. And above all, for this is the incontestable lesson of *The Future of Hegel*, one should not, ever, treat this word 'event' too lightly. This word, one should not 'see it come' into view too quickly. One should not too hastily apply it to the demonstration here put forth by Catherine Malabou. At the turbulent and paradoxical heart of this book, which projects nothing less than an unheard history, a history of time as a 'history of the future',[3] and hence as a history of the 'event', there lies a powerful demonstration. It comes to itself and is formed precisely from this fold: as soon as an idea of the event is advanced, a discourse or a text on the event is proposed, and at the very moment when a history of the event is designated, there is, already, creation and formation of *an* event.

How may we anticipate the formation of this form? What does it *announce* in itself? What does one see coming in this *annunciation*? The chance of this expression, 'to see (what is) coming',[4] will traverse the enigma of this book. It seems to be linked to some sort of *equivocacy*, but in truth it remains profoundly dialectic, in a sense where the dialectical here thought is thought over, re-thought, from what could resemble a fortuitous chance. We need time and time again to meditate this quasi-automatic alliance between chance and necessity, between accident and essence. Catherine Malabou gives all its chances to this chance of and in the idiom itself, and thus claims all that is announced from another idiom, following Hegel's 'imperative to philosophize in one's idiom'.[5] Literally making this Hegelian imperative her own, following it and pursuing its commandment in her own language, French, at the very point where it commands the literality of the letter and to the point where it remains almost untranslatable, Catherine Malabou *invents* an idiom. This really means she *recovers* and brings to light, she brings about and retrieves, from a place where it was never really abandoned but where something like a 'farewell' had somehow banished it, dismissing it without ever giving it its leave, the double and contradictory sense of this strange French expression 'to see (what is) coming' ('*voir venir*'). 'To see (what is) coming' is to anticipate, to foresee, to presage, to project; it is to expect what is coming; but it is also to let what is coming come or to let oneself be surprised by the unexpected, by the sudden appearance of what is un-awaited. 'To see (what is) coming' means *at the same time* to anticipate and to let oneself be surprised, to bear *and, at the same time*, I mean precisely *at the same time*, *not to* bear the unexpected. In other words, the surprise *in* what is coming, the event *of* what is coming: the future.

This 'goodbye', this 'until we meet again', which you have just been talking about, and which I don't read as a farewell, an adieu or a salutation which marks an eternal separation; she, it seems to me, does not talk about it. Now, beyond the fact that this 'to meet again' intrigues me, in so far as it seems to appeal to a 'seeing', a 'seeing of what is coming', together with all the equivocal and dialectical character which you bring to this phrase, I wonder what is the scene of this exile or of this slumber. I wonder where is to be found, to take up your expression, this 'leave'. In what sense has the double meaning of 'to see (what is) coming' been banished, retreated or taken its leave? Which is the scene of this goodbye to which, without ever having said farewell, we are now returning? Would it not be some sort of unconscious? Would it not be some sort of cunning performed by the unconscious (here understood as the unconscious proper to language) of which Freud said both that it renounces nothing and that we must reckon with it when we attempt to interpret the 'contradictory meanings' of the celebrated 'primal words'? An unconscious about which he even said, rightfully so or not, that it remains indifferent both to logical contradiction and to temporality? In any case, to temporality understood as that which is constituted within the ego of a phenomenological consciousness or as that which is constructed by the self-relation of *Dasein*, that is, by the '*mineness*' (*Jemeinigkeit*) proper to *Dasein*.

We shall speak again of these differences between goodbye and farewell, that is, between all of *these farewells*. Each in its proper time, and it will always be at that very time when we shall have to say 'goodbye' or 'farewell'. Freud? Yes, if this book never names him *per se*, everything in it seems to address him, point by point, in each and every word, almost as if he was already participating in a major and seriously worked out explication. There is so much more to be learned here about the Freudian discourse on life and death, and thus on so many modalities of Freud's analysis, than in a host of books explicitly psychoanalytical.

I shall continue to speak a little while longer. Not so much because I wish to put forth a sort of meta-discursive monologue, but rather in order to let myself be caught or trapped in the snares of language and to take on a certain risk here involved, the risk of *my* idiom. I will have to do this while always remaining deliberately *on the edge* of this book. After all, what we are doing here is to put forth an invitation, an invitation to read a book too rich in its content to be explained, paraphrased or analysed in a few pages. *The Future of Hegel* bears such a strong relationship to its own writing and its own idiom that it constitutes on its own a kind of philosophical *œuvre*. That is, at least, what I wish here to show: it is a unique *œuvre* on which any meta-linguistic dialogue very quickly experiences its own limitations and its own simulated nature. This experience, as it unfolds, we shall make our own.

By 'reinventing' an idiom, by coining this phrase 'to see (what is) coming', by revealing the power and the virtual economy of its 'unconscious', if you like, and by making it the organizational figure of an immense problematic, Malabou's strategy, as I see it, achieves three feats in one: (1) She transposes or translates the Hegelian imperative ('to philosophize in one's idiom') thus displacing it into the history of French language and philosophy. (2) She puts into practice – and thus to the test – this other Hegelian motif: the very possibility, or chance, of a *speculative* language, or rather, of inserting the *speculative* in language when language measures itself to the very capacity of condensing two contradictory meanings in one single syntagm. Two antinomical meanings *at the same time* concentrated in one and the same verbal formation (verbal, again, in a double sense: consisting of two words and two verbs: '*to see (what is) coming*'). The Hegelian *Aufhebung* is not only an example of this possibility: it is its very concept. Between the two contradictory senses of 'to see (what is) coming' there is an *Aufhebung*, or a *sublation*, of one meaning into its other. (3) Finally, the factor, the modality, that demonstrates this mobile and self-contradictory ambiguity of 'to see (what is) coming', is its *plasticity*. The 'to see (what is) coming' is plastic. Before inquiring into the immense breadth of this conceptual word, *plasticity*, before interrogating the very plasticity of this conceptual word which is what it states and states what it is, which is precisely what it thinks and reflects, before specifying its very opportunity which is discovered and offered by Malabou's philosophical writing, we should remark that plasticity is not a secondary concept, another concept which, conjoined with the expression 'to see (what is) coming', would form a sort of hermeneutical couple in *The Future of Hegel*. It is the same concept in its differentiating and determinating process. Because of its own dialectical self-contradiction and mobility, 'to see (what is) coming' is itself a plastic concept, it allows us to see coming plasticity itself. Since its self-interrelating with its own difference also passes through the *Aufhebung*, we would almost be tempted to recognize in it the Hegelian concept, the very concept itself, the concept of the concept. In any case, without going too fast or too far at the moment, we should recall that it is in order to define this expression 'to see (what is) coming', the future and the structure of its anticipation or again the Hegelian subjectivity, that the *Introduction* of this book associates the dialectical, time and plasticity. And since the Hegelian subjectivity, the Hegelian concept of subjectivity, incorporates the whole and entire history of *being-subject*, the becoming-subject of all subjectivity, what must be thought here is the very subjectivity of the subject and what happens to the subject, that is, the experience which exposes a subject to what comes to it, to what happens to it, to what it 'sees coming', in the double sense of what can be anticipated and what remains impossible to anticipate. And what happens to the subject who 'sees coming' will be for it as essential as accidental, as essential as the necessity of its *telos*, as accidental as an unanticipated accident. At the heart of Malabou's thought, that is of a certain non-empiricist idea of contingence or of a certain responsible empiricism with renewed radicality, we will always find the same commitment: the 'becoming essential of accident' and, *at once, at the same time and in the same time*, the 'becoming accidental of essence'. The paradox or formal *aporia* here raised is revealed by the dialectical plasticity or the self-contradiction in the expression 'to see (what is) coming'. Towards the end of the book, this feature will become more and more apparent, especially in the discussion of Hegel's profound repetition of the Aristotelian notion of *automatos* or *automatismos*, the self-being of that which necessarily moves in and of itself (*aus sich selbst*), but also, *at the same time*, the self-being of what happens in and of itself by chance or by accident.[6] Without both, without the conjunction of the essential or teleological necessity and, *at the same time*, of the aleatory accident, of the 'may-be' inherent in contingence, no event would or could ever come forth or happen. This is where we must return, to this 'may-be' or to this 'perhaps', for it is without doubt the most difficult and most audacious thesis of this book. The syntagm *at the same time*, which I shall underline again in the following passage, declares *at the same time* the conceptual indissociability and a singular synchrony, the one of temporality itself together with the transformation of a form – at once spatial and conceptual. 'At the same time' emphasizes the power of language, others would say, the genius inscribed in such and such *play* with language, the capacity or the aptitude to conjugate in itself two contradictory meanings at the same time, in the same stroke, within the same time, all at once and in one time. More than one time at the same time – and these times (*fois, feiz*, *vices*) are also successions of strokes, they are all 'plays'.

> The dialectical composition of such concepts as the 'future', 'plasticity', and 'temporality' form the *anticipatory structure* operating within subjectivity itself as Hegel conceived it. To distinguish this structure from the future as it is ordinarily understood, we will name this structure 'to see (what is) coming', obeying Hegel's injunction to philosophize in one's idiom. '*Voir venir*' in French means to wait, while, as is prudent, observing how events are developing. But it *also* [I emphasize, J.D.] suggests that there are intentions and plans of other people which must be probed and guessed at. It is an expression that can thus refer at *one and the same time* [I emphasize again, J.D.], to the state of 'being sure of what is coming' and of 'not knowing what is coming'. It is on this account that 'to see (what is) coming' can represent that interplay, within Hegelian philosophy, of *teleological necessity* and *surprise*.
> (p. 13)

This 'interplay' of necessity and of surprise does not only happen once in language, as if by chance, as if it resulted from a simple accident of and in the idiom. Language must be able to play, there must be within it the very display of its aptitude to play, the habit of conjugating, and of holding in itself and for itself, in the very body of its syntax and of its lexicon, the constant mark of this transformation, something like the permanent *habitus* of this alteration. In other words, it is of the essence of language, of what we call an idiom or a dialect,[7] that its vocation be dialectical or, if one prefers, that its calling be essentially plastic. The idiom itself must be a subject capable of 'seeing what is coming'. In both cases, in the very alternative proper to the 'at the same time', all depends on the coming, if I may say, of 'what comes' and of what we are sure is coming as if 'what will come', and of what slips away from being seen, from what is to be had and from what is to be known. It is what comes that is here the issue, and hence the event or the advent, of invention or of adventure. Where it comes to the subject and where the subject, the essence of the subject comes to itself and sees itself come. The question becomes then, and will remain obscure: how can (and may we) see *ourselves* coming to *ourselves*, to the double meaning of 'to see (what is) coming'? What is the *ipseity* of this 'self' who sees itself come, and hence, constitutes itself *at the same time* in the teleological development of itself and in absolute surprise? For, let us say it simply: there would, without the future, be no more history, and there would be no more future, no event to come, without the very possibility of an absolute surprise (that is, without this 'to see (what is) coming' blind to all anticipation); but there would also be no future, no future as such, no novelty at all, without some sort of historical link, memory, retention or tradition, thus without some sort of synthesis. This synthesis has already claimed the future anterior and the 'to see (what is) coming' of anticipation, it has already called for the teleological structure which must dampen surprise itself or novelty in order to make it possible: as if it were a surprise *without* surprise. A continual transformation and radical interruption, a process and an explosion, plasticity and gelignite. But also *physis* and *techné*, nature and culture, nature and the technological, nature and art, if you like: on the one hand, the natural or organic transformation of living forms, their own plasticity and, on the other hand, plastic artificiality and art, and the synthetic, indeed prosthetic technology of 'plastic matter'. Such would be, at the heart of the 'to see (what is) coming', the two antithetical forms of the plastic and the plasticity of these two contradictory forms.

Once again, let us start again. This book sculpts a multiplicity, both powerful and organized, this book formulates thousands of impatient, troubled and anxious questions on what the word 'annunciation' can mean in the various modalities of prophecy, of prevision, of information or of prediction, of prefiguration, of protention, all within the horizon of phenomenology or of ontology, on what can be meant by the expression 'to see (what is) coming', precisely, when we are more or less 'sure of what is coming'; but it also asks, this book, at the same time, what it can mean for there to be an interruption of this 'to see (what is) coming' by *its* other, the 'to see (what is) coming' which does not know what is coming. This book can be read as a meditation on what could mean a form, a process of formation or a formalization of form, or its very plasticity, which corresponds to the first instance of the expression 'to see (what is) coming'. But it can also be read as an interruption of this formative or informational plasticity by the irruption or the explosion of some sort of gelignite dynamite, a meditation, we might say, on 'to see (what is) coming' that which could never be seen or known, on what it could mean 'to see (what is) coming' as an absolute surprise or an unpredictable accident. What is here announced, we may have already seen it, is not exactly a question of posterity, but rather the question of the future, the question of the condition, if we may say so, of what is to come in itself, of what comes in the event which is coming, of everything which presents itself or which absents itself in the word or the experience of 'to come'.

Here, then, a work which is from one end to the other obsessed by this same question: what can it possibly mean this 'coming', this 'arriving', and most of all, this '*to see (what is) coming*' and thus also, 'being born', appearing', and even before 'being born' and 'appearing', what can it possibly mean to 'take', to 'conceive', 'to take or give a form', to 'arrive' and to 'arrive onto oneself''? And why does this matrix of questions bring us back or lead us to the question of plasticity? To the plasticity of a form, of course, to the plasticity of another form, to the plasticity of a form involved in its process of formation, to the plasticity of the unformed, to the plasticity of 'plastic matter', but also to the plasticity of gelignite, of what can at any time explode or threaten to explode, for example, the self-identity of the present? Yes, it is the expression 'to see (what is) coming' and plasticity, both thought together, as if they were inseparably intertwined, as if everything we needed to say could and would be said in these few words, that would be the genius of this book: it can launch a real event in the world of thought by inventing the very reinvention of one, two or three words, to 'see (what is) coming' and 'plasticity', in order to think in both their common or shared possibility and in order to recall their very presence not only in one but in more than one language. At the philosophical frontier between many languages, by putting to the test a desire for a speculative translation.

If I understand correctly, what you find admirable in this book is that, at the same time, it is a gift of idioms and a particular type of philosophical writing.

Yes, and also, which is extremely rare, the art of cultivating something like a performative writing of which the force be philosophical or, better, reflexive: reflecting upon the very possibility of the philosophical. Without ever surrendering to aestheticism, without ever striving for 'stylistic effects', this book achieves a sober beauty which I would want to call plastic, precisely where it takes *shape*, the same *shape*, singular and unique, as the *thought* of plasticity, and the European genealogy of this concept. *The Future of Hegel* opens precisely the way to a thought of the corporeal, it engages it in the very manner plasticity is treated, plasticity which 'works on and within the body of the systematic exposition' (p. 18).[8] Here, in the very same horizon as this problematic, what is being discussed is plasticity *as a schema* in Hegel. Since Being 'schematizes itself', empirical or sensuous existence is not to be dissociated from the movement and the unity of the concept. Therefore, it has the right to demand a systematic exposition of its own. The system is thus its scene, its home, and hence the very scene or home of the sensuous body. This is one of the strategic justifications, we shall return to it, which Malabou offers for the extensive and systematic treatment of a notion which, in the end, appears only very rarely, and in a self-contained manner, within the Hegelian corpus, never at its heart, or at least not at first glance. (A possible title for an imaginary chapter: *on body and corpus*.) Malabou has just called it the *schematization of being* in Hegel, in the *Phenomenology of Spirit*: 'The singular individual is, on its own terms, the transition of the category from its concept into external reality: it is the pure schema itself.'[9]

Then, in order to justify her choice, and the privilege bestowed to this motif, Malabou connects it to what she names the 'motor' of a 'strategy' (motif or motor, word or concept, concept of a schematization movement, this is what would be plasticity):

> Being schematizes itself, and the unification of the concept with empirical existence cannot be explained by anything external to the system. The scarcity of the references to the concept of plasticity is thus evidence of its distinct mode of presence, which is that of the originary synthesis, maintained only in the interval between presence and absence. It is for this reason, because plasticity works *on and within the body* of the systematic exposition, without ever extending above it or over determining it, that it is revealed as the concept capable of accounting for the incarnation, or the incorporation, of spirit.[10]

Following the rich and significant examples which Malabou offers from the first words of her *Introduction* (which also refers to Hegel's *Aesthetics*, the *Lectures on the Philosophy of History*, the *Lectures on the History of Philosophy*, as well as to the Prefaces of the *Phenomenology of Spirit* and of the *Science of Logic*), we cannot help sensing the many occurrences of this term, occurrences which are all clearly symptomatic. Perhaps neglected, but wrongly so, and in this regard *The Future of Hegel* is inaugural. Although Malabou does not linger on this, it seems to us (for this is the hypothesis I would like to suggest here) that the major philosophical and strategic decision of her book consists in emphasizing the Hegelian *schema*, the Hegelian notion of a *schema*, that is, the Hegelian thesis which holds that being *schematizes itself*. (Being or God, one or the other, either one – God who thus sees himself coming while leaving, departing and separating *himself from himself*, all the while, '*farewelling himself*', but let us not anticipate what we see here coming.)

The concept gives itself or receives *from itself* its own sensuous figures, its own rational imagination, its own intellectual intuition, etc. This giving and receiving, this giving to oneself to receive, which is the very process of plasticity, the very movement of being as becoming-plastic, this would be the speculative and reflexive power of the Hegelian concept. The Hegelian concept assimilates itself and exceeds in itself the opposition between giving and receiving, between giving and taking. It is here that we could find its ontological plasticity, at once its essence and its schema, the historical schematization of its being. This schematization is entirely historical, and the word used to speak of it, here, is a Greek word. For, if to 'see (what is) coming' is a French idiom with Latin roots, 'plastic' is before all and initially Greek. This word embraces deeply in its memory, if we may say so, keeps and holds in the immense stratification of an invisible archive, a privileged relationship to art, the 'very birthplace of plasticity' (p. 8);[11] it penetrates and informs, hence, if not all European languages, but certainly the Romance, the Slavic, Germanic and English languages. The name of the philosophical form of this dual penetration proper to plasticity, that is to say, the form which receives just as much as it gives, this *plastic* form, is nothing but that enigmatic *betwixt and between* called a *schema*. It is, between Kant and Hegel, the scene of so many fundamental questions and debates, some explicit, some less so, questions and debates which have, in any case, shaped (I could hardly say here *schematized*) a philosophical legacy far greater than us all.

The very invention of *The Future of Hegel* has occurred, among so many things (for we are still only on the edge of this book), at the philosophical intersection between the expression 'to see (what is) coming' and *plasticity*, precisely where each of these two 'terms' dialectically *conjugate telos and surprise*, anticipation *and* eruption, metamorphosis *and* absolute explosion. To invent, and most particularly understanding invention as an event, means here to rediscover what was there without being there, both in language and in philosophy; it is a question of finding, yes, but of finding for the first time what was always there and what had always been there, to find again, almost to re-find, something in its (contradictory) fusion and in its (atomic) fission where it had never before been seen, to invent it almost as one would invent a bomb, but to discover it also almost like the excessively obvious evidence of a purloined letter: never seen, never known, never waited on or for, never expected as such, while all the while only expecting it and not expecting anything else but it, the unexpected ('*Plasticity*' will be presented as the 'unforeseen of Hegelian philosophy'[12]). The letter will have been *there*, in other words, have been *truly* there in truth, and if we reflect on this and read carefully what it means, it will have been there *everywhere*, everywhere where plasticity itself, everywhere where the lexicon and the concept of plasticity operates within the moments and the corpus of the history of philosophy, even before Aristotle and after Hegel, but especially in those towering figures, at the intersection of philosophy and science, of genetics and of politics, in short, at the very centre of the *Encyclopedia*. To invent and to formulate invention as an event, in this case, is to find for the very first time, and to show or demonstrate what is there to be found within the family, the genealogy, the resources of a lexicon, and by this gesture, to institute, in a manner which shall never again be effacable, the modality in which words become concepts and confirm thereby their theoretical legitimacy. It is, in other words, formulating the scene of an idiom as a philosophical *topos* through which we will have to pass hereafter. Such words which seemed lost, hidden away in language, almost asleep in language, but asleep with one eye open, here they appear leaping into the centre of the stage, organizing and playing a lively and vigilant role. These words are almost like animals. A profound thought or conception of animal life animates this entire book. It almost gives it its breath. Such ephemeral meanings, such auxiliary predicates or attributes which seem barely determinable, in so far as they are spoken of as neither determinate nor indeterminate, but plastic, and 'seen in their coming', actually arrive at the highest position and maturity of major concepts. It is into this very conceptual scene that we are called, to which we are already indebted, without however knowing the extent of our debt but, more than ever today, in debt towards it. Here, then, is a rare book, an uncommon, unusual, and ambitious book which meets the importance of its ambitions to the fullest and which, from its inherent doubleness, from the pair of concepts it puts forth, the two families of words it presents, words which have been largely invisible and unthought – 'to see (what is) coming' and 'plasticity' – takes on the difficult task of rethinking precisely what constitutes the *event-ality* of the event: what comes in the event, what comes forth or comes again in an event, what can be seen as coming in what comes and thus what can be seen as coming in the future itself – at the same time, always, in both senses of the expression, that is between teleological anticipation and the explosive surprise.

But again, once again, why Hegel? Why '*The Future of Hegel*'? And what does plasticity or what does the expression 'to see (what is) coming', or again, what does the inherent plasticity of the expression 'to see (what is) coming', have to do with Hegel's time?

The question cannot be limited or restricted to what one could or would want normally to categorize or include simply in the history of philosophy, even though, it must be said, Catherine Malabou treats this history with great rigour and unquestionable attention. No, nothing in the world can be in this way determined or pre-determined, for almost two centuries, whether or not we are aware of it or know about it (and in general we are aware of it, or believe we are aware of it), that does not entertain some sort of relation with the living tradition embodied by Hegel. It is simply not enough to recall the names of Marx and Heidegger, or the themes of the 'end of history', of 'absolute knowledge', of the 'dialectic', of the *ends* of this and the *ends* of that, the 'death of God', the 'death of Man', etc. These terms and themes are Hegel's terms, we always finish by finding Hegel at the very origin of all these thematized or schematized *ends*. We are all the inheritors or the descendants of Marx, of Heidegger, and a few others, and we often, perhaps always, have lived, for many decades, in the reassuring certainty that the Hegelian legacy is over and done with. Even though we may always and do always recognize the unequalled power and force of this thought, we always maintain that this thought has assigned to itself its own fate, which, as every fate, belongs to the past, to what already has passed (fate is precisely being already a part of the past, of what is passed and of what has passed away in everything that comes or could come). More profoundly, Hegel's thought would have assigned to itself this final fatefulness of fate, this very finality of the end and of what remains final, of which the only temporal determination is the 'past', what 'has already passed away'. It is in this sense, simply because it has thought time itself, to have it in this manner thought about time, that Hegel's thought would have, above all, renounced any future for itself as all future itself. This is, at least, the common belief or the widespread interpretation, in truth the accusation which Malabou re-interrogates and re-questions to submit it, first of all, to an intractable and obstinate trial. With as much acerbity as patience, Malabou first reconstitutes, in all of its breadth and range, the history of this interpretation, the history of an interpretation which has become dominant, the history of its hegemonic-becoming. Having become hegemonic, almost held as a common or current currency, held as the only accredited interpretation, it becomes something like our universal coin. This interpretation, as a universal coin, is legal tender everywhere and universally. Why here insist on this image, an image of a universal currency which could *flow* everywhere? And all the while referring to Heidegger, who is, as we know, the one responsible for coining this interpretation in its most striking and most profound way. It is he, Heidegger, who combines the two interpretations of Hegelian temporality, one according to which time has always 'passed' (and is thus without any future) and the other, which cannot be dissociated from the first almost as its own premiss, according to which the Hegelian concept of time is the current or ordinary (which is, as we know, the current translation of the German word *vulgär*)[13] way one understands time, for it refers to the image of a 'course of time' (*Lauf der Zeit*). Let us start with the second of these interpretations: 'Hegel's concept of time presents the most radical way in which the vulgar understanding of time (*des vulgären Zeitverständnisses*) has been given form conceptually, and one which has received too little attention.'[14]

As we know, despite the extreme radicality demonstrated in this conceptual elaboration, Heidegger only sees in the Hegelian discourse a 'paraphrase' of Aristotle's *Physics*, precisely where Aristotle had previously determined time as the 'flow of a current', or again, as a succession or flux of moments.

> Time appears to the vulgar understanding (*für das vulgäre Zeitverständnis*) as a succession of nows constantly 'present-at-hand' (*vorhandenen*), that pass by and arrive at the same moment (*zugleich vergehenden und ankommenden Jetzt*). Time is understood as a sequence, as a 'flux' of nows, like the 'stream of time' (*als 'Lauf der Zeit*').

Why has this interpretation of time as a figure of succession, as a modality of what is 'cursive', as something which must be read as a 'course', a 'transition' or a 'passage', become the *current* interpretation? Why has this interpretation of time become generally accepted, dominant, hegemonic, self-evident, and even legitimate, accredited as such and at face value? And most of all, why has it come to deny and even erase or forbid all thought of a future? Well because, by passing through its passage, the 'course' of time would only *follow* the series of present moments, the very essence of the present, all of the nows here present (the actual present, but also, the past present and the future present), and this along the same line of succession. This sequential representation, and often linear depiction, would render it impossible for anything to *take place* or *arrive*, anything which has not yet been in advance reduced or which would not yet be reducible to what Husserl, the last inheritor of this tradition, would have called the originary form (*Urform*) of temporalization, the 'living present'. This present would give its basic form to all that could be 'seen coming' or to all that might be 'bound to come'. It is the anticipatory act of 'seeing what is coming', the very dampening act of the absolute surprise inherent to the future. The future will thus be the present which will then become the present past or the past present. If the future disappears or vanishes, for Hegel, it is because, according to Heidegger, he would have all too well understood the very essence of that cursory and cursive, current and general, interpretation inherited from Aristotle; Hegel would have carried to their limits the consequences and taken to its finest accomplishment this very tradition of which and in which he still belongs. With admirable but yet questionable intrepidness, Hegel would have arrived at the conclusion that the future itself is finished! He would have reached the end point where every event can only be as such reduced to the cursive and cursory passage that follows being as it 'becomes past' or as it 'passes away'. This is at least the thesis Heidegger advances in his 1930 lectures on the *Phenomenology of Spirit*, a thesis which 'follows' the same interpretative line formulated in the famous Note of *Sein und Zeit*, where the Hegelian interpretation of time is assimilated to a paraphrase of Aristotle's *Physics*:

> Undoubtedly [Hegel] occasionally speaks about having been, but never about the future. This silence fits with the fact that (for him) the past is itself the decisive character of time, and for a good reason: time is both the passing itself and what passes; it has always passed away.[15]

Malabou argues that she is not here 'proposing a confrontation between the Hegelian and Heideggerian interpretations of time'. And, without doubt the elegant modesty of this assertion points to a certain truth: *The Future of Hegel* does not organize or set out such a 'confrontation'; it is even less an attempt at mediating a *direct* debate or a *thematic* conflict on the *concept of time*. But in truth, we shall progressively see it, all is much more complex. As are the matters at stake.

On the one hand, behind the modesty, behind the moderation, behind the *measure*, we must recognize the cunning of a deliberate strategy: take on the questions differently and displace the horizon in which one can or may think them, and above all, do not precipitate oneself into the conceptual and thematic antagonisms. Malabou distinguishes, in what we could call her discourse on method – or her discourse on war – the *theme* and the *strategy*. She does it precisely in order to justify her recourse to the couple 'plasticity' – 'to see (what is) coming', terms which designate, not so much thematic concepts, but rather operative *figures*, motifs or 'motors'. As figures or 'schemes', these must keep something like a sensuous body in the translation of the categories. Irreducibility of this sensuous translation – which is, of course, more than a simple translation, more than a translation in the current sense of the word, and which orchestrates the plastic beauty of the philosophical writing we have been speaking of earlier. Malabou translates it herself (we should here analyse the foundation or the limits of this analogy) in Kantian language, especially when she calls it a 'hypotyposis'.

> In this regard, our approach shall be not so much thematic as strategic. It is a strategy driven by the two concepts – of *plasticity* and 'to see (what is) coming' – whose construction is the keystone of this project. *An economy of sensuous translation* – to borrow the Kantian definition of hypotyposis (1) – is itself figured sensuously by these concepts. This translation of the concept into the form of the sensuous is in essence systematic, an operation which cannot be *pinned down* in a transcendental deduction.

1. 'All *hypotyposis* consists in making a concept sensuous, and is either *schematic* or *symbolic*.' Kant, *Critique of Judgment*, §59[16]

The autopresentation of this 'method' is written in a remarkable and marked manner. It shows itself to itself as entirely 'plastic' and urges itself to manifest itself as the 'formation of concepts'. It underlines an added point in that the concepts ('plasticity' and 'to see (what is) coming') it calls into play constitute a sensuous figurality, which necessarily calls them to formulate the great question (post-Kantian or post-Hegelian, let us say, Marxist) of time as an un-sensuous sensibility. While insisting on the strategy rather than on the thematic, it recalls that the warrior's strategy is necessarily required by all dialectical thought, that is, by all conceptual opposition: 'The dialectical process is plastic . . . the process of plasticity is dialectical.'[17] But here, strategy does not mean polemic, and the question here posed by the antagonism does not in any way resemble some sort of philosophical victory. The thought implied in the expression 'to see (what is) coming' is much too plastic and in itself contradictory, stretched out between surprise and anticipation, too attentive to what comes in the future, to the future of what is coming, to come back and say 'I have come to see . . .'; and even less to conclude simply on some sort of *veni*, *vidi*, in the past of a 'I have conquered . . .'.

On the other hand, this strategic insistence on the schematic hypotyposis of the expression 'to see (what is) coming' or of 'plasticity' can but provoke, in depth, a radical transformation of the whole horizon. This is the hypothesis I would like here to expose, in four points, four headings, while proposing, perhaps, another mode of reading.

1 The choice of the strategy, of *this* strategy, does not, in this case, only have a beneficial value. As the book demonstrates, this strategy does not only have a simple exemplary *operative* value, for the strategic motif itself is precisely justified by the figures or the hypotyposis themselves radically inseparable from the expression 'to see (what is) coming' and from the notion of 'plasticity'. This choice has an *exemplary general* value, we should even say, a universal methodological value if we could at least agree on surrendering the concept of method to a Hegelian mutation. It should not suffice then to hold method, as Hegel himself thought, for something other than a system of predetermined rules or regulations, but as the very experience of the path tracing its own history; we should also interpret this experience from the motifs of plasticity and the expression 'to see (what is) coming'. And this dialectical experience commands the very 'strategy' of this work, if I may say so, inasmuch as it is structured, from its most speculative form, as and by work, practice, as and by a philosophical writing which effortlessly adapts the languages to the corpus rather than to some sort of theoretical view, rather than to some 'to see (what is) coming' which

would be limited only to the category of 'seeing'. For, let us say it without any further delay, the dialectical and plastic complexity of the expression 'to see (what is) coming' does not only refer to the paradox of 'waiting for itself without ever waiting for itself', of 'waiting for what comes' without ever seeing or knowing 'what we are waiting for'. We must go further than this paradox: in both terms of the alternative, in both figures of the expression 'to see (what is) coming' the theoretical and theatrical privilege of 'seeing' can also be suspended or see itself suspended. All of the senses are put into play here, and beyond the sensuous passivity, 'all' of the gestures are 'active'. We can anticipate while 'seeing', but we can also anticipate without ever 'seeing', and first of all, because we can only truly anticipate something or someone if we go beyond what can be perceived, or what can present itself in the present tense of sight; we may no longer be capable of anticipation, let ourselves be surprised, because we no longer see or because we see without ever seeing what comes. In other words, within the expression 'to see (what is) coming', the anticipatory prevision must go beyond the category of 'seeing', must go beyond the present act of seeing the visible; furthermore, within the same expression 'to see (what is) coming', the exposition to surprise, the non-anticipation can paradoxically have the same effect: the surprise can be so explosive that it cannot even constitute itself as an *object* for the category of 'seeing'. In both cases, as irreducible and as contradictory as they are and as they seem one in the face of the other, we only *see coming* if we no longer *see*: whether without seeing anything at all (the apprehension of the surprise), whether by relating to the future of what comes through the perception of what is and remains visible, in the full thematic and intuitive actuality of what is given to sight. The expression 'to see (what is) coming' is also plastic for it passes from one sense to the other and is not, from one end to the other, the affair of sight: to see coming, in the end, would always mean to see coming *without ever seeing*, whether we see beyond the visible present, whether we see nothing at all, whether again, what is announced or what surprises without ever being announced has nothing to do with the category of sight and is never given at all to sight. In all cases, there needs to be some sort of blindness. And hence, beyond theoretical *perception* or *thematic* intuition, beyond the *object*, there needs to be *strategy*. This paradoxical stance of 'sight' in the expression 'to see (what is) coming' without ever 'seeing what comes' perhaps responds to another strategic necessity. As we have suggested it, beyond the simple commentary, it allows us to conjoin the intrinsic plasticity of this expression, 'to see (what is) coming', to all living beings in general, whether they be endowed with the faculty of seeing or not seeing, to all animals, human or not (not all animals are endowed with sight, and not all sensitivity to light can be considered as sight). Plasticity characterized all sensibility or irritability as a moment of subjectivity in general, and, we shall come back to this,[18] the 'plastic' contraction of all habit (or *hexis*). In the strong conclusion of her book, devoted to the 'event of reading', that is of what has just taken place, of what has hence happened as to the unveiling of Hegel, and by fidelity to the Hegelian Law, Malabou takes into view this alliance of 'sight', of the category of 'sight' and of the blindness inherent in the expression 'to see (what is) coming'. How 'to see (what is) coming', how reading is 'seeing without ever seeing':

> The Hegelian idea of *plastic reading* confers on the notion of 'to see (what is) coming' its real meaning. 'To see (what is) coming' denotes at once the visibility and the invisibility of whatever comes. The future is not the absolutely invisible, a subject of pure transcendence objecting to any anticipation at all, to any knowledge, to any speech. Nor is the future the absolutely visible, an object clearly and absolutely foreseen. It frustrates any anticipation by its precipitation, its power to surprise. 'To see (what is) coming' thus means to see without seeing – a wait without awaiting – a future which is neither present to the gaze nor hidden from it. Now isn't this situation of 'in-between' *par excellence* the situation of reading?[19]

In the spirit of a book largely devoted to the plasticity of the living in general,[20] we could here prolong the weight and the extension of this remark with regard to the possibility of genetic deciphering. On the DNA strands, even before the constitution of animal organisms without vision, the decoding operations suppose no vision or visibility as such.

What is being said here of reading, and of the possibility of reading the living being *per se*, should we not also say it of *death*? If we were to ask how to name or categorize the event which a living being always 'sees coming' (letting it come to it as that which in any way will be an absolute surprise and thus be entirely unsubjective), sees coming without ever seeing it come, that is to say, without ever being able to see or foresee it, and hence without ever knowing and without ever having any power over it, an event which remains for it the place marked by an absence of all power and as itself impossible, how can we not name that death, as obscure as this event remains or the thing designated as such? The ultimate unity of 'to see (what is) coming' and 'not to see (what is) coming', of the 'to see coming without ever seeing what comes in the act of seeing what comes', the 'seeing without ever seeing', and thus of the *without* everywhere and anywhere this word articulates something, whatever it is, to itself, is that not what we ought or should call or name death? The plasticity of death at the heart of the 'to see (what is) coming', is that not also (as the root of habit) a kind of mourning? Or mourning itself? What we understand or determine as the work of mourning? We would then only have to relate this language, and 'the Hegelian concept of a plastic reading', to Hegel's great discourse on the work of death or the work of the negative as the life of spirit.

Amongst the many moments where death enters the scene in *The Future of Hegel*, there is one which seizes the very definition of the expression 'to see (what is) coming'. It is at the end of the prodigious analyses of habit, in the first part ('Hegel on Man: *Fashioning* of the second nature'). After having twice quoted Hegel, who regularly joins death to habit ('Man also dies from habit', *Philosophy of Right*; 'it is the habit of life which gives way to death, or, if we take this movement in a purely abstract manner, which is death itself', *Philosophy of Spirit*), Malabou writes:

> Since habit is the precondition for the existence of self-feeling, without habit there would be literally *nobody* to live or to die. Human beings are those who, in order to be, must observe that speculative clock which is habit, a clock which makes it possible to 'see (what is) coming', meaning that the end can be brought forward and, at the same time postponed. The soul analysed in the early sections of the *Anthropology*, a soul not yet habituated, cannot see itself dying and does not know it is finite: it is, therefore, insane. But the real soul, on the other hand, knows how to tell time.
>
> *Substance-subject returns in the death of man.*[21]

This insanity of the soul which does not see itself dying and which does not dispose of any measuring element, this 'seeing what comes' which does not see death coming, is it *an* insanity, *a* madness *in* the act of 'seeing what comes' (an anthropological moment, that of the 'soul not yet habituated') or *an* insanity, *a* madness *of* the act of 'seeing what comes' in general, of the act of 'seeing what comes' in itself, and thus that always *differs from itself*?

2 It is also a great consequence that this strategy is organized or seems to be organized, from the first lines of this book, around and beyond the Heideggerian verdict according to which there is an absence of any future in Hegel's thought. A whole horizon, our own landscape seems here to have changed, our philosophical territory, the European scene and much more than only the French. Before marking the reason for this change, it should be noted and underlined that the privilege given to the Heideggerian reading is not only a consequence of its powerful modality or of the explicit denegation it proposes with regard to the question of a future in Hegel or in the face of the future of Hegel. The entire deconstruction of the onto-theological finds in this reading, as we know, its cornerstone. Let us stress it once again, the privilege given or attributed to this reading incites us to put on a second plane the two other readings of Hegel, and to marginalize them

by attributing them less than two pages[22] (a gesture that some could consider or even judge violent and much too economical in regard to readings that could seem so close to the very thesis this book puts forward, but we shall explain precisely why for us such an interpretative gesture could be justified). It concerns thus two readings proposed and put forth in France, with the influence we know, by two thinkers who were neither French nor German, but of Russian origin. Both of these thinkers, Koyré and Kojève, recognized, contrary to Heidegger, the 'prevalence' or the 'primacy' of the future on the present in the *Jena Lectures*. They did this in a non-equivocal manner and with strong and powerful formulas.[23] Malabou points to these – and reminds us that these two readers of Hegel were attentive to a profound affinity between the young Hegel and the (not so old) Heidegger. There is certainly much more than a simple coincidence or a fortuitous affiliation here. We should also not forget that Koyré and Kojève were amongst the first readers of Heidegger; they also recognized this influence in their interpretations of Hegel. One of the reasons (there are more than one) which authorizes Malabou to treat these two analyses so rapidly, is that both lead to a contradiction, which in itself would not be surprising nor even worrisome, but, which is worse, both lead to a non-dialectical contradiction, that is a contradiction which remains 'non-resolute' and 'without solution'.[24] Hegel would pass in judgement before a dialectical tribunal for having sinned, in his thought of the future, against the dialectical itself! Here, by the way, in a few pages, a whole conjuncture, a whole 'field' or 'horizon' of the French 'reception of Hegel' is questioned again. Another chart is established, whose lines are traced from this point: a *seemingly* non-dialectical contradiction in the thought of the future. This phase of objections or inhibitions, the 'Koyré–Kojève' phase (paradoxically under the direct or indirect influence of Heidegger, Malabou perhaps does not state this enough), would have reached its end and been revoked by a 'new wave of French commentators':[25] Bourgeois, Labarrière, Lebrun, Souche-Dagues, etc. Between both of these phases, both of these times, we could ask ourselves why Jean Hyppolite remains unspoken for, as a great absentee in this book, never named, even, to the point where this silence screams for some sort of justification. Particularly for those of my generation.

3 But what sense is there in speaking, as I just have – capitulating to convention – of a 'French reception of Hegel'? For in the end, before and after the Second World War, what did not belong to some 'horizon' or other, directly or indirectly? Who could possibly escape from subscribing to one or the other 'field of interpretation'? And furthermore, has there ever been something to delimit in such a manner, that is, have there ever been such 'interpretative fields'? Without speaking of those whom Malabou calls the 'French commentators', there were few who did not situate their thought in the shadow of Hegel and in the legacy left by Kojève's and

Koyré's meditations. And not only in the more or less academic discipline of philosophy (Lévinas, Sartre, Merleau-Ponty, but also Breton, Bataille, Klossowski, Lacan, and so many others) and not only in that generation: Althusser, Foucault, Deleuze, Lyotard, all shared at least, with a few others, a sort of active and organized allergy, we could even say an organizing aversion, towards the Hegelian dialectic. They all shared this trait, of situating themselves philosophically, and they did this explicitly, *from* this rejection. The structure of this 'field' is determined and, we should say, complicates itself at the same time and as soon as we come to say something analogous, or even identical, about a 'reception of Heidegger'. Whether acknowledged or not, it was also as common, and if it ever crossed the first, it was above all with Kojève[26] and Koyré. This would or could suffice in understanding the privilege given to Heidegger's reading of Hegel in a book which at the same time analyses, brings to light and transforms in depth a great philosophical trial, the same one which gave way to a dominant configuration in 'French philosophy' formed and shaped for almost half a century and that reigned over two or three generations. It was in this manner formed and shaped, let us say it now, in a 'plastic' idiom, by giving to itself and receiving a form, the true form of genealogical crossing and on the basis of the French spiritualist tradition, of a Hegel and a Heidegger both reinterpreted together by these two great Russian immigrants. In this landscape dominated by wars and European revolutions, to re-question and re-interrogate the Heideggerian interpretation of Hegel, precisely on the fundamental theme of time and history, and in this way, to think and to re-think in its very principle the Heideggerian 'deconstruction', that is, the entire perspective it puts forth, that of an onto-theology understood by and from the privilege of the 'present-now', and hence of 'vulgar' temporality – this is a strategy of great scope. It precisely points to and aims at disturbing a very specific lever of this device, but also sets its sight on a much larger range: there is nothing in this configuration that is to remain unchanged, un-reinterpreted or un-transformed. Plastically – and beyond any kind of plastic surgery, any kind of *Aufhebung*, *sublation* or 'lifting' of Hegel.

In order to limit ourselves to this trait, one of the first consequences of this 'plastic' re-evaluation of the expression 'to see (what is) coming' in the hegemonic history of subjectivity may concern the privilege attributed to the 'ecstasy' of the 'future' in the *Dasein Analytic*, and all which depends on it, that is to say, it would be easy to show, almost everything. What if the primacy of the future were to transform the existential analytic, regardless of all the numerous de-negations which could here be invoked, the analytic of a novel figure of subjectivity? Yet again another moment in the history of the subject, perhaps the last and penultimate one? Precisely where the *Dasein Analytic* is identified with the analytic of *mineness* or with the *egoity* (*Jemeinigkeit*) of an 'I am' which is not indifferent to his

Being, or with a 'we' which justifies the exemplary privilege of the *Dasein* in its openness to the question of Being and which is defined by a '*we*-who-is-capable-of-questioning-ourselves', etc.? And above all, where the privilege given to the ecstasy of the future seems inseparable, more so than any other *existential*, from the 'Being-for-death', that is, from the possibility of the impossible: perhaps from something akin to a farewell, a certain kind of farewell, if not a certain kind of mourning. In all, from something similar to what we were suggesting earlier on in regard to the possibility of seeing what is coming without ever seeing what is coming, as in the apprehension of death. This would perhaps offer us a supplementary confirmation.

As many of our contemporaries are divided on this question, even if each bends and amends it in their own way, I shall not insist on the temptation of reinscribing *Sein und Zeit* and the existential analytic in the transcendental or ontological tradition of subjectivity, or even of the Cartesian *cogito*. I shall only note here that this hypothesis is given great force, great conviction, we may even say, a new and novel force, from the modality of the expression 'to see (what is) coming', that is in the plastic ambiguity of a Hegelian history of subjectivity. Given that the existential analytic has played an indispensable role in all current interpretations and in all interpretations to come of onto-theological metaphysics, we can see coming all of the perturbations that could be unleashed by this *subjectal* logic inherent in the expression 'to see (what is) coming'. Even more so that in this reinterpretation of Hegel, this *subjectal* logic, this movement of plastic *subjectivation* would not or should not be considered simply as an anthropological or even theological stance. It would begin with life itself, within its very first contraction and with the first idealization of animal *habitus*. With the very apparition of life, hence, that is to say, with that which is not or should not be constitutive of the Heideggerian *Dasein* but which opens the way for so many more rich and fruitful analyses of *ipseity*. For, right from the *Philosophy of Nature*, where the plant ignores all 'self-feeling' and all 'return to itself', there is an animal subjectivity which finds its elementary form: 'The organization, in general, of the animal represents the physical elements reconstructed in one single individual.' (*Philosophy of Nature*, §398). Or again, 'organic individuality exists as *subjectivity* if the specific exterior of the figure is idealized (*idealisiert ist*) in its elements and the organism in its external process maintains in itself its own unity' (§350).[27]

4 Perhaps there is something graver, something much more radical, precisely where one should not, in the first place or in the last instance, challenge or even take on Heidegger. What does Malabou do when she states that 'it is not my purpose here to stage a confrontation between the Hegelian and the Heideggerian conceptions of time'? She perhaps does not

content herself by recognizing a necessary limit or a methodological frontier in her reading. It is possible, and likely, that she also claims, if I may say it openly, that time really is not the question. Time is not the fundamental theme of the difficulty. It is but a formal and abstract determination, the 'time-form' of which we will speak of later, the vacant middle of a process in which we must recognize so many more determinations, all the other processual determinations, and in particular what we here designate under the dialectical terms of the expression 'to see (what is) coming' and of 'plasticity'. As the whole demonstrative tissue of the work would be here, let us retain only one consequence of this other displacement, one which points once again towards Heidegger, or at the very least towards *Sein und Zeit*, the time of *Sein und Zeit*. What do we call or name time in *Sein und Zeit*? It would be, on the one hand, a determined *moment*, that of a circumscribed period in which Heidegger had proposed a contestable interpretation of time according to Hegel (as a paraphrase of Aristotle's *Physics*, as a 'vulgar' concept or a 'current' concept dominated by the schema of the flux, by the succession inherent to the current of the present 'nows', etc.). The time of *Sein und Zeit* (which shortly precedes the 1930 Seminar on the *Phenomenology of Spirit* and the verdict characterizing Hegel's conception of time as that which has 'passed away') is also the choice which makes time the 'transcendental horizon' of the question of Being. What did Heidegger do (distance himself from . . .? Interrupt . . .? Displace . . .?) when he engaged his thought in ways or paths which could seem here to be so different? This is one of the questions *The Future of Hegel* can help us elaborate. A certain reduction of 'time as the transcendental horizon of the question of Being', the suspension of the abstract theme, in the end, of the pure movement of temporalization, this is perhaps what happens, later on, in *Zeit und Sein* (1952), where Heidegger speaks of this modality of giving to receive when he writes '*es gibt die Zeit, es gibt das Sein*'. But it is also perhaps what happens in *The Future of Hegel*.

Perhaps, or should we say, *maybe*. Before coming back to the modality of this *maybe*, to truly come back to it, we must here, jumping provisionally above the immense trajectory of the book, conjoin two propositions or two states of the same proposition, which we had left in the dark.

It concerns what I here propose to call a certain *salutation to time*. Another salutation: between a certain goodbye and a certain farewell or *adieu*.

Let us here remember the moment in the Introduction where what was being questioned and re-questioned was, first, the Heideggerian thesis according to which Hegelian time supposedly always had 'passed away': 'Hegel's explication of the genuine concept of Being – in the passage just indicated, where time is mentioned – is nothing less than a *farewell to time* on the road to Spirit, which is eternal.'[28] (I have underlined '*adieu au temps*' ('*farewell to time*'.) Catherine Malabou quotes a French translation.[29] The word 'adieu' in French, which she keeps and will also use herself in her exposition, is used to translate the German word *Verabschiedung*: the leave-of-absence (taken or given), a separation or a departure. *Sich verabschieden* means to separate, to take one's leave, say goodbye or to present one's farewell. This French translation poses many problems, to which I am sensitive, for the word 'adieu' in French is to be distinguished in at least two ways from the German *Verabschiedung*:

1 Besides being a noun, the word 'adieu' is also sometimes used as an exclamation or a performative verb when, for example, it serves as an address to the other: 'adieu!'.
2 It also refers quite evidently, but rather strangely, to the name of God. In spite of these problems, and for other reasons, which will become clearer as we progress, I will also keep and use the French word.

Retort or reply, Malabou responds by questioning, after quoting Heidegger:

> Hasn't Hegel's 'farewell' *to* time simply been converted to time's farewell *to* Hegel? Indeed, could it be that time as it exists for speculative philosophy is not actually time at all, but rather the flattening or the levelling down (*Nivellierung*) of time, of that authentic time called by Heidegger 'primordial' or 'originary temporality' (*ursprüngliche Zeit*)? Primordial time cannot be conceived in terms of the present for its most fundamental 'ecstasy' is the future. Primordial temporality, Heidegger writes, 'temporalizes itself *primarily* out of the *future*' (*Being and Time*, p. 302). Thus the authentic future, for Heidegger is no longer a simple moment of time, but becomes almost indistinguishable from time itself. It is not my purpose here to stage a confrontation between the Hegelian and the Heideggerian conceptions of time.[30]

Hence, to give a future back *to* Hegel, the strategy does not consist here in simply demonstrating that the future has the place that we often deny it *in* Hegel's philosophy. In a more subtle and underhand manner, we will here neglect this worry or this proposition, which was precisely that of Koyré or Kojève.[31] We will attempt to think *differently* – to think *otherwise* – a certain radicality of the future. *Otherwise*: that is to say, and such is the radicality of the 'farewell' or the 'adieu', a different radicality or a radicality otherwise more radical than a simple 'moment of time'. The future, *what is yet to come in the future*, is not simply reducible to what is *imminent* in the future, and this very difference reveals plasticity itself, the condition also for there to be some kind of sense in speaking, as we have been from the beginning, of a 'history of the future':

> to posit the future as 'plasticity', amounts to *displacing* the established definition of the future as a *moment of time*. And indeed in the title such a displacement has already been announced: 'the future', that which is 'to come', will not be restricted in meaning by the immediate, ordinary connotation, that of the 'future' as a 'tense'.
>
> (Ibid. pp. 5–6)

Why insist again on this equivocal logic proper to the 'farewell' or to the 'adieu'? It is because the very movement of *The Future of Hegel* follows its course in order to reveal, in Hegel himself, the *abandonment* of the 'all too common' definition of the future as that which is simply imminent, that which is simply reducible to imminence. Let us underline the word 'abandonment', which immediately follows the above quoted passage in the text, and let us underline this word because it says something of what is done or of what passes in and with the 'farewell', that is, a certain kind of desertion, of abandonment, of *aban-donation*, if we could say:

> It is not a matter of examining the relations between past, present and the ordinary of the future, presented in the discussions of time in Hegel's different versions of the *Philosophy of Nature*. Rather these texts themselves *demand* that we *renounce* the 'well known' and familiar meaning of the future and, as a consequence, the *'well known' definition of time*. The possibility that one temporal determination – the future – can be thought differently, beyond its initial, simple status as a moment of time, of 'that which is now to come' – makes it immediately clear that time for Hegel cannot be reduced to an ordered relation between moments. By 'plasticity' we mean first of all the *excess of the future over the future*; while temporality, as it figures in speculative philosophy, will mean the *excess of time over time*.
>
> (Ibid. p. 6)

There is thus a farewell to time in Hegel, an abandonment of time, as Heidegger states, but it is not the one we believe; it is only a farewell to 'the "all too common" definition of time'. And perhaps of farewell itself: is farewell something inherent or proper to time? Is it a salvation of time within time? In time beyond time? Perhaps, we should even say *maybe*, we ought to think of different farewells, and different times for farewells. These will often be difficult to discern. As it will often be difficult to distinguish the movement which consists of, in Hegel's name, this time, we have just heard and seen it, 'displacing the all too current definition of the future as a *moment* of time', of the Heideggerian movement according to which, according to Malabou's own words, 'the authentic future is no longer a simple moment of time'. What will be the difference between each of these two farewells, inasmuch as neither one can be understood as a 'moment of time'? And that each, in its own manner, says farewell to the future as a simple 'moment of time'?

Perhaps neither? Perhaps a silent but vertiginous move in the use of the word 'time'. Is the question 'what is time?' something else, something other, something richer than the question 'what does the noun time mean or mean to say?' What do we mean to say here when we name time itself? And when we speak of a farewell to time? And of a 'moment of time'? These questions are here more than ever to be thought as abstract, particularly when we cease to consider them as easy games, and attempt to comprehend them as phrases which seem to contradict themselves, phrases which 'I see coming without ever seeing them come' or to quote Malabou: 'By "plasticity" we mean first of all the *excess of the future over the future*; while temporality, as it figures in speculative philosophy, will mean the *excess of time over time*.' In both cases, and from both sides of an excess, if we may say so, the excess of thinking as the excess to be thought will have inscribed a mutation, or even better, an absolute heterogeneity between the two senses or meanings of the same word, between the two concepts, and the two concepts of time, and the two concepts of the future. There would otherwise be no excess. One says farewell to the other. One meaning of time says farewell to the other, and to one sense of the future, and, without doubt, to one sense of the word farewell. Is that the only question, the only problematic, the only stake of this 'speculative philosophy', in the Hegelian sense? And what about this excess – of time on time, of the future on future – is it something other than time itself? Is it something other than the future itself? The farewell of one to the other, does it mean saying the same word?

Here, I will allow myself to interrupt you. At length. I am wondering if this excess passes or goes through the limit between two concepts. Would it not pass or go through the limit *of* the concept, in language itself, of *all* possible concepts, pre-Hegelian or post-Hegelian, and even of this inconceivable concept which Hegel speaks of here and there? And if, as I see what meaning the word 'farewell', the words 'salvation', 'salutation', and the expression 'good-bye' import to you, must or should we not say that these nouns always imply an address to someone, to some other, to the other, to otherness, to the absolute other, at the very moment when we can 'abandon' something, 'abandon' a 'what', and not necessarily a 'who', time itself or the future. The absolute interruption, surprise itself marked by one of the plastic senses or meanings of the expression 'to see (what is) coming', its explosive sense or meaning, the plastic dynamite, does it not come from the Absolute Other as much as death, which we see coming without ever seeing it come and of which you were speaking of earlier? Time and the future *as such*, if this is possible, would have then to be seized from this 'who' proper to the Absolute Other, from this Absolute Other to whom we say farewell, or even adieu, a farewell, an adieu or a salutation which absolutely renounces the possibility of 'seeing again', which unequivocally relinquishes or abandons the assurance of repetition or of redemption, a 'salutation' which must begin by refusing all the assurances of salvation. This renunciation, this relinquishment, this abandonment or this refusal, which would be the very condition of the 'farewell' addressed to the other, the condition of time and of the future to which it is exposed, is that not what, in the expression 'to see (what is) coming', does not only suspend the act of 'seeing' by a sort of internal blindness, by a sort of blinding stain or wink which while participating in the modality of the expression 'to see (what is) coming' and to its horizon, would regularly shut or close sight itself, from one instant to the other, by some sort of obscuration, and would stop sight itself from seeing in front of itself, would limit the horizon in order to see in front of itself, in sight of seeing in front of itself, while providing sight to sight, while procuring for sight the spectacle or the scene before which all spectacles, scenes or objects could be seen? No, there would be an even more radical interruption of sight in the expression 'to see (what is) coming'. It would affect all and any finite beings which present themselves upon it from *behind* or *vertically*, from a very high stance, in truth, from the height of a height much higher than height itself or any height whatsoever. What would hence 'come to me' would fall upon me or would look at me and would see me come, perhaps, from this scene without symmetry nor synchrony, without ever giving or offering me the possibility of seeing it come or of exchanging with it a glance, without ever giving or offering me the possibility of waiting for it or of preceding it – not even, at the very moment where I no longer seek to precede it, would even allow me to be affected by a surprise which would still come before me, etc. You see what I mean here to say, don't you? I am not letting only one theologian speak, I am not only allowing for the one preoccupied by the transcendence of an Absolute Other which we do not see, nor see coming, not even as the Messiah (which, by the way, as the future itself, as what comes in the future itself, can conjoin both meanings of the expression 'to see (what is) coming': we wait for it without ever waiting for it, it can or may come as it can or may not come – at every single moment or instant, as death itself) express himself. I also let a certain psychoanalyst speak. This last one would in fact be doubly interested: by a past stronger, much stronger than the future, much more powerful than any (representational or conscious) memory and also, by what joins and conjoins the event to a sort of repetition, a kind of compulsion of repetition which would have absolutely nothing to do with habit. This event can or may come from that which is the highest but it may also come from 'behind', from what comes and comes back from behind me, always, as if it came in my back, from behind my back, without ever presenting itself in front of me, in, so to say, the face of my face, not even as the face of the other: the coming of an event which, to have taken place, would never ever present itself, has never presented itself and will never present itself. It would come to me, this event, if we are entitled to believe it can or may come *to me*, not only without prevision or without being called or recalled to my attention, but without even presenting itself *to me*. If I may allow myself a confidence here, I often ask myself if it is not precisely this which, without ever being able to accustom myself to it, happens to me in all that I recognize happening to me. When I say 'recognize', it is a very *schematical* way of speaking. I recognize rather what comes to me only if I recognize nothing of which comes to me, and I should even add, only if I do not recognize myself recognizing that which comes to me. I no longer know if it comes to me or if it arrives at me, comes or arrives unto me, unto someone who knows and understands what he says when he pronounces the words 'me', 'I', or even 'myself' – let alone when he proclaims the 'I-subject' of a phrase or of whatever else that may be. What would you do with that? Is it in any way comprehensible for a subject or even reducible to any subjectivity? Does it still belong in a history of the 'becoming-subject'? And most of all, what would you do with the fact that I don't even believe of any future for myself and feel at the same time both faithful and radically amnesic?

Let us persist a little while longer in this direction which you will easily recognize, and from which you, without doubt, already see me coming from (but would this suffice to discredit it in advance?). The event which we do not see coming, in front of which we do not stand in so far as it does not expose itself nor announce itself in the face of sight or to some sealing of the eye, this event does not arrive necessarily from behind or from above, as I have just suggested. It can or may all too simply not come at all from an exteriority (in front of . . ., in back of . . ., from above . . ., or, from below . . .), from this *in front of* . . . more or less before us and from which we always believe events come to us, but it can or may come from *within*, from the *within* within the within which would not and never convert itself or be converted in some sort of without, some sort of outside or exteriority and in any case would render this opposition 'within–without', 'inside–outside', 'interiority–exteriority' radically null and void. Graver still for the figure or the scheme of the expression 'to see (what is) coming', and perhaps for all figures in general, for its opening to sight, to speech, to hearing, what would come in this manner would have no essential relation to the future, but with an absolute past which would be irreducible to the now-present form as the future you have been speaking of. We would then have to emancipate what comes (the event), the very concept of the event, from all relation to the future. And perhaps even with a semantic of *what comes* and of the *coming*. And with the whole rhetoric which gives it its tropes, its schemes, its *hypotyposes*. An 'Unconscious', a 'God', the One or the Other would then only be names or nouns, amongst so many others, for this Thing. What would then become of the scheme or of the *hypotyposis* inherent to the expression 'to see (what is) coming'? What would become of its possibilities? Will it suffice to enrich them of one more turn, of one more figural power? And should we not imply this one more turn in the very night which exposes the prevision implicit in the expression 'to see (what is) coming' to the self-abandonment inherent in the 'to see (what is) coming', the self-abandonment to surprise, to the other who is no longer *its* own other? To the menace of sight, without even having the time 'to see (what is) coming', the plasticity of the plastic exploding in the very hands of all and any 'subject' as a bomb whose timer remains uncontrollable? A bomb which would no longer be regulated or programmed by this 'speculative clock' through which the effective soul, you were saying, the one which is not crazy, can tell the time, indeed a bomb without the timer that lies within the clock of the 'speculative subject'? And which could not in any case let itself be domesticated or appropriated, reset by habit, or in another words, be re-subjectivized? At the very moment where we could no longer say, as in the phrase you were quoting before, that 'the substance-subject returns into the death of man'? If I did not fear to waste your time, I would risk analogous hypotheses on the concept of decision. If all decision, to be what it is and to say what it says, must settle on a background of indecisiveness (for example, between the two 'plastic' senses of the expression 'to see (what is) coming' and of plasticity: apprehension or concept of anticipation *and* surprise, proposition or pre-position *and* exposition, the given or received form *and* explosion etc.), then it cannot even be the essential or accidental modification of a subject. Can such a being as a subject, a subject as such, ever decide on whatever is? As all which comes or arrives to it, must not its 'own' decision affect it from the Other, as always, and always explosive decision of the Other in it? Such is a folly, would you say, this passive experience in regard of ones own decision, a decision which I claim and assume freely the responsibility. Unless it is the impossible? But what could possibly *come* other than this to a subject?

Perhaps. Perhaps this is one of the most secret or one of the most discreet motifs of this book, which ends, as a matter of fact, on an allusion to the atomic bomb (*Plastikbombe*) and on these other technical figures of death, of the non-living, of the artifice and of the synthetic, all of which are the plastic, the *plastification*, the plastic matter. Perhaps I have not known how to read it, and read it well, to offer it to one's reading, to invite one to read it. But before leaving you with the book on the edge of which I stand, I would like to come back on the 'perhaps', on the 'may-be' which marks all of our propositions. Hegel did not care very much for the 'perhaps' or for the 'may-be'; he had only irony or sarcasm for whoever (for example for poor Krug) pretended to give a philosophical dignity to this category, which he judged to be empirical, in fact empiricist, of the possible, of the eventual, of the accidental or of the aleatory. Nietzsche confronted, we know it all too well,[32] this great Hegelian tradition, this great dialectical tradition, tradition of fear, tradition of a terrified metaphysics, according to him, in the face of what he called 'the dangerous may-be' to which are promised the philosophers of the future and all future philosophers (*Philosophen des gefährlichen Vielleicht*). It is a question here of a 'may-be' which the 'possible' as much as the 'Being', or their conjunction, would perhaps not correspond to any traditional philosophical modality, unless it responds again, more profoundly than ever, to what remains still in reserve, still repressed, held in respect by that which is called philosophy.

It is the convention of this all too-well-received idea, in this interpretative scene, in this historical perspective which is finally taken on by Malabou in her book. To say, so easily and all too simply, that there is no contingence or no 'pure accident' for Hegel, and hence – I translate – that a 'perhaps' has no place and no philosophical dignity, is an error: 'Such a reading is erroneous.'[33] For in the speculative automatism, the cause of the Self or the foundation of the Self, in the relation of Self to Self, only is or becomes what it is, its own Self, only to divide itself, only to become in and for itself in splitting itself between a passive Self and an active Self. In order to take into account this process (which forms the ground of plasticity and of the expression 'to see (what is) coming'), Malabou quotes Hegel. Hegel speaks of a 'passivity posited by its own activity' and shows, in a first moment, that the absolute substance 'repels itself as necessity from itself'. We could be tempted here to object, in a classical or traditional manner, that it is still an activity which *poses* passivity, that this *Setzung*, this position, this auto-position, this presupposition of the self is still or already a necessary and automatic act of this *ipseity*. But Malabou entices this necessity into its own abyss, the abyss where it loses itself, that is to say, into its own necessity, the necessity of necessity, which would be a *fact* or a *Faktum*, the *fact* of a necessity which remains as a fact, in itself, not necessary, and in any case not comprehensible as the necessity which he *founds by depriving it of its own foundation*. To recall Hegel's text to this abyss of a foundation which founds its necessity in concealing itself, claims its *fact* to this self-necessity, is a right which Malabou has the right to demand without our accusing her of betraying Hegel. But to demand this right in her reading is the only chance of giving a chance to chance itself in Hegel's thought. That is to say, of placing a '*point of sheer randomness*' in the heart of Being, at the *origin* of essence or of substance:

> A *point of sheer randomness* dwells within essential being, within the 'original substance'. This is the perspective we need to understand, the claim that the essence of necessity is contingency. The becoming accidental of essence originally stemmed from the process whereby necessity sets itself up as an event.[34]

A just demand of reading, the very one we are here calling for but which the contingent limits here imposed forbid us from respecting fully, should command a step-by-step reconstitution of all the methodical developments which follow and which precede. More or less abstractly, I will underline *three phases* in the interpretation of this *point of sheer randomness*.

1 First, far from leaving this *point of sheer randomness* to its own contingence, and although 'Hegel, contrary to a common opinion, does not deny contingence', it is the alternative or the opposition of the necessary and of contingence that the *sublation* constrains to *let go*, or *let fall*:

> Contingency and necessity support one another in such a way that spirit itself liberates itself from their division, and can let its two-sided claim – it could have been otherwise, it could not have been otherwise – simply go. It would be useless to want to determine some ontological priority of essence over accident or accident over essence, for their co-implication is primary.[35]

That a *sublation* can liberate itself in this way, that is, that it can *let go* or *let fall* that which it *sublates*, abandoning it in a 'farewell' or an 'adieu', giving what it *sublates* its leave – nothing is less surprising for an 'habituated' reader of the Hegelian dialectic. But perhaps this also pronounces or dictates a 'farewell' to the 'perhaps' – not in order to save it, in order to keep it, but rather in order to *keep oneself from it*.

More surprising, but then much more thought-provoking, would perhaps be one of the consequences, all very rich, which Malabou underlines in regard to the post-Hegelian *tradition* (notably Heideggerian) of the very concept of *tradition*. This consequence touches Absolute Knowledge itself. Not Absolute Knowledge as a self-enclosed knowledge, or Absolute Knowledge as a non-knowledge, but rather Absolute Knowledge as knowledge of its own limit, of its proper (?) limit, of the limit of knowledge as knowledge, in two words as *knowledge (of that) of which no knowledge is to be had*. The Absolute Knowledge would still *know* that there is nothing to know, especially no object, beyond the *form of knowledge*. And the *form of knowledge* of Absolute Knowledge would still be a limit, its own, and that it still knows, on its own edge, but beyond which there would be nothing knowable, only a heterogeneous unknown to all knowledge. Would we then say this of all that is to be seen coming? Am I translating justly and faithfully what Malabou intends, by underlining yet again this 'at the same time', with which we have not ceased to deal with since the beginning? Each time, 'at the same time' synchronizes or symmetrizes 'in the same time', *simul*, in the Same, two contrary, sometimes two contradictory *salutations*, one which would want to save, the other which would renounce in saving by relinquishing, one more 'saving' than the other, two salutations to time, to farewells two adieux, or two goodbyes to one or the other of the meanings inherent in what is 'seen coming', perhaps even to the very expression 'to see (what is) coming' in general:

> Hegel explains that a philosophical tradition refers to two things *at once*: to the movement through which a particular accident (for example, something that arises in its own place and time, like the birth of philosophy in Greece) becomes essential (i.e. it becomes *fate*) *and* to the way a destiny, standing for the essential, then actualizes itself in its accident, i.e. in its epochs and its stages. Whether one is prior to the other is not something that can be known. This is what Absolute Knowledge *knows*. Hegelian philosophy assumes as an absolute fact the emergence of the randomness in the very bosom of necessity, and that the random, the aleatory, becomes necessary.[36]

2 Whatever could be meant here by '*assumes* as an absolute fact', and even if this expression does not reform, as it could be imagined, the classical figure of Hegelianism, even if Spirit had to let go or let fall, abandon, say farewell or adieu to the alternative between 'it could have been otherwise' and 'it could not have been otherwise', the dialectical *sublation* of the 'time form' would still leave time itself, an 'empty time', the time inherent in the expression of 'to see (what is) coming' and to think that *it could have been* otherwise. This conditional, however, would be the time of an 'alienation'. Must we conclude from this that all of *our* experience of 'to see (what is) coming' belongs to a time left behind by this 'empty time' and is conditioned by alienation? What would *to assume* then mean in regard to this time?

> Dialectically sublating 'the time form', Spirit removes the tendency to question whether a *wholly different origin* might have been possible, whether there could be an origin and a *destination wholly different* from those that actually come to pass. At the stage of Absolute Knowledge, the time which is sublated – that empty time posted outside itself by consciousness giving the unfolding of Spirit, the appearence of 'a free contingent event', leaves us always *time to think what might otherwise have been*. In this fact, Hegel believes, there remains the possibility of *alienation*, theoretically something that is due to the feeling of lost necessity.[37]

What is meant by *to leave*, what is meant when we say we are *leaving* this time *left behind*, and especially when we have already *left* or *let go*, *let fall* time itself? What is the time inherent in this *rest* of time *left behind*? Is there still an essential link or alliance between this 'leaving' and that which in the expression 'to see (what is) coming' still lets or allows come what comes, from beyond what can be seen, what can be foreseen, what can be known? If all farewell, all adieu, all goodbye, all salutation are all different modalities of 'leaving behind', how is it still possible to equate them here with what is so well described, as an alienation, under the traits of feeling, a 'feeling of lost necessity'? We should even ask ourselves here if such a feeling still lets itself, as such, *sublate,* know, comprehend dialectically.

3 For what we see coming without ever seeing it come, in any way (and regardless of whether or not these 'events' are analysed in this book), the *uncontrollable* as such, and the *inevitable*, and the *unsteadiness*, still seem incorporated within the same necessity, the necessity of the Same. From this necessity of the Same would emerge the inevitable, uncontrollable and unsteady question of the other itself, of the absolute other. This question of the other shares these very same traits (the *uncontrollable*, the *unsteadiness*, the *inevitable*) with the question of the origin, of the origin of the speculative – and hence of all this dialectic – as a question emanating from the Absolute Other. The passage I have chosen to quote immediately follows the preceding one, and I would have liked to dwell extensively within this proposition which seems not to constitute a center of gravity but which, I would say, signifies yet another sign of farewell, another adieu (to abandon, to leave, to leave behind, say goodbye, perhaps, salute in leaving, with or without any promise of a redemptory salvation: *to detach oneself*). I thus formulate for the first time my question: why, as it is said, and how does Spirit detach itself from itself, by itself, from an uncontrollable, inevitable and unsteady question? Why not think or say the contrary? Let us first read:

> To know the *provenance* of the speculative is a question *beyond any possible scope*; thus, by itself, spirit abandons it. [It is the conjunction performed by this *thus* which surprises me, you see, as much as the 'by itself': 'thus, by itself, spirit abandons it.] For Heidegger to claim, more than one century later, that it is as impossible as useless to ask about the possibility of a wholly different 'guise' (*Weise*) of Being from the one which occurred in the metaphysical tradition as a 'forgetfulness of Being', Hegel's entire work on the essence of history and tradition was needed. [Would there be then some sort of secret affinity between the movement inherent in the farewell in which Spirit detaches itself from a 'question *beyond any possible scope*' and the 'forgetfulness of Being in metaphysics'?].
>
> The question of the wholly Other – something that cannot be thought without a feeling of vertigo – is always in fact a question about an origin that could have been wholly otherwise. A vertigo

> of thought, this is still a solicitation that is not to be avoided, one not coming from without, but rather from the Same. 'It is because it is' – the formal and immediate tautology of necessity – and 'it could be otherwise' – the *heterology* of contingency: in Hegel's thought these reveal their original and inherent complicity, shown in the two meanings of the phrase: 'what arrives from itself/what happens on its own'.
>
> Everything begins in the same moment, where the becoming essential of the accident and the becoming accidental of essence mutually imply one another. There is nothing beforehand. The dialectic is primordial, indeed, it is the origin.
>
> (pp. 163–4)

Inasmuch as spirit does it 'by itself', it which knows so well from what it detaches itself (the uncontrollable, the inevitable, the unsteadiness), would we then say that it abandons or that it leaves behind that which it detaches itself from? That it gives it or takes its leave from it? It would be a form of farewell, of adieu, and also a kind of salutation. Or else will we say that, within the speculative automatism in which by itself it detaches itself from itself, it still keeps, retains, *sublates* and recalls within itself, saves and interiorizes that which it seemingly says farewell or adieu to – another form of farewell or adieu, another time of the farewell or of the adieu – and which in truth will have never been absolutely other but yet another figure of the Same? Both of these salutations, both of these adieux, would then be, as essential figures of Spirit, as already participating in the self-relation of spirit, two experiences of mourning, of an *originary* mourning, of a possible mourning as that which is impossible. Is there not some sort of plasticity of mourning? This plasticity, would it not consist in saying farewell to itself while always giving and receiving for itself yet another form, while always interiorizing, incorporating, *sublating*, idealizing, spiritualizing that which we abandon or which abandons us? The dialectical would be this plastic of mourning – or of melancholy, of the pathologies and of the 'folly' which the Hegelian problematic so carefully and remarkably interrogated from the first chapter of the first part of this book.[38] Let us radicalize the theme in following the *motif* of *mourning* (a word which, as long as I remember, is not present in this book but which haunts it in so far as this book is also, thematically, a book on death and even on the death of God). May we not say that all plasticity is engaged or involved in some sort of mourning, in a mournful experience or a work of mourning, and to begin with the very one which divides and opposes to itself the expression 'to see (what is) coming'? And when it fails to recall, or to bring back, within Sameness, when it falls short of interiorizing, of assimilating (etc.), the other, the 'uncontrollable', remember, the 'inevitable', the 'unsteadiness', the question of the 'Absolute Other', then the failure of this work of mourning would urge to leave, *abandon* (see above), to salute with a certain farewell or adieu, and hence *to mourn mourning itself*. Precisely where mourning is impossible. From one farewell to the other. There is always more than one farewell, more than one adieu, in the farewell or the adieu; one renounces the future, the other hopes or promises, but the more it is assured or given (as the salutation inherent to salvation), the more the promise becomes a calculation, that is the more it is lost – as future. That is why the time of these multiple farewells remain so difficult to think: it never gathers or draws itself with itself or in itself.

In both cases, we then have the impression that the possibility of the future is at the same time promised and refused by this farewell. I could demonstrate it, but I do not have here the time or the space necessary for such an exploration. We will have to interrupt *ourselves* or let ourselves be arbitrarily interrupted, at the forefront of this book, as if by accident, an accident or a contingence which no internal or essential justification could ever comprehend, and hence save.

You have not privileged this ambiguous word 'farewell' (synonym of this other equivocal word, 'salutation'), you have not let resonate 'farewell' with 'mourning' without the economy of some sort of calculation, without some kind of strategic presumption. I am not sure of seeing it come. Would we only say farewell to death? Does God ever say farewell or adieu? Does he ever mourn himself? Does he ever mourn himself from himself? And the 'death of God', is it a way for God to manifest himself, to incarnate himself, to say himself, to name himself in saying to himself *Adieu, adieu to God*?

Having had to stay on the edge of this book and since nothing will ever absolve us from following step by step, page by page, the extraordinary trajectory of *The Future of Hegel*, well, I looked for a virtual guiding question which, at least in principle, if I had to now explain or teach this book, would allow me to propose a deduction of its three main parts (Hegel on Man, Hegel on God, Hegel on the Philosopher). Not, of course, the 'deduction' refuted from the very beginning of the book,[39] but rather an order that would be at the same time faithful to the strategy and to the idiom of the book without however simply reproducing, imitating or repeating. I have hence attempted to put to the test, with this discourse on mourning and farewell, another idiom which at the same time accords with the intentions of the author, in truth with the gift of what she is giving, to accept it, subscribe to it or countersign it and, at the same time hence, surprise (a little, perhaps) in this gift something to interrupt in the expression 'to see (what is) coming'. To add one word, in all, only one word, in truth a strange word, a word at the same time of mourning and of salutation (farewell, farewell to oneself, farewell of God unto God) which enters in its turn in this double game of the 'at the same time', precisely where it works and at the same time interrupts the work of the expression 'to see (what is) coming', gives and receives plasticity, but also plastic explosives. In short, a concern for plasticity everywhere you look, and however you write it.

For this I would have started again from the middle of the book (second part: Hegel on God: The *Turn* of the Double Nature), but not simply in a Hegelian manner, from the meditation or the middle term of a syllogism – although it is quite rare and symptomatic to use God, as it is the case in the architectonics of this book, without transcendental dialectic, as a scene of the passage between Man and the Philosopher. At this junction point of the book, an immense debate rearticulates itself, with such precision, such finesse, such economy, on what I here propose to name or surname, since the word does not figure, if I remember correctly, the farewell, a certain farewell to God, and the farewell of God to or unto God.

It is always the question of interpreting the Hegelian interpretation of the death of God and of this *kenosis* in which, according to Paul's expression, Christ 'emptied himself of himself'. By translating *kenosis* by *Entäußerung* ('the separation of the Self through an externalization'), Luther designates a sort of exit outside one's self in one's self, a farewell to one's self, an abandonment of one's self. A taking leave of one's self in one's self. And most of all he opens the way for a tradition in which the Hegelian dialectic inscribes itself (originary division of judgement, alienation, exteriorization, exit of God outside of himself: *Entzweiung*, *Entfremdung*, *Entäußerung*)[40] and out of which the great modern discourse on the 'death of God' would lose its meaning and its memory. Theologians and thinkers of faith who protested against Hegel are numerous and their arguments are diverse. Malabou scrupulously gives to each the occasion to speak, and she does so with a precision I shall not attempt to reconstitute here. To translate, to gather or formalize the blame in my own way, I would say that all, Protestants or Catholics, seem to reproach Hegel for having systematized a farewell of God to himself. Unique realm of a requisition that deploys itself in multiple consequences: *on the one hand* this thought of a farewell to one's self receives and accepts too easily the negativity in God (this was already the reproach some advanced in regards of the Hegelian reading of Aristotle);[41] *on the other hand* the farewell of God to himself turns God towards the past ('Hegel's God has no future', has no transcendence). *Finally*, above all – and this is a phenomenon at the same time more singular and more resistant to any formalization – the deprivation of the future is to be deduced from two premises which may seem contradictory. This God who says farewell to himself would have no future, precisely because, in leaving and in emptying himself, he could no longer promise or give. This inaptitude would be due, at the same time, to the *negativity* in God (to that which separates itself from itself, impoverishes itself of itself, in what Malabou calls an 'originary penury',[42] and which would contradict all generosity) *and* (a typical Heideggerian argument, as Malabou justly remarks) to its *absolute presence*: in the farewell *to one's self*, which is nothing else but the salvation of an auto-revelation, the infinite presence, the *parousia* of God would also forbid this other present which is also the gift to the other, the offering, the future of a promise or of a donation. God would have no future, he would not even be able to promise or give himself both because he leaves and impoverishes himself (he says farewell to himself) and because, while leaving himself, he still does not leave himself, he does not abandon himself (he says *to himself* farewell, that is to say, to *his* own *self*, within a strange reflexivity of the Self, of the accusative or the dative: to say to one's self, to say to one's self farewell, to one's self or for one's self, in his proper name, farewell, a*dieu*). Is it surprising then that all these debates on the farewell to the other as a farewell to one's self are circumscribed within this alliance: *kenosis* and the Eucharistic? Too much emptiness, too much fullness. On one side, we reproach Hegel for having dialectically interpreted, as negativity, the emptiness of a God separating himself from himself and losing himself. On the other, we reproach him for having, as an uncontrollable Lutheran, too fully or too perfectly interiorized, of having dialectically interpreted the communion, the trans-substantialization, the assimilating consumption, by abusing organic metaphors of appetite, of interiorizing digestion – and of having been fascinated by the 'mysteries of eating' (Balthasar).[43] We should then accomplish one more step, add a supplement of farewell to this Hegelian farewell, and say farewell to this farewell of God to God.

I once again urge all to read this book. No more than I did with the objections which she judges both 'penetrating' and 'illegitimate', I will not here present Malabou's own answer, an answer marked by the themes of a 'divine plasticity' and of 'the essence of modern subjectivity as *kenosis*'.[44] Not only in order not to betray the richness and the subtle folds of her references, but above all because my – experimental – question is rather to suggest that the infinite logic, unusable and originally in mourning, the logic of the farewell to God, of the farewell to the farewell from God to himself, etc., continues to deploy itself from *all* sides of the discussion, and hence also, from the side of the answer to all the above mentioned objections. This logic would, in this way, infinitely attempt to fold itself (for it is a fold without any outside, any outside/inside, a fold on oneself) but to fold itself *at the same time* in plasticity and *to* plasticity. One may as well say that plasticity is an experience *of* farewell. Having said this, however, almost as a gesture towards this formal structure which is not some sort of meta-language but in which there would be no such thing as a meta-language, I do not believe I am opposed to what Malabou says, in order to respond to the objections addressed to Hegel, in her reinterpretation of Hegel's reading of the death of God. 'God himself is dead': Hegel has never ceased to return to this phrase whose Lutheran provenance he understands all too well (and we have the feeling that to read Hegel without Luther is as blinding as to read, say, Heidegger without Luther – and without Meister Eckhart;[45] even if we are unlikely to believe it in this last case). For in following all the occurrences and all the interpretations of this phrase 'God himself is dead',

Malabou intends to conclude that 'the divine negativity, thought in its most radical form, does not manifest (as it might have been objected) the lack or the passivity, but rather the *plasticity* of God'.[46] At the very moment when she shows that according to Hegel, 'the death of God appears as a moment within God's Being' and the 'advent of the "metaphysics of subjectivity"' (a proposition which, taken on its own, Heidegger would probably not have repudiated), Malabou follows a path whose very necessity is marked by this reflexivity of the farewell of God to his own self, an infinite reflexivity of the infinite farewell to one's self which does not by some chance end in finitude, in the 'situation of an absolute finitude characterized by modern philosophy'. Inasmuch as the death of Christ is the *Mittelpunkt* around which all turns and according to which begins the 'conversion of conscience' and the true 'faith' (the 'apprehension by Spirit, as the spirit of truth, the Holy Spirit'),[47] we arrive at this thought, which is at the same time a philosophical and religious thought: the negation is in God. And more so, fatal doubling, this negation in God passes by the experience of a farewell to salvation, 'the loss of all salvation', the 'feeling of complete irretrievability', the very salutation to salvation or the farewell to all and any farewell.

> *God has died* (*Gott ist gestorben*), God is dead (*Gott ist tot*) – this is the most frightful of all thoughts (*der fürchterlichste Gedanke*) that everything eternal and true is *not*, that negation itself is found in God. The deepest anguish, the feeling of complete irretrievability, the annulling that everything that is elevated are bound up with this thought.[48]

The farewell to this renunciation, to the death of God, would only be the first moment of the negation, a first negation which must double itself and return in itself as a farewell to this farewell, that is to say as a death of death itself (*mors mortis*, Luther's expression which seems to me, more literally than any other, since it concerns the very death of God, to justify the syntagm of this farewell to farewell, of this farewell to the farewell to God, etc.). Inasmuch as we must pass through the death of God and by the name of God in order to think the negation of the negation, the speculative idealism would also represent a gigantic effort, in truth a superhuman effort, to understand, with the name of God, of course, what we say when we say 'farewell'. In French, and in a few other Latin languages, in some Slavic languages also, but not in German, nor in English, where precisely the French word as such, the interjection or the exclamation rather than the name, allows itself sometimes to be used in a certain manner – rare, precious and literary.

The words of *return*, of *doubling*, and of *reduplication*, which I have just underlined to describe this infinite reflexivity of this farewell, of this negation of negation as a 'farewell', we find them first in Malabou's writing, precisely where she raises the question of the death of God as the death of death itself and as the negation of negation:

> The Death of God thereby appears for Hegel as a moment in the divine being in the form of a *first negation*, logically destined to be reduplicated and reversed: 'Rather, a reversal takes place: God, that is to say, maintains himself in this process, and the latter is only the death of death (*der Tod des Todes*).' The expression *mors mortis* is found many times in Luther's writing, but the singularity of the Hegelian version shows itself in the way he interprets this death of death as a 'negation of negation'. Supported by such an interpretation we can already predict the transition from the theological signification of *kenosis* to its philosophical meaning.
> (Ibid. p. 107)

This interpretation of the death of death itself (that which I call farewell to farewell) as the negation of the negation allows us, according to Malabou, to move from the 'theological signification of *kenosis* to its philosophical meaning' (ibid.). The process which assures the 'mutual fashioning' (this is a deliberate plastic expression) of the two instances of *kenosis*, the divine and the human, that of God and that of the 'modern subjectivity', would be a process inherent to the *Vorstellung*, that is of a representation which *at the same time* exteriorizes and interiorizes (*Entäußerung/Erinnerung*). In exteriorizing, in extra-posing its object, it alienates and empties itself, it sacrifices itself, according to a movement which already belongs to the Being of God and hence is in this way represented. The representation effectively represents it and not as a simple figurative projection. Constantly, and this is one of the major motifs of this book, as we have already noticed, this insistence concerns the difference between the schema and the figuration of the image. And precisely at the point where the analysis is of this representation as a representation *of* God (as an objective genitive) which, in its first instance, represents a representation *of* God (as a subjective genitive), we find these formulas that encourage us to speak again of farewell – and of farewell to God as a farewell to one's self, farewell *of* God *to* God. God must distance himself from God in order for everything to begin, in order for this process to proceed: that which we would or could call the history of Being, the history of Spirit, the history of God, the history of time and of the future. God *proceeds*, he moves forward by parting himself from God, even though it is to return or rejoin himself. Such is the pace with which he progresses. The pace of God which says and could only say there will be no God. God leaves and separates himself from God. This is why Hegel saw to which point the same accusation that can today denounce *pantheism*, precisely where earlier it was worried at revealing a form of *atheism*.[49] And as Malabou will say, in accordance with this meaning, 'God stands afar from God', are we not here entitled to think that, at the very height of God, a distance between God and God ('God . . . afar from God'), a distance between one's self and one's self, for God, must be infinite? And, with or without, a possible return as a farewell? Must God not take leave from God but also give himself the chance of taking his leave and effectively leaves, from and of himself, that he separates of and from himself, and finally dies of himself to himself? The name of God as farewell: does it not name something else? Malabou will have quoted Hegel at length, of which this last phrase:

> Although we consider the idea of God this way in the philosophy of religion, we at the same time also have before us the mode of God's representation. God represents only himself and does so only to himself (*er stellt sich nur vor und stellt sich selber vor sich*). This is the aspect of the existence (*Dasein*) of the absolute.

And then interpret and conclude: 'What appears from this passage is that consciousness only represents God because *God re-presents himself*; consciousness is only at a distance from God because God distances himself from himself.'

How is it possible to take or to give one's self its leave? As the plastic form itself, a leave is taken, is received or is given. I have just used the word *leave* (the leave of God! The leave which he gives himself or which he takes by himself, in his very name!) for it always signifies a movement, the pace of a passage (*commeatus*, from *commeo*), the passage through which we may pass, come and go: become a passer, past or to come. The leave that we take or give one's self (*commeatum sumere*), is the possibility, the permission of passing, of coming, of going: come now! Go! Go away! No future without leave. And hence without this separation in departure which we have here named or surnamed *farewell*.

How did the word 'leave' come to impose itself, almost in passing or by chance, in *The Future of Hegel*? If at the end of this great treatise on 'Hegel's God' – which we again invite the reader to follow step by step, at a much slower pace than what can be performed here – the figure of the 'crossing' here imposes itself, if it reminds us of the Cross and places us at the crossroads of a way (the way of the Cross or at a Greco-Oedipean crossroads: the violent death of a father or of a son is at each time inscribed in the part), if at the crossroad of two ways we ever cross ourselves and leave ourselves *at the same time*, we salute one another in saying to each other farewell (farewell as good-day or good-bye in the Midi) what can then be said of a 'crossing of times'? For it is in this way that Malabou defines the Hegelian God. 'In itself a synthesis between the Christan God and the Aristotelian God', he 'situates himself at the *crossroads of times*'.[50] The dialectical *sublation* of temporality in Absolute Knowledge would not have been possible without the teleological and circular Greek time in which one can identify the end and the beginning. Conclusion, the leave: 'This is a time which can dismiss that other time, the one which does not *lie ahead*. At the very moment where we believed time had been dismissed, *the two times* meet and unite.'

Taken, given or received, this leave of time to time, is it a farewell or a 'good-bye, until we meet again'? A farewell since they leave themselves (infinitely), but a 'goodbye, until we meet again' since they will return to themselves and already see themselves return. But who can ever distinguish between a farewell and a goodbye, until we meet again? No more than a promise, this distinction will never be appropriable by some knowledge, and especially not by an absolute knowledge and all of its *criteria*. Always and forever, 'farewell' and 'goodbye, until we meet again' will continue to haunt each other. One will always remain the ghost of the other, the spectre itself.

A precipitation without ever seeing it come. To God go! Epilogue and prolegomena on the edge of this book, an edge which, respectfully, we have held on to and on which we have been standing all along. Take leave, now, in abandoning one question. It would concern the divine plasticity but also this 'future' which would have to be saved through or beyond the 'future of God'. To give a form to this question, let us start, as always, by quoting:

> Consequently, God's inner negativity can no longer be interpreted as passivity, unless we are to understand by this passivity the passivity of time itself. But since the passivity of time is also a *gift* of form, plasticity is demonstrably the right word. Invoking this name brings into play the future of God – God as the one 'who sees (himself) coming'.[51]

What can it possibly mean, here, 'into play'? There would then be for God a more truthful name than God. There would be, in any case, a predicate that 'would be more just' in order to define the essence of God, the negative or the passive donation of form. Plasticity would be the best word for this donation. And to say this 'future of God' as 'seeing (himself) coming'. So here is the question (and it is always, as in the word *farewell*, that of the name of God and of the 'schema' that we give it or that it gives itself, that we hear or pronounce this word 'schema' as we wish, in Greek or in Hebrew where it names the name and appeals to the appellation itself): if God is dead, is it an accident? Is he dead by accident? Such an accident, would he have seen it, and seen it come – or not? Would or could he have seen it come in this sense (foresight) or in this other sense (unexpectedness) of the plasticity inherent to the expression 'to see (what is) coming'? If this accident becomes essential, the expression 'to see (what is) coming' would have been the future anterior of some sort of providence or of theodicy (the *felix culpa* is not very far, and it is a good example for the expression 'to see (what is) coming'): no more explosive surprise, no more letting come, farewell to the future! For the future to have a future, and because God himself remains still to come, should not his death, if it has ever taken place, be *purely* accidental? Absolutely unpredictable and never re-appropriable, never re-essentializable, not even by some endless work of mourning, not even, and above all, by God himself? A God who would have, without ever seeing it come, let an infinite bomb explode in his hands, a God dead by some hopeless accident, hopeless of any salvation or redemption, without essentializing *sublation*, without any work of mourning and without any possible return or refund, would that be the condition of a future, if there must be such a thing called the future? The very condition for something to come, and even that of another God, of an absolute other God?

Who could or would possibly be ready or able to subscribe to such a history, I ask you? Neither Hegel, nor the theologians or thinkers of faith who believe they are opposed to him.

And yourself?

I do not know anymore. Here. We must believe, if we must believe, that at this point the word 'accident', as that which it opposes itself without being opposed, essence, I mean to say, and Being and all of those concepts, this word, these words belong to an idiom which I am not sure any more of being able to understand. It is as though, in history, in my history, a strange accident happened to the word 'accident' (and hence to the word 'essence'), an accident of which I am no longer sure, of which no one can be sure of being able to *sublate*. 'Farewell', the noun or the exclamation (the *performative* salutation! Yet another plastic connotation!), in the plasticity of these idiomatic values, a mobile and reflexive, specular or speculative plasticity (and so dangerous), I have not used it in the time of this dialogue, because, as the 'perhaps', it has occupied me at great length these times, but in order to let one understand, in *this* idiom, my own incomprehension, a certain increasing and stubborn non-intelligence, on this stubbornness precisely, of an idiom, of more than one idiom, perhaps, at the crossroads of the Greek and of its other, go wonder . . .

Translated by Joseph D. Cohen

ACKNOWLEDGEMENTS

This book is a revision of my doctoral thesis, which was completed under the supervision of Jacques Derrida and defended on 15 December 1994 at the École Normale Supérieure. The jury was presided over by Bernard Bourgeois and composed of Denise Souche-Dagues, Jacques Derrida, Jean-François Courtine and Jean-Luc Marion. The perspicacity of their reading made the defence of this thesis a decisive event for me and, in many respects, shaped the future path I have pursued.

Bernard Bourgeois did me the honor of not only recognizing the validity of an interpretation of Hegel not without its contentious aspects, but also of perceiving, better than I could, the direction it was taking.

Jean-Luc Marion showed me his trust, his support, his benevolence. He knows all that I owe him. I can here only tell him once again of my friendship and my admiration.

Jean-François Courtine has been a remarkable reader and re-reader of my work. He has been unstinting with advice and encouragement during the revision I undertook. I am very grateful to him for including my book in his series.

I thank my family and friends, in particular Lucette Finas and Hervé Touboul, for their unfailing support during the difficult period in which *The Future of Hegel* was conceived and written.

I completed this book while in my first year of teaching at the University of Paris-X. I hope my new colleagues will know how much the warmth of their welcome has made my task easier.

Alain Pernet, from the CNRS, has been extremely helpful in the finalizing of the manuscript. I am sincerely grateful to him.

In everything essential my work is beholden to the writings, the teaching, and the friendship of Jacques Derrida. I trust that this book – did he ever see it coming? – will show him the extent of my debt.

PRELIMINARY REMARKS

Aufhebung has been systematically translated by *sublation*, *aufheben* by *sublate*, modifying the actual translations. *Begriff* has always been translated by *Concept*. The title of the third volume of Hegel's *Science of Logic* has been translated as the *Doctrine of the Notion [Concept]*. Two major difficulties were encountered in the translation of Catherine Malabou's text. These concern the French expressions 'voir venir' and 'devenir essentiel de l'accident/devenir accidentel de l'essence'. 'Voir venir', which means at the same time to anticipate while not knowing what comes, has been translated by the phrase 'to see (what is) coming', the parentheses marking the reserve inherent in waiting itself. As for the second expression, it has been translated as 'the becoming essential of the accident/the becoming accidental of essence'.

INTRODUCTION

The Problematic

The philosophy of Hegel: is it a 'thing of the past'?

The title, *The Future of Hegel*, can be read as an affirmation, as if anticipating a positive response to the question: Does Hegel have a future? At the end of the twentieth century, this question must inevitably be asked. While philosophy, willingly celebrating the greatness of Hegel, acknowledges how much it is in his debt, speculative idealism has been suspected of totalization, and even of having totalitarian designs. If it has not been entirely repudiated, it has at the very least been kept at a distance. It is impossible to consider Hegel's future today as something already guaranteed, established and recognized. This future itself is still to come. It remains to be demonstrated and discovered. Such a demonstration is what the present work intends to provide.

By 'future of Hegel', one must understand first of all the future *of* his philosophy. 'Future' (*avenir*), in the ordinary sense of the word, means the time to come (*futur*), what lies ahead. Etymology confirms this connection: the future (*l'a-venir*) means that which is to come (*ad-vient*). But it denotes also that which is capable of lasting: to 'have a future' is to have the right to posterity. Now, and this is the fundamental problem, does the philosophy of Hegel have legitimate descendants? How can it still hold out a promise? How can it continue to play a leading role in our time, when history has shown it to be an enterprise that brings time to an end?

Time: everything began with time. And it is on the account of time that the divorce between Hegel and contemporary philosophy was decreed. The famous conclusion to the *Phenomenology of Spirit* signed the death sentence, so to speak, of Hegelianism:

> Time is the concept itself that *is there* and which presents itself to consciousness as empty intuition; for this reason Spirit necessarily appears in time, and it appears in time just as long as it has not

> *grasped* its pure concept, i.e. has not annulled time. It is the *outer*, intuited pure self which is *not grasped* by the self, the merely intuited concept; when this latter grasps itself it sublates its time-form (*hebt seine Zeitform auf*), comprehends this intuiting, and is a comprehended and comprehending intuiting. Time, therefore, appears as the destiny and necessity of spirit that is not yet complete within itself (*der nicht in sich vollendet ist*).[1]

Many interpreters have concluded from this analysis that time was for Hegel nothing but *a passing moment*, something to be left behind. And it does appear that time itself, unwilling to forgive Absolute Knowledge for having ordained its dialectical suppression, has demanded reparations. In philosophy this demand has been articulated most forcefully by Heidegger, who argues that when time is sublated (*aufgehoben*) by spirit at the moment of Absolute Knowledge, this is in fact simply the *vulgar* or common notion of time. The 'vulgar understanding of time' is a conception that Heidegger believes has dominated the entire history of metaphysics and now ends with it. The stereotype is complete: 'Hegel's concept of time presents the most radical way in which the vulgar understanding of time has been given form conceptually'.[2]

It was initially Aristotle who developed the concept of this 'ordinary understanding of time', which he understood as a sequence of 'nows'. Aristotelian time passes by without beginning or end, constituting the uniform flux within which the sequence of events unfolds: 'Time appears to the vulgar understanding as a succession of nows constantly "present-at-hand (*vorhandenen*)", that pass by and arrive at the same moment. Time is understood as a sequence, as a "flux" of nows, like the "stream of time".'[3]

According to Heidegger, the paragraphs devoted to time in the *Encyclopedia of the Philosophical Sciences* simply reiterate point by point the Aristotelian problematic of the στιγμή[4] developed in Book IV of the *Physics*. Hegel may have perfected the classical idea of 'instantaneousness', giving it the conceptual determination of 'punctuality' (*Pünktlichkeit*). It is Hegel who maintains that:

> The negativity which relates itself to space as point (*die sich als Punkt auf den Raum bezieht*) and develops its determinations within it as line and plane, exists also as something for-itself and for its determinations in the sphere of externality (*des Äußersichseins*); yet at the same time as positing those determinations in the external space, it appears indifferent to the immobile juxtaposition (*das ruhige Nebeneinander*) of space. Posited thus for-itself, negativity is *time*.[5]

A spatial determination – the point – serves to characterize a temporal determination – the instant. But such a concept of time, seeming to reduce temporality to nothing but the form of juxtaposition, strikes us today as stripped of all future.

The ordinary understanding of time is what constitutes for Heidegger the unity of the philosophical tradition summed up for him in the name 'metaphysics'. Metaphysics, in this view, was ruled by a certain determination of *being*, understood in the sense of *presence* (οὐσία, *Anwesenheit*), and that is tantamount to privileging the present tense (*Gegenwart*) with respect to the other dimensions of time. Consequently, the past and future must necessarily appear as either a *present* time which is just past,[6] or a *present* which is to come ('that which is not-yet-now'). In Heidegger's view, the conception of time as a homogeneous milieu in which events occur dominated philosophy from the Pre-Socratics to Husserl. Hegel stands out however from the other philosophers because he takes to its logical conclusion this traditional privilege of the present. In the speculative conception of time, the future is not even *a time like other times*: it lacks the power to *preserve* itself, succumbing to the advances (that is to say, the ontological priority) of the past understood as the previous modality of the present.

In his lectures of 1930 on *Hegel's Phenomenology of Spirit*, Heidegger claims:

> Undoubtedly [Hegel] occasionally speaks about having been, but never about the future. This silence fits with the fact that (for him) the past is itself the decisive character of time, and for a good reason: time is both the passing itself and what passes; it has always passed away.[7]

Time for Hegel is understood as the past tense of spirit: spirit must pass over (*übergehen*) into time in order to fulfil its own identity with itself as absolute and eternal. That identity, in its turn, is itself a past but a past not yet temporally passed away.[8] It is the timeless antiquity of 'presence', the '*parousia*' of the absolute. From its standpoint, everything that occurs can be only the indication of what has already come to pass; everything still in the future is simply a potential return to itself.

In fact, for Hegel, isn't it the case that everything that occurs has done so too late? Isn't youth itself, in its very novelty, already belated? In the *Philosophy of Spirit* of *The Encyclopedia of Philosophical Sciences*, at the moment where he analyses 'the natural course of the ages of life', Hegel makes it clear that the characteristic of youth is to believe in the future, to think that the world is not yet all it really is: 'The exalted spirit of the youth does not recognize that the substantial universe, in its essence, has already achieved in this world its development and its actuality (*Wirklichkeit*).'[9] The youth must wait to grow old to understand that the world 'possesses the absolute power to actualize itself and that it has done so in our time; that it is not so impotent that it needs first to await its effective realization.'[10]

The absolute does not wait, was never expected (*ne s'est jamais attendu*), will never be awaited. The tension towards the unexpected (*l'inattendu*) is only one of youth's illusions, one which Hegel himself remembers as his own before the crisis of his Frankfurt period. But too late. In its twilight discourse, at the beginning of its night, philosophy may be nothing but the announcement of this truth: it is too late for the future.

At this announcement, don't we begin to feel constricted, as if ontology has closed in on us? The System: doesn't it seem to be a tight loop which envelops everything – all exteriority, all alterity, all surprise? Hegel asserts that spirit has no absolute other than itself, *for the absolute there is no absolute alterity*: 'For spirit, nothing exists which is absolutely other than itself'. That is why: 'All spirit's activity is nothing but a grasping of itself, and the aim of all genuine science is only this, to know that spirit recognizes in itself everything there is in heaven and on earth.'[11]

Spirit, whose task is to comprehend itself, to anticipate itself in everything that is now and is to come, can never encounter anything wholly other, can never come face to face, one might say, with the *event*. How, then, could there be room in Hegelian thought for the question of the future, if everything has already been permeated by spirit and, in this fashion, already completed?

Scattered throughout recent philosophical texts, any number of analyses note this rigid, fixed, and deadening character of speculative thought. Kojève himself, while committed to stress the timeliness of Hegelian thought as a means with which to think the future, nonetheless defines Absolute Knowledge in terms of 'the end of time'.[12] But can there be any temporality which corresponds to this 'end of time' except time's stasis in the congealed form of a *perpetual present*? Heidegger states: 'Hegel's explication of the genuine concept of Being . . ., is nothing less than a farewell to time on the road to spirit, which is eternal.'[13]

Hasn't Hegel's 'farewell' to time simply been turned around to time's 'farewell' to Hegel? Indeed, could it be that time as it exists for speculative philosophy is not actually time at all, but rather the flattening or levelling-down (*Nivellierung*) of time, at least of that authentic time called by Heidegger 'primordial' or 'originary temporality (*ursprüngliche Zeit*)'? Primordial time cannot be conceived in terms of the present, for its most fundamental 'ecstasy' is the future. Primordial temporality, Heidegger writes, 'temporalizes itself *primarily* out of the *future*'.[14] Thus the authentic future, for Heidegger, is no longer a simple moment of time, but becomes almost indistinguishable from time itself.

It is not my purpose here to stage a confrontation between the Hegelian and Heideggerian conceptions of time. However, the notion of the future has changed in the course of the twentieth century in ways it would be impossible to overlook. If we fail to be aware that the idea of the future has, as it were, a 'future', then we would be ourselves guilty of 'levelling-down' that very future and, in a sense, lagging behind it.

Now, whatever else is risked in the undertaking I am beginning here, what I want most of all to avoid is the reactionary, nostalgic tone. The success, the 'future', of this approach will depend on its capacity to remain open to those arguments that oppose it. In particular it must remain open to that analysis which claims that the absence of a conception of the future *in* Hegel implies the absence *of* a future *for* the philosophy of Hegel. To say, with Heidegger, that Hegel never speaks about the future amounts to saying that Hegel does not have a future. The present work contests the validity of Heidegger's assertion, while recognizing what it means and the philosophical concerns it continues to provoke. Against this claim, we affirm that there is indeed a 'future of Hegel'.

The promise of plasticity

With this end in view, our plan is to form a concept, that of 'plasticity', as foreshadowed in the title: 'The Future of Hegel, *Plasticity*, Temporality, Dialectic'. To 'form a concept' in the sense intended here means first of all to take up a concept (*plasticity*), which has a defined and delimited role in the philosophy of Hegel, only in order to transform it into the sort of comprehensive concept that can 'grasp' (*saisir*) the whole. Here the double sense of *grasp* as 'seizing' (*prendre*) and 'understanding' (*comprendre*) is authorized by the etymology of the word 'concept'. Transforming plasticity into a concept is a matter of showing that plasticity 'seizes' (*prend*) the philosophy of Hegel and allows the reader to 'comprehend' it, appearing at one and the same time as a *structure* and as a *condition of intelligibility*.

Second, to form a concept means to take an instance with the power *of giving form* to whatever it grasps, and then to elaborate (*élaborer*) it. Hegel repeatedly insists on this feature of the concept: although it is a logical form, the concept must not be considered like an empty receptacle, rather as a power that can fashion its own content. By giving plasticity a mediating position between 'future' and 'temporality', my title: 'The *Future* of Hegel: Plasticity, *Temporality*, Dialectic' – already indicates that *plasticity* will be envisaged as the 'instance' which *gives form to* the future and to time in Hegel's philosophy. That is to say, their relationship is constructed in the mode of plasticity; time and the future are mutually involved in a dialogical process governed by plasticity. From this it follows that the concepts of future and of plasticity need to be treated concurrently, one clarifying the other as a title is clarified by its subtitle.

But this relation of synonymy needs to be reversed into a relation of *asymmetry*. Indeed, to posit the future as 'plasticity' amounts to *displacing* the established definition of the future as a *moment of time*. And indeed in the title such a displacement has already been announced: 'the future', that which is 'to come', will not be restricted in meaning by the immediate, ordinary connotation, that of the 'future' as a tense. It is not a matter of examining the relations between past, present and the conventional sense of the future presented in the discussions of time in Hegel's different versions of the *Philosophy of Nature.*[15] Rather these texts themselves demand that we renounce the 'well-known' and familiar meaning of the future and, as a consequence, the 'well-known' definition of time. The possibility that one temporal determination, the future, can be thought differently, beyond its initial, simple status as a moment of time, from 'that which is now to come', makes it immediately clear that time for Hegel cannot be reduced to an ordered relation between moments. By 'plasticity' we mean first of all the excess of the future over the future; while 'temporality', as it figures in speculative philosophy, will mean the excess of time over time.

These preliminary remarks indicate that my work will not follow the path set out by Koyré and Kojève, although both do pursue this question of the 'future' *in* Hegel's philosophy. Koyré, in his article on 'Hegel in Jena',[16] and Kojève, in his *Introduction to the Reading of Hegel*,[17] recognize that in the 'Systems' of the Jena period, the future has a 'prevalence' or alternately, a 'priority', over the past and the present. Thus both writers show here the proximity between the thought of the young Hegel and that of Heidegger. But the kind of project they represent, as significant as it is, does not give us the means to respond to the question of the future of Hegel. Besides the fact that the problem of an 'orientation towards the future' is in no respect a Hegelian problematic, this way of reading Hegel leads, as Koyré and Kojève both admit, to an impasse. They conclude that there is an unresolved contradiction in the philosophy of Hegel: it can only grant the future a priority over the other moments of time by *suspending* at once all future yet to come.

Koyré, on the one hand, argues that for Hegel, 'time is dialectical and . . . is constructed from the vantage point of the future', but on the other hand, he asserts that

> the philosophy of history – and in that respect the philosophy of Hegel as a whole, the System, so to speak – can only be a possibility if history has come to an end, if it has no more future; if time can stop.[18]

Hegel was never able to 'conciliate' the two meanings that the notion of the future takes on in his System: on the one hand, a chronological future, whose dynamic is the foundation of all historical development, and, on the other hand, a future as the logical 'happening' of the concept, i.e. the concept in the 'act-of-coming-to-itself (*Zu-sich-selbst-kommen*)'.[19]

Kojève, for his part, maintains on the one hand that 'Time for Hegel is characterized by the primacy of the Future',[20] but, on the other hand, 'man' when he achieves the standpoint of Absolute Knowledge has no future left:

> Man who no longer relates himself . . . to an object given externally, thus has no further reason to *negate* it for the sake of remaining in existence and conserving his self-identity. And Man who no longer negates has no real future.[21]

A supposed contradiction which, by its very nature, could not be dialectical as it remains irresoluble: it was common for early twentieth-century interpreters of Hegel to draw attention to this 'discovery'. But the work of a new generation of French commentators – Bernard Bourgeois, Pierre-Jean Labarrière, Gérard Lebrun, Denise Souche-Dagues[22] – establishes on the contrary that 'historical becoming' and 'logical truth' form a dynamic unity in Hegelian philosophy. Admittedly these studies have not resolved the problem of the relation between 'eternity' and 'historicity' in Hegelianism, but they have sufficiently clarified it that it no longer needs to be thematized here as a *subject*. If my approach does not return to this problematic, neither does it take the form of an analysis of the structural relation connecting the *Phenomenology of Spirit* and the *Science of Logic*. Nor, finally, does it undertake the examination of the relation between a philosophy of history and the immanent derivation of the concept within the confines of the System. These problems will be continually referred to in the course of my inquiry, but they do not constitute its *themes*.

The possibility of affirming the 'future of Hegel' – in the double meaning of a future 'of' his philosophy and the future 'within' his philosophy – depends in the first instance on posing the question of the future where one does not expect it. Henceforth it is *plasticity* which will be presented as the 'unforeseen' of Hegelian philosophy.

To this extent, the future of the concept of plasticity itself must be put into play. Its viability depends on the success of an epistemological operation which resembles, in its method, that defined by Georges Canguilhem in terms that would become famous:

> To elaborate (*travailler*) a concept is to vary both its extension and its intelligibility. It is to generalize it by incorporating its exceptions. It is to export it outside its original domain, to use it as a model or conversely to find it a model, in short it is to give to it, bit by bit, through ordered transformations, the function of a *form*.[23]

Such an operation will guide us, throughout the scope of this work, in testing the very plasticity of the concept of plasticity itself.

Hegelian philosophy and the test of plasticity

Plasticity in its ordinary meanings

To elaborate (*travailler*) the concept of 'plasticity' will, following Canguilhem's usage, amount to 'giving the function of a form' to a term which itself, in its first sense, describes or *designates the act of giving form.* The English and French substantives 'plasticity' and *plasticité* and their German equivalent, *Plastizität*, entered the language in the eighteenth century. They joined two words already in use which had been formed from the same root: the substantive 'plastics' (*die Plastik*), and the adjective 'plastic' (*plastisch*).[24] All three words are derived from the Greek *plassein* (πλάσσειν), which means 'to model', 'to mould'. 'Plastic', as an adjective, means two things: on the one hand, to be 'susceptible to changes of form' or malleable (clay is a 'plastic' material); and on the other hand, 'having the power to bestow form, the power to mould', as in the expressions, 'plastic surgeon' and 'plastic arts'. This twofold signification is met again in the German adjective *plastisch*. Grimm's dictionary defines it thus: 'that which takes or gives shape, or figure, to bodies' (*körperlich . . . gestaltend oder gestaltet*).[25] *Plasticité*, or 'plasticity', just like *Plaztizität* in German, describes the nature of that which is 'plastic', being at once capable of receiving and of giving form.

These definitions help to clarify the 'hermeneutic circle' in which this undertaking is caught, since we cannot complete the formation of the term 'plasticity' without giving it a definition and, in this case, the defining and the defined are identical. Admittedly, if we are to separate one from the other, 'the extension must vary'. But these alterations themselves take advantage of the signification of the term 'plasticity': indeed, the word's evolution in the language reveals already its 'exportation outside its original domain'. Plasticity's native land is the field of art. Plasticity characterizes the art of 'modelling' and, in the first instance, the art of sculpture. The plastic arts are those whose central aim is the articulation and development of forms; among these are counted architecture, drawing and painting. Hence, by extension, plasticity signifies the general aptitude for development, the power to be moulded by one's culture, by education. We speak of the plasticity of the newborn, of the child's plasticity of character. Plasticity is, in another context, characterized by 'suppleness' and flexibility, as in the case of the 'plasticity' of the brain. Yet it also means the ability to evolve and adapt. It is this sense we invoke when we speak of a 'plastic virtue' possessed by animals, plants, and, in general, all living things.

The 'extension' I have been drawing out must be understood in a particular way. By analogy to a malleable material, children are said to be 'plastic'. However, the adjective 'plastic', while certainly in opposition to 'rigid', 'fixed' and 'ossified', is not to be confused with 'polymorphous'.

Things that are plastic preserve their shape, as does the marble in a statue: once given a configuration, it is unable to recover its initial form. 'Plastic', thus, designates those things that lend themselves to being formed while *resisting* deformation. From this it is possible to understand a further 'extension' of this term into the terrain of histology, in which 'plasticity' represents the ability of tissue to re-form itself after a lesion.

Plasticity's range of meanings is not yet exhausted, and it continues to evolve with and in the language. *Plastic material* is a synthetic material which can take on different shapes and properties according to the functions intended. 'Plastic' on its own is an explosive material with a nitroglycerine and nitrocellulose base that can set off violent detonations. The plasticity of the word itself draws it to extremes, both to those concrete shapes in which form is crystallized (sculpture) and to the annihilation of all form (the bomb).

Hegel's idea of plasticity

To form the concept of plasticity as it figures in Hegel's philosophy requires first of all that we uncover the way in which Hegel himself constructs this idea. When we take this further, we find that three areas of meaning are mutually implicated. In each case that double connotation of the adjective 'plastic' reappears: a capacity to receive form and a capacity to produce form. It is this double signification which enables us to treat the adjective as itself a 'speculative word', in Hegel's special sense.

The first relevant field of signification is that of the 'plastic arts'. The words *plastisch* and *Plastik* appear frequently in Hegel's discussions of Greek art, especially in the *Aesthetics* where sculpture is defined as 'the plastic art par excellence'.[26] This more familiar sense of 'plasticity', invoked and extended, authorizes the philosopher to develop his notion further: it acquires a greater range and complexity in its second signifying field, where it applies to those entities he entitles 'plastic individualities' or 'plastic characters'. In Hegel's account, 'plasticity' describes the nature of those Greek figures who represent an individuality he names 'exemplary' (*exemplarische*) and 'substantial' (*substantielle*). 'Pericles . . ., Phidias, Plato, and above all Sophocles, as well as Thucydides, Xenophon, Socrates', are 'plastic individuals': 'They are great and free, grown independently on the soil of their own inherently substantial personality, self-made, and developing into what they (essentially) were and wanted to be.'[27]

Hegel insists on the fact that:

> This sense for the perfect plasticity of gods and men was pre-eminently at home in Greece (*dieser Sinn für die vollendete Plastik der Göttlichen und Menschlichen war vornehmlich in Griechenland heimisch*). In its poets and orators, historians and

> philosophers, Greece is not to be understood at its heart unless we bring with us as a key to our comprehension an insight into the ideals of sculpture and unless we consider from the point of view of their plasticity not only the heroic figures in epic and drama but also the actual statesmen and philosophers. After all, in the beautiful days of Greece, men of action, like poets and thinkers, had this same plastic and universal yet individual character both inwardly and outwardly (*diesen plastischen, allgemeinen und doch individuellen, nach außen wie nach innen gleichen Charakter*).[28]

These 'plastic individualities' give form to the 'spiritual in its embodiment' (*Körperlichkeit des Geistigen*). Thus the theme of plastic individuality itself represents a middle term, a mediation between plasticity in its first signifying domain, that of sculpture,[29] and its third, that of *philosophical plasticity*.

The expression 'philosophical plasticity' must be understood in two different ways. On the one hand, it characterizes the philosophical attitude, the behaviour specific to the philosopher. On the other hand, it applies to philosophy itself, to its form and manner of being, that is to say, to that rhythm in which the speculative content is unfolded and presented.

In the 'Preface' to *the Science of Logic* of 1831 Hegel states:

> A plastic discourse (*ein plastischer Vortrag*) demands, too, a plastic sense of receptivity and understanding on the part of the listener (*einen plastischen Sinn des Aufnehmens und Verstehens*); but youths and men of such a temper who would calmly suppress *their own* reflections and opinions in which 'the need to think for oneself' is so impatient to manifest itself, listeners such as Plato imagined, who would attend only to the matter at hand (*nur der Sache folgender Zuhörer*), could have no place in a modern dialogue; still less could one count on readers of such a disposition.[30]

The plastic individuality of the Greeks thus acquires the value of a model for the ideal philosophical attitude.[31] Plasticity here designates primarily the ability of the philosophizing subject to attend to the content, the 'matter at hand', by purifying the form of all that is arbitrary and personal, all that is immediate and particular. However, as we have seen, 'plasticity' does not mean 'polymorphous'. The philosophical reader and interlocutor are of course receptive to the form, but they in their turn are led to construct and form what they hear or read.[32] In this sense they become comparable, Hegel reasons, to the Greek 'plastic individualities'. If, like those models, the ideal philosophers are both 'universal and individual', this comes from the way they acquire their formative principle from the universal – the concept – while at the same time bestowing a particular form on the universal by *incarnating* it or embodying it. Thus the individual now becomes the 'Dasein', the 'being-there' of spirit, the form in which the spiritual is translated into the materiality of sense. Consequently, plasticity appears as a process where the universal and the particular mutually inform one another, and their joint outcome is that particularity called the 'exemplary individual'.

These remarks lead us to think further about the second connotation of philosophical plasticity. For what is a 'plastic discourse' (*ein plastischer Vortrag*)? A passage from the Preface to the *Phenomenology of Spirit* helps clarify this definition: 'Only a philosophical exposition that rigidly excludes (*streng ausschlösse*) the usual way of relating the parts of a proposition could achieve the goal of plasticity (*diesjenige philosophische Exposition würde es erreichen plastisch zu sein*).'[33]

As a philosophical proposition is normally understood, the subject of the proposition is thought of as a fixed instance: it is given predicates from outside, and is not able to produce them itself. 'To exclude rigidly the usual way of relating the parts of a proposition' implies a reconceptualizing of this relation, which is now to be understood as a process of substance's 'self-determination' (*Selbstbestimmung*). Substance's relation to its accidents changes from one conception to another, and this Hegel interprets as the transition from the *predicative* proposition to the *speculative* proposition.

Elevated into its speculative truth, the relation between subject and predicates is characterized by 'plasticity'. Within the process of self-determination, the universal (the substance) and particular (the accidents as something independent) give form to each other through a dynamic like that at play in the 'plastic individualities'. The process of self-determination is the unfolding of the *substance-subject.* In the process, substance withdraws from itself in order to enter into the particularity of its content. Through this movement of self-negation substance will posit itself as subject.

As Bernard Bourgeois remarks,

> the subject is that infinite activity, or, more precisely, negativity, whose identity is in this way made true, concrete, and mediated, and which actualizes itself in its internal self-differentiation, in its division or original scission (*ursprüngliches Teilen*), that is to say, in its 'judgment' (*Urteil*). The identity that belongs to the subject affirms itself in its difference whereas the identity at the level of substance can only be affirmed in the negation of difference which is also implicit in that identity.[34]

Self-determination is the movement through which substance affirms itself as at once *subject* and *predicate* of itself. In the *Encyclopedia*'s *Science of Logic* Hegel defines the 'relation between substantiality and accidentality', or the 'Absolute Relation', as the 'activity-of-form' (*Formtätigkeit*).[35] Indeed it is this 'activity' that clearly indicates the very *plasticity of substance* itself, its capacity both to receive form and to give form to its own content. With this consideration of self-determination, seen as the 'originary operation of plasticity', we arrive at the very heart of the present study.

'To see (what is) coming' and the Dialectic

The rhythm of this pulse becomes clear through the third term, the last in my title – 'The Future of Hegel: Plasticity, Temporality, *Dialectic*'. The foundation of the dialectical process is in fact a movement, the movement of self-determination. Its energy flows from the contradictory tension between particular determinacy as it is held and preserved, and the dissolution of everything determinate in the universal. In the *Science of Logic* Hegel demonstrates that this same tension is operative in the way a 'first term', posited 'in and for itself', a moment which has the appearance of 'self-subsistence' (*Selbstständigkeit*)', displays itself as 'the other of itself' by dissolving the fixity of its position.[36]

In the logical unfolding of the 'substance-subject', the possibility of this dynamic of preservation and dissolution takes shape, as a passage in the Preface to the *Phenomenology* shows clearly: 'On account of its simplicity or self-identity (*Sichselbstgleichheit*), substance appears fixed (*fest*) and enduring (*bleibend*). But this self-identity is no less negativity, therefore its fixed existence passes over into its dissolution (*Auflösung*).'[37]

The dialectical process is 'plastic' because, as it unfolds, it makes links between the opposing moments of total immobility (the 'fixed') and vacuity ('dissolution'), and then links both in the vitality of the whole, a whole which, reconciling these two extremes, is itself the union of *resistance* (*Widerstand*) and fluidity (*Flüssigkeit*). The process of plasticity is dialectical because the operations which constitute it, the seizure of form and the annihilation of all form, emergence and explosion, are contradictory.[38]

The connection linking the three concepts, 'Plasticity', 'Temporality', and 'Dialectic', now becomes clear: it is nothing less than the *formation* of the future itself. Plasticity characterizes the relation between substance and accidents. Now the Greek word συμβεβηκός, 'accident', derives from the verb συμβαίνειν which means at the same time to follow from, to ensure and to arrive, to happen. Thereby it can designate *continuation* in both senses of the word, as *consequence*, that is, 'what follows' in the logical sense, and as *event*, that is, 'what follows' in a chronological sense. Self-determination is thus the relation of substance to that which happens. Following this line of thought we understand the 'future' in the philosophy of Hegel as the relation which subjectivity maintains with the accidental.

To understand the future otherwise than in the ordinary immediate sense of 'a moment of time' requires by the same token an opening-out of the meaning of time: an extension made possible by the very *plasticity* of temporality itself. The deployment of the Hegelian conception of time is not fixed by reference to the places and the times – to the 'moments' – of its treatment within the System. Time is a dialectically differentiated instance; its being divided into definite moments determines it only *for a moment.*

The dialectical composition of such concepts as 'the future', 'plasticity', and 'temporality' forms the *anticipatory structure* operating within subjectivity itself as Hegel conceived it. To distinguish this structure from the future as it is ordinarily understood, we will name this structure 'to see (what is) coming' (*le 'voir venir'*), obeying Hegel's injunction to philosophize in one's own idiom. 'Voir venir' in French means to wait, while, as is prudent, observing how events are developing. But it also suggests that other people's intentions and plans must be probed and guessed at. It is an expression that can thus refer at one and the same time to the state of 'being sure of what is coming' ('être sûr de ce qui vient') and of 'not knowing what is coming' ('ne pas savoir ce qui va venir'). It is on this account that the 'voir venir', 'to see (what is) coming', can represent that interplay, within Hegelian philosophy, of teleological necessity and surprise.

The structure of 'to see (what is) coming' creates its own demarcations. From the *internal* side, the concept is determined by the way it functions *within* Hegel's thought; on the *external* side, it is decisive for the future *of* Hegel's thought. To elaborate as a whole all the instances of the Hegelian concept of plasticity implies the task of 'varying the intelligibility' of this concept, 'extending' its signification 'through ordered transformations'. This amounts to the following: revealing the link between these two sides, internal and external, and, no less, discovering the manner in which 'form' happens (*la manière dont la forme prend*) in the Hegelian System and after it.

Plasticity is, therefore, the point around which all the transformations of Hegelian thought revolve, the centre of its metamorphoses.

The two stages of time in Hegel

Time, as deployed in this philosophy, is neither a univocal nor a fixed concept. In fact, Hegel works (in) on two 'times' at once. Paragraph 258 of the *Encyclopedia* stands as a proof of this. 'Time', Hegel states in this paragraph, is 'the being which, in being, is not and in not-being, is'.[39] A *dialectical* understanding of this phrase brings out its necessary 'double meaning'. Normally, it can be understood in the first and primary way: time is and is not to the degree that its moments cancel each other out; the present is a 'now' which exists, but as it is something which passes, it will soon, almost immediately in fact, exist no longer; this is the present as an instant hanging between two non-existents, the past and the future. Further, Hegel writes in the next paragraph, §259: 'The dimensions of time, present, future, and past, are the *becoming* of exteriority as such, and the resolution (*Auflösung*) of it into the differences of Being as passing over into nothing, and of nothing as passing over into Being.' But to understand 'becoming' as the co-implication of presence and nothingness, as a twofold negation of 'nows', while it is accurate, remains incomplete. If time is 'the being which, in being, is not and in non-being, is', then this also means, rigorously put: 'Time itself is not what it is.' Time is not always (simultaneously, successively, and permanently) the same as itself. The concept of time has its own moments: it differentiates itself and thus temporalizes itself.

Logical differentiation

This differentiation becomes immediately apparent on a careful reading of §§258 and 259. Here time is *simultaneously* presented both according to its classical Greek, or more precisely, Aristotelian determination and according to its modern, that is to say, Kantian determination. If the analysis of the now, the definition of time as 'a being which, in being, is not', is effectively borrowed from *Physics* IV, the definition of time as 'the pure form of sensibility' (Hegel writes in fact: 'Time, like space, is a pure form of sense or intuition; it is the non-sensuous sensuous (*das unsinnliche Sinnliche*)') obviously comes from the *Critique of Pure Reason*.

By claiming, in the Remark to §258: 'Time is the same principle as the I = I of pure self-consciousness (*das selbe Prinzip als das Ich = Ich*)', Hegel absorbs the conclusions of Kant's analysis and recalls the identity of the 'cogito' and time itself. This identity of time and the 'cogito' cannot be reduced to a continuum of instants; rather it appears as a synthetic unity, that is as a 'seeing of (what is) coming'. It is evident that by defining time as a 'sensible non-sensible' – a reference to the Kantian definition of the pure form of intuition – Hegel is not reducing the understanding of time to a mere series of nows. In this connection, Jacques Derrida remarks that Heidegger utterly ignores the fact that Hegel introduces Kant 'into his paraphrase of Aristotle'. Heidegger fails to 'relate this Hegelian concept of the "sensuous non-sensuous" to its Kantian equivalent'.[40]

The Hegelian analysis of time is not aimed at the single 'now'; nor does time appear in it as 'that in which' becoming has its place. Hegel clarifies this: 'It is not *in* time that everything comes to be and passes away, rather time itself is the *becoming*.' Derrida comments: 'Hegel took multiple precautions of this type. By opposing them to all the metaphorical formulations that state the "fall" into time, . . . one could exhibit an entire Hegelian critique of intratemporality (*Innerzeitigkeit*).'[41]

The same conclusions can be drawn about the reference to Aristotle. Hegel clearly adopted the Aristotelian problematic of the στιγμή. In defining time, he followed the first phase of the *aporia* set out in *Physics* IV: time is composed of 'nows'. But Hegel also takes on, although not explicitly, the second part of the *aporia*: time is not composed of 'nows'. Derrida directs our attention to this point precisely. In the second phase of the *aporia*, Aristotle argues that it is impossible for the parts of time to coexist with one another: 'A now cannot coexist, as a current and present now, with another now as such.'[42] Derrida concludes:

> The impossibility of co-existence can be posited as such only on the basis of a certain co-existence, of a certain *simultaneity* of the nonsimultaneous, in which the alterity and identity of the now are maintained together in the differentiated element of a certain sameness (*un certain même*) . . . The impossible – the co-existence of two nows – appears only in a synthesis . . . in a certain complicity or complication *maintaining* (*maintenant*) together several current nows (*maintenants*) which are said to be the one past and the other future.[43]

The writer draws attention to the little word *hama*, which appears five times in *Physics* IV, 218a, and means 'together', 'all at once', 'both together', and 'at the same time'. This locution 'is first neither spatial nor temporal'. The *simul*, here, 'says the complicity, the common origin of time (the possibility of the synthesis of the co-existence of the nows) and space (the potential synthesis of the co-existence of points), appearing together as the condition for all appearing of being.'[44]

The exposition of *Physics* IV allows us to see how Aristotle understands time at the same 'time' as a sequence of nows and as an instance of synthesis.

In Hegel's analysis of the relation between space and time, he shows that the same conception of the synthesis applies. In reference to space he writes:

> It is inadmissible to speak of *spatial points* as if they constituted the positive element in space (on account of its lack of difference), space is merely the possibility, not the positedness of a state of juxtaposition and what is negative.[45]

Space, to the degree that it is a synthesis, is the originary *possibility* of separation.[46] Much the same is true for time, whose synthetic unity is called by Hegel 'a negative unity'.[47] The dialectic of 'Sense Certainty' in the *Phenomenology of Spirit* explicitly reveals the difference between the 'here' and the 'now' understood on the one hand as punctual phenomena, and on the other as that synthesis which represents the 'now which is many nows'.

In this capacity to differentiate itself from itself time displays the marks of its plasticity. Yet this differentiation itself requires a twofold understanding. For it is, on the one hand, synchronic: the Hegelian concept of time cannot be reduced to a singular meaning. And on the other hand, it is diachronic: to say that time is not always what it is also means that it temporally differentiates itself from itself, that it has, to put it another way, a *history.*

Chronological differentiation

In the *Encyclopedia* paragraphs on space and time, the implicit references to Aristotle and Kant make it possible to clarify a fundamental characteristic of Hegel's thought. 'To see (what is) coming', the structure of subjective anticipation which is the originary possibility of all encounter, is not the same in every moment of its history, it does not 'see (what is) coming' in the same way, it does not have the same future. Subjectivity 'comes itself' (*advient*) in two fundamental moments: the Greek moment and the modern moment, which prove to be, both in their logical unity and in their chronological succession, 'subject as substance' and 'substance as subject'. Hegelian philosophy synthesizes two understandings : (1) οὐσία-ὑποκείμενον, the Greek substance-subject; (2) *subjectum-substantia*, the modern subject-substance.

In the advent of Christianity, which he saw as the 'axis on which the history of the world turns',[48] Hegel saw the emergence of the modern conception of subjectivity which dialectically sublates the earlier Greek conception. The subject thus differs from itself chronologically and logically. First the 'substance-subject' shows itself as a *substance*-subject, then as a substance-*subject;* one needs to respect the accentuation here, insisting on, to repeat the terms of Bernard Bourgeois, 'The substitution of the primacy of Christian thought, which is subjectivist ("the subject is substance") for the primacy of pagan thought, which is substantialist ("substance is the subject").'[49]

Our objective here is to clarify the way in which 'to see (what is) coming' exists in two operative forms, each a matter of logical as well as chronological differentiation, and to bring to light the way these stand, in Hegel's philosophy, for the two great moments of subjectivity's 'coming-to-be' that are paradigmatic for their times: the first being the epoch identified with the name of Aristotle, the second, the one which belongs to Kant.

The power of Hegel's thought comes from the transformation of these two modalities of the movement inherent in 'to see (what is) coming'; what was historical succession becomes a *philosophical face to face.* The first modality arises from what it is possible to call the originary synthetic unity of a teleological movement in potentiality and in action. The other modality stems from the originary synthetic unity of apperception, the foundation of representation (*Vorstellung*). It is the double sense of the locutions 'in itself' and 'for itself' which demonstrates this claim. The speculative content itself follows the movement shaped by this contrast between the 'in itself' and the 'for itself', a movement conceivable in two ways. On the one hand, it opposes what is 'potential' to what is 'actual';[50] on the other hand, it opposes the truth known in the form of 'certainty' (truth's subjective moment) to the truth known in the form of 'truth' (truth's moment of objectivity).

At the core of his philosophy Hegel sets up a speculative relation between teleological circularity and representational linearity, recalling representation to its Greek past and announcing *a posteriori* to Greek philosophy its representative future. In return, Greek thought appears as much as the future of representation as representation appears as the future of Greek thought. This game of the double meaning of 'to see (what is) coming' makes reading Hegel more trying than reading almost any other philosopher. Reading Hegel amounts to finding oneself in two times at once: the process that unfolds is both retrospective and prospective. In the present time in which reading takes place, the reader is drawn to a double expectation: waiting for what is to come (according to a linear and representational thinking), while presupposing that the outcome has already arrived (by virtue of the teleological ruse).

No study has yet appeared which is dedicated to uncovering what these two 'great moments of subjectivity' promise: nothing less than the immanent temporalization of the System. For these two moments do not belong to the same time. By configuring itself in both perspectives, Hegelian thought announces the arrival (*l'advenue*) of a new time. And here waits the underlying question of my work. If there is a time that is the synthesis of its own content, thus as much a logical form as a chronological one, how can we explain its nature?

Speculative exposition and transcendental exposition

Already in the *Philosophy of Nature* time has been driven out of the natural world, revealing that the concept of time goes beyond its initial definition. This excess of meaning is not, however, presented for its own sake within the System. No moment of the speculative exposition can occupy the overarching position: there is no speculative '*arche-moment*'. No transcendental status can be attributed to the movement of 'seeing (what is) coming)'. Any transcendental instance necessarily finds itself in a position of exteriority in relation to that which it organizes. By its nature, the condition of possibility is other than that it makes possible. Yet the Hegelian conception of a system implies precisely the opposite: the absence of any 'outside' of the System. Dialectical philosophy is *systematically non-transcendental*. There is no place, in Hegel, for a specific analysis of the concept of time, one that would demonstrate its plastic character.

In this regard, our approach shall be not so much thematic as strategic. It is a strategy driven by the two concepts – of 'plasticity' and 'to see (what is) coming' – whose construction is the keystone of this project. The sensible translation of an economy of sensible translation – to borrow the Kantian definition of '*hypotyposis*'[51] – is itself represented by these concepts. This translation of the concept into the form of the sensuous is in essence systematic, an operation which cannot be pinned down in a transcendental deduction.

In the *Phenomenology of Spirit*, Hegel declares: 'The singular individual is, on its own terms, the transition of the category from its concept into external reality; it is the pure schema (*das reine Schema*) itself.'[52] Being schematizes itself, and the unification of the concept with empirical existence cannot be explained by anything external to the System. The scarcity of references to the concept of plasticity is thus evidence of its distinct mode of presence, which is that of the originary synthesis, maintained only in the interval between presence and absence. It is for this reason, because plasticity works on and within the body of the systematic exposition, without ever extending above it or overdetermining it, that it is revealed as the concept capable of accounting for the incarnation, or the incorporation, of spirit.

A reading of the *Philosophy of Spirit*

At this point we can bring together the different hermeneutical trajectories which determine the strategy of this reading. The *voir venir* stands for the operation of synthetic temporalizing in Hegel's thought, which means it is the structure of anticipation through which subjectivity projects itself in advance of itself, and thereby participates in the process of its own determination. Plasticity for its part guarantees the differential energy which traverses the very heart of the movement inherent in 'to see (what is) coming', appearing as the condition of possibility for this projection.

This movement is differentiated, and in two ways. Logically: it gathers together the different significations of the Hegelian understanding of time: a whole and a relation of moments (past, present, future), a synthetic structure (self-determination), a sensuous translation of the concept. Chronologically: it has itself a history, which is unfolded *in* history without being reducible to it. The substance-subject 'sees itself coming' (*se voit venir*) through two moments of its own identity, the Greek and the modern. These two major moments each possess their own conception of the relation between the *extases of time*, one having a conception of it as synthesis or self-determination; the other of it as hypotyposis. Furthermore, the 'infinite elasticity of the absolute form (*unendliche Elastizität der absolute Form*)'[53] from which follows the temporalization of the 'process' of the substance-subject, is that which can determine, in every moment of the substance-subject, its 'form' (*Form*). The form, we can say, is the 'relation (*Verhältnis*) which self-consciousness takes to the body of truth'.[54]

To study how this device (*dispositif*) functions in each of its epochs, we will enter into the 'forward march of spirit', embracing its temporal deployment in the places where time is supposed to be absent: viz., in the *Philosophy of Spirit* of the *Encyclopedia of Philosophical Sciences*. The last edition of 1830 will be the basis for this reading. In his Remark to §387, Hegel displays the process of *spiritual anticipation*:

> and so in spirit every character under which it appears is a stage in a process of specification and development, a step forward (*Vorwärtsgehen*) towards its goal (*seinem Ziele*), in order to make itself into, and to realize in itself, what it implicitly is. Each step (*jede Stufe*), again, is itself such a process, and its product is that what the spirit was implicitly at the beginning (and so for the observer) it is *for itself* – for the special form, what spirit has in that step. . . . In the philosophical vision of spirit as such, spirit is studied as self-instruction and self-cultivation in its very essence, and its exteriorizations (*seine Äußerungen*) are stages in the process which brings it forward to itself (*seines Sich-zu-sich-selbst-Hervorbringen*), links it to unity with itself (*seines Zusammenschließens mit sich*), and so makes it actual spirit.'[55]

In the course of this reading particular attention will be paid to that structure within the *Philosophy of Spirit* which leads from the 'sleep of spirit' (*Schlaf des Geistes*) – the 'passive νοῦς' of Aristotle'[56] – to the 'intelligence which thinks itself' – the citation from Aristotle's *Metaphysics* which closes the *Encyclopedia*.[57]

The life of the *Philosophy of Spirit* lies here, in the space between νοῦς and νοῦς. However, in another realm, between potentiality and act, we find another type of temporality, one which does not move forward according to a teleological deployment. This is the time of representation, 'which gives to the elements of the content of the absolute spirit, on the one hand, a separate being, making them presuppositions towards each other and phenomena which *succeed each other* (*aufeinander folgender Erscheinungen*)'.[58]

At the heart of our analysis is the way these two perspectives, Greek and modern, are constructed and detailed.

The Hegelian exposition of Aristotle's passive νοῦς is found in the section *Anthropology*; the exposition of the temporality of representation in *Revealed Religion*; and it is the citation from the *Metaphysics* which brings *Philosophy* to its completion. The substance of the present work will consist of a reading of these three moments of the *Philosophy of Spirit*: the first the moment of subjective spirit; the penultimate and the final moments those of absolute spirit. These three times of our reading will be entitled respectively: 'Hegel on Man' (*L'Homme de Hegel*); 'Hegel on God' (*Le Dieu de Hegel*); and 'Hegel on the Philosopher' (*Le Philosophe de Hegel*).

The choice of this triad – 'Man, God, Philosopher' – is intended to allude explicitly to Heidegger's articulation of 'onto-theology'. The challenge here is to produce an interpretation of this triad that uncovers all the surprises it has in store for a reading concerned to present Man, God and the Philosopher not as if they were fixed and substantial entities but as perspectives open to the crossroads of time.

What does that mean? Man, God and Philosopher, to adopt Hegel's own phrase, need to be considered as the 'steps' (*Stufen*) in the development of the substance-subject. One could think about this as if 'steps' implied at once a process of progressive intensity and a succession of stages, as if the life of the concept were governed by the rhythm of Man, God, Philosopher, as if the concept, although it manifests itself in history, remains without history.[59]

But in fact, Man, God, Philosopher, far from being subjects constituted in advance, turn out to be the sites where subjectivity forms itself. They are the *plastic instances* (*instances plastiques*) where the three great moments of self-determination – the Greek, the modern, and that of Absolute Knowledge – give themselves the 'form' of moments, in other words, where they create their own specific temporality. From this perspective, the notion of 'step' loses its evaluative content, and only signifies the break or interruption – the operation of breaking – in the self-formation of time itself.

To begin with the idea of such interruptions invites a discourse not content to argue either for the unity of the logical or the chronological genesis, but rather trying to locate their common origin within the speculative movement. Such a discourse – where the times meet and intersect – is beholden to the very thing it is trying to describe: that speculative *suppleness* which is neither passion nor passivity, but plasticity.

In what follows, at each moment of this triad, we will select and study a primordial modality of substance in its self-determination and its recurring negativity. By doing this, we set ourselves in opposition to any approach that believes it can discard the anthropological, theological and philosophical material whose novelty Hegel brings to light. For it is within this material that the unique perspective of a philosophy of the event can be uncovered. Further, if we take this thought to the limit, we offer Hegel's philosophy the possibility of inscribing itself as an event.

Encountered through such a discipline of plasticity, this text, the *Encyclopedia*, the ultimate expression of Hegelian thought, discloses itself in all the gentleness of its maturity.

Part I

HEGEL ON MAN: FASHIONING A SECOND NATURE

INTRODUCTION

The 'False Dawn' of the *Anthropology*

Not many commentators have responded to the strange beauty of the *Anthropology*.[1] Yet it forms a central moment in the development of the *Philosophy of Spirit*. For we meet here the first human being within the system: the first man as he awakes, rises to his feet, begins to walk and speak. The *Anthropology* marks the birth of the living creature called *man* and as such constitutes his first appearance in the exposition of the *Encyclopedia*.

In all probability, the lack of interest shown by the commentators for this initial moment of the *Philosophy of Spirit* can be explained by the disappointment its first reading produces. The twenty-five paragraphs that comprise its development force the reader to follow a long and steep path that leads only to a definition which, on the face of it, appears rather impoverished, and indeed far from original. Under the heading – 'the knowledge of man's genuine reality – of what is essentially and ultimately true and real'[2] – not very much is revealed: man is a being whose essence consists of 'the upright posture, the formation of the limbs . . ., especially the hand, as the absolute instrument, of the mouth, laughing, weeping, etc.', and finally 'speech'.[3] Does such a rich development justify only this sort of conclusion? Isn't this simply the rediscovery of the most traditional of all definitions of the human as 'animal rationale', midway between the animals and God?

The Addition to §396 establishes the boundaries of this situation. The animal, Hegel says, 'does not have the power to actualize within itself the genus in its true form'.[4] Its immediate, abstract individuality remains permanently in contradiction with its generic universality. Now the universality in question is further characterized by Hegel as 'divine reason', 'fulfilled from time immemorial'.[5] What is 'proper to Man' is to maintain itself between, on the one hand, the animal's incapacity, and, on the other, the perfect actualization which is divine. For this reason Man is 'perfectly able to present the genus'.[6]

What does 'perfectly able to present the genus' mean? If we examine Hegel's response to this question, we find a second reason for disappointment.

It is largely in §396 that his response is developed, in an exposition of the 'natural course of the ages of life'. The pace here is striking: Hegel presents human life with a sombre briskness. From the dawn of birth to the eternal night, first the child, then the youth full of ideas and projects, give way to the mature man ripe but disenchanted, broken in by social obligations, finally to the old man exhausted and drivelling.[7]

Childhood is the immediate and natural unity of the individual and the genus. But it is necessary, Hegel says, 'that this immediate and therefore non-spiritual, purely natural unity of the individual with its genus and with the world generally, must be sublated (*aufgehoben*); the individual must go forward to the stage where he opposes himself to the universal. . . .'[8]

This opposition to universality defines the period of adolescence. The young man feels 'stirring' in himself 'the life of the genus' which 'seeks satisfaction'. However, Hegel states, the youth believes wrongly that this satisfaction is to be attained by transforming the genus itself and by actualizing his own ideal. Only the mature man is able to recognize 'the essential nature of the world already in existence, completed'.[9] Through work, the mature man 'finds his place in the world of objective relationships and becomes habituated to it and to his tasks'.[10] He makes himself thereby 'conformable and adequate to the universal' and it is in this fashion that he can 'present perfectly the genus'. But by this very fact his vitality begins to wane and he becomes an old man.

'Abandon hope, all who enter here': Is this not the covert inscription which decorates the pediment of the Hegelian *Anthropology*? What is the end of youth if not a dismissal of the ideal? To live out one's life to the end, by deferring to the force of circumstances, would amount to renouncing any introduction of the new and unexpected into the realm of the actual. Man, to the degree that he only 'creates what is already there',[11] will be condemned to verify the absence of the future. As the ages of man pass by in their course, the future disappears in the false light of distant horizons.[12]

The role of habit

A close reading of the *Anthropology* may reveal however that the procedures of habit serve not only as a force of death but also as a force for life. Because, if habit represents the dulling of life which gradually weakens the power of resistance and dynamism itself, it constitutes at the same time, in the course of its development, the vitality and persistence of subjectivity. Hegel declares: 'Habit is, like memory, a difficult point in the organization in mental organization; habit is the mechanism of self-feeling, as memory is the mechanism of intelligence.'[13] He continues: 'The form of habit applies to all kinds and grades of mental activity.'[14]

The exposition of habit[15] is a moment which marks a decisive turn in the economy of this section. By focusing on its transitional position we will be able to give a new and wholly different slant to the reading of the *Anthropology*, eclipsing the apparent poverty of its conclusions.

It is critical to make habit a turning point, and this for three fundamental reasons. First, if we do this, we can open up an original perspective on the *history* of subjectivity, where this history has the double sense of the dialectical constitution of the individual subject and the evolution of the concept of 'subject' itself. Reversing all 'pragmatic anthropology', Hegelian anthropology returns us to the founding Greek moment of the 'substance-subject'.[16] Second, habit emerges as the fundamental anthropological determination in so far as it is a 'mechanism of self-feeling'. This mechanism, by its very structure, presupposes a particular modality of the reduplication of the negative. Third, habit fashions the human 'as a work of art of the soul',[17] a transformation which will bring us back to plasticity.

The Greek moment of the substance-subject

How can we justify our claim that the Hegelian *Anthropology* finds its seminal conception in this moment? In the first place, there is the fact that Hegel explicitly asserts that he intends to locate his analyses outside the framework of both empirical psychology and rational psychology,[18] and that he will be guided in his presentation of 'the concrete knowledge of spirit' by the *De Anima* of Aristotle:

> The books of Aristotle *On the Soul*, along with his discussion on its special aspects and states, are for this reason still by far the most admirable, perhaps even the sole, work of philosophical value on this topic. The main aim of philosophy of spirit can only be to reintroduce unity of idea and principle into the theory of spirit, and so to reinterpret the lesson of those Aristotelian books.[19]

The soul, the analysis of which controls the entire development of this section, is for Hegel spirit in its *natural* state. The 'concrete determinations' of the soul are those already uncovered by Aristotle. Further, the notion of habit formulated by Hegel includes, as its central determination, the Aristotelian definition of 'ἕξις', way of being or permanent disposition.

In the second place, the definitive characterization of man as 'the work of art of the soul' has behind it the Hegelian conception of classical Greek sculpture, the privileged site of anthropomorphism.

Habit: a particular modality of the reduplication of the negative

The importance of habit emerges within the dialectical process which leads from the *Philosophy of Nature* to the *Philosophy of Spirit.* The transition between the two poses a genuine problem because it concerns the only moment of Hegel's philosophy where the same term plays the role both of result and of origin. The *Philosophy of Nature* ends with the study of the soul and its functions; the *Philosophy of Spirit* begins with the study of the soul and its functions. This difficulty is brought out with exemplary clarity by Bernard Bourgeois:

> How was Hegel able to join under the same designation the two extremes of the essential difference at the heart of the absolute's realization, to know through it both the termination of nature and the exact commencement of spirit?[20]

The response proposed here will be the following: the transition from nature to spirit occurs not as a sublation, but as a *reduplication*, a process through which spirit constitutes itself in and as a *second nature*. This reflexive reduplication is in a certain sense the 'mirror stage' of spirit, in which the first form of its identity is constituted. Man appears as the inverted lining of the animal and not as its opposite. The concept of 'second nature', synonymous with habit, allows us to bring to light the great originality of the *Anthropology*.

Plasticity

As Hegel's mode of attack is to confront dualism in every arena, he adopts the Aristotelian definition of the soul: the soul is the principle of the living organism and 'the form of a natural body with life as its potentiality'.[21] The anthropological 'I' or 'Self' emerges as the end of a project of mutual self-fashioning performed jointly by soul and body, engineered specifically by the efforts of habit. Habit, a process whereby the psychic and the somatic are translated into one another, is a genuine plasticity. It fashions the human by an incorporation (*Verleiblichung*) or rather an incarnation of the spiritual, similar to an *hypotyposis*. The 'exemplary individuality' which is man 'sculpted' by habit discloses, as if in a Greek statue, the unity of essence and accident. 'Plastic individuality' makes it possible to imagine the 'conformity' of singularity with the universal by means of a perspective totally different from that of pure and simple subordination.

The itinerary

After having presented the *Anthropology*'s movement as a whole, we will introduce the Hegelian reading of Aristotle. The *Anthropology* is an astonishingly powerful reading of the subtle link that unites, in *De Anima*, the categories of *habit* (ἕξις), *man* (ἄνθρωπος), and *spirit*. This interpretation ensues from an original comprehension of the relationship between the active and passive νοῦς, between being acted upon (πάσχειν) and acting (ἐνεργεῖν). This noetic plasticity directs the Hegelian comprehension of auto-determination in its Greek moment. What is important is that we consider the relationship of auto-determination to its sensible medium, man, and see the way in which man's habit-formed soul marks the birth of the spirit. The analysis of noetic plasticity and of the role that habit plays in it will allow us to shed new light on the question of the 'the proper of man (*le propre de l'homme*)'[22] and of the limits, animal and divine, that reserve for him his place.

1

INTRODUCTION TO THE *ANTHROPOLOGY*

The course of the *Anthropology* as a whole explicates the process whereby originary substance, leaving behind the natural world, progressively differentiates itself until it becomes an individual subject. This movement unfolds in three moments which structure the exposition: self-identity, rupture, return to unity. The meaning of this division organizes itself in the process of the soul's *singularization* which, from its beginning in the 'universal' (understood as 'the immaterialism of nature' or 'simple ideal life'), moves progressively towards self-individuation until it becomes 'singular self'. From the 'sleep of spirit'[1] to the 'soul as work of art'[2] the genesis of the individual is accomplished, that individual which, configured as the 'Man', finally stands forth in the guise of a statue.

If the anthropological development appears to be a progressive illumination, it does produce some abrupt returns to obscurity, some moments of trial and error, some aberrations. The spirit that awakens knows also crises of somnambulism, delirious manias; at times it consults the stars or magnetizers, at times it weeps endlessly over those it has lost whom it never managed properly to mourn. It haunts its own depths, its own night, failing to commit to the individuation which will be its definitive splendour.

The unfurling of the process of individuation is the constitution of the 'Self' (*Selbst*), the founding instance of subjectivity. But this process does not follow a smooth path. Between nature and spirit there emerges a space of latency, a state of spiritual hypnosis corresponding actually to a time prior to the 'I' which, on this account, precedes man as such. It is as if Hegel is combining here the confident, regular movement of the constitution of individual subjectivity with the disorder of its pathology. The meaning of this conjunction will only be discovered if one takes into account the logical remedy of this originary hypochondria: habit.

Three periods structure the self-differentiating movement of the soul. The soul is first of all 'natural soul' (*natürliche Seele*),[3] which unfolds itself again in three moments: that of the 'natural qualities (*natürliche Qualitäten*);[4] that of the 'natural alterations (*natürliche Veränderungen*)';[5]

and, finally, that of 'sensation (*Empfindung*)'.[6] The second stage is the time of 'the feeling soul (*fühlende Seele*)',[7] itself divided into three moments: that of 'the feeling soul in its immediacy',[8] that of the 'feeling of Self',[9] finally that of 'habit (*Gewohnheit*)'.[10] The last stage, called 'the actual self (*wirkliche Seele*)', is much shorter and is the subject of the last two paragraphs.[11]

This threefold rhythm is the same as that of the *concept* which, according to the expositions of the *Science of Logic* of the *Encyclopedia*, includes the moments of the *universal*, the *particular*, and the *singular*.[12] The concept (which is at once the whole and a moment of the whole) in its turn develops into the moments of concept, judgement (the originary division and separation of the particular from the universal), and syllogism (reconciliation and dialectical unity of the divided terms, emergence of genuine singularity). To observe closely this formation of form in its full presentation in the *Anthropology* prevents us from losing our way in the rich but distracting development of subjectivity.

The 'natural soul' or the moment of the concept: elemental equality

The 'universal soul'

The first stage of the *Anthropology*[13] – the 'natural soul' with its 'qualities' and its 'alterations' – corresponds to the *concept* in its undifferentiated and systematic universality, where the concept simply and immediately contains its three moments of universality, particularity, and singularity. The 'natural soul', as the 'universal immateriality of Nature . . . the simple ideal and natural mode of life', is the soul 'which only *is*'.[14]

Nonetheless, Hegel does not return to the Aristotelian notion of a 'world soul': 'The *universal soul* must not be fixed on that account as *anima mundi*, as if a single subject; it is rather the universal *substance* which has its actual truth only as *individuality*, subjectivity.'[15]

Hegel uses the notion of the 'universal soul' to designate life in its simplest, most elementary form: an original vitality (prior to the sundering which introduces particular forms) which has not yet arrived at the stage of division which characterizes particular forms. Universality is here in every sense of the word the most primitive stage of the soul; it can only achieve 'its actual truth as *individuality*'. For the moment it is simply the 'sleep of spirit', the passive νοῦς of Aristotle, which is potentially all things.[16]

The soul as substance is not, however, an empty and formal identity. Nature in the form of soul is already reflected into itself and hence virtually differentiated. Hence the 'universal soul' will contain within itself the moment of particularity.

Particularity of the 'natural qualities'

The soul's determinations are in the first instance the 'natural qualities' which make up its initial 'being-there (*Dasein*).'[17] According to the *Encyclopedia Science of Logic*, '*Being-there* is being with a *determinacy*, that is [given] as immediate determinacy or as a determinacy that [simply] is: *quality*.'[18] But what, for the *Anthropology*, are these 'qualities'?

They are divided into three types following a hierarchy based on their degree of differentiation. The first type includes such qualities as 'differences of climate, changes of the seasons, times of the day, etc.', connected to 'the general planetary life'. Spirit lives this life 'in agreement with it'[19] – an expression which translates the German word *mitleben*, literally, 'to live with', implying here an immediate and elementary harmony, a 'sympathy' with nature. These first natural qualities can be classified under the generic term of 'influences',[20] in the original sense of that physical and fluid force believed by ancient physics to proceed from the heavens and the stars and act upon men, animals and things. These 'physical qualities' determine the soul's correspondence to 'cosmic, sidereal, and telluric life'. They can be felt above all 'in those morbid states, to which insanity belongs', but also in instances of superstitious attitudes, divinatory practices, and 'prophetic visions'.[21]

The second group of 'natural qualities' contains those of the specialized 'nature-governed spirits' (*Naturgeister*) which constitute the 'diversity of races'.[22]

The third set of 'qualities' consists of those which can be called 'local spirits' (*Lokalgeister*).[23] These are 'shown in the outward modes of life (*Lebensart*) and occupation (*Beschäftigung*), bodily structure and *disposition* (*körperlicher Bildung und Disposition*), but still more in the inner tendency and capacity (*Befähigung*) of the intellectual and moral character of the peoples'.[24]

The singularity of the individual subject

It is in this manner, according to Hegel, that 'the soul is further differentiated into an *individual subject*'. But

> this subjectivity is here only considered as a differentiation of nature's determinations. It is a natural subjectivity in so far as it provides the *modes* of human being in its diversity: differences of temperament, of talent, of character, of physiology, and the other dispositions and idiosyncrasies found in families or single individuals.[25]

At this stage of the analysis, singularity is understood as an immediate unity of *essence* – the simple and ideal life of nature, the substantial basis of all further individuation – and *existence* – 'being-there', which acts as the differentiated foundation of natural qualities. In its abstract form, singularity 'is only in itself or immediately the unity of essence and existence'.[26] In this sense it is still a potentiality: it '*can* act in an effective way', but this is only a potentiality, it does not yet 'produce' itself 'as its own effect'.[27] In the *Anthropology*, this singularity without effect appears in the shape of 'idiosyncrasy'. An individual's idiosyncrasy is an immediate disposition to feel the influence of other agents or universal principles in a way unique to itself.

The 'immediate judgement' or 'natural changes'

The movement of singularization is now pursued into the domain of 'natural changes', three types of 'differences' which are 'at once physical and spiritual'. The first 'alterations' are inherent in the 'natural process of the ages of life'. The second set of alterations are linked to the 'sexual relation (*Geschlechtverhältnis*).'[28] The third depend on 'the distinction between waking and sleeping'.[29]

In the process of individuation, these 'natural changes' represent a higher stage. These already begin to manifest the difference between identity and alterity. Hence, these natural alterations can be seen as an early experience of temporality. However, because they are simply natural, such alterations have not yet achieved their full measure of actuality. To achieve that will require a prolonged and violent repudiation, where the power of those influences (something simply given) struggles against that moment of free existence which characterizes the spiritual. In this opposition, subjectivity arrives at its critical moment.

'Sensation', 'sentiment', 'feeling of self': the moment of judgement or the crisis of individuality

The formation of individuality represents a crisis. It is clear that in the word 'crisis' we hear the double meaning of the term 'judgement' – as a rupture and as a decision.[30] The *self-critique* of the *Anthropology* is a long and complex process.[31] In fact, the further the 'self' advances in the movement which constitutes its own formation, the more it finds itself dispossessed of itself, to the point of becoming truly mad. It seems that spirit does not leave its initial state of self-hypnosis, its original slumber, except to sink further into alienation.

In the terms presented in the first moment of the *Anthropology*, 'the soul is singularized as an *individual subject*'.[32] This singularization becomes actualized only through a threefold process: 'sensation', 'the feeling soul', and 'feeling of Self', a process which puts into motion the birth of the Ego. Ideality, in the way Hegel discusses that in §403, is no longer 'the simple life of nature'; it is, rather, the possibility of the individual's reflection on itself, when it feels itself identical and the same in its numerous determinations. The emergence of the 'Ego' is connected to the process through which alterity is interiorized. With sensation arises the possibility of the self's relation to itself as a unity of identity and difference. In so far as it 'feels', 'the soul is no longer a simply natural, but an inward individuality'; the individual is in a position to 'realize its mastery over its own'. Finally, in the 'feeling of self', the individual becomes 'a sensitive totality'.

But the gradual formation of the 'I' is paradoxically accompanied by a loss of fluidity, leading to 'ruin and disaster within the conscious spirit'.[33] This crisis results from the fact that the subject, being constituted in a free relation to the self, feels at the same time like 'an other', and this tension pushes it into a state of 'trembling (*durchzittern*)'.[34]

Sensation

From its original state, elementary, simple, and indivisible, substance becomes the basis and support for individual subjectivity. Thus the soul of nature becomes the nature of the soul. And it is sensation which marks the first stage in this process. In the sensations which arise from the individual's encounter with external objects, the soul begins to awaken to itself. 'On waking we find ourselves at first only quite vaguely distinguished from the outer world generally. It is only when we start to have sensations that this difference becomes a *determinate* distinction.'[35]

The soul, in so far as it is feeling, appropriates the determinations which come from the external world, and welcomes them as if they were its own. Alterity is the mediation through which the reflexive relation is articulated:

> In this examination [i.e. in that discrimination which is the act of sensation or feeling], we do not relate ourselves directly to the Other, but *mediately*. Thus, for example, *touch* is the mediation between myself and the Other, since though it is distinct from these two sides of the opposition, yet at the same time it unites them. . . . This linking of the soul with itself is the progress made by the soul, which in waking had divided itself, by its transition to sensation.[36]

The relation between the soul and its corporeality, posited here, now appears to be the prototype of all relation to alterity:

> What the sentient self finds within it is, on the one hand, the naturally immediate, as 'ideally' in it and made its own. On the one hand and conversely, what originally belongs to the central individuality (which as further deepened and enlarged is the

> conscious ego and free spirit) is determined as natural corporeity (*Leiblichkeit*), and is so felt.[37]

The idea of embodiment, *Verleiblichung*, incarnation as a 'translation into corporeity', makes here its first speculative appearance. The reflexive relation between body and soul is analysed in its circularity: those determinations which come from the external world are interiorized by the soul, and those which come from the soul are translated into corporeity.[38]

The body and the soul form a 'system' consisting of two distinct subsystems: on the one hand, that formed by the five senses ('simple system of specified corporeity'); on the other hand, that which enables the regulated functioning of the determinations originating internally and given bodily form ('system of inward sensibility').[39] To show the fundamental unity of these two economies, Hegel insists on the necessity of producing a science whose object would be the reciprocal relation between the physical and the psychical, a science he names 'psychical physiology'.[40]

As the relation between soul and body becomes systematized, a 'reflective totality (*reflektierte Totalität*)' is created, and this is the subject of the following section, 'the soul which feels'.[41]

The feeling soul

No longer is the feeling soul an individuality simply in the natural sense; it is now something internal and interior: 'The individuality which in the merely substantial totality was only formal has to be liberated and made independent.'[42]

The relation of the elementary substance to immediate individuality is presented as a relation between the individuality and its own personal being, its own 'Self'. From this point on, the soul is, on its own account, both *substance* and *subject*. Hegel insists on this outcome: 'As *individual*, the soul is, in general, exclusive, and it posits all difference as *a difference within itself*: . . . In this judgement, it is always subject: its object is its substance, which is at the same time its predicate.'[43]

Henceforth the soul is a critical instance and, as such, an autonomous individuality. Subjectivity originates in the possibility of self-solicitation, its own power to address itself: the 'Self' is the instance which guarantees the unity of the relation of the same to the other.

Yet it is this dialectical structure of identity and alterity which, constituting itself, immediately causes its own dissolution. The strength of the Hegelian analysis emerges here, for it is uniquely capable of producing a synthesis both in the presence of a unifying form and in its absence. At this moment of the analysis Hegel raises simultaneously the possibility of co-existence in real form (as in the co-existence of identity and difference; the constitution of the soul as a 'Self'), and the impossibility of such co-existence (as in morbid or sick states of the soul where identity and difference can remain only in an irreducible tension). This strange synthesis of synthesis and non-synthesis is more originary than the simple synthesis of the 'Self'; in fact, it precedes the 'I'.

At first there is a mixture, a primordial composition of sickness and health: this represents thought in its infancy. The effect of returning to this infancy is a shock, explosively destroying the noetic unity already formed and forcing it to reflect on its own makeup. It is only because 'the development of the soul' has already occurred, in its ulterior determination as consciousness and understanding, that it can 'once again sink into the abyss (*wieder herabversinken kann*)'.[44] This reconduction of thought to its own origin provokes a dual movement: first, an aggravation of the moment of crisis; then the announcement of the liberating instance which will render the synthesis possible: habit.

The aggravation has three degrees: the 'magical relationship', 'magnetic somnambulism and its cognate states', and 'clairvoyance, or the prophetic'. These three moments reveal a 'Self' still unable to sustain itself as an individual; substance and subject appear to it as two diverse entities, and this sort of co-existence brings about two types of diseased conditions. On the one hand are the diseases of 'tautology', or forms of 'idiocy' caused by the fact that the soul here has no relation with anything but itself and cannot succeed in producing its own self-differentiation. On the other hand are the diseases of 'heterology', or forms of 'alienation' in the literal sense, resulting from the soul's inability to forge a relationship to itself as persisting as an identity. The two types of diseases are developments of that primal 'magical relationship', that is, of the soul's hallucinatory relationship, entertained with a 'phantasmatic alterity':

> This standpoint can be called the *magical* relationship of the feeling soul, for this term connotes a relation of inner to outer or to something else generally, which dispenses with any mediation; a magical power is one whose action is not determined by the interconnection, the conditions and the mediations of objective relations.[45]

The 'magical relation' is the dialectically sublated determination of influence. There is no longer a body which exerts the force of action at a distance over another body, but a spirit which attracts another spirit whose course of thought and actions it determines. Here an individual relates to itself as if it were a being external and controlled, an 'other' it has deprived of freedom. Successively, this 'other subject' reappears in various forms: in the relation between mother and child in the womb;[46] as the 'individual and his genius';[47] as the phantom of the somnambulists;[48] and as the prophetic soul with its visions.[49]

Subjectivity presupposes a primal synthesis of identity and difference: without this, differences could not be absorbed. Such a synthesis is indeed present as far as form is concerned: the 'Self' is already constituted. But this form lacks its own content. There must be a structure inherently capable of accepting alterity, and the soul is not and does not yet possess such a power. From this moment on, Hegel will proceed to intensify the dissociation between alterity and the self, forcing the consequences of this severance to their extremes.

The 'feeling of Self' in its immediacy: spirit deranged

The moment of crisis deepens. Unquestionably, the birth of a 'feeling of Self'[50] marks an advance in the constitution of individuality. However, Hegel will very quickly present to view the *derangement* which inhabits this sense from the moment of its origin.[51]

The subject has effectively gained possession of itself and now we see it is subjectivity which becomes the home of *auto*-differentiation:

> The sensitive totality is, in its capacity as an individual, essentially the tendency to distinguish itself in itself, and to wake up to the *judgment in itself*, in virtue of which it has *particular* feelings and stands as a *subject* in respect of these aspects of itself. The subject as such gives these feelings a place as *its own* in itself. In these private and personal sentiments it is immersed, and at the same time, because of the 'ideality' of the particulars, it combines itself in them as a subjective unit. In this way it is *self-feeling*. . . .[52]

However, to the degree that corporeity and spirituality cannot be fully distinguished, the feeling of Self is still immediate and 'although the subject has been brought to acquire intelligent consciousness, it is still susceptible to disease, so far as to remain fast in a *special* phase of its self-feeling, unable to refine it to "ideality" and get the better of it'.[53]

The feeling of self itself becomes a personal and specific feeling. Even if there is a possibility of bringing together feeling's manifold material, that possibility *itself* becomes part of the objective content. The form needs to be the content of all that it forms: subjectivity does not reside in its own being, it 'haunts' itself. The soul is possessed by the possession of itself.

> The subject finds itself in contradiction between the totality systematized in its consciousness, and the particular determination which, in itself, is not fluid and is not reduced to its proper place and rank. This is mental derangement (*Verrücktheit*).[54]

The singularity Hegel analyses here is incapable of synthesizing itself: 'the Self isolated in its aspect of particularity' cannot adapt itself or remain consistently related to 'its individual position and its connection with the external world'. Strictly speaking, this leads to the condition of 'idiocy', where an excessive particularity dominates the self. Idiocy may be described as an imprisonment within the Self. The idiot's behaviour is to remain 'seated, quiet, looking straight in front of himself', without saying a word.[55] Idiocy is clearly nothing but the inverted figure of alienation. Insanity proper begins when

> the natural spirit which is shut up in itself . . . acquires a *definite* content and this content becomes a *fixed idea*, the spirit which is not as fully self-possessed becoming just as much absorbed in it as in *idiocy* it is absorbed in its own self, in the abyss of its *indeterminateness*.[56]

Mental illness is explicable in the same way as physical illness, since they share the same cause: a paralysis in which the organism's vitality becomes fixated onto a single aspect or part and this paralysis threatens the fluidity of the whole. In the *Philosophy of Nature* Hegel writes:

> The organism finds itself ill, when one of its systems or one of its organs, troubled by a conflict with the forces of the inorganic, retreats into itself and continues to aim its own actions antagonistically against the interests of the whole, and the fluidity of the whole comprised by all the processes moving through the individual parts is thereby disturbed and brought to a halt.[57]

For this reason, the treatment of madness, like that of organic illness, will consist in putting back into circulation that vital mobile energy.[58] But is there a way to explain more fully the spirit's restoration from bondage?

Habit and the syllogism of the 'Self'

The route to recovery is the work of habit. Alain, in his commentary on the *Philosophy of Spirit*, strongly emphasizes this factor:

> When freedom comes it is in the sphere of habit. . . . Here the body is no longer a foreign being, reacting belligerently against me; rather it is pervaded by soul and has become soul's instrument and means; yet at the same time, in habit the corporeal self is understood as it truly is; body is rendered something mobile and fluid, able to express directly the inner movements of thought without needing to involve thereby the role of consciousness or reflection. . . .[59]

With habit, a new form of the soul's relation to its body comes into view, and this delivers the spirit from the threat of madness. In the etymology of the word 'habit' we discover the Latin word *habere*: habit is a way of 'having', and, in this sense, a kind of possession, a property. We see the same semantic connection between the Greek word ἕξις which derives from the verb ἔχειν. This verb means 'to have', but as soon as it is followed by an adverb, it changes its meaning to include 'the state of *being* in one way or another'. Ἔχειν is therefore a particular kind of having which becomes a way of being. Hegel brings out here the sense of a 'having' derived from a 'mechanism'. Habit is in truth 'mechanism of self-feeling' (*Mechanismus des Selbstgefühls*).[60]

It is habit which gives the soul the possibility of escaping from the two kinds of mania previously described: idiocy – the self over-concentrated on itself – and alienation – where a particular part of the self is clung to. Habit emerges as a liberating process, saving the soul from the two forms of dissolution – either lost in the emptiness of ideality or absorbed in a determinate part isolated from the whole:

> The soul's making itself an abstract universal being, and reducing the particulars of feeling (and of consciousness) to a mere feature of its being, a determination that is no more than a simple *thing*, is habit. In this manner the soul possesses the content, and contains the content in such manner that in these features it is not active as sentient, nor does it stand in relationship with them as distinguishing itself from them, nor is it absorbed in them, but as having them and moving in them, without feeling or consciousness of the fact.[61]

Dialectically sublating the anthropological moment of judgement, habit represents an example of the dialectical syllogism, restoring the unity of subject and predicate. For the syllogism is a synthesis of the universality of the concept and the particularity of judgment, producing as its result a singularity which is no longer merely immediate but actual.[62] Soul has become the place for the creation of a structure joining particularity ('particularity of feeling') and universality (those same particulars having become the 'forms' in which spirit is active). Reducing particularity to 'a mere feature of its being' through the effects of habit, the soul no longer suffers from that mad presumption of universality we have seen earlier. In the same fashion, universality has ceased to be a sphere of complete abstraction and has become something objective and actual. The structure of the syllogism is achieved when soul, neither distinguishing itself from nor confusing itself with its specific features or expressions, comes to enjoy a position between abstraction and rigidity.

The characteristic of habit is to substitute for an immediacy which is natural a second immediacy, an immediacy 'posited' by soul. This repeated immediacy (*immédiateté redoublée*) rightly deserves the name of 'second nature'. Specifically, the work of habit consists in 'integrating and moulding the corporeality (*eine Ein- und Durchbildung der Leiblichkeit*) which enters into the modes of feeling as such and into the determinations of representation and volition so far as they have taken corporeal form (*als verleiblichten*).'[63]

The formation of corporeal aspect of the determiantions is the product of their 'repetition' (*Wiederholung*); similarly, the 'generation of habit' is the work of 'practice'.[64] Habit is the plastic operation which makes the body into an instrument: 'In aptitude (*savoir-faire*) corporeality is rendered completely pervious (*durchgängig*), made into an instrument (*zum Instrument gemacht*).'[65]

This interpenetrability of the psychic and the physical has immediate consequences for time. When nature passes over to its second nature, this implies, by the same token, that 'natural time' – the simple exteriority of moments linked to one another as if in a pure linear sequence – is interiorized and acquires a totally different shape. Subjectivity, henceforth capable of appropriating difference to itself, now appears as what it truly is: the originary synthetic unity linking its determinations and, at the same moment, putting them into sequential form. When the soul succeeds in idealizing the corporeal, it also gains the power to make itself a 'simple and ideal unity', that is to say, to be only with itself. This ideal 'substance', says Hegel, 'is not yet a Self', but it is the possibility of a Self. As a synthesis of spirit and nature, it opens up for the subject the horizon into which it will progress – the horizon of *Bildung*, of culture, of development. It liberates the subject from the obstacles and the limitations of that state where nature is still too intensely influential. With the 'pure act of intuition'[66] the subject is now opened to the possibility of 'seeing (what is) coming'.

Engaged precisely in that way with his own future, soul and body fashioned by habit, Man appears as he is at the conclusion of the *Anthropology*: the incarnation of spirit.

2

ON NOETIC PLASTICITY

Hegel's reading of *De Anima*

The threads that unite spirit to its exemplary incarnation, man, are forged in the course of the *Anthropology*. But how does this happen? To answer this question requires an exposition of Hegel's interpretation of Aristotle's *De Anima* which underlies the entire anthropological discussion. However, if this is our aim, it will take more than simply listing those Aristotelian elements Hegel retains and transforms. Such a comparative procedure, as useful as it may be, remains at a simple descriptive level. What is important is to understand how, for Hegel, Aristotle's text presents a mirror of the psyche, in which spirit recognizes something essential about itself, a vision which necessarily involves the coming into being of man. It would be too hasty to claim that all Hegel is doing is taking the Aristotelian distinctions between 'souls' and forming them into a dialectical hierarchy, as if Hegel's purpose were nothing else but the assimilation of the noetic soul to the human spirit, thereby presenting the achievement of the ζῷον λογικόν (or *animal rationale*) as the ultimate goal of all philosophy of spirit. There are two fundamental grounds for immediately dismissing such an interpretation as insufficient, even irrelevant.

The first is that *De Anima* is not an anthropology. The ἄνθρωπος is never treated as an entity in itself. The human is not its concern. Even the noetic soul itself is not clearly and definitively linked to the human. Of course, such a connection can be inferred, but it is never explicit.[1] To argue otherwise is to do violence to the text itself. Nor is it possible to accuse Hegel of such intentions since, in the *Lectures on the History of Philosophy*, where he discusses *De Anima*, he never speaks at all of 'man' and never takes Aristotle's text as the starting point of an anthropology.[2]

The second reason can be deduced from the marginal position Hegel allots to νοῦς in the presentation of the *Anthropology*. 'Passive νοῦς', in fact, functions as the absolute beginning of the *Anthropology*'s development. As 'substance or absolute basis of all the particularization and individualization of spirit',[3] it exists before any individuation and appears before the entrance of man: from this alone it is clear that man and the noetic soul are not co-extensive.

Why then should we make *De Anima* the central reference point of the *Anthropology*? If we focus all our attention on the passive νοῦς and the position it occupies, a tentative answer can be suggested. For isn't there something odd about this position? What appears to be the ultimate and final point according to Aristotle – the passive νοῦς appears at the end of *De Anima* (Book III) – has become, for Hegel, a starting point. Even if one considers the Hegelian circle for which beginning and end meet, such an inversion leaves a lot to think about. It is here that we must begin the task of interpretation, because it is here that we see Hegel interpreting.[4]

Hegel's understanding of νοῦς

The intellect and its 'way of being'

Passive νοῦς is 'the *sleep* of spirit, and *potentially* all things'.[5] The conclusion of this phrase is almost a literal translation of a fragment from *De Anima*:

> In fact thought is, on the one hand capable (τοιοῦτος) of becoming all things [this is the passage translated by Hegel], on the other it is capable of producing all things; this is a sort of positive state like that of light: in one sense, light makes potential colors into actual colors.[6]

Examining Hegel's treatment of this passage will help us to discover his actual understanding of *De Anima*.

In the first place, the passage presents the notion of what we can call the *originary plasticity* of νοῦς The expressions πάντα γίνεσθαι, πάντα ποιεῖν (the 'becoming of all things', the 'making of all things'), express in turn the aptitude to be 'fashioned by all', or of 'receiving form', and the aptitude to 'fashion all', or to 'give form (εἶδος)'. For Aristotle, it is a question of showing in the final instance the process of νόησις νοήσεως, 'knowing the known', or of 'the thinking of thinking', which assumes the identity of thought with the process of thinking itself.[7] If it is true that thought must be ' thinkable *per se*', that it is not 'in virtue of something other than itself that it is thinkable', then it must be shown that it is, in a certain sense as stated by Hegel, the subject and object of itself, that which 'suffers' or submits itself to its own activity. The two verbs πάσχειν ('to be acted upon') and ἐνεργεῖν ('to act'), are on several occasions used by Aristotle to define the νοῦς.

This noetic power both to make and to undergo, to fashion and to be fashioned, is characterized by Aristotle as an ἕξις. In the French translation, the expression, 'similar to a state of being like light', translates the Greek ὡς ἕξις τις, οἷον τὸ φῶς. This is the main deduction: νοῦς is a capability similar to an ἕξις which should not be given the impoverished translation of 'state', but of 'way of being', with the implication 'a way of being which is habitual'. The verb ἔχειν when modified by an adverb does not simply mean 'to have' but also 'to have in a particular way'. Consequently, the way of being proper to νοῦς is to be understood through its 'having', that is to say, through its plastic ἕξις. This way of being with a double sense – of fashioning and of being fashioned – is constantly interrogated in *De Anima*. The connection which joins plasticity and habit has certainly not been ignored by Hegel. What he interprets as the '*sleep* of spirit', that which sleeps in spirit when spirit sleeps, is precisely this same mode of possibility (δύναμις) that Aristotle characterizes, in *De Anima*, as ἕξις.[8]

At this point the term ἄνθρωπος makes its appearance. Since Aristotle presents this term as defining that entity most likely to develop habits, it will serve in two cases as a privileged example. To explain the originary unity of πάσχειν and ἐνεργεῖν Aristotle uses the example of the man who acquires the habit of knowledge. Leaving behind his initial state of ignorance, man is subjected to the effects of his apprenticeship, his learning. But, as soon as knowledge is actually gained, this 'subjection' becomes the possibility of an actualization, and hence of an action: man has the power freely to exercise his knowledge.

In the *Anthropology*, Hegel brings to light the fact which is never explicitly addressed in *De Anima*: the idea that ἕξις is the only theoretical moment where there is anything specific or privileged claimed for the ἄνθρωπος. Nonetheless, as we shall see, man is not the only entity able to acquire ἕξις. For the moment, the most important point to note in the problematic of the originary plasticity of spirit is the solidarity uncovered between ἄνθρωπος, ἕξις and the 'example'.

It may be that such a reading distorts the meaning of the expositions of νοῦς, whether Aristotelian or Hegelian. To such an objection, we can only retort that any account of νοῦς which takes on the delicate issue of πάσχειν and ἐνεργεῖν must inevitably be an interpretation, and all the more so because the traditional distinction between 'passive νοῦς' or 'intellectual' and 'active νοῦς' is not truly an Aristotelian distinction.[9] A synthetic totality, νοῦς itself was interpreted by the commentators in a twofold manner: one being the power to be acted upon, the other the capacity to produce. Given the manner the commentators have chosen of presenting the text, the possibility of a single totality with two forms of action is forestalled by an intepretation which pre-empts the process by the names it gives to the titles of the sections. To speak of 'passive νοῦς' requires that one speak of an 'active νοῦς', for the two are irretrievably linked together. But on the other hand, investigating how Hegel interprets the noetic entity of Aristotle is a delicate matter: the present examination of the 'νοῦς' touches on the most controversial point of Hegel's reading of Aristotle.[10]

Hegel's 'misreading'

Passion of the νοῦς

Book III of *De Anima* is devoted to the noetic soul, ie, 'the part of the soul with which the soul knows'.[11] The problem is to know whether the noetic soul has a separate existence. In the course of the argument we are presented with the first analogy: by way of comparison to the logical functioning of sensation, we can isolate the noetic economy:

> If thinking is like perceiving, it must either be a process in which the soul is acted upon by what is capable of being thought, or a process different from but analogous to that. Thought must . . . bear itself in relation (ἔχειν) to what is thinkable, as sense is to what is sensible.[12]

Perceiving and thinking are not explicable in terms of the ordinary, everyday varieties of shaping such as, say, manufacture or the way a form is impressed on a medium. Yet it is by analogy with these procedures (which thus constitute the terms of reference for the second analogy) that Aristotle proposes to reveal the signification of those forms of πάσχειν and ἐνεργεῖν which are inherent in the mechanisms of sensation and intellection. Thus the image of the imprinting of a ring in wax and that of the writing tablet serve as explanatory paradigms for both processes. This analogy itself follows from a third analogy, which places πάσχειν and ἐνεργεῖν in relation to motion itself (κίνησις). Aristotle says accordingly at II, 5, 417a:

> To begin with let us speak as if there were no difference between being moved or affected, and being active, for movement is a kind of activity – an imperfect kind, as has elsewhere been explained. Everything that is acted on or moved is acted upon by an agent which is actually at work.[13]

But do these analogies permit the further deduction, of *plasticity* as the 'genuine' and 'authentic' character of νοῦς? Wouldn't the carefulness of Aristotle's argument be invalidated by the violence of such a gesture, where a procedure that is no more than aporetic is transformed into the rigidity of a thesis? What is said on the subject of νοῦς makes for a response to these questions extremely difficult. It must be the case, Aristotle insists, that 'this part of the soul be, while impassible (ἀπαθές), is capable of receiving the form of an object (δεκτικόν (. . .) τοῦ εἴδους) that it must be potentially identical in character with its object without being the object'.[14]

How can we reconcile the fact that intellection must be imagined as a πάσχειν, a 'passivity', subjected to the action of the intelligible, while at the same time this 'passive receiving' doesn't put into doubt its fundamental impassivity, its (essential) systematic incorruptibility?

In order to make intelligible the modality of πάσχειν that is relevant here, Aristotle gives himself the task of isolating a type of *alteration* (ἀλλοίωσις) which is not at the same time a *corruption* (φθορά), which implies a fulfilment rather than a diminution of the subject's way of being. Now ἕξις matches very closely this definition of an alteration which does not corrupt. For example, the possession of knowledge or science (which draws man from his initial state of ignorance up to the state of the knower, and thus creates an alteration): this is certainly not a measure of deprivation but a change for the better. It is for this reason that Aristotle can say about νοῦς that it is 'potentially like a ἕξις'. The example of the man who becomes a wise man sheds light on the meaning we must give to ἕξις as in the case of 'the ἔχειν of νοῦς'. Ἕξις is defined as a degree of δύναμις. Πάσχειν should therefore be understood here as a mode of potentiality: that of 'thinking' in so far as it is not *actually* thinking at the moment.

However, this further explanation of ἕξις only throws us back into the same difficulty. Even if we were to know henceforth that any alteration experienced by νοῦς in so far as it submits to its own action is not in fact a corrupting ἀλλοίωσις, is that enough to justify us in maintaining that it is indeed acted upon? Aristotle asserts: 'We cannot help using the incorrect terms "being acted upon or altered" of the two transitions involved as if they were the correct terms',[15] which implies that they were not correct, at least on initial consideration! On the other hand, any ἀλλοίωσις suggests motion and change (μεταβολή); and Aristotle says of movement that it is 'a certain act, although an imperfect one'. How, accordingly, is it possible to allow, except analogically or through a misinterpretation, that there is movement and change within νοῦς?

Hegel's interpretation

Most of Aristotle's commentators have accused Hegel of this very misinterpretation. Hegel's reading of *De Anima* is consistent with his overall interpretation of Aristotle, in particular of the *Metaphysics*. The passage from the *Metaphysics* which concludes the entire movement of the *Encyclopedia* is devoted to that intelligence 'which thinks itself in grasping the intelligible' and defines 'God' as 'that actuality itself'. Commenting on the *Lectures on the History of Philosophy*, Pierre Aubenque recalls that Hegel interprets 'the union of thinking and what is thought' as 'activity (*Tätigkeit*)', which is 'movement and reaction', and goes on to claim:

> We may be astonished that Hegel, translating ἐνέργεια by *Tätigkeit* and assimilating activity to movement, misunderstands several Aristotelian texts, beginning with those which define movement

> as an 'incomplete act' (thus prohibiting any assimilation of the pure Act to movement in general), and also those in which Aristotle clarifies the divine act as an act of immobility (ἐνέργεια ἀκινησίας). If Hegel considers himself authorized to posit the identity of the divine act and that of movement, it is because he interprets the immobility expressly attributed by Aristotle to the Prime Mover as 'self-generating motion' (*Selbstbewegung*) or circular motion (*Kreisbewegung*).[16]

It is true that in the *Lectures on the History of Philosophy* Hegel does define the Aristotelian 'pure act' as 'that which moves in itself' and interprets it as 'the circle of reason which returns solely into itself'.[17] As for Aristotle's 'great definition', his idea of the 'unmoved which causes movement', Hegel explains that it is 'the Idea which remains self-identical, which, while it moves, remains in relation to itself'.[18] Now this relation to itself is defined as 'the self-relating negativity', which is, he argues, 'a principle of individualization'.[19] Here, Aubenque insists, Hegel is in error because

> in reference to God Aristotle never speaks of an 'activity relating itself to itself', because relation, even if it is to oneself, presupposes a duality and therefore an element of potentiality, incompatible with the purity of the divine act.[20]

Hegel would be wrong to interpret so literally the Aristotelian assimilation of the pure act to a life. In fact 'it is not possible to know whether the biological metaphors which Aristotle so much enjoys should be taken as anything more than approximations'.[21]

In the light of such statements, and in response to the questions raised earlier, we could argue that in *De Anima* all the passages developing the ideas of 'being acted upon' (πάσχειν) and 'acting' (ἐνεργεῖν) which are intended to clarify the process of νόησις νοήσεως are best understood as attempts at exemplification, metaphors in themselves 'necessarily partial and inadequate'.[22] As a consequence, all the importance we have been proposing to grant to these matters could well be exorbitant, indeed illegitimate. Aubenque recalls that potentiality and movement can only be attributed to sublunary existences, and that the 'pure act', 'free from all potentiality', has nothing do with 'the laborious, needy and discontinuous activity', and much less with the capacity of developing habits, which characterizes 'the creatures of the sublunary world'.[23] Hence, to move from ἕξις and ἄνθρωπος to the plasticity of νοῦς would be absurd.

By concluding his analysis of νοῦς and 'intelligence in action' with the claim that 'for thinking, that which is moved and that which moves are the same thing', and thus by conceiving movement and the immobile as an identity, Hegel is actually 'theologizing the sublunary experience of life',[24] and 'telescoping' the 'second and third stages of the Aristotelian universe, conflating the First Empyrean and the Prime Mover'.[25]

There is no doubt that these objections to the Hegelian interpretation must be taken into account. Yet even if a certain literal reading of the text does support them, they fail to be convincing when one looks more closely at their fundamental rationale. Can we be so sure that the biological 'metaphors' used by Aristotle to characterize the divine as living are nothing but 'approximations'? Or that there is a proper sense only remotely affected by its metaphors? To take this point a bit further, it is by no means certain that Hegel could have let himself be 'deceived' by these metaphors; in this connection we may also have to dispute the judgement of Dominique Janicaud, who concludes that Hegel is responsible for an interpretation of Aristotle which is 'excessively mobilistic'.[26]

Rather than opposing a 'true' interpretation of the meaning to a misinterpretation, can't we contrast one kind of textual fidelity to another? Must we see Hegel's interpretation of the divine act as 'a negativity relating itself to itself': as an abuse of the habit of dialectical systematization? Could it not be a matter of inscribing into God himself the mark of the *virtual* by introducing an element of potentiality into his very essence? Using the idea of a *noetic plasticity*, it is this direction that we shall pursue.

By inserting the passive νοῦς at the opening of the development of the *Philosophy of Spirit*, indeed making it the extreme counterpart to that quotation of the *Metaphysics* which stands at the conclusion, Hegel forces the two notions, in their dialogue, to act as a mirror to one another. To introduce negativity into the state of the pure act or 'absolute substance' reveals the process of *auto-determination* at work via the interplay of πάσχειν and ἐνεϱγεῖν. It is precisely this interplay which deserves the name of *plasticity*. The *Anthropology* will give it its first concrete enactment, relating the ontological sense of plasticity to its anthropological content, and asking, in particular, what transformation Hegel will impose on the Aristotelian treatment of exemplification in *De Anima*.

At this point we might recall Aristotle's example of the human aptitude for contracting an ἕξις as his central instance of an alteration which does not corrupt. Now, in Hegel, the close relation between human being and habit helps to explain the specifically spiritual process of giving and receiving form. In so far as Hegel has no room for the problematic of transcendence as it is commonly understood, noetic plasticity can only be conceived through the concrete determinations of spirit, namely, in this case, man. This refusal of transcendence logically entails a refusal to make a division between the transcendental and the empirical: the absolute never exists separately, never occupies an overhanging position. Consequently, since the concept of plasticity must also be understood in this way, it finds here its second meaning, as a mutual giving of form between the empirical and the noetic.

Book II of *De Anima* – Sensation

Presentation of the argument

We must now revisit *De Anima* to look at section 5 of Book II, entitled 'The Faculty of Sensation'. The overall problem is as follows: 'Sensation depends on a process of movement or change from without . . ., for it is held to be some sort of alteration (ἀλλοίωσίς τις).'[27] Initially Aristotle will explain why it is not possible to understand the general mechanism of sensation without involving, at least hypothetically, the couple of being affected and being active. But the issue he must clarify is the question of 'alteration'. What is of real importance is the detailed characterization of the type of alteration (ἀλλοίωσις) produced by sensation in general.

Aristotle begins by articulating a difficulty: 'Here arises a problem: why do we not perceive the senses themselves, or why without the stimulation of external objects do they not produce sensation?'[28]

The senses do not sense on their own, sight does not see, hearing does not hear. Hence it is impossible simply to claim that 'the like is affected only by the like', as certain philosophers nonetheless assert. Vision is necessarily the vision of something other than itself. Consequently, we must go back to the processes of πάσχειν and ἐνεργεῖν in order to explain the phenomenon of an 'affection' that can create an identity between that which senses and that which is sensed. Just as the 'combustible', as Aristotle says further, 'can never ignite itself spontaneously',[29] sensation cannot be explained except as the affection of the sensory or sentient organ, that is by the action of the sensible, or of the sensed.

This movement of πάσχειν and ἐνεργεῖν is made parallel to the twofold process of receiving and giving form:

> Generally, about all perception, we can say that a sense is what has the power of receiving into itself the sensible forms of things without the matter, in the way in which a piece of wax takes on the impress of a signet-ring without the iron or gold; what produces the impression is a signet of bronze or gold, but not qua bronze or gold: in a similar way the sense is affected by what is coloured or flavoured or sounding not in so far as each is what it is, but in so far as it is of such and such a sort and according to its form.[30]

Sense perception can only perceive what is other than itself; consequently, the sensible in so far as it is sensed is an alteration of that which senses. The like cannot be affected by the like; one must thus admit an originary receptivity, a passivity of the organ of sense towards that which is not itself. Yet this alterity cannot be a radical alterity. Without a certain communality (κοινόν τι) between that which senses and that which is sensed, sensation would never come about. Accordingly, the passivity which characterizes the sensory organs cannot be passivity pure and simple, like that of the wax, indifferent to the nature and quality of the form it receives. This is the point noted by Hegel in the *Lectures on the History of Philosophy* when he asserts:

> The wax does not, indeed, take in the form, for the impression remains on it as external figure (*äußerliche Gestaltung*) and contour, without being a form of its real essence (*keine Form seines Wesen*). If it were to become such, it would cease to be wax. The soul, on the contrary, assimilates (*assimiliert*) this form into its own substance, and for this reason the soul is in itself, to a certain extent, the sum of all that is perceived by the senses.[31]

If that which senses and that which is sensed were completely alien to one another, no sensory reception would be possible. The search for a 'mean' (μεσότης) between the two instances dominates the philosopher's entire approach and brings him to the conclusion that the 'agent' and the 'patient' which are at issue here can neither be utterly alike, nor completely unalike.[32] Aristotle claims:

> Hence it is that in one sense, as has already been stated, what acts and what is acted upon are like, in another unlike; for the unlike is affected, and when it has been affected, it is like.[33]

Hegel concludes from this that 'the manner in which the soul receives [is] just as truly activity of the soul (*Aktivität der Seele*); for after the perceptive faculty has received the impression, it abrogates the passivity, and remains thenceforth free from it'.[34]

One could certainly say that what is sensed alters that which senses. But this alteration needs to be understood as an achievement. According to a paradox which is only too obvious, it is solely through the work of this alteration that sensation can actualize its potential, that there can be the entelechy of vision. Already the terms used in this conclusion permit us to anticipate the outcome of the analysis. For it is now that Aristotle can let himself take up the examination of the couple δύναμις–ἐνέργεια, since sense must have two meanings, 'potential sense and actual sense'.[35] However, the distinction is not yet sufficient and needs to be clarified further. In so far as it is a matter of establishing how sensation can be a type of alteration, since it is ontologically continuous with ἐντελέχεια, we must distinguish different degrees of δύναμις and ἐνέργεια. At this point the example intervenes.

The example: ἕξις and ἄνθρωπος

> We can speak of some being as a knower either as when we say that man is a knower, meaning that man falls into the class of beings that know or have knowledge; or when we are speaking of a man who possesses a knowledge of grammar. Each of these has a potentiality, but not in the same way. . . .[36]

Man, the ἄνθρωπος, appears just at the moment when the different degrees of actuality and potentiality are being analysed, in order to characterize an ἀλλοίωσις which would not be a privation. Now it is ἕξις which will provide the necessary definition, because it represents the specific case of an intentionally produced alteration. At the beginning of the passage it is clearly indicated how ἄνθρωπος comes to characterize the neutral term, the ἐπίστημόν τι, by giving it a particular form. The human way of 'possessing' knowledge functions as a paradigmatic expression of the capacity of sense or intellect to receive form. Man is exemplary because of his own specific way of appropriating things. Because he is 'capable of knowledge', knowledge has the power to become for him a ἕξις.

Examining the different meanings one can give to the statement that a man is potentially a knower brings us back to the question of ἕξις and with it, to the question of the various degrees or gradations proper to actuality and potentiality. We need to distinguish the meaning of 'potentially' in the case of the man who knows 'potentially' from the meaning of the same phrase in the case of the man 'who already possesses a knowledge of grammar'.

> The one because his kind or matter is such and such, the other because he can reflect when he wants to, if nothing external prevents him. And there is the man who is actually reflecting – he is a knower in actuality and in the most proper sense is knowing . . .[37]

The transition (μεταβολή) from the first case to the second is nothing like the transition from the second to the third. The man who emerges from his condition of ignorance by learning something 'has been acted upon through a change of quality, has passed through repeated transitions (πολλάκις) from one state to its opposite'. This change is of a different nature than that by which ἕξις is realized, where a state of actuality (ἐντελέχεια) in the proper sense has been achieved. In fact, in the second case, the knower actualizes his potentiality by passing 'in another way by the transition from the inactive possession of sense or grammar, without exercising them (μὴ ἐνεργεῖν), to their active exercise'.[38] Hence Aristotle concludes:

> The expression 'to be acted upon' has more than one meaning; it may mean either the extinction (φθορά) of one of two contraries by the other, or the maintenance (σωτηρία) of what is potential by the agency of what is actual and already like what is acted upon, as actual to potential.[39]

Something can be acted upon by the action of either of the two types of action, both of which are included in the notion of ἀλλοίωσις. On one hand, being acted upon can be understood as a corruption or as a destruction; on the other hand, it can be understood as a conservation or an accomplishment: 'We must recognize two senses of alteration, viz, the change to conditions of privation (στερητικὰς διαθέσεις), and the change to a thing's dispositions (ἕξεις) and to its nature', says Aristotle.[40] Hegel renders this conclusion as follows: 'There is one change which is privative; and another which acts on the nature like a permanent energy (force and habit, ἕξις).'[41]

The accomplished act confirms a presence that has pre-existed, albeit withdrawn into itself. This 'presence in a state of withdrawal' is what characterizes a thing that is possessed, as if 'having' becomes the same as being-in-withdrawal, suspended being. This withdrawal or suspension of being is the other name of ἕξις.

Between the fact of being blind and that of always being able to see, there is a kind of 'not seeing' which is still the power to see, just as between ignorance and knowledge applied there is a third term which represents the mere possession of knowledge. By claiming that sensation is 'potentially in act' before anything has been sensed, Aristotle defines sensation precisely as that which at every moment has the possibility of bringing itself to completion. Seeing could not be seeing without possessing such a possibility. If seeing were simply and absolutely identified with the act of seeing, then it would be a kind of blindness. Without the power to close one's eyes, the gaze would be impossible. Hence it follows that the withdrawal of sensation which is inherent to sensation itself paradoxically testifies to the constancy of sensation, the things that can be sensed, and to sensing itself: it keeps open a critical space without which neither distinction nor identity could ever become manifest.

To demonstrate the difference between the first μεταβολή (the transition from ignorance to knowledge) and the second (the transition from possessing to actualizing), Aristotle uses a comparison between childhood and adulthood in terms of the degree of potentiality possessed:

> At present it must be enough to recognize the distinctions already drawn: a thing may be said to be potential in either of two senses, either in the sense in which we might say of a boy that he may become a general or in the sense in which we might say the same of an adult . . .[42]

Just as in the *Anthropology*, 'the natural course of the ages of life' is made to function as a *hypotyposis*, the sensory translation of a logical process. Because man goes through changes in age, it is he who embodies the degrees of potentiality as if in a translation into temporality. The distinctions internal to the signification of δύναμις and ἐνέργεια, distinctions identified by Aristotle, correspond in fact to what is captured in the 'process of temporalization' shown by the example.

In this context, man provides a reference, that is, a paradigmatic case of 'pathos'. Man is the παθητικός, the being to whom things happen. *De facto*, that which is kept, or reserved by ἕξις, would appear as a 'reserve of the future', a possibility of future time which runs ahead of presence (*entelechy*) even though presence is logically prior to it. Because he has the capacity of contracting ἕξις, man has the capacity to place energy in reserve. Aristotle's example allows him to introduce a condition into the economy of rest and movement which is neither one nor the other: an intermediate position, ontologically muted, a middle term between passivity and activity.

The human capacity to contract ἕξις or habit makes of man, properly speaking, a sensory medium; in other words, the human incarnates the originary synthesis of δύναμις and ἐνέργεια. But the problem that immediately arises is this: the 'natural course of the ages of life' is embedded so intimately in the speculative analysis of actuality and potentiality that it is at once possible and impossible – always a sign of plasticity as we have already defined it – to speak of a childhood and a maturity belonging to δύναμίς itself. How far and in what way does real temporality affect the ontological structure of potentiality, and with that, the structure of νοῦς itself?

Book III of *De Anima* – Understanding

At this point we must return to the distinction – at the same time a non-distinction – between the 'passive intellect', 'passive νοῦς'. and the 'active intellect', 'active νοῦς'. Between the processes of sensory perception and those of understanding, the difference lies in the fact that, in the case of sensation,

> the objects that excite the sensory powers to activity, the seen, the heard, etc., are outside, . . . while what knowledge apprehends are the universals, and these are in a sense within the soul itself. That is why a man can think when he wants to, but his sensation does not depend on himself: a sensible object must be there.[43]

The process of νοῦς thinking itself is an internal process, to be analysed in Book III, where a similar argument will be applied.

How can νοῦς think itself without being acted upon? The difficulty will be resolved by means of a distinction between the two understandings of 'being acted upon' linked to the two forms of alteration. In addition, this distinction is itself made possible through the earlier distinction between potentiality and actuality: it must be admitted 'that thought is in a sense potentially whatever is thinkable, though actually it is nothing until it has been thought'. The metaphors of the medium and the inscribed impression are once again introduced in the shape of the famous example, that of the writing tablet: 'What it thinks must be in it just as characters may be said to be on a writing-tablet on which as yet nothing actually stands written.'[44] Hegel resists the common misinterpretation of this comparison: the conceptualization of spirit as a '*tabula rasa* on which characters are first traced by external objects'. The philosopher insists that

> that is the very opposite of what Aristotle says. . . . The understanding . . . has not the passivity of a writing-tablet (for then all concepts would be forgotten). It is itself the actuality (*die Wirksamkeit selbst*). The comparison is confined to this, that the soul has a content only in so far as actual thought is exercised. The soul is this unwritten book, and the meaning is that the soul is all things implicitly (*an sich*), but is not in itself (*in sich selbst*) this totality: just as from the perspective of possibility a book contains all things, but in actuality it contains nothing until it is written on.[45]

While he does not develop further the principle of the non-corrupting ἀλλοίωσις Aristotle does return twice to the example of the potential and actual knowers, although he touches on it only in an elliptical and abbreviated manner. Once again, the problematic of the ἕξις is mobilized. It occurs first at 429b:

> when thought has become each thing in the way in which a man who actually knows and is said to do so (this happens when he is now able to exercise the power on his own initiative), its condition is still one of potentiality, but in a different sense from the potentiality which preceded the acquisition of knowledge by learning or discovery: and thought is then able to think of itself.[46]

The second occurrence is the analogy between the understanding (νοῦς) and that 'sort of positive state (ἕξις) analogous to light', which is pursued in the section commentators have called 'the active intellect'. As does light, the understanding 'converts' the contents of thought (νοητά) which are potentially contained within it, transforming them into those that exist in actuality. Following this point, Aristotle turns to a comparison between 'potential knowledge' and 'actual knowledge' within an individual.[47]

Aristotle's concern here is to think a difference, that is, an element of difference between the intellect and the intelligible, understanding and what is understood, which would render possible the very appearance of all forms (εἶδος). According to Aristotle, there can be nothing prior to this element of difference; it is the most elementary position, that which is of all things the most simple. Being acted-upon (πάσχειν) does not precede that which acts (ἐνεργεῖν); nor does the acting precede the acted-upon.

νοῦς and negativity

How will Hegel understand this originary synthetic instance? He resolves the question by positing νοῦς as a 'differentiated unity': 'Therefore there is a self-differentiation within it (*ein Verschiedenes von ihm in ihm*) and at the same time, it is pure and unmixed (*rein und unvermischt*).'[48] For Hegel, there can be no doubt that the plasticity of νοῦς, articulated in this act of its auto-differentiation, constitutes its very essence. This can clearly be seen in the following passage, which concludes the examination of passive νοῦς:

> This opposition, the difference within activity and the sublation of that difference, is expressed by Aristotle in saying that νοῦς thinks itself in the reception of thought, in those things which have become thought. νοῦς thinks itself through the reception of the thinkable; this thinkable only comes into being as something touching and thinking, it is first engendered when it touches – this is the way it is for thinking, in the activity of thinking.[49]

This passage sums up the exegetical 'lines of force' criticized by the Aristotelian commentators. According to them, the same 'misreadings' are equally manifest in Hegel's interpretation of Book XII of the *Metaphysics*. On the subject of the 'Prime Mover' Hegel argues that

> God is pure activity (*reine Tätigkeit*). . . . [He is] the substance which in its potentiality also has its actuality, the substance whose essence (*potentia*) is itself activity and in which the two are not separable; in it, possibility cannot be distinguished from form (*Form*), and it is that which itself produces (*produziert*) its own content, its own determinations.[50]

His interpretation has been subjected to two fundamental criticisms. The first one, discussed above, accuses Hegel of not respecting the Aristotelian distinctions between ontological levels. For the second, the problem is that his interpretation is tainted by anachronism.

For Aubenque, who represents the first line of criticism, Hegel's understanding of ἐντελέχεια as *Tätigkeit* rests on a series of misunderstandings. By characterizing the 'divine νοῦς' as 'the absolute which, in a state of rest, is simultaneously absolute activity', Hegel 'dynamizes' the Aristotelian concept of activity. It would be 'wrong' to attribute 'to the divine those palpitations of life which are at once exteriorization and return to self', and wrong to substitute 'for the perfection of the pure act the *aorist* of an activity that would be an infinite movement of self-constitution'.[51] The second line of criticism is formulated by Dominique Janicaud: 'the metaphysical horizon of speculative idealism . . . comes to impose itself, indeed to superimpose itself, on the Aristotelian text.'[52]

The two issues become one. Either Hegel has let himself 'be carried away' by his desire for 'systematization', and the projection of a dogmatic and anachronistic 'idealist' conception of subjectivity onto a philosophy totally uninterested in the concepts of the 'substance-subject' and 'auto-determination' is grounded on an uncritical presupposition. Or his interpretation of Aristotle's text is grounded on an even more elaborate position, no less than the foundational principle of Hegel's philosophical system: viz., the idea of subjectivity as support of its own ontological history, that is, of its own temporal self-differentiation. If we follow the argument suggested by Hegel's principle, the possibility of one epoch's 'superimposition' on another epoch's way of thinking, far from being the result of a *parti pris* alien to thinking itself, is on the contrary inscribed within substance's very way of being. If this were not the case, Hegel believes, it would be impossible to understand how subjectivity, while remaining as it is, continues all the time to change its meaning, this being the evolution responsible for the very idea of a history of philosophy.

By introducing into νοῦς an 'element of potentiality' Hegel accounts for the subject's ability to differentiate itself in time, thus enabling the translation of Aristotelian philosophemes into the language of speculative idealism. It may be the case that Hegel does not abide by the separation of ontological levels important to Aristotle's thinking; yet, by this exegetical *coup de force* he insists that absolute substance cannot be understood outside of its own auto-differentiation. This is tantamount to saying that substance as it is conceived by Aristotle can include among its own attributes the possibility – that which will be its fate, or its future – of being interpreted through conceptual determinations which are not those of Aristotle. The play of πάσχειν and ἐνεργεῖν within νοῦς must be interpreted, from a Hegelian perspective, as providing the possibility for substance to 'see (itself) coming'.

If Hegel does introduce movement into substance, it is not because he is 'infatuated' with motion (a *maniac* for the dialectic) as his opponents seem to suspect, but because the principle of auto-differentiation is identical with the principle that allows subjectivity, through the element of time, to develop its concept. This claim helps us to picture more precisely the problem of a pure noetic habit or primal ἕξις by which substance can make itself by itself. This is the very operation we call plasticity. In this context we need to repeat Hegel's phrase which locates ἕξις at the centre of νοῦς:

'νοῦς acts receptively, and what it receives is οὐσία, thought: its receiving is active, producing as appearance what had been received – it becomes what it has (*so fern er hat*)'.[53]

The process of substance's auto-differentiation as Hegel conceives it can only be possible if there is admitted within it an element of virtuality: substance possesses in itself its future actualizations. The outcome (logical and chronological) of substance's actualizations contains the principle of substance's internal differentiation, the principle without which the concept of 'spiritual development' would be unintelligible. Hegel imagines the existence of a *noetic habit*, or pure ἕξις, inscribing within substance the very possibility of its history.

In the *Lectures on the History of Philosophy*, the philosopher insists on the fact that the negativity revealed within substance is not a form of pure and simple nullity:

> With Plato the affirmative principle, the Idea as only abstractly identical with itself, is the major consideration. In Aristotle there is added the moment and emphasis of negativity, but not as change nor as nullity (*als Nichts*), rather as difference (*aber nicht als Veränderung, auch nicht als Nichts, sondern als Unterscheiden*).[54]

This negativity manifests itself as virtuality. Ἕξις, in so far as it is something possessed and held in reserve, falls outside the scope of that category called by Hegel 'abstract negativity'; it is rather instead a negation which preserves that which it negates (ἀλλοίωσις without corruption). From this it follows that negation is in fact a modality of what the Greeks knew as the μὴ ὄν – that which might not be – the non-existent as a problematic way of being: distinguishing it from the οὐκ ὄν – that which is not – signifying the absolute lack of being. The negative adverb μή indicates a case where negation is accompanied by a doubt, as opposed to the adverb οὐκ which denies a certain fact.[55] Hegelian negativity, the nature of a being which is suppressed 'but has not definitively disappeared', of a 'state midway between being and nothing',[56] requires this modality of the μὴ ὄν which is one of the central meanings of virtuality. In the logical process of the *Aufhebung*, the essential idea of a mode of preservation – a form of preservation identified by Hegel in several different places through the Latin adverb *virtualiter* – is clearly associated with the Aristotelian concept of ἕξις. Ἕξις describes the manner in which substance entertains the reality of its *future* actualizations as if they were its 'possessions' or properties.

Aristotle's commentators find something scandalous or, at the very least, improper in this introduction of negativity at the very core of impassivity, for it implies a process which, in a certain manner, leads it towards passivity. From this it seems possible to interpret this 'passivity' as an 'originary passivity', if not as temporality itself, in so far as this 'passivity', being subject to the past (*le passé*) as such, is truly the past from which all time has emerged. Yet this passivity could by the same token be called the true form of 'the Self's seeing itself come' ('*le voir venir du Soi*'). Substance's internal auto-differentiation, which governs the division into subject and object, is at the same time a self-differentiation of the concept of division itself. In this is contained *both* the Greek *and* the modern understandings of the 'face to face'. Negativity programmes substance.

Habit and Temporality

Through a consideration of the *temporal* dimension of habit, in the human contraction of habits, it becomes possible to explicate both plasticity and the immanent temporalization of νοῦς. In his attempt to clarify the specific nature of ἕξις in relation to the other types of disposition, Aristotle frequently introduces the factor of time. In *Metaphysics* IV, 19, 20, he argues that ἕξις is 'a way of being, or habitual state' like science or virtue, as opposed to διάθεσις, a transient disposition (e.g. illness, health, warmth, chilling), and also as opposed to πάθος, a simple and superficial affection which quickly passes away.[57]

Habit is a mode of presence that cannot be reduced to the present time of the now. In this way it is temporally unique. For I can easily say that at a certain moment I possess this or that knowledge, this or that talent, without at that moment making use of it. But everything which is, so to speak, held within me, can also at any moment have a different outcome, falling outside this fragile slice of a 'now', or of an instant. It is impossible to give a date to habit. Habit is a memory which, like all memory, has lost the recollection of its own origin. We never know exactly when habit began or when it actually ceases to exist. It might have disappeared before the day at which we notice its absence, notice that we could no longer do something, that we were no longer adept.

In a certain sense the notion of ἕξις defines a kind of time within time, as if time (χρόνος) could, in the transition from a simple πάθος to the μεταβολή that belongs to the process of ἕξις, exhibit a strange ability to double itself. For ἕξις, as second nature, involves a second nature of time which no longer is part of nature. Nature is repeated because it is transformed; ἕξις is a power elevating time itself to the second power. If Hegel does indeed treat habit as the determining moment of the *Anthropology*, it is because habit makes possible the transition of nature into spirit, revealing and putting into perspective a temporality no longer belonging to the simple rule of time.

Something we possess as a kind of ἕξις (for example, knowledge) is not strictly speaking present, if by present we mean something which is standing there and here, in front of us, ready at hand. Habit is in fact *virtuality*. Now the *virtual* is just that – what is never exactly 'here'. In what place and time does the expectation of its actualization occur? No tangible schema can claim to show the location of a specific piece of knowledge, for example, when it is not being exercised but is still kept in reserve.

The process of θεωρεῖν, a verb which in this context means both 'to contemplate' and to 'exercise', elucidates this odd play of time which links virtuality and actualization. Θεωρεῖν is a circle. The pupil learns while contemplating the teaching. Yet this contemplation is already and by itself an exercise, a practice. It is not something to be put into practice only when the pupil has become 'practised'. From this it is obvious that ἕξις is as much the result as the condition of the exercise. If it rightfully precedes the actualization and seems to be something that has already happened beforehand, it is also the task of this actualization, since one must practise and hence already have actualized an aptitude in order that habit (ἕξις) may come into being. If the novice always finds himself in an impossible situation at the start, caught between the contribution of spontaneity and the contribution of receptivity, it is this impossible bind which reveals time's second nature, its chronology suspending chronology. Ἕξις is a kind of virtuality engaged in three extases of time at once, without one dominating the others: the *past* (habit is prior to its being put to work), the *present* (habit is itself a modality of presence), and the *future* (habit takes the form of a task which must be fulfilled, of an expectation that rules the direction of what is to come).[58]

Conclusion

In the course of moving from one mode of time (the noetic) to another (the time of human habit-forming), Hegel has completed the trajectory of Greek subjectivity. In a close examination of his reading of *De Anima*, we have been able to show that the development and evolution of the *Anthropology* is determined by a dialectical movement itself controlling the relations between the noetic process and its exemplification. Man, he who has the power to acquire habits, provides the singular example of spirit in its incarnation.

It has become clear that when Hegel attempts to conceive negativity and potentiality as existing within the very heart of the divine intellect, he is by no means simply taking Aristotle's 'biological metaphors' in a crude, literal sense. However, it remains to be seen whether or not the radical transformations which Hegel gives to the conclusions of *De Anima* amount to an anthropological interpretation of substance itself. In other words, the example must be pushed to the limit at which it can be thought.

3

HABIT AND ORGANIC LIFE

In the *Principles of the Philosophy of Right* Hegel claims that man has the power to 'transform his first nature into a second, spiritual nature, in order that every spiritual element becomes for him something habitual'.[1] Man's potential to duplicate his nature emerges from this as the defining anthropological attribute. Does this mean that the ability to develop habits is sufficient on its own to distinguish a 'proper of man' within the element of living things?[2]

When Hegel reopens the analyses of *De Anima* does this entail an anthropological conception of habit? The *Philosophy of Nature*, with its concentration on the notion of 'organic life', immediately invalidates such a conclusion. The account developed here shows that, for Hegel, nature is always *second nature*. In this context, we must reverse the preceding questions: it will be difficult to determine whether in Hegel's thought there is a privileged place for this reduplication of nature. If all animals are habituated animals, how do we distinguish the boundaries of that exemplary living being called man?

The homelands of habit

When we undertake a detailed examination of habit and its functions, both as understood by Aristotle and his followers and as brilliantly rethought by Hegel, we will see that such an operation is not exclusive to man. According to its Greek definition, habit is a way of being which is general and permanent, or, to cite Ravaisson in his work *On Habit*, it is 'a state of existing understood either as the ensemble of its parts or as a temporal succession'.[3] Given these conditions, the notion of existence extends beyond any strictly anthropological rendering. To what beings other than man can it apply?

For Aristotle, habit implies the aptitude for change, along with the possibility of preserving the modifications inherent in such change. As the *Eudemian Ethics* explains, if we throw a stone many times in the same direction, it will not keep a single trace of each alteration of place: 'The body remains always the same with reference to this motion, even if it has been marked on it one hundred times.'[4] Ravaisson, commenting on this passage, argues: 'Habit does not simply introduce mutability into something that would otherwise continue without changing; it suggests change within a disposition, within its potentiality, within the internal character of that in which the change occurs, which does not change.'[5]

In the *Lectures on the History of Philosophy*, Hegel emphasizes the dual principles of change and preservation as Aristotle had formulated them:

> That which is changed is only the sensuous and perceptible; forms and figures, as capacities, and *habitus* (habits like virtues and vices, for example) are not changed; 'Forms etc. arise and disappear in a thing, but what rises and disappears, is not changed'.[6]

In Hegel's view, Aristotle believes in a 'pure ideality of change' in the sense that change appears to be neither a simple corruption nor a movement towards non-being. Instead it is revealed as the principle of internal differentiation.[7]

Because inorganic bodies are incapable of this self-differentiation, they lack the power to develop habit. On the other hand, each and every organic being, living 'with itself as its own end'[8] and which must 'preserve within itself the unity of the self',[9] is always a being of habit.

Auto-differentiation assumes a measurable length of time between the living being's originary principle and its ultimate end, an 'action lying in the middle between its first and last stage'.[10] The organic being is characterized by its effort in maintaining its own unity through the synthesis of differences: the difference between the organism and its environment and the difference between the heterogeneous elements which make up the organism. Such an effort is nothing less than habit itself: from the beginning to the end of the organism's life, habit is busy applying its power from the inside, fulfilling the individual development of the organism's faculties.

'Adaptation' is the proper term for this process of development and actualization. In this context it is easy to see why habit can be defined as a

> general phenomenon of biological and even physical adaptation, consisting in the fact that a being, once it has experienced for the first time some kind of modification, will preserve that modification so that even if the action is repeated or continued, there will be no additional modification like the first one.[11]

For Hegel, adaptation and auto-differentiation are phenomena visible already in the vegetable kingdom.[12] In the plant, the mechanism of assimilation on which it is dependent is inseparable from the process of adaptation: 'in every vital process, natural and spiritual, the essential factor is assimilation'. Assimilation is 'the substantive change and immediate transformation of one external or particular material into another'.[13] In the syllogism Hegel entitles 'the syllogism of the plant' (division, growth, reproduction), one finds an 'internal process of the plant's relation to itself', which can be divided up into two acts:

> One side of this is the substantial process, involving immediate transformation whether of the nutrients absorbed into the specific nature of the plant, or the formless liquids (the vital sap) which inside are directed to the production of forms (*Gebilde*); on the other hand, there is a process of the organism's mediation with itself.[14]

Thus for Hegel it is not impossible to refer to a vegetative habit. However, it is with animals that habit becomes something explicit. In the *Philosophy of Nature* Hegel refers to Bichat who claims that 'in animal life everything is modified by habit'.[15] Fundamental to the animal organism is the relationship between habit and auto-differentiation, a relationship to which the notion of habit contributes four distinct features: contraction, internal disposition, conservation of change, reversibility of energies.

Contraction and *Habitus*

The first determination concerns the way the living organism interacts with the inorganic world. The very materials of the inorganic, subjected to an immediate contraction, are what make up the organism. In the core of its being, the living organism is nothing but the reduction and condensation of the elements of its environment: water, air, the molecules of nitrogen and carbon. What results from such a contraction is, literally, *habitus*, at once the internal disposition and the general constitution of the organism.

Hegel's entire *Philosophy of Nature* is organized according to the logic of this contraction. Hegel intends to show how the living organism summarizes everything that precedes it: inert matter, the elements, chemical processes, all the constitutive moments which are dialectically conjoined in the *Philosophy of Nature*.[16]

If the plant world already knows the synthesis of inorganic substances, the animal world takes this even further, contracting all that comes before it. In the *Philosophy of Nature* of 1805–6, Hegel writes that 'the organization, in general, of the animal represents the physical elements reconstructed in one single individual'.[17] Such a reconstruction turns the organism into a *habitus*, meaning that it is provided with an internal disposition at the organic level. Following Cuvier, Hegel defines the animal *habitus* as 'the connection (*Zusammenhang*) which determines how all the parts are constructed'.[18]

Contraction is intimately connected to the formation of *habitus*. In the animal organism, this connection represents the elementary shape of subjectivity.[19] 'The animal organism is the reduction of the divided nature of the inorganic into the infinite unity of subjectivity.'[20] Lacking a German equivalent for the concept of contraction,[21] Hegel takes advantage of the more powerful notion of 'idealization': 'Organic individuality exists as *subjectivity* if the specific exterior of the figure is *idealized* (*idealisert ist*) in its elements and the organism in its external process maintains in itself its own unity.'[22]

Idealization, because it represents the process of preservation and suppression, simultaneously appears as condensation and synthesis, or as a twofold abstraction–contraction.

Contraction and 'theory'

The dialectical movement uniting the inorganic components of the environment to the components of the organism is what Hegel calls 'theoretical'. Every vital mechanism of adaptation is already in itself a certain modality of θεωρεῖν in the double meaning Aristotle emphasizes: to contemplate and to exercise. The living being is at once identical to and different from its non-living origins and surroundings. Because sameness and alterity are related, habit becomes a condition of adaptation in a double sense, being a form of *contemplation* – absorbing the environment, passively lending itself to what is given – and a kind of *exercise*, informing and transforming the surroundings, appropriating the given conditions for its organic functions.

In *Difference and Repetition*, Gilles Deleuze formulates the relation between contemplation and contraction with admirable precision:

> A soul must be attributed to the heart, to the muscles, nerves and cells, but a contemplative soul whose entire function is to contract a habit. This is no mystical or barbarous hypothesis. On the contrary, habit here manifests its full generality: it concerns not only the sensory-motor habits that we have (psychologically), but also, before these, the primary habits that we are; the thousands of passive syntheses of which we are organically composed. It is simultaneously through contraction that we are habits, but through contemplation that we contract.[23]

How are we to understand the precession of contemplation over contraction, as seems to be assumed by the phrase 'through contemplation we contract'? *Proceed* must be substituted for *precede*, as the following assertion invites us to do: 'We do not contemplate ourselves, but we exist only in contemplating – that is to say, in contracting that from which we come.'[24]

An initial 'situation' (*une situation de départ*) in Deleuze's analysis is portrayed by him in the following terms: 'We are made of contracted water, earth, light and air – not merely prior to the recognition or representation of these, but prior to their being sensed.'[25] We depart *from* and *in* the inorganic and the four elements – by contraction. The more complex the living thing becomes, the more it adds to the number, extent, and quality of its contractions, and it does this in three ways: through a passive and active structuration, an ongoing aptitude for acquisition, and a multiplying reduction.

For example, an animal will form the *habitus* of sight by determining how luminous stimuli, otherwise scattered and diffuse, are reproduced on the privileged surface of its body. 'The eye binds light, it is itself a bound light.'[26] The activity of binding difference (in this case, the perception of light) is dual. On the one hand it is contemplative, for vision is achieved only by seeing, hence by submitting the eye to the action of the sensible. But on the other hand, it is also active: for it is by submitting itself that the eye paradoxically acquires its form and exercises itself. In a certain sense, the eye is produced by the material it contracts and invests in during the process of contemplation.

Contraction and concentration are the work of the plasticity of life, initially in the sense that life is responsible for the donation of the vital forms, but also in the sense that each of these forms, to the degree that it is made of a concentrated energy, provokes an explosion. Bergson, in the same connection, will say about the animal that

> all that the effort it can do, then, is to make the best of a pre-existing energy which it finds at its disposal. Now it finds only one way of succeeding in this, namely, to secure such an accumulation of potential energy from matter, that it can get, at any moment, the amount of work it needs for the action, simply by pulling a trigger (*en faisant jouer un déclic*).[27]

The animal finds the stored energy it needs. Initially passive towards that energy, it can liberate it by exercising its vital functions.

> It feeds itself on substances which are . . . reservoirs of energy. Formed from complex molecules which contain a considerable sum of chemical energy in the potential state, these substances are like explosives, needing only a spark to set free the stored-up force.[28]

This explosion of vitality, joined to the process of contraction, indicates at the same time continuity and rupture. The more complex the living being, the more its organism contracts its elements: in this sense, increasing contraction marks continuity on the scale of beings and forms an evolutionary line. But at the same time, this evolution is a sequence of ruptures. Between plant and animal, for example, there is not so much a transition as a break. Hegel explains this very well: 'A point occurs at which the continuity of mediation, a gradual progression which could be either a chemical or mechanical development, suddenly breaks off and becomes impossible. This point is everywhere and penetrates everything. . . .'[29]

Continuation ('this point is everywhere and penetrates everything') and halt ('breaking off'), contraction is simultaneously mediation and explosion.

Conservation of change and reversibility of energy

Necessarily, mediation and explosion imply both change and the conservation of change. If repeated change produces a difference in the subject experiencing it, this means that change coming from the outside has altered into a change emerging from the inside. The law of this alteration is the law of reversibility of energies, or reciprocal transformation of passivity into activity.

The animal is a genuine individual in the sense that it relates at the same time to itself and to an other as 'its' other. The syllogistic process that constitutes it determines the relationship between activity and passivity within its organism. Hegel explains it as follows:

> As living universality, the animal organism is the concept which passes syllogistically through its three determinations . . . (a) as the individual idea, which is simply self-related in its process, and which inwardly coalesces with itself, i.e. shape (*Gestalt*); (b) as idea which relates itself to its *other* (*ihrem Anderen*), its inorganic nature, and posits the ideal nature of this other within itself, i.e. assimilation; (c) as the idea relating to an other which is itself a living individual, and thereby relating itself to itself in the other, i.e. the generic process.[30]

According to Hegel, those 'developed determinations', which make up the concept of the organism and constitute the animal's characteristics and specific properties, are three in number: sensibility, irritability, reproduction. These three determinations 'have their reality' in three systems, the nervous system, the system of the blood, and the digestive system.[31] As these interpenetrate, they train the organism's general system of action and reaction in response to the pressures exerted by the environment. Forming the capacity Hegel calls 'organic elasticity', they constitute an activity in which 'the individual repels itself from itself'. This activity is itself the sublation (*relève*) of a twofold propensity: a receptivity towards excitation coming from outside the organism, and, inversely, a reaction towards this excitation.

The disposition of a living being is constantly and repeatedly being modified to welcome and transform nature. Inherent in irritability is the same law of action and reaction, inducing receptivity to diminish and spontaneity to increase. The more these actions are repeated, the higher the level of appropriate response, the more the organism familiarizes itself with its circumstances, with that environment in which external and contingent elements 'continuously threaten the sensitive being and surround it with danger'.

Impressions, Hegel insists, lose their force to the degree that they are reproduced. Under the action of habit, 'immediate feeling is treated as indifferent'. From this arises the power to become 'inured against external sensations'. Desires and impulses are 'by the *habit* of their satisfaction deadened'.[32]

What was initially only submission becomes, with repetition, the power to initiate movement. The blunting of sensation has as its correlative an increase in judgement and discrimination. For example, the more the animal develops and becomes stronger, the greater its skill at discovering the places where water is readily to be found. The animal senses the power of water through signs unlike the signs that alert the thirsty animal to its need. As the displeasure caused by thirst becomes something habitually acknowledged, the animal becomes capable of interpreting its warning signs, and through these signs it can advance a step beyond its immediate surroundings. Thus the animal becomes a being who invents.[33]

Animal habit and its improbable limit

Because the animal can transform its environment through the active power its organism acquires by developing within processes of adaptation, it is not completely a prisoner of natural circumstances. Instead, the animal exhibits a rudimentary aptitude for interpreting, a sensibility to non-sensuous signs, and a power to trigger off the energy which, without this aptitude, would always remain captive to the inert elements that are its reserves.

In reference to animal life, Hegel speaks of a *Bildungstrieb*, or even of a *Kunsttrieb*. Literally, these expressions mean 'formative tendency' and 'artistic tendency'.[34] Augusto Vera, the first French translator of the *Philosophy of Nature*, used an expression which is not the literal equivalent of these terms, but nonetheless gives us a translation both interesting and pertinent: *Bildungstrieb* is rendered as 'plastic instinct'. To what does this refer? To the fact that 'the animal, consuming the things it needs, using natural materials to build its shelter or its lair, uses no more of that material than is necessary, so that it leaves the world in its being, without entirely destroying it'.[35]

The animal allows the surroundings in which it lives to subsist, which transforms those surroundings already into a 'world': something unified, a space remade to suit. Accordingly the 'habit' of the animal already functions as a way of 'inhabiting' the world, and thus involves a particular relation to temporality.

Habit is what gives a being the impression of its existence as something continuous, and this Hegel calls the 'impression of selfhood'. Habit makes it possible to *retain* the changes that occur and to expect that they will recur. Invoking the past and the future, habit brings becoming to life. In return, the individual feels the weight of its own existence. The animal is already the subject of such a mechanism. Thus we can recognize in the animal an elementary form of seeing what is coming, of the *voir venir*. Need, appetite, desire, the accumulation of such retentions and expectations, are themselves proof of the fact that the animal is concerned to ensure the perpetuation of its own life.

The previous chapter on the human contraction of habit uncovered determinations which are not strictly speaking anthropological: the relation to contemplation and activity, the possibility of holding energies in reserve, the introduction of a time which is not the time of nature. Habit is not essentially a property of man. Nevertheless, it cannot be denied that it plays a decisive role in the development of the *Anthropology* and that it signals the gap between man and animal. How, then, can this gap grow wider?

One measures this gap by its effects. Hegel remarks that the animal experiences an 'awareness' of its own 'deficiency (*Mangel*)',[36] an awareness which motivates it to reproduce itself. This feeling arises from the tension (*Spannung*) between the 'inadequacy (*Unangemessenheit*) of its single actuality' in relation to the genus. Such a tension reveals itself as an 'urge to attain the sentiment of itself in another member of its genus, to integrate itself (*integrieren*) and through this mediation to link itself (*zusammenschließen*) with the genus, thus bringing it into being: this constitutes generation (*Begattung*)'.[37]

However, propagation (*Fortpflanzung*) only leads to a spurious infinite progression (*mauvaise infinité*). Because the animal cannot establish its singularity as universal by cancelling the discrepancy between them, the animal cannot on its own 'become the absolute genus'. In fact, 'the genus preserves itself only through the perishing of the individuals, who have fulfilled their determination in the sexual act and, in so far as they have no higher determination than this, pass on to death.'[38]

But what kind of mediation does the animal lack, which thus authorizes its retreat in favour of man, who now approaches his speculative birth?

4

'THE PROPER OF MAN' IN QUESTION

Human Specificity and Plastic Individuality

There is one immediate and obvious response to that last question: it is language that could act as the cutting edge between the death of the animal and the birth of man. For what else but the power of speech could enable man to 'present perfectly the genus'? There are passages in Hegel's *Anthropology* that would support such a conclusion, pre-empting the inquiry already underway: 'Seen from the animal world, the human figure is the supreme phase in which spirit makes an appearance. But, for spirit, it is only its *first* appearance, while *language* is straightaway its perfect expression (*sein vollkommener Ausdruck*).'[1]

The notion of 'expression' is striking here. Indeed, at the end of the *Anthropology*, man comes onto the scene as the 'free shape' of the soul, with its 'human pathognomic and physiognomic expression'.[2] But how are we to understand this notion of *expression*? If expression is to be understood as a kind of direct emanation, the phrase 'to present perfectly the genus' would mean that spirit speaks in the man when man speaks; human individuality would be simply a medium for the speculative broadcast. The genus would reach its perfection in the limpid form of a word and a singular physiognomy.

However, if this were the case, and human subjectivity were for Hegel something immediate like a transparently reflecting crystal, how could it have a place for delirium, madness, the primordial night? Why would the anthropological development take so long, concluding with language rather than beginning with it? And on this account, what would be the role of habit?

If we avoid a hasty reading of the human relation to its *habitus*, then a patient reflection on the material will reveal that human *expression* does not reduce to a pre-constituted *expressed*. The economy of signification that appears at the end of the *Anthropology* has been dialectically liberated from the initial and natural economy of the sign which originally governs man. In the transition from one economy to the other, in a passage which involves the formation of our 'plastic individuality', it becomes possible to encounter the real role of language.

'Interior' and 'exterior': the natural economy of the sign

Human 'nature' is, for Hegel, always and already 'second nature':

> The form of habit applies to spirit in all its degrees and varieties. Of all these modifications, the most external is the determination of the individual in relation to space; this, which for man means *an upright posture*, is something which by his will he has made into a habit. Adopted *directly, without thinking*, his upright stance continues through the persistent involvement of his will. Man stands upright only because and in so far as he wants to stand, and only as long as he wills to do so without consciousness of this. Similarly, to take another case, the act of *seeing*, and others like it, are concrete habits which combine in a single act the multiple determinations of sensation, of consciousness, intuition, understanding, and so forth.[3]

However, the preceding analyses have shown that the ability to contract habits cannot be the only distinguishing feature of the anthropological. If second nature is always present in organic nature, what is human habit and what does it mean?

Between animal habit and human habit, the real distinction lies in the way human habit has an innate tendency to conceal its identity as habit. Such a tendency springs from human *habitus* itself. In the case of the animal, influences from the outside world are immediately 'intro-reflected'.[4] With the human organism, on the other hand, such a reflection back onto the self is not an immediate action, body and soul not forming so instantaneously that 'simple ideal unity' which is required by self-feeling.

Accordingly, the individual first considers himself to be a being divided into an 'exteriority' – the body – and an 'interiority' – his inner being, which Hegel calls in the *Phenomenology of Spirit* its 'intrinsically determined original character'.[5] In the section '*Observing Reason*', this blindness of man to his own lack of an 'originary' nature is brought into view. There is no way that the human organism can be treated as something simply natural and instrumental, as we understand from the dual meaning of the Greek *organon*, at once an organ and an instrument. Yet the difficulty is that man does not know this about himself. 'The simple lines of the hand, the timbre and volume of the voice',[6] the features of his physiognomy, although these do not predetermine the individual from birth, seem to possess the power as signs to *express* and manifest the inner self.

At this level of analysis, 'the outer (*das Äußere*) is merely the expression (*Ausdruck*) of the inner (*des Innern*)'.[7] This economy of expression, according to which 'this outer, in the first place, acts only as an *organ* in making the inner visible or, in general, a being-for-another', constitutes a natural state of signification and, as a result, the state of nature of a second nature. Indeed, the organs which function as immediate signs represent natural expressions, physical expressions, of the soul. Hence the individual who believes, on this evidence, that his 'exteriority' reveals his 'inner being', that everything is there to be seen, interpreted, made meaningful, has in fact made himself a prisoner of this state of nature. When the organs 'become a sign' they place the subject at the mercy of the gaze of others. Man sees himself being seen and seeing: he has become doubled and, at the same time, multiplied perspectivally.

This state of absolute transparency is the paradoxical result of a phantasm of opacity. Following the logic of this immediate 'transformation into sign', the interior becomes something 'invisible' which, although expressed by the organs, remains ineffable, non-existent, and merely intended. Given an interiority posited as *referent*, the phantasm of opacity must follow. This conception of the sort of expression generated by the referential illusion is precisely what Hegel understands as the *negative of language*, language, or a part of it, having come on the scene concurrently. In fact, the 'individual characteristic of speech',[8] i.e. immediate physical expressiveness, precedes language itself as a consequence preceding its premisses.

The individual confronts a 'signifying act which is double and contradictory (*doppelte, entgegensetzte Bedeutung*)'; the individual is at once 'the inner individuality and *not its expression*'; and 'something external, a reality *free from* the inner', hence 'something quite different from the inner'.[9] This contradiction demands the ironic characterisation of a Lichtenberg, as Hegel notes: 'You certainly act like an honest man, but I see from your face that you are forcing yourself to do so and are a rogue at heart'.[10] The quote illustrates how signifier and signified, constrained by the purely imaginary status of the referent, fail to coincide. The sign with which we have to deal 'in truth signifies nothing (*in Wahrheit nichts bezeichnet*)', and Hegel concludes: 'for the individuality, it is as much its countenance as its mask which it can lay aside'.[11]

It has become obvious that natural expressivity, by its own operation, must lose what appeared to be its assigned role:

> But, since the individual is at the same time only what he has done, his body is also the expression of himself which he has himself produced; it is at the same time a sign (*Zeichen*) which has not remained an immediate thing (*Sache*), but something through which the individual only makes known what he really is, when he sets his original nature to work.[12]

Human *habitus* signifies the fact that it signifies nothing. Indeed, as Hegel puts it, 'we can say with equal truth that these expressions express the inner too much, as that they do so too little'.[13] Immediate 'signifying' can only lead to a 'science of conjectures, according to which the reality of man is his face'.[14] This science, physiognomy, developed by Lavater, takes as its mission the task of manifesting something that doesn't exist: natural man. Against this enterprise,

> the *being* of spirit cannot in any case be taken as something fixed and immovable. Man is free; it is admitted that the *original being* consists merely of *dispositions* about which a man is free to do much as he wishes, or which require favourable circumstances for their development; i.e. an *original being* of spirit is equally well to be spoken of as a being which does not exist qua being.[15]

Man appears as the being who must come to experience the non-referentiality of expression, or, in other words, signification's impossible state of nature. Through this experience he recognizes the lack of any ontological guarantee outside of the play of signification. But this lack had initially disturbed the structure of reflexivity inherent in the notion of an 'immediate signifying process'. In turn, that disturbance produced those pathological states of spirit described in the *Anthropology*. Spirit is not that which is expressed by its expressions: it is that which originally terrifies spirit. The individual's ability to express his genus cannot adhere to an indexical type, but, on the contrary, involves an economy of auto-referentiality.

With the help of habit in its dialectical work on itself, we have been able to pass from one signification to another. Speculative anthropology is a revelation man's reduplication of his own nature does indeed correspond to a 'reduplication of the reduplication', and human habit appears as the passage from second nature to a second second nature.

'The soul's work of art' and the arrangement of signification

In its origins, human *habitus* is characterized as a surplus of (non-)meaning. If in the state of nature meaning had no sense, here it is replaced by the speculative signification: something that appears when 'individuality gives up that *reflectedness-into-self* which is expressed in lines and lineaments, and places its essence in the work it has done'.[16] Man is only what he does and only expresses what he *forms*.

At the end of the *Anthropology*, man is defined as 'the soul's work of art', in direct reference to Greek sculpture. Habit's contribution to the work of formation and culture is presented as analogous to the moulding gesture of the sculptor, whose vocation is to 'resolve the question of how the spirit . . . may be incarnated in the corporeal and thereby gain a form (*Gestalt*)'.[17]

At first glance, this argument involves a contradiction, since the statue does not function 'mimetically' and must refrain from representing any particular bodily form.[18] Yet, in juxtaposing the notion of the work of art against that of 'human pathognomic and physiognomic expression', Hegel is by no means inconsistent. Rather, he draws out the deeper meaning of traditional anthropological categories. Human characteristics are not a given: they emerge as the result of a process of formation of which art is the paradigm.

The task of sculpture is to strip from the human organism all traces of 'immediate signifying', so that the mutual translation of spirit and embodiment is achieved in stone and marble. The sculptural body, like the body of man which appears at the end of the *Anthropology*, becomes 'the sign of the soul'.[19] Hegel describes this state of plasticity as a meeting between the habitus and the ideal: 'This sort of attitude and movement in their specific appearance (*habitus*) and expression provide a clearer understanding of the situation in which the organic and the ideal, which can never be merely the ideal in *abstracto*, are apprehended.'[20]

In his work, the sculptor achieves the unification of the organic and the idea, as he knows that 'each organ must in general be considered from two points of view: the purely physical one and that of spiritual expression'.[21] This twofold perspective is also what we have seen in the case of human habit. Through its power of self-repetition, habit creates in man the condition for the reversibility of psychic and physical attributes. The features of the soul, as they acquire a physical means of expression, cease to function as a separate world, or a 'mysterious inner space'. Similarly, the body, as it is made into an instrument, will no longer act as a natural 'immediate externality' and a 'barrier':[22] 'In the initial stages, the body shows itself intractable, its movements are uncertain and are either too strong or too weak for the task at hand.'[23]

From the interpenetration of the psychic and the physical achieved as a result of repeated exercise, man is able to discover the correct measure of his powers. If 'naturally' deprived of nature, the soul regains nature through the mechanisms of habit: 'Habit is the mode of feeling (as well as intelligence, will, etc., so far as they belong to self-feeling) made into a natural and mechanical existence.'[24]

In constructing the mechanism that allows man to liberate himself from a phantasmatic relation to referentiality, repetition and exercise play an important part. In so far as the influence of habit causes a translation of soul into body and body into soul, these two will form a unity-in-separation, an absolute union without fusion, a union which forms, by its self-referentiality, the structure of speculative meaning. Between container and contained, a reversible relation abolishes the partition between exterior and interior, allowing soul – henceforth constituted as a 'Self' – to relate to the world, the real externality. From here the next step is the awakening of consciousness. The actual soul, 'with its sensation and its concrete self-feeling turned into habit', enters into relationship with the 'world external to it, but in such a way that in the world, it is immediately reflected into itself – *consciousness*'.[25]

Habit and thought

Even as it blunts the vivacity of external impressions, habit plunges the soul into a certain kind of slumber. But that increase of passivity is in fact the condition for the progressive development of an internal activity. Unconsciousness (*la non-conscience*) is necessary for the emergence of consciousness: the soul, no longer immersed in the particularity of external determinations, is 'open to be otherwise occupied and engaged – say with feeling and with mental consciousness in general'.[26] At the end of the Addition to §410, Hegel explains with even more striking detail the mechanism that makes consciousness possible:

> We see, therefore, that in *habit* our consciousness is at the same time *present* in the subject-matter (*Sache*), *interested* in it, yet conversely *absent* from it, *indifferent* to it; that our Self just as much *appropriates* the subject-matter as, on the contrary, it draws away from it, that the soul, on the one hand, completely pervades its bodily activities and, on the other hand, *deserts* them, thus giving them the shape of something *mechanical*, of a merely natural *effect*.

The mechanism described here is what endows the activity of sign-producing intelligence[27] with its condition of possibility. The structure of presence–absence is discovered again in intelligence which, giving an objective, fact-like character to external intuition (determining 'as an *existent* that which, in it, has been perfected to concrete auto-intuition'), transforms that into signs, into material to which it is indifferent, all the while 'making itself *be* and be a *thing*.'[28] The fact that consciousness withdraws from the concrete action of signifying (the translation of the intuition into a sign) liberates the possibility of signification itself.

Habit allows the soul to appropriate a certain content without losing itself or becoming immersed in that content, but also without being indifferent to it: neither within the soul nor outside it. Moving between the inside and the outside, between 'interior' and 'exterior', the soul establishes its 'rational liberation': 'Thinking, too, however free . . . no less requires habit and familiarity (*Geläufigkeit*) (this impromptuity or form of immediacy), by which it is the property of my singular Self.'[29]

Habit and will

The effect of unreflective spontaneity on the will is decisive. At the practical level, the plastic operation of this dual 'psychical–physicality' is critically important. For within the organs, increasingly permeated by the soul, the tendencies are formed that will bring ideas into action. If an external change is repeated, it turns into a tendency internal to the subject. The change itself is transformed into a disposition, and receptivity, formerly passive, becomes activity. Thus habit is revealed as a process through which man ends by *willing* or choosing what came to him from outside. Henceforth the will of the individual does not need to oppose the pressure of the external world; the will learns gradually to want what is. The ideal ceases to appear as something which ought to be, which 'might be but is not yet'. To the degree that the objective merges with the movement towards it, the ideal is achieved.

Now we can see the full meaning of the story of Hegelian affirmation as told in the 'natural course of the ages of life', where man releases himself from his ideals through the habitual tasks he accomplishes within the actual world, now takes on its full meaning. By erasing the 'innumerable mediations' that lie between the initial conception of one's ideal aim and its eventual actualization in the real, habit abolishes the two extremes at once. Habit creates a virtual being, acting as a middle term in this oppositional structure, and reducing the distance between the contraries.[30]

Transformed by the work of habit, soul and body form the sensory medium of the spirit. The individual as singularity, a realized unity of the formal universality of the spiritual determinations and the particularity of somatic affects, arrives through the process of mutual translation between psychic and corporeal manifestations. Individuality is from this point on a 'plastic individuality'.

The becoming essential of the accident

Plastic individuality

Psychosomatic unity results from an auto-interpretation independent of any referent. This is shown by the 'plastic individuals'. The adjective 'plastic' indicates the nature of what is at once universal and individual. If Hegel calls spirituality 'plastic', it is on the grounds that it is 'at the same time substance and, within its universality, individual'.[31] Such a synthesis becomes visible in sculpture,

> which has to present (*darstellen*) only the permanent (*das Bleibende*), universal and regular elements in the form of the human body, even if there is a demand so to individualize (*individualisieren*) this universal element that what is put before our eyes (*vor Augen stellen*) is not only abstract regularity but an individual figure most closely fused with it.[32]

The man transformed by habit is presented as the soul's work of art, in so far as his way of being, like that of the statue, displays substance universalized only as an individual figure. Contrary to the logic of immediate 'signifying', which implies the illusion of referentiality, incarnate spirit assumes an absolute coincidence of 'interior' and 'exterior'. 'Substantive individuality' (*die substantielle Individualität*), as Hegel calls it in the *Aesthetics*, displays 'a complete concordance of inner with outer (*ein vollständiges Zusammenstimmen des Innern und Äußeren*)'.[33] This harmony appeared at its utmost perfection in the example of those 'plastic individuals' who, for Hegel, represent the greatest of the men of ancient Greece: 'In the beautiful days of Greece men of action, like poets and thinkers, had this same plastic and universal yet individual (*allgemein und doch individuell*) character both inwardly and outwardly.'[34]

The exemplary nature of these men comes out in the way they embody the synthesis of the particular with the genus. Such individuals are called 'free' in so far as 'they are grown independently on the soil of their own inherently substantial personality': they express the genus only by, in turn, forming what it is. That is what is meant by the expression: 'self-made and developing into what they essentially were (*sich aus sich erzeugend*) and wanted to be'. If there is anything that still remains of the accidental in such exemplary individuals and their particular shape, it has acquired such a *formative* power that it is impossible to know, or say, of Thucydides, Phidias, Plato and others cited by Hegel, whether they are men or gods. They have become 'ideal artists shaping themselves, individuals of a single cast, works of art standing there like immortal and deathless images of the gods in which there is nothing temporal and doomed'.[35]

Such individuals *signify* themselves. This auto-referentiality is for Hegel the fundamental characteristic of classical art: 'Classical beauty has for its inner content the free *independent* (*selbstständige*) meaning, i.e. not a meaning *of* this or that but what means itself and therefore bears in itself its own interpretation (*das sich selbst Bedeutende und damit auch sich selber Deutende*).'[36]

If a work signifies itself, this implies that there is no 'outside' of the work, that the work acts as its own referent: it presents what it interprets at the same moment it interprets it, forming one and the same manifestation.

Following the example of the Greek statue, the 'plastic individual' is not a simple indexical or external sign of the spiritual element which is alive in it. In the plastic individual, spirit makes itself visible not in a transparent way, but through *style*. Style, the deictic or ostensive aspect of individuality, represents a distinctive *manner* (*façon*) of being or acting that represents the universal, that brings the ordinary and general onto the scene in a form appropriate to it. Accordingly, the 'plastic individual' has, through the impact of his style, the power to transmit or imprint (*imprime*) what he expresses (*exprime*). Speculative *expression*, in Hegel's idea of it, must create as its counterpart a power of making *impressions*. This is the sense in which the 'plastic individual' is 'plastic', for he can render the universal as a 'type'. The spiritual bestows form, but only because it is itself formed in return. Thus, 'habit's reunion with the ideal' has a twofold meaning: the ideal, becoming embodied, gives its spiritual form to the singular subject which, for its part, sculpts the ideal into form.

At a number of significant junctures Hegel will emphasize the role of such singular *interpretations*. Classical beauty, he wants to say, cannot be a 'purely universal norm (*allgemeine Norm*)': 'such a conception', he continues, 'is simply foolish and absurd. For the beauty of the ideal consists precisely in . . . essentially having individuality and therefore a particular character.'[37]

In this way individual and genus support one another in a mutual *hermeneutic*.

The ontological meaning of habit

The mutual fashioning of soul and body has led to the formation of man as the sensuous medium of spirit, and this same process illuminates the movement of substance's determination of itself. It is this latter movement which Hegel conceives of as spiritual incorporation or embodiment. In the *Aesthetics*, he says that spirit's various moments, the moments in its own development, are equal to 'bodily forms (*Leiblichkeit*) of spiritual individuality'.[38] Hence, the process of substance in its self-determination finds itself translated into the sensuous through this 'psychosomatic hermeneutic'.

Man, who forms himself in order to become a substantial individuality, represents the paradigmatic instance of this movement whereby substance is self-differentiated. Habit has helped man to acquire the 'plastic character', making him at once 'universal and individual'. This is exemplary for the way spirit's universality, in its different moments, acquires concreteness and actuality through its incarnation in those individual forms. Thus in Hegel, the notion of an 'individual' does not merely apply to man, but ultimately can apply also to a nation, an artistic epoch, a philosophy, or a moment of the 'substance-subject'. Subjectivity is not a reality existing in advance of the process whereby it becomes self-differentiated: each of its moments emerges from an independent interpretation of its own being.

Just as Hegel's notion of habit cannot be called anthropological, so his use of man as paradigm does not include an anthropologizing notion of substance. In truth, what is exemplary about man is less human-ness than his status as an *insistent accident*. If the animal is not able fully to present the genus, the flaw is not in the genus, because the genus will always be in excess over its individual way of being: rather it is due to the accidental nature of the example. Because the individual animal is nothing but a natural accident it can only respond to the genus in its substance by means of another accident: the generation of another animal.

In contrast, the 'plastic individual' has the power to add to the accidental the very integrity and ontological constancy of a genus. This power is the power of habit. 'Plastic individuals' are those who synthesize in their very 'style' the essence of the genus and the accident which has become habitual. What in the beginning was merely an accidental fact – Plato's commitment to philosophy, Pericles' to politics, Phidias' to sculpture – is changed through continual repetition of the same gestures, through practice, achieving the integrity of a 'form' (*eidos*). Effected by habit, the singularity of the 'plastic individual' becomes an *essence a posteriori*.

The process of habit ends by canonizing being's improvisations on its own themes. The philosopher, the political man or sculptor, are determinations which could not have been anticipated just by the simple generic definition of man: they are destinies contained *virtually* in the genus 'man', but remain there as something unpredictable. By forming themselves, by undergoing repetition and practice, these determinations ultimately construct a state which is habitual and accordingly *essential*. Habit is the process whereby the contingent becomes essential. Man can 'present the genus' to the degree that habit is the unforeseen element of the genus. Habit, then, appears as the *future* of the undifferentiated genus.

Habit would not have this power of plasticity if it did not, in the process of bringing the possible to actuality, manifest a virtuality already inscribed within essence itself. This virtuality authorizes essence in its free 'interpretations' in the same way as the 'type' legitimates the sculptor's improvisations. The investigation of 'plastic individuality' brings out one of the fundamental aspects of the Hegelian theory of substance: the recognition of the essential status of the *a posteriori*. The speculative meaning of the *Anthropology* transcends the particular anthropological horizon, becoming part of the ontological principle at its foundation.

Man is exemplary because the human formative power can translate the logical process into a sensuous form. In this case, the logical process is the path by which the accident becomes essential. If this possibility did not exist, there would be no way to understand the movement of the substance-subject, the dialectical identity of subject and predicate. Hegelian man owes his 'proper' essence (but is it still a matter of the 'proper', of authentic human properties?)[39] to the way he *appropriates* this non-human development. Through the forms of human plasticity, substance informed by its modifications (*substance accidentée*) gains something else: a face.

CONCLUSION

The 'becoming essential of the accident' describes the Greek moment of subjectivity, as interpreted by Hegel. It is a moment marked ontologically by its insistence on the first part of the speculative proposition: the substance-subject. Within this process, one that assumes a mutual giving of form from spirit to its example and vice versa, the role of man is clearly decisive, but not fundamental. If Hegel had granted man such a substantive ontological status, there would only remain an anthropological conception of substance. Yet the entire *Anthropology* is devoted to destroying such a status.

Man does not have a substance. There is no human substance. The Hegelian man is above all a man of habits, and that means, paradoxically, a disappearing subject. The more closely habit is studied, the more it becomes clear that human subjectivity is constituted in self-forgetting; consciousness and will, under the influence of repeated practice, win their force through a kind of self-absenting. When man makes his entrance into the speculative narrative he does so in the guise of a farewell.

At the moment when the soul has perfected itself as a 'work of art', it ceased to be a soul: 'The soul, thus setting in opposition its being to its (conscious) self, absorbing it, and making it its own, has lost the meaning of mere soul, of the *immediacy* of spirit.'[1] In its highest moment, the soul has turned itself into spirit. In this expiring, it is also man who has become exhausted and died, leaving nothing behind except the part created by habit, that is, the mechanism of self-feeling, which will live on as the foundation of all the forms of theoretical and practical spirit.

After the *Philosophy of Spirit*, man will no longer be the subject of the speculative development. This means that subjectivity, on its way to its fulfilment as absolute spirit, no longer bears a human shape and severs itself from any strictly anthropological basis. There is only one moment at which man returns as a question and as one of the essential moments in the *Encyclopedia*, and that is the religious moment, which introduces the idea of the Incarnation. But between the *Anthropology* and *Revealed Religion*, subjectivity abandons the human soul first appearing at the dawn of spirit.

Habit murders man. And it does so just as surely as it makes man live. If habit collapses the distance that divides the aim from its realization, if it makes accomplishment a real fact, it is also a force of death which, once the aim is achieved, puts the individual to death:

> Human beings even die as result of habit – that is, if they have become totally habituated to life, and spiritually and physically blunted, and the opposition between subjective consciousness and spiritual activity has disappeared. For they are only active in so far as they have not yet attained something and wish to assert themselves and show what they can do in pursuit of it. Once this is accomplished, their activity and vitality disappear, and the loss of interest which ensues is spiritual or physical death.[2]

Habit makes teleological accomplishment possible, yet renders that achievement null and void. Once the end is reached, the subject disappears: 'it is the habit of living which brings on death, or, if put quite abstractly, is death itself'.[3] What fulfils, destroys. Living is exhausting, and building the mechanisms of body and spirit also brings exhaustion. That is why the motions of body and spirit must be channelled into the shape of habit. For it is habit that draws the line between using and exhausting one's forces; it offers leisure in the midst of carrying on, establishes a reservoir of potential energy to guarantee that the individual can continue. Yet at the very moment that habit awakens and restores, it puts to sleep.

Since habit is the precondition for the existence of 'self-feeling', without habit there would be literally nobody to live or to die. Human beings are those who, in order to be, must observe that speculative clock which is habit, a clock which makes it possible to 'see (what is) coming', meaning that the *end* can be brought forward and, at the same time, postponed. The soul analysed in the early sections of the *Anthropology*, a soul not yet habituated, cannot see itself dying, and does not know it is finite: it is, therefore, mad. But the real soul, on the other hand, knows how to tell time (*sait lire l'heure*).

Substance-subject returns in the death of man. Habit, as it is traditionally understood from Aristotle on, is in fact difference repeated and made productive, connected in the closest possible way to being itself. Until now it is only this complex of meanings that has been pursued, and the deadening principle of habit has been left in the shadows. Nevertheless, the murderous power of habit has an ontological significance beyond the immediate anthropological level.

Under the guise of 'possession' (ἕξις), subjectivity embraces in itself its future ways of being, the ways it will become actual. But ἕξις as something virtual inscribes in substance the moment where the virtual will cease to have an ontological signification. This realization is essential in forming the transition from the Greek conception of subjectivity to the modern, and it is this conception which we must now bring to light.

Part II

HEGEL ON GOD: THE TURN[1] OF THE DOUBLE NATURE

INTRODUCTION

To take God as the subject

Historical-philosophical perspectives

To rest our inquiry into the modern concept of subjectivity on a reading of *Revealed Religion*, the penultimate section of Hegel's *Philosophy of Spirit*, may seem questionable. Isn't there something clumsy about an approach that cuts abruptly across centuries and speculative moments?

Yet history and philosophy intersect, an intersection that immediately justifies this approach. The emergence of modern subjectivity is, for Hegel, fundamentally and profoundly connected to the advent of Christianity. In the *Lectures on the Philosophy of History*, he traces the evolution from the Greek to the Roman world where the principle of 'spiritual inwardness' first comes into view – though only as the condition of abstract 'personality' or ego.[2] With such a principle, 'humanity has the sphere of free spirituality in and for itself' and delimits 'the place where the divine spirit has its inward abode and presence'.[3] Spiritual inwardness is the condition of *freedom*, the 'higher principle' and the content revealed in Revealed Religion.

For Hegel, modern philosophy retrospectively furnishes the conceptual realization of the 'principle of subjective freedom'. In fact, philosophy could not 'develop except on the basis of religion'.[4] Consequently, it is incumbent on philosophy to redeem and set free the speculative content of Christianity by raising it to the absolute concept, that of subjectivity. Given its form by Descartes, radicalized in its significance by Kant, the subject will henceforth appear as an independent principle and as the absolute autonomy of thought.

In his book *God as Mystery of the World*, Eberhard Jüngel analyses the terminological shift affecting the concept of the *subject* in modernity.[5] He recalls how the formulation of the trinitarian doctrine relied on the Aristotelian concept of substance, understood as a 'being independent of all others'. Jüngel argues that

> substance was originally . . . only another name for subject. The identity of essence (οὐσία) and foundation (ὑποκείμενον) is expressed in the term *substantia*: the being which, as distinguished from this, fails to serve as its own foundation, is explained as having a difference with respect to *essentia*.[6]

Christian doctrine was formulated in these terms, yet all the while the ingredients of an important change were in being. The doctrine of the Trinity affirms that the divine essence (that which God is: his οὐσία) is undoubtedly independent with respect to the non-divine, to alterity; however this independence occurs in three distinct modes of being, even if these modes are equally and supremely linked one to another. 'Because, with reference to the New Testament, these three hypostases would be represented as persons: Father, Son and Spirit', Jüngel asserts, 'there is implicitly operating a terminological change which will conceive *subjectum* as a Self, a "subject" in the modern sense of the word.'[7]

This shift was created as much by philosophy as by theology. Descartes conceptualized the subject as an autonomous instance who would become the foundation for certainty, establishing the objectivity of all other objects. It must be remembered that there are many occasions when Hegel celebrates the decisive importance of Cartesianism, most notably in the *Lectures on the History of Philosophy*:

> Descartes begins . . . with the 'I' as indubitably certain. . . . By this, philosophy is at one stroke transplanted to quite another field and to another standpoint . . . To consider the content in itself is not the first matter; only the 'I' is the certain, the immediate.[8]

The freedom of thought and the definition of the subject correlative to that thought find expression, for Hegel, in the formula 'I=I':

> In the expression *I=I* is enunciated the principle of absolute *reason and freedom*. Freedom and reason consist in this, that I raise myself to the form of *I=I*, that I know everything as mine, as 'I', that I grasp every object as a member in the system of what I myself am.[9]

This principle is raised by Kant to the highest expression of which speculation is capable. It is Kant's virtue to have raised the 'I' to the form of a pure concept, thus achieving for thought the state of absolute freedom. In the *Science of Logic*, Hegel writes:

> Among the insights in the *Critique of Pure Reason*, one of the most profound and true is the idea that the *unity* which constitutes the

> *essence of the concept* is the synthetic unity of apperception, formulated as the unity of the 'I think', or of self-consciousness.[10]

The position of the subject as pure and absolute autonomy implies the rejection of habit, which will henceforth lose its Aristotelian significance and stand simply for something mechanical, alien to human freedom.[11] From the point of view of modern philosophy, freedom never becomes habituated to itself.

The specificity of the religious moment in the Encyclopedia

If we want to register the mutation of subjectivity's meaning during the modern period, it would certainly be possible to remain within the historical-philosophical perspective. Yet this perspective, while indispensable for the understanding of *Revealed Religion*, differs to a degree from the point of view of the *Encyclopedia.* The *Encyclopedia* exposition is neither dictated by the historical concerns relevant to revelation in its 'positive' character – this is the concern of the *Lectures on the Philosophy of Religion* – nor by philosophical consciousness applied to the meaning of revelation – the point of view of the *Phenomenology of Spirit.*

The adjective 'revealed' (*geoffenbarte*) in the title *Revealed Religion* already confirms the specificity of this religious moment in the *Encyclopedia.* The *Phenomenology* treats Christianity as the example of 'the revelatory religion' (*offenbare Religion*). The *Lectures on the Philosophy of Religion* present the analysis of Christianity under the heading: 'The consummate or revelatory religion: Absolute Religion'. Now 'revelatory' qualifies the way God is here presented to consciousness. The *Lectures* also present the point of view of consciousness, but 'Absolute Religion' embraces the *fact* of revelation as well. It is a concept whose content depends on the actual history of the Christian religion and the concrete textual statements imparted by Scripture.[12]

On its own account, the *Encyclopedia*'s exposition presupposes at the same time both the subjective and one-sided view of consciousness and the 'objective' point of view taken by the *Lectures on the Philosophy of Religion.* But it cannot be reduced to either of these. The adjective 'revealed' specifies the *divine revelation of God by himself,* the *absolute self-revelation.*

Accordingly, the *Encyclopedia* brings out the point presupposed in all the other discussions of Christianity within the System: viz., that the possibility of the modern conception of subjectivity, in both the religious and philosophical senses, was already *in the divine subjectivity itself.* While the text of *Revealed Religion* provides the foundation for an analysis of this modern concept of subjectivity, it is not simply a matter of extracting from it the relevant characteristics but, even more, of showing how such characteristics are present in God. Framing the question in these terms will lead us to consider more closely the way Hegel takes God for a subject, both in the sense of a 'subject of the exposition' and 'the constitution of God as a subject.'

Revealed Religion develops the concept of the Trinity as a movement conforming to the logical development of the substance-subject. God the Father – who is the moment of substance in its potentiality – undergoes an auto-determination, producing the moment of God the Son; the moment of Spirit completes the reconciliation of that split thus created. All the philosophical attributes of the modern concept of subjectivity can be deduced from the process presented by this speculative proposition. It is in God and as God that we see manifested the 'becoming subject' of substance. This is, in fact, the moment of substance-*subject*.

The Critique of Speculative Theology

God in dependence

The identification of such a 'becoming' could not of course escape the reaction of Hegel's theological readers who, whether Catholic or Lutheran, find the perspective of the divine substance 'becoming-subject' an inadmissible prospect. Doesn't the affirmation that God is subjected to the concept of the subject thereby deny his freedom as creator? How can God be made a subject among other subjects without submitting him to the logical necessity of the speculative proposition, thereby making him fully and exhaustively something thought and thinkable?[13]

Such objections, for the most part, rest on the same arguments offered against the Hegelian reading of Aristotle. It is in fact the introduction of negativity into God which seems unacceptable to the theologians. Just as the Hegelian recognition of negativity within the Prime Mover appeared to betray its ontological meaning, so the application of the logical dialectic to the heart of the Trinity imports into the essential being of the God of revelation an inconceivable injury.

This injury is made clear in the Hegelian concept of a *divine alienation*, central to the dialectical conception of *kenosis* and its principle. '*Kenosis*' means the lowering or humbling of God in his Incarnation and the Passion. The word '*kenosis*' derives from the Greek κένωσις (from κενός, empty) which means shedding the skin, annihilation, pulling down, and from the Pauline expression ἑαυτὸν ἐκένωσεν (*Letter to the Philippians*, 2, 7): Christ 'emptied Himself of Himself', which the Latin translates as *semet ipsum exinanivit* – from which comes the word 'exinanition', synonymous with '*kenosis*'. Luther translates κένωσις as *Entäußerung*, literally 'the separation from the self through an externalisation'. Now from this *Entäußerung* or 'alienation', Hegel forges a logical movement which becomes constitutive of the development of the divine essence. God necessarily departs from himself in His self-determination; in this way He, with every other 'ego-self', is put to the test of judicative partition.

A God without future

The theologians' objections to this approach converge on a single issue: Hegel's God is *without future*.

By linking (*en enchaînant*) God to the necessity of the concept, Hegel in fact removes from Him the mystery of His *coming to be* (*advenir*), or, in other words, His *transcendence*. With the plenitude of his possibilities removed, God would be reduced to a being without the power either to give himself or to promise himself. A God we no longer await, how could such a God have a future?

As Hegel sees it, negativity belongs essentially and properly to God, in so far as God must produce Himself, and the moment where negativity is repeated is a moment necessary to this self-production. The theologians infer from this process of negativity that an *innate poverty* is ascribed to God who, through successive mediations, would be able to affirm Himself only in the end as a positivity. They reproach Hegel for having introduced into God something of an *originary lack* that contradicts, at first glance, his generosity.

The fulfilment of onto-theology

It is surprising to observe that many of the contemporary theological interpretations of Hegel's philosophy of religion repeat, whether intentionally or not, certain motifs of Heidegger's discussion. The speculative God is without future on account of his *presence*. In his desire to think God as absolute presence (implied by the concept of self-revelation), Hegel ultimately misses out on God in the *present*, that is, in the time of his genuine offering of himself. This argument echoes the Heideggerean claim that Hegel's theological thinking carries to its logical conclusion the traditional idea of God as *parousia*, a conception which lies behind all of metaphysics.[14]

Heidegger assimilates 'speculative theology' to the 'ontology of absolute being (*ens realissimum*)'.[15] This ontology, ever since its Greek origins, has conceived of presence as something atemporal, for it bases its concept of time solely on the priority of 'present' time. On this line of thinking the Hegelian concept of self-revelation seems to affirm the idea of presence in the strongest sense, and God appears as the supreme being: a collector who joins together the totality of being which time has dispersed and scattered afar.

From the divine passivity to the divine plasticity

If in the final analysis, these arguments represent the only possible account of speculative theology, then we would have to admit that speculative theology's ability to reach completion requires either an inconsistency or an absence of thought. The Hegelian idea of *parousia* – God's absolute presence-to-self – could in fact only be sustained by admitting into God an original *passivity*: the possibility of His submission to the same constitutive negativity that marks all subjectivity. This would be an unacknowledged radicalization of Origen, who had already written: 'God the Father himself is not impassible!'[16]

If our concern is the modern instance of substance-subject, are we then obliged to refuse passivity in all its modes as condemning presence to a lack of future?

A close reading of *Revealed Religion* forbids that refusal. The concept of 'alienation', carefully dissected, shows us that if God does accept the form of subjectivity, if He does submit himself to being a subject, it is He who gives subjectivity the very form He receives from it. In alienating himself, God imprints subjectivity with a special type of self-extension, an 'exteriorization'. He gives himself this same form, the form of development. Thus alienation must be seen from both sides, as a receptivity and a spontaneity in God.

Obviously the notion of passivity is not sufficient on its own to describe this dual aspect. Consequently we must return to the idea of *plasticity*, in its twofold meaning of a receiving and a giving of form. An example of originary synthetic unity which lends itself to all it creates, the subjectivity of God, from the perspective of plasticity, appears not as an absolute presence paradoxically deficient in its relation to itself, but as the living source of a process of *temporalization*.

The Itinerary

This process confers a specifically modern character on substance-subject's movement of 'seeing (what is) coming'. In virtue of the three determinations of plasticity, the modern moment (1) presupposes a certain *form* (self-consciousness in its relation to speculative content); (2) corresponds to a particular notion of *self-determination* (the *subject* in relation to its *accidents*); and (3) determines a certain modality of *hypotyposis*, i.e. the translation of the spiritual into sensuous form.

After tracing the stages of *Revealed Religion*, we will consider the objections raised by the theologians. By replacing *passivity* with *plasticity* as the interpretative key to the divine negativity, we will suggest a new reading of the relation between divine subjectivity and philosophical subjectivity, based on the double sense of the Death of God. By the time we come to the end of our questioning, through an examination of the movements of the double nature (*les tours de la double nature*), divine and human, the divine temporality – God's plasticity – will have come fully into view.

5

PRESENTATION OF *REVEALED RELIGION*

In its entirety, the movement of *Revealed Religion* respects the triple logical exposition of concept, judgement and syllogism.[1] The introductory paragraphs[2] expose 'the concept of religion', stressing the meaning of 'self-revelation',[3] then pointing to the specificity of the mode of religious representation[4] in order to present in detail, at the end, the three 'special spheres' of representation.[5] These three correspond to the three logical moments of the deployment of the concept of religion itself.

The Trinity in the element of 'pure thought or the abstract medium of essence' characterizes the religious moment of the *concept*.[6] The moment of *judgement* appears next in its triple articulation: creation, birth of the 'only Son', and introduction of evil.[7] Then, the three *syllogisms* of Revelation follow: (1) the syllogism of the Incarnation, the Death and Resurrection of the Son (*kenosis* in the Incarnation and Death of Christ); (2) the syllogism of the identification of the faithful with the glorious Death of Christ;[8] (3) syllogism of the cultic community.[9] The conclusion of this movement announces the sublation of the representational form by speculative thought, thus initiating the dialectical transition from *Religion* into *Philosophy*.[10]

The 'concept ' of religion

Self-revelation

In its concept, true religion is self-revelation (*Selbstoffenbarung*). According to Hegel, Christianity is the religion that has become absolute manifestation, without any secret residue: 'It lies essentially in the concept of religion – the religion whose content is absolute spirit – that it be *revealed* and, what is more, revealed by *God*.'[11] This implies necessarily that 'God is out and out manifestation' and that it is not possible to ascribe *envy* to God.

> The old conception – due to an abstract understanding – of Nemesis, which made the divinity and its action in the world only

> a *levelling* power, dashing to pieces everything high and great, was confronted by Plato and Aristotle with the doctrine that God is not *envious*. The same answer may be given to the modern assertions that man cannot ascertain God.[12]

The 'careful and thorough speculation (*gründliche Spekulation*)' that demands such a knowledge of revelation includes three 'propositions': 'God is God only so far as he knows himself: his self-knowledge is, further, a self-consciousness in man and man's knowledge *of* God, which proceeds to man's self-knowledge *in* God.'[13]

The 'spheres' of representation

In the next paragraph, Hegel describes the 'form' of this knowledge:

> When the immediacy and sensuousness of shape and knowledge is sublated, God is, in point of content, the essential and actual spirit of nature and spirit, while in point of form (*der Form nach*) he is, first of all, presented to subjective knowledge as a *representation* (*Vorstellung*).[14]

The first part of the phrase refers back to the previous moment of Absolute Spirit, *Art*, in which the spiritual content is presented in the immediate, sensuous or intuitive, form of the image. The dialectical suppression of this immediacy marks, psychologically, the birth of representation (*Vorstellung*). And representation is, for Hegel, the medium through which the religious moment of spirit has its immediate and initial expression.

Representational knowledge gives to each moment of the notion a separate being, and 'makes them presuppositions towards each other, and phenomena which *succeed each other* in a relationship that is a series of *events* (*einem Zusammenhang des Geschehens*) according to *finite reflective categories*'.[15]

Representation, thus, first appears as a process which temporalizes the conceptual content. The concept's logical moments would appear as chronological moments. Such a linear temporalization is echoed by a movement of spatialization. Indeed, representation separates (*trennt*) the speculative moments by juxtaposing them to each other, by solidifying the elements which form the living whole of the concept endowing them with an autonomous existence. Hegel defines these moments, now placed side by side, as 'spheres (*Sphären*)': 'In this act of separating, the *form* parts from the *content*: and in the form the different functions of the concept part off into *separate spheres*, in each of which the absolute spirit exposes itself.'[16]

The Trinity in the element of pure thought

The exposition of these spheres constitutes the developments that follow. Paragraph §567 establishes the 'moment of *universality*'. This is the 'sphere of pure thought or the abstract medium of essence'. God is initially 'the concept of God'. In his conceptual identity with himself, God is not yet involved either with time or with space. His element is pure thought, principle of truth and reality. This first moment is the *Father*, the God of the Old Testament.

God's self-identity is, however, not formal and empty. Even in the conceptual element God is already differentiated, and does not remain 'aloof and enclosed within himself'. As 'underlying and essential power',

> he . . . only begets *himself* as his *Son*, with whom, though different, he still remains in original identity – just as, again, this differentiation of him from the universal essence eternally sublates itself, and, through this mediating of a self-sublating mediation, the first substance is essentially as *concrete individuality* and subjectivity – is the *spirit*.[17]

God's identity with himself is thus, in its concept, the intra-trinitarian difference. The absolute idea manifests itself initially as the eternity of the *Logos* and the triune God. The intra-trinitarian difference is the movement of the *self-determination* of God, which presupposes the logical deployment of the concept of God as substance-subject.

Extraposition of the created: the world and evil

Divine subjectivity now immerses itself in its critical moment, knowing the rupture of the judgement as it becomes particular: 'in the moment of *particularity*, of the judgement, the eternal concrete being is presupposed, and its movement is the *creation* of the phenomenal world.'[18] The actual creation (*Erschaffung*) of the phenomenal world posits that world in its alterity. Essence departs from itself, in a movement of dislocation that goes as far as 'shattering, the rupture (*Zerfallen*) of the eternal moment of mediation'. This is the moment of the *Son*, the conclusion of the first syllogism.

Finite spirit is shattered, interiority manifests the most profound division and negativity of the absolute. Now God becomes manifest to finite consciousness as another finite consciousness: 'elementary and concrete nature' confronts 'spirit standing in relation (*Verhältnis*) to it'. Finite spirit 'completes its independence (*verselbstständigt*) as wickedness', and man is torn between his temptation to do evil and his relation to the eternal.[19]

Reconciliation: The three syllogisms of Revelation

The moment of the Spirit, or singularity, is articulated in three syllogisms.[20]

The first syllogism of Revelation

The first syllogism contains Christology proper, meaning *Incarnation, Death and Resurrection.* Its movement corresponds to the articulation of the qualitative syllogism or syllogism of 'being-there' (*Schluß des Daseins*), presented in the *Encyclopedia Science of Logic*: 'The first syllogism is the *syllogism of being-there* or *qualitative syllogism*, . . . S–P–U: that a subject as something singular is *concluded* with a *universal determinacy* through a *quality*.'[21]

The middle term of this syllogism is immediate particularity, the particularity of 'sensuous existence'.[22] The minor premiss (S–P) is the individual self-consciousness of Christ (S), posited in the natural element of temporal existence (P). This is the Incarnation: 'The *universal* substance is actualized out of its abstraction into an *individual* [*singular*] self-consciousness . . ., in the eternal sphere he is called the Son, and is transplanted into the world of time (*in die Zeitlichkeit versetzt*).'[23]

The major premiss (P–U) announces the painful sundering of this sensuous existence (P) through its negative identification with the universality of divine essence (U). This is the death of Christ who 'poses himself in (the originary separation of) judgement and expires in the pain of *negativity* (*in den Schmerz der Negativität ersterbend*)'.

From such premisses, the conclusion (S–U) is the absolute return, but again on the level of immediacy, in which individuality and universality are reconciled in the Idea of spirit which is present in the world in its eternity. It is Resurrection, the 'absolute return' of the Son, who 'has realized his being as the Idea of the spirit, eternal, but alive and present in the world'.[24] God's appearance in the actual objective reality of the world makes history the very place of redemption and reconciliation.

The second syllogism of Revelation

This is the syllogism of the negative identification of the believer with Christ's transfiguration.[25] Its movement corresponds to the articulation of the 'syllogism of reflection' in the *Science of Logic*, its formal structure being U–S–P:

> The mediating unity of the concept has to be posited, no longer as abstract particularity, but as the *developed* unity of singularity and universality, indeed, as first the *reflected* unity of these determinations. . . . This kind of middle term gives us the *syllogism of reflection* (*Reflexions-Schluß*).[26]

The middle term of this syllogism is the singularity of 'all the *singular concrete* (*konkrete*) subjects' who make up the reflective universality. These subjects are here the believers, united in what Hegel calls in the *Encyclopedia Science of Logic* 'allness (*Allheit*)'.[27] The minor premiss (U–S) is the relationship of the believers with the universal, or 'objective totality (U)'. This is 'for the *finite* immediacy of the singular subject (S) . . . at first an *other*, an object of *intuition*'.[28] The major premiss (S–P) is the following: by the witness (*Zeugnis*) of spirit, and by means of faith, that is, of 'faith in the unity, in that example (i.e. Christ) implicitly accomplished, of universal and individual essence', the singular subject (S) appropriates, through his 'self-will', the death of Christ, throwing off his own 'natural immediacy (P)', determined as natural man and as evil. From these two premisses arises the conclusion (U–P): the movement of the singular subject, now dispossessed of his particularity (P), is to 'close himself in unity, in the pain of negativity', with 'that example (*mit jenem Beispiel*)' – Christ crucified and resurrected – thus 'to know himself made one with the essential being (U).'[29]

The third syllogism of Revelation

The third syllogism is the worshipping community. It corresponds to the articulation of the 'syllogism of necessity (*Schluß der Notwendigkeit*)' whose form is P–U–S.

> This syllogism has *the universal* as its middle term . . . posited as essentially determinate within itself. Initially (1) the *particular* is the mediating determination, in the sense of the determinate *genus* or *species*, – this is the case in the *categorical* syllogism. Then it is (2) the *singular* in the sense of immediate being, so that it is both mediating and mediated – in the *hypothetical* syllogism. (3) The mediating *universal* is also posited as the totality of its *particularizations* and as a *singular* particular [or as] excluding singularity – in the *disjunctive* syllogism. So that there is one and the same universal in all these determinations. . . .[30]

The middle term here is the substantial link unifying the community, gathering together the totality of its particularizations. The minor premiss (P–U) is the negation of all natural finitude and of all particular representation (P) by universal essence (U). The major premiss (P–U) is the universal essence (U) living from this point on within the form of self-consciousness (P): 'This essence . . . through this mediation brings about its own indwelling (*als inwohnend*) in self-consciousness, and is the actual presence of spirit being in and for itself the universal spirit and self-subsisting spirit.'[31]

Conclusion: from religious faith to philosophic thought

Representational form is dialectically sublated in the gathering of the cult and the simplicity of thought: that is, in the return into the self and the mental assimilation of the death of Christ by the singular concrete subjects. Self-revelation has, for one aspect, the representational form of successive and objective events, but as its other aspect, it has the form of subjective absorption in the community of faith. At the end of §565, this conclusive moment is already announced: 'such a form of finite representationalism is also sublated in the faith which believes in one spirit and in the devotion of worship (*in der Andacht des Kultus*)'.[32] The gathering and contracting of the self in devotion makes possible the transition to speculative thought, to pure and non-representational thought. Henceforth, 'in this form of truth, truth is the object of *philosophy*'.[33]

6

GOD WITHOUT TRANSCENDENCE?

The theologians contra Hegel

In the eyes of Hegel's theological readers, the *Encyclopedia*'s presentation of the religious moment of spirit leads, in an unprecedented manner, to the forced 'submission' of God to logical necessity. In its development, *Revealed Religion* is punctuated by the concept of 'alienation' (*Entäußerung*), which undergirds not only the dialectical understanding of *kenosis*, but even, as a consequence, the comprehension of *faith* and *representation*.

First of all, to consider *kenosis*. Recalling Luther, the concept of *Entäußerung* in Hegel continues to designate the 'divine sacrifice'.[1] However, he interprets this sacrifice as God's genuine '*becoming other*', and this justifies the French translation of this concept by '*aliénation*'.[2] In the *Lectures on the Philosophy of Religion*, Hegel indicates that the act whereby the Son, 'having come into the world', acquiring his determination as 'Other' – an act brought to its fulfilment by his death –, is understood as the work of *Entäußerung*. The Incarnation is 'the alienation of the divine (*Entäußerung des Göttlichen*)', and Death, the 'alterity of the divine (*Anderswerden des Göttlichen*)'.[3] In the *Encyclopedia* Hegel makes the point that the world, as created, is 'separated by its *Entäußerung* from the divine being'.[4] For the theologians, this dialectical interpretation of *Entäußerung* introduces lack into God and ruins the *superabundance* of the Father.

As far as *faith*: in the *Encyclopedia*, Hegel thinks of faith as the movement by which the believer 'throws off (*entäußert*) his immediacy, his natural man and his self-will, to close himself in unity with that example (Christ)'.[5] Through this alienation, the believer repeats the movement of *kenosis*. As the theologians see it, the attitude of the believer theorized in this way no longer includes the expectation of God.

For representation. For Hegel, the concept of *Entäußerung* characterizes the very process of religious representation, which constrains the religious consciousness to experience its relation to God merely as separation: 'The consciousness of God has two sides, one being God, the other the pole of consciousness proper. Both are in the first instance alienations (*Entäußerungen*) in the element of the finite. . . .'[6]

Philosophy takes on the dialectical sublation of this separation and of representational thinking in general. In the objections of the theologians, such a sublation reduces the transcendence of God to the eternal present of thought.

The speculative ruin of the Father

Hegel's concept of self-revelation and of the absolute *presence* of God which it implies, providing an ontological guarantee in the sense that God is *absolutely* and always present, seems on the contrary to the theologians to occult God's giving himself as (a) *present*. If God reveals himself incessantly and unreservedly, holding nothing back, he is never, in reality, *giving* himself. Under such conditions, he could not make a 'present' of himself. In his study of *Hegel's Christology*, Emilio Brito asserts: 'The Hegelian God is exhaustively manifest; as a result, He is completely hidden.'[7]

A God without envy would overflow with abundance, unmotivated generosity, grace. Yet the Hegelian God does not seem to be conceived as total plenitude. As the theologians claim, the definition of divine essence as 'the sphere of pure thought, the abstract medium of essence . . . underlying and essential power'[8] results in the supposition that 'Revelation is only, and exclusively, a manifestation of its Origin in all its emptiness and need', emerging from the 'hardworking dynamism of freedom, and, in the end, rejecting everything that belongs to the contemplative'.[9] If God, in his original moment, is no more than 'immediate indeterminacy', he will divest himself of himself as a matter of necessity, not out of goodness or love.

Now at first glance these claims could sound surprising. How could one possibly doubt the speculative generosity of the Hegelian God? To conceive of God as absolutely present to thought should logically lead to the conclusion of his infinite goodness. Nonetheless, it would seem impossible to imagine generosity without the presence of an originary plenitude. And is it not the case that dialectical necessity will inscribe 'lack' in the divine potentiality, thus depriving it of all power to give? Hegel's God would, on this account, be jealous not in the sense that He wishes to protect the exclusive nature of his power over against humanity, but in the sense that the logical economy of the concept would adapt itself to an economy of need, a need to which the emptiness of *kenosis* can be assimilated. What would be the meaning of such an emptiness, such an avidity, if not the desire to possess, hence jealousy? The God who reveals Himself, as Hegel conceives Him, must, in order to avoid speculative 'envy', be no less dialectically *consuming* (*dévorateur*).

The Hegelian conception of kenosis

In the idea of *kenosis*, the mystery of the union of divine and human natures in Christ returns.[10] The voluntary privation of Christ initially occurs in the very event of the Incarnation, and it continues in the saviour's humiliation and obedience unto death. By taking on an inferior nature, that of a slave (μορφὴ δούλου, the form of human nature), Christ does not merely renounce the divine rank to which he is entitled as God, but further, he accepts the task of leading a human life, engaging fully in the course of a life of obedience, humiliation and pain.

Patristic exegesis always related *kenosis* to the Incarnation, whether through attributing *kenosis* to the pre-existing Logos or to a subject who is both divine and human. This is the crucial point that allows us to appreciate the difference between a Catholic and a Lutheran interpretation of *kenosis*. For Catholicism, *kenosis* is the *kenosis* of a pre-existing Logos,[11] and not simply the humiliation of Christ in his being as human. Privation flows from the will which was present in Christ as pre-existent, and annihilation is related to the actual fact of the Incarnation:

> Paul thinks of Christ as a single person in three states: the state of pre-existence in which, subsisting in the form of God, the Saviour does not view his equality with God (the rank to which he is entitled) as a prize he must guard jealously; the state of voluntary humiliation in which he renounces the divine rank by taking on the form of a slave (*status exinanitionis*); the state of exaltation (*status exaltationis*) in which the Father makes reparation for the voluntary humiliation of his Son.[12]

In contrast to the exegesis of the ancient Church, Luther interprets the passage from *Philippians* 2, 6, not as the description of the Pre-existent prior to the Incarnation, but as the work of Christ made man, earthly Christ.[13] His interpretation relies on the doctrine of the *communicatio idiomatum*. 'Idiom' (from ἴδιος, one's own) designates what belongs to one or the other of the two natures of Christ. The 'communication of the idioms' declares that whatever belongs to one of the natures belongs also to the other: it is by virtue of the 'communication of the idioms' that one is able to say 'God is created', 'God is dead', 'God is resurrected'. Protestant kenoticism draws the consequences of this 'communication' to the limits of what Catholicism would consider an 'exaggeration': in the Protestant account, *kenosis* occurs not just within the human element, but also in the divine.[14] The first version of the *communicatio idiomatum* declares that it is correct that 'This, which in a literal sense is only the property of a nature, be attributed not just to the nature *qua* separated, but to the entire person at once God and man.'[15]

Hegel is faithful to the Lutheran tradition when he argues against the understanding of the unity of two persons in Jesus Christ as an abstract union. If God has become man, it must be that, within the person of Jesus Christ, the divine and human natures are to be thought of as communicating, so that their union in his person is to be conceived as the differentiated unity of one and the same event. The *Lectures on the Philosophy of Religion* are unequivocal on this matter: 'The necessity of the unity between the divine and the human natures (*Einheit der Göttlichen und menschlichen Natur*)' implies that 'both would sublate their reciprocal abstraction', so that the truth lies in their 'identity' understood not as the 'unity of the abstract and rigid Being-in-itself', but rather as a process which is, in itself, 'concrete (*das Konkrete*)'.[16]

Yet even Lutheran theologians would not recognize the validity of such a conception of *kenosis*. Since it derives its impetus from the energy of the negative and not from the originary superabundance of God, the dialectical *Entäußerung* contradicts the freedom of the divine. From this vantage point, the sending of the Son would no longer be a gratuitous act, or an act of love. It is on these grounds that Ernst Jüngel, despite his belief in Hegel's fidelity to the Lutheran doctrine of *kenosis*, points to a principle of profound dissonance. For as the Lutheran interpretation would have it,

> the union (of the natures) must exclusively be ascribed to the person of Jesus Christ. Hegel's definition argues that, on the basis of the Incarnation and Death of God, an absolute spirit has arisen which transforms the union of the divine and human natures into a universal truth and condition: for that reason it must be disputed by theology. . . .[17]

What is inadmissible is to identify *kenosis* with a logical process. The sending of the earthly and mortal Son is for Hegel the 'shattering of the eternal moment of the mediation', and the moment of *kenosis* has for its dialectical expression the transition from God as being-in-itself (substance) to being-for-itself (subject):

> The in itself and for itself of the eternal consists in its self-imparting *(sich aufzuschließen*), self-determining (*zu bestimmen*), in judging (*zu urteilen*) and positing itself in the form of a difference (*sich als Unterscheidenes seiner zu stehen*); but this difference, this distinction, is also always and eternally sublated, so that in and for itself the eternal is reconciled with itself in its return to self; only thus is it spirit.[18]

Thinking of God as a being 'in itself' leads to an unacceptable conclusion that implies something abstract and incomplete.

The Hegelian conception of the Trinity

Yet couldn't the meaning of 'gift' and 'God as gift' be understood in another way, through the idea of an 'absence' affecting plenitude, an absence which would give the gift its own authenticity? One thinks here of negative theology, in particular of the idea we find in Plotinus, essentially that 'The Good gives what it does not possess'.[19] In our context, however, such references are ineffectual. The traditional vocabulary of *ousia* and *hypostasis*, from the point of view of a Hegelian theology, falls short of the life of spirit.

As Hegel says in the *Lectures*, it is natural to consider the moments of the Idea as numbered. This is something we can learn from the determinations of Father, Son and Holy Spirit. They are Three and at the same time One (*drei gleich eins*). Of course, the traditional representation and its form can only conceive of the inwardness of this idea in an external way: putting it into numbers, which are immediately something external, goes no further than abstract reflection. Yet, even if this remains within the specific forms of dogmatic consciousness, it is still a genuine representation of the absolute as it appears for speculation. Hegel distinguishes two levels in the comprehension of number: first, that of the understanding (*Verstand*), bound to the natural and immediate exteriority of things; and second, that of speculative reason which discerns, beneath the moments of summation and division, the movement of the concept which unifies through singularization: 'They are three in God.' This affirmation, nonetheless, will only disclose its absolute meaning in the concept itself, and it is via its light that the traditional doctrine of the Three Persons is illuminated.

The word 'person' (*Person*) was first adopted by Tertullian.[20] In Hegel's view, this conception remains insufficient to explain the speculative content of the intra-trinitarian difference. Indeed, 'person' always in his view retains the technical sense it bears in Roman law, of a 'formal and abstract' freedom. This is a 'person' who is to be understood solely in reference to the juridical order. Hegelian theology only extracts the truth of the trinitarian doctrine, the doctrine of the 'three divine persons', by assigning it to the sphere of representation and thus abandoning it to the theological tradition as a moment in Christian thought which is clearly necessary and significant but, by the same token, inadequate.

Speculative thought has for its task the recovery of the trinitarian representation in the very 'imperfection' (*Unvollkommenheit*) of its conception.[21] In its most immediate form, this representation grasps the movement of spirit as an event in history, returning with it to the *gnosis* of early Christianity:

> In Philo, the ὄν is the first, the inconceivable, the uncommunicative, the silent god, the god one does not name. . . . In the second place comes the Logos, especially νοῦς, the deity who reveals himself, who manifests himself to the outside world: ὅρασις θεοῦ, the σοφία, the λόγος and then the archetype of humanity as the man who is the image of celestial revelation, the eternal image of the hidden divinity, as φρόνησις. . . . Valentinius and the

> Valentinians named this unity Βυθός, the 'abyss'. . . . Necessarily preceding all things was the revelation of the hidden god. Through his self-contemplation . . . he engenders the only-begotten (*der Eingeborene*), who is the Eternal become comprehensible . . ., the first conceivable Being, the principle of all determinate existence. . . . The *Monogenes* is actually the Father, the founding principle of all existence. . . . The Βυθός is in and for itself ἀνονόμαστος, the other is the πρόσωπον τοῦ πατρός.[22]

Without adopting this gnostic abstraction, Hegel sees in this dual principle, contained in the 'Abyss', 'the major disagreement between the Christian churches of the East and the West'. But at this moment of his analysis, he commits a 'strange mistake' (*faute étrange*), writing that this disagreement concerns the question of knowing

> if the Holy Spirit proceeds from the Son, or from the Father and the Son (*ob der Geist vom Sohne, oder vom Vater und Sohn ausgehe*), the Son being only the one who actualizes, who reveals – thus from him alone the Spirit proceeds.[23]

The two confessions of East and West disagree about the Holy Spirit, whether it proceeds from the Father alone, or from the Father and the Son, but not, as Hegel puts it, from either the Son alone or from the Father and the Son.[24] It is an extremely uncommon error for this philosopher. Either it stems from ignorance (Hegel, according to a number of commentators, was only mediocre as a theological scholar),[25] or it is a 'revealing' *lapsus*. It is the second hypothesis which the theologians consider the more plausible. This 'mistake' must clearly show that Hegel attempts absolutely to reduce the originary superabundance of God the Father.

The dialectical formulation of the Trinity seems to lend itself wholeheartedly to such a reduction. If Hegel's trinitarian theology separates itself from the scholastic doctrine of the procession of the Spirit *ab utroque tamquam ab uno*, it also abjures the Greek point of view which holds that the Father is the first origin of both Son and Holy Spirit. The speculative content of religion is not longer attached to the idea of 'hypostasis', but it is not attached to the idea of 'person' either. The concept of a 'substance-subject' neither refers to the principle of a hypostatic substance (literally, ὑπό–στασις, *Sub-stanz)*, as the Greek Fathers argued, nor to the subjective person (*persona*, *Person*, *Subjekt*) of the Latin Church. In Hegelian thought, apparently, there is absolutely no place for the doctrine that the Spirit proceeds from the Father alone. Nor is there even, more fundamentally, a place for the idea of 'procession'. The 'path' – whether as a process or μέθ–οδος – or as a 'path' in the sense of 'procession' or πρό–οδος – requires two different conceptualizations. The path of procession is a trajectory lacking those conceptual linkages demanded by the dialectical process as presented in the last paragraphs of the *Encyclopedia Science of Logic*, where the three moments of speculative method are defined as the 'beginning' or the 'first' (*Anfang*); the 'progression' (*Fortgang*); and the 'end (*Ende*)'.[26]

Instead of the classical language of the Trinitarian doctrine, Hegel substitutes terms previously foreign to theological thought. Of these, the most significant is 'difference' (*Unterschied*), articulating the relation of the three conceptual instances which the language of representation signifies in the names of Father, Son and Spirit. Dialectical 'difference' is the key term of a conceptual chain that finds figures for all the stages of God's departure out from himself: *Entzweiung*, *Entfremdung*, and, of course, *Entäußerung*.

Faith according to Hegel, or 'the appetite of the concept'

According to the theologians, Hegel's understanding of the faith is dominated by a further idea, that of a divine 'avidity' and neediness, ascribed to a God who must fulfil, through the dialectical process, his own essence and being. Hans Urs von Balthasar interprets this idea as an 'autophagia' in God, an ontological insatiability. In his *Prometheus*, Balthasar writes: 'Kant is a legislator, Fichte a judge, Schelling a seer. But Hegel has only one desire, that of appropriation. He returns constantly to the mysteries of eating.'[27]

Balthasar submits this evaluation in response to the Hegelian interpretation (in the *Lectures on the Philosophy of Religion*) of the 'for us (*pro nobis*)' in the formula 'Christ was given *for us*'. Hegel says: 'On the basis of this death the assertion is justified that Christ (was) given *for us*, [and that his Death] may be represented as a sacrificial death, as the act of absolute satisfaction.'[28] To explain the meaning of the *pro nobis*, Hegel uses the example of organic assimilation:

> If the individual human being does something, achieves something, attains a goal, this fact must be grounded in the way the thing itself, in its concept, acts and behaves. If I eat an apple, I destroy its organic self-identity and assimilate it to myself. That I can do this entails that the apple in itself, already, in advance, before I take hold of it, has in its nature the character (*Bestimmung*) of being subject to destruction, having in itself a homogeneity with my digestive organs such that I can make it homogeneous with myself.[29]

The meaning of the example is clear: Christ's death can only 'be satisfactory (*genugtuend*)', can only be significant *for us*, because it, like the apple, is digestible and assimilable to the organs which receive it.[30] The metaphor of alimentary assimilation is for Hegel the sensory translation of the conformity between religious truth and the human spirit.

A God conceived as something *to be consumed* is in Balthasar's view an unacceptable concept of God. These 'mysteries of the act of eating' extend their darkness in every direction, embracing not only the *Entäußerung*, the divine self-abasement, but also the *Erhebung*, the elevation of man to God. Could it not be claimed that Hegel's way of conceptualizing self-revelation must make religion the site of the mutual devouring of God and man, each attracted to the other by their respective *hunger for being*? It is worth remembering the arguments of the *Philosophy of Nature*, which maintained that 'in every process, organic and spiritual, assimilation (*Assimilation*) is the most essential factor'.[31] Not even God will escape from the rule prescribing ingestion and digestion; even He finds himself submitted to the '*substantial* change, i.e. the general *immediate* transformation of one external or particular material into another'.[32]

Lutheranism gone too far?

It may seem obvious that Catholic theologians would reject the idea that divine truth is *assimilated* by human beings, given its source in the Lutheran understanding of Eucharistic communion. Hegel's theory of assimilation, in this context, appears simply to conform to the Mystery of the Eucharist as preached by the Protestant faith. At the very least, the Remark to Paragraph §552 of the *Philosophy of Spirit* encourages such an inference. Here Hegel compares the Catholic Mystery of Transubstantiation to the Protestant idea of 'Commemoration':

> In Catholicism this spirit of all truth is in actuality set in rigid (*starr*) opposition to the self-conscious spirit. And, first of all, God is in the 'host' presented to religious adoration as an *external thing* (*als aüßerliches Ding*). (In the Lutheran Church, on the contrary, the host as such is only first consecrated in the process of enjoyment (*im Genüsse*), i.e. in the annihilation of its externality, and in the act of faith, i.e. in the free self-certain spirit.)[33]

Similarly, a fidelity to the spirit of the Reformation, with its insistence on the inwardness of the spirit, can be detected in Hegel's claim that the truth of faith is found in the act of assimilation, or absorption.

That the *Encyclopedia* passage is interpretable in these terms is what Jean-Luc Marion suggests in his *God without Being*. 'Hegel', writes Marion, 'sees precisely in its notion of Eucharistic consciousness without real mediation the immense superiority Lutheranism enjoys over Catholicism.'[34] Indeed, Hegel believes that for Catholics, the process of Communion does not take place 'in spirit, but only through the external object (*Dingheit*) that mediates it'.[35] Now, for Marion, such a deliberate and reductive cancellation of exteriority will paradoxically lead to the very 'idolatry' it intends to avoid:

'It is this criticism of Hegel's which, more than anything else, enables us to understand, *a contrario*, how only the real presence (guaranteed by a thing independent of consciousness) has the power to avert the most extreme kind of idolatry.'[36]

The 'present which Christ makes us of himself' is something irreducibly external. Thus it alone can guarantee the absolute break (*écart*) which opens for the believer the horizon of divine transcendence, by the same token forbidding any conception of faith as a kind of assimilation. It is this break (*écart*) which proves that God is free from 'beingness' (*étantité*): God is not *there* (*là*). God's *present* (understood as a gift) does not present itself in the modality of 'now'. To this quality of the un-presentable, Marion gives the name 'distance'.[37]

Because it is based on the reduction of the divine presence to a present entity, a 'thing' (*res*), the Hegelian critique of a reified divine presence runs into an unavoidable paradox. For as 'thing', accessible in the here and now (*hic et nunc*), this presence would be more immediately *assimilable* than the Eucharistic host, understood as a symbol and promise of the body of Christ. In essence, the dialectical notion of God permits the very thing which Hegel in other respects shows to be impossible: a presentation of the divine presence as sense certainty. A gift to the believer in the proximity and absolute intimacy of the present, no longer mediated through the actual and reified dimension of the host, the divine essence would become an *object possessed* intimately, enjoying a proximity to the self which no spatial reason – no relation to the external – could begin to change. If we understand the Hegelian argument in this fashion, we will be led to the following conclusion:

> On the evidence it appears that the eucharistic presence never finds itself as definitively subordinated to metaphysics as in the conception that criticises the theology of transubstantiation as metaphysical: in this conception the primacy of the present (as the *here and now* of an ontic disposability) and that of the primacy of human temporal consciousness are at play in the open and in full.[38]

Karl Barth's response

While this analysis is of great interest, it must be noted at once that Lutherans themselves also reject the idea of a God who, to adopt the formulation of Karl Barth, 'would let himself be entirely understood'.[39]

The Lutheran understanding of Communion in no way presupposes the logic of assimilation. Barth's insistence on divine freedom, understood as 'grace', testifies to its own refusal of that logic and all its implications, its organic metaphors of hunger, satisfaction, and digestion. Hegelian concepts have no purchase in what is, strictly speaking, the theological domain. That Hegel fulfils and surpasses the philosophy of the Enlightenment is, as

Barth admits, beyond doubt: 'He brought the great conflict between reason and revelation . . . to a highly satisfactory conclusion' and 'brought to an end the arguments against theology'.[40] Nevertheless, 'the Hegelian demand is unacceptable to theology for good reasons',[41] chiefly because Hegel considers it essential that God be conceived 'not as an incomprehensibly new beginning', but as an essence, an idea that can be 'delegated to the authority of mind'.[42]

If God can be delegated in such a way, this will necessarily imply that divine presence can be linked to acquisition; indeed the self in Hegel is constituted by just such a seizure in so far as it understands itself as including the other, as appropriating and grasping the other. However for Barth, on the contrary:

> The identification of God with the dialectical method, even if it did not signify that He was identified with man's act of life, implies a scarcely acceptable limitation, even the abolition of God's sovereignty, which makes even more questionable the designation of that which Hegel calls mind, idea, reason, etc., as God.[43]

By thus being 'identified' with speculative truth, God becomes assimilable by man just like any other knowable content.

Any erasure of the uniqueness of the divine is declared unacceptable, again in the name of a problematic of the gift. If no movement is acknowledged as belonging strictly and exclusively to God, doesn't this amount to a questioning of God's own being as originary gift? Moreover, according to Barth

> Hegel, in making the dialectical method of logic the essential nature of God, made impossible the knowledge of the actual dialectic of grace, which has its foundation in the freedom of God. Upon the basis of this dialectic, the attempt to speak of a necessity to which God himself is supposed to be subject would be radically impossible.[44]

The logic of conceptual linkage (*enchaînement conceptuel*) would destroy God's free superabundance. A God who is 'at the least, prisoner of himself'[45] can give nothing.

Barth as he appears here is fundamentally much closer to Marion than to Hegel. He also would understand the gift as a 'present' which does not let itself be presented, as the promise of an event, as, in a word, a future. It emerges from the Barthian analysis that divine freedom must be conceived as an offering. Yet the possibility of freely giving to another would be completely covered over by the logic of dialectical assimilation and appropriation. Was it not Luther himself who affirmed that 'the form of the syllogism can understand nothing of that which is God'?[46]

The fate of representation: Philosophical rationality as the future of Religion

We are approaching the last stage of our investigation: the question of the dialectical sublation of the representational form and its correlative, the religious stage of spirit, as these have been intepreted by Hegel's theological critics. For Hegel, the representational form is sublated in both religious contemplation and the simplicity of thought: 'In this form . . ., truth is the object of philosophy'.[47] The return to the simplicity of thought occurs when 'the unfolding of the mediation' demonstrates substance as subject. The 'absolute result' marks the dialectical identity of subject (Father) and predicate (Son). The intra-trinitarian distinction resolves itself into the movement of a speculative proposition. But wouldn't such a thought spell the ruin of any idea of divine *transcendence*?

When the different writers we have been looking at invoke the idea of the 'incomprehensibility' of God, they resist any implication of obscurity, obscurantism, or unintelligibility. They do not contrast what Hegel calls the 'homely pictures of faith'[48] to speculative insight. They concentrate on what, in God, cannot be comprehended, what cannot be seized, possessed, or assimilated. Not because spirit – by some flaw, by some fallibility – is impotent to constitute the divine as object of knowledge, but because he is not simply a matter for knowledge. God is not a concept.[49]

The 'secret' of God, the test of his superabundance, of his power to give, is not something hidden from reason or knowledge, but something which is not of the *order* of reason or knowledge.[50] From this irreducibility of God to knowledge it is possible to understand the place of *mystery* in the arguments of the theologians, particularly in the case of Barth who claims that we cannot 'allow Hegel to submit to the control of thought the mystery of evil and salvation, the possibility of illuminating the twofold mystery'.[51]

'Mystery' must not be understood here by reversing Hegel's sense, as if mystery were another name for the understanding's inability to grasp the religious content in a properly speculative framework. The theological claim of mystery rests less on a gnostic principle (e.g. God must be inaccessible to human understanding) than on the recognition that God has a particular way of appearing. The *phenomenon* of God's presence does not cause a failure of knowledge but a 'breakdown of assurances, of guarantees'.[52] It creates a relation to the secret, but not to the secret in the sense of something 'secret to the understanding'. The secret as understood here belongs to the manifestation of God himself and could not be interpreted as a sign of his jealousy.

For a philosopher such as Marion it is not a question of using the concept of 'distance' to promote the idea of a 'beyond', or an 'evasive transcendence'.[53] Rather it is a question of showing how the divine presence is incommensurable with the ontical. Hegel's speculative reduction of the 'beyond' seems, on the contrary, to reflect a desire to put presence back at the centre, hence to attach God's being to the 'present' time and place of the supreme *entity*. On this point Marion echoes Derrida, who writes in *Glas*:

> Because it still has an object, a desire, or a nostalgia, absolute religious consciousness remains [for Hegel] in the opposition, the split. Reconciliation remains a beyond. The temporal motif (the movement of transcendence, relation to a non-present future or past, de-presentation), is the truth of a metaphorically spatial motif (the 'distant', the non-proximate, the non-proper).[54]

But by repudiating the beyond in its temporal and spatial schema, doesn't Hegel simultaneously repudiate time and space themselves, as well as the ontological distance that constitutes them? Has he forgotten that there may be a *non-representational* presentation of the beyond, one that is irreducible to the representational *Entäußerung*, indeed a speculative meaning of transcendence? If there is one, one conceived as *pure difference*, it would mark the irreducibility of God to the status of a pre-constituted entity, to an onto-theological God. It would no longer refer back to the promise of an 'other world', to something 'outside the system'.

An impossible future

The claim that Hegel's God lacks a future is based, in the final instance, on three main arguments. First, according to the theologians, the transparency implied by the speculative concept of self-revelation is a transparency without surprise. In so far as the dialectical process of God's coming to himself assumes the sublation of the temporal form intrinsic to the representational process, it would seem that God can neither *occur* nor *arrive*. The necessity to which the *Entäußerung* of the movement of *kenosis* is submitted, is a necessity which deprives the Father of his fullest possibilities. Accordingly, Hegel's God is a God who does not *promise*.[55]

Second, this God who does not promise is not anticipated. The believer is led to renounce all hope of his coming. The alienation through which God dispossesses himself of his 'determination as immediate nature' seems to confront him with the paradox of an escape from the self without any outside.

Third, this absence of transcendence, established by the philosophical sublation of the representational form, indicates the omnipotence of the concept, ie., the complete victory of self-presence.

From the emptiness of its first conception to the closure of its syllogistic conclusion, the Hegelian God may make himself present without ever happening.

7

THE DEATH OF GOD AND THE DEATH OF PHILOSOPHY

Alienation and its double fate

For all their insight, these interpretations of Hegel's religious thought are nevertheless illegitimate. In Hegel's philosophy, as it happens, neither the subjectivity of a revealed God nor the modern philosophical notion of the subject can be seen in isolation. Yet the theologians persist in dis-associating them. *De facto*, the notion of divine alienation detached from its philosophical replica, where alienation is understood as a movement of and within *reason*, could certainly point to a lack. The negativity at play within the essence of the divine, if we were to separate it from its philosophical destiny (*advenir*), can clearly appear as the sign of an absence of *future*. Nonetheless this apparent shortage of futurity and the lack it implies will cease to be relevant when the divine subject and the subject of modern philosophy are restored to one another.

The close affinity of these two subjects appears most vividly in the Hegelian theory of the 'Death of God'. Starting with the publication of *Glauben und Wissen* (*Faith and Knowledge*), the idea of the Death of God revealed its double articulation as both theological and philosophical. On one hand, the Death of God, the event of the Crucifixion, represents one moment within the absolute Idea; on the other hand, the Death of God appears as the truth of human subjectivity, a subjectivity that constitutes the 'absolute principle of modern philosophy'.[1] In at least one essential aspect, the Hegelian concept of the Death of God is linked with the consideration of a certain condition or state of philosophy (*état de la philosophie*), namely, that established and realized in the ideas of the Enlightenment: 'The feeling that God himself is dead (*das Gefühl: Gott selbst ist tot*) is the sentiment on which the religion of modern times rests.'[2]

The suffering of God and the suffering of human subjectivity deprived of God must be analysed as the recto and verso of the same event. There is a fundamental relationship between divine *kenosis* and the tendency of modern reason to posit a beyond which remains inaccessible.[3] The *Encyclopedia* makes this relation visible by presenting the Death of God at once as the Passion of the Son who 'dies in the pain of negativity'[4] and the human feeling that we can know nothing of God.[5]

If we insistently stress this relation, it is because it allows us to show that for Hegel, the divine negativity, conceived in its most radical form, does not manifest the lack or the passivity, but rather the *plasticity* of God.

'God himself is dead': a divine event

In the concluding section of *Faith and Knowledge* Hegel establishes the philosophical meaning of the statement 'God himself is dead'. 'That from the start this implies a Christological proposition', Jüngel writes, 'is something Hegel only reveals indirectly, but he knows it.'[6] Later, in the *Lectures on the Philosophy of Religion*, Hegel makes it explicit to his readers that the phrase comes from a Protestant hymnal. As he puts it: '"God himself is dead", it says in the Lutheran hymn.'[7]

However, this 'Lutheran hymn' is not a hymn of Luther's.[8] Rather it is from the second stanza of a passion hymn written by Johannes Rist in 1641 and added to a Church chorale (of Catholic origin), 'O Traurigkeit, o Herzleid', well known in Würzburg since 1628. While the Catholic hymn was heard accompanying the liturgical rite where Christ, in the form of the host, is placed in his tomb, these words would resound: 'O great woe, God himself lies dead. On the cross he has died; And thus he has gained for us, by love, the kingdom of heaven.'[9]

As Jüngel remarks:

> This phrase: 'God himself lies Dead' was known and discussed as the authoritative expression of Lutheran doctrine: so much discussed that, for example, in the hymnal of Dortmund, the authors preferred to soften it to a less shocking version: 'the *Lord* is Dead'. In the faculties of theology scholarly arguments raged about the dogmatic correction of the chorale.[10]

These discussions can be connected to the doctrinal tradition and debates of the early Church. For the theologians it was a question of how far it could be asserted that God the Father would have suffered and died on the Cross. If Tertullian, in a text where he mentions the Death of God, employs the formula 'The crucified God (*Deus crucifixus*)',[11] he nonetheless declares that it is enough to say: 'The Son of God is dead, and that only because it is thus written.'[12] Athanasius, on the other hand, considers it a sign of heresy not to confess the Crucified as God. However, he also writes that Christ 'would have suffered for us not in his divinity but in his flesh'.[13] The Reformation did not limit itself to the discourse on the Death of God as discussed by the early Church. The idea of a God who dies is not foreign to the mystical tradition. Meister Eckhart states: 'God is dead in order for me to die in regard to the entire world and in the face of all created realities.'[14]

The philosophy of the young Hegel is still inscribed within the tradition of such controversy. But between *The Spirit of Christianity and its Fate* and in *Faith and Knowledge* there is a divergence which must be emphasized and it is, historically speaking, remarkable. In the text from 1798–99, Hegel still considers it scandalous that 'the form of a servant, the humiliation in itself' – rather than being something simply provisional – is 'supposed to remain fixed and permanent in God, belonging to his essence'. He argues that 'this blemish – humanity – is something quite different from the configuration proper to God'.[15] During this period, Hegel conceives the Death of Jesus as the suppression of divine *kenosis*, while later it will seem to him to be the ultimate event of *kenosis*. The very thing which is rejected in the Frankfurt period has become, in 1802, thought's essential requirement (*une exigence de la pensée*).

The feeling that 'God himself is dead' must be understood as a moment of the supreme Idea. Before Hegel, no one had philosophically interpreted the Death of God as the event of his self-negation, that is, as a moment of truth within God himself. *Faith and Knowledge*, the *Phenomenology of Spirit* and the *Lectures on the Philosophy of Religion* are the three essential texts where this interpretation is developed and elaborated.

Faith and Knowledge

In this work, Hegel does not mention the source of the expression 'God himself is dead'. But in the conclusion the Christological subtext does become recognizable, as the citation is linked to the discourse on the 'Speculative Good Friday' and the Resurrection. This same connection helps to clarify the transition from the theological meaning of the Death of God to its philosophical meaning. Death is analysed as a moment in the idea of God: 'The feeling upon which the religion of modern times rests – the feeling that God himself is Dead . . . – is purely a moment of the supreme Idea'.[16]

But this feeling, exacerbated by modern philosophy, has 'come to exist historically in the formative process of culture'. From this point on it will be the role of speculative philosophy to manifest it 'in all its truth': 'The absolute Passion (*absolute Leiden*) or the speculative Good Friday, that was once an historical event . . . can and must arise again in the serene freedom of its form.'[17]

The Phenomenology of Spirit

In the *Phenomenology of Spirit*, the Death of God is explicitly presented as a moment in the 'becoming-subject' of substance. Spirit, in the Revealed Religion, 'reveals itself as self-revelation'. It is this aspect which distinguishes a revealed religion from a 'natural religion (*natürliche Religion*)' or from a 'religion of art (*Kunstreligion*)'. In 'natural religion' (the religion of the Parsees and early Indian religions), 'spirit knows itself as its object in a natural or immediate shape'.[18] In the 'religion of art' (Greek religion), consciousness produces itself in the form of a 'Self', so that when consciousness admires its object, it is in fact intuiting itself, as we see in the beauty of classical art. Here 'naturality' (*Naturalität*), formerly the religious object for spirit, is annulled. But it is for the first time in Revealed Religion that the spirit's attainment of self-knowledge is actually *incarnated* in a man, a determinate self. From this point on, spirit becomes *self-consciousness* while the divine essence becomes human.

The development of the 'substance-subject' is accomplished through this sequence of religious 'shapes' and figures.[19] In natural religion, spirit only knows itself as substance, as self-identity, and immediate unity between interior and exterior. Only through the distinction of the self – the difference that governs the division of substance and subject – can the spiritual content of religion be fulfilled. Since it has not yet arrived at such a distinction, the 'wisdom' of natural religion is 'scarcely intelligible' and remains attached to 'this ambiguous being which is a riddle to itself'.[20] In the religion of art spirit manages to escape and distinguish itself from itself: 'Through the religion of art, spirit has advanced from the form of *substance* to assume that of *subject*'.[21] Spirit is involved here in the 'free becoming of the self' in so far as substance becomes for it a material amenable to creative fashioning on which it can imprint its own form. Art 'is the night in which substance was delivered over and betrayed (*verraten wird*) and has made itself into subject'.[22] Through the artistic act of fashioning, spirit recognizes the way it has formed itself while distancing itself from itself. Hegel understands this transformation of substance into subject as the beginning of a process of 'humanisation of the divine Being (*Menschwerdung des göttlichen Wesens*) which starts from the statue'.[23]

However, if what is other to the self is only, from the subject's point of view, an object to be formed according to its own image, the subject is in fact only in relation to itself: the other remains the same. The subject, as Hegel writes, possesses nothing more than 'the thought of its self'. Ultimately, such a situation is the fate of the unhappy consciousness. Here the subject, lacking any objective and actual relation to the other, tests through its own experience 'the Stoic independence of thought'. And this condition, passing through the journey of sceptical consciousness, 'finds its truth in that shape we have called the *unhappy consciousness*'.[24]

Unhappy consciousness:

> is the loss of all *essential being* in this certainty of itself, and of the loss even of this knowledge about itself – the loss of substance as well as of the Self; it is the grief which expresses itself in the hard saying that 'God is Dead'.[25]

The Death of God appears as a moment of God's being. As such, the concept is intuited immediately as something *necessary* for consciousness. Revealed Religion differentiates itself from other religions precisely through this insight into the necessity of development, within which substance completes itself as self-consciousness, 'and for that it is spirit'.[26] This development *is* precisely the speculative meaning of *kenosis*. In it, the simple being of substance 'alienates itself from itself, yields to death, and thereby reconciles absolute essence with itself'.[27] Christ's Death is thus at once the death of the God-man and the Death of the initial and immediate abstraction of the divine being which is not yet posited as a Self.

The Lectures on the Philosophy of Religion

The point of view adopted in the *Lectures on the Philosophy of Religion* allows the positive, historical content of revelation to be synthesized with the absolute content of the Idea:

> With the Death of Christ, however, the reversal of consciousness begins. The Death of Christ is the midpoint (*Mittelpunkt*) upon which consciousness turns; and in its comprehension lies the difference between outward comprehension and that of faith, which entails apprehension by the Spirit, from the Spirit of truth, the Holy Spirit.[28]

It is because God himself is present in the individual human existence of his Son that the Death of Jesus Christ acquires not only a religious but also a philosophical meaning:

> *God has died* (*Gott ist gestorben*), *God is dead* (*Gott ist tot*) – this is the most frightful of all thoughts (*der fürchterlichste Gedanke*), that everything eternal and true is *not*, that negation itself is found in God. The deepest anguish, the feeling of complete irretrievability, the annulling of everything that is elevated, are bound up with this thought.[29]

The Death of God thereby appears for Hegel as a moment in the divine being in the form of a *first negation*, logically destined to be reduplicated and reversed: 'Thus a reversal takes place: . . . God maintains himself in this process, and the latter is only the death of death (*der Tod des Todes*).'[30] The expression '*mors mortis*' is found many times in Luther's writings, but the singularity of the Hegelian version is marked in the way he interprets this death of death as a 'negation of negation'. On the basis of such an interpretation we can already predict the transition from the theological signification of *kenosis* to its philosophical meaning.

'God himself is Dead': the advent of the 'metaphysics of subjectivity'

The new meaning of the opposition of knowledge and faith

If the phrase 'God himself is dead' indicates the event of God's negation of himself, it equally brings us back to the situation of modern philosophy with its absolutizing of finitude. It is this signification which has in effect 'been transferred (*verlegt*)' from the theological domain to that of philosophy.

> Culture has raised the most recent era (*die letzte Zeit*) so far above the ancient antithesis of reason and faith, of philosophy and positive religion, that the opposition of faith and knowledge has acquired quite a different sense and has now been transferred into the field of philosophy itself.[31]

Initially this change took place in the domain of culture (*Kultur*); its significance for philosophy had not yet, in Hegel's view, been fully brought out. Only by keeping up with what it saw to be the fashion of the times did modern philosophy take as its own content this new modification: 'Through this whole philosophical revolution . . . the metaphysics of reflection has at first glance merely taken on the hue of inwardness, of the latest cultural fashion (*der modischen Kultur*).'[32]

Still, this transposition of the theological into the speculative must be made philosophically explicit. Hegel distinguishes three major stages of the evolution of the relationship between faith and knowledge: (1) faith and knowledge as a harmonious and non-conflictual distinction within theology itself; (2) faith and knowledge as an antagonistic distinction between theology and philosophy; (3) faith and knowledge as a distinction within philosophy itself.

The transposition of the quarrel between faith and knowledge into the inner domain of philosophy seems to be a victory of the discourse of the Enlightenment (*Aufklärung*).[33] But:

> Enlightened Reason won a glorious victory over what it believed, in its limited conception of religion, to be faith as opposed to reason. Yet it seems in a clear light the victory comes to no more than this: the positive element with which reason busied itself to do battle is no longer religion, and victorious reason is no longer reason. The new born peace that hovers triumphantly over the corpse of reason and faith, uniting them as the child of both, has as little of reason in it as it has of authentic faith.[34]

The expression 'God himself is dead' acquires its meaning, philosophically speaking, from this event of mutual debasement and bastardization of both philosophy and religion.

With the Enlightenment, philosophy 'has acknowledged its own nothingness'.[35] It is precisely this event of the self-annihilation of philosophy, the correlative of the divine self-negation, that determines the transposition of the traditional opposition of faith and knowledge into the very core of philosophy. For what else can this acknowledgement of its own nothingness mean to philosophy except that reason itself is now no longer merely the critic of religion, but the critic of itself? The Kantian critical philosophy – just like the philosophies of Fichte and Jacobi which Hegel considers to be its continuations – ordains reason as a tribunal which dictates to itself where its limits are to be drawn:

> After its battle with religion the best reason could manage was to take a look at itself and come to self-awareness. Reason, having in this way become mere intellect, acknowledges its own nothingness by placing that which is better than it in a faith outside and above itself, as a 'beyond' (*Jenseits*) to be believed in. This is what has happened in the philosophies of Kant, Jacobi and Fichte. Philosophy has made itself the handmaiden of a faith once more.[36]

The present outcome is in fact identical with that of the past, and the division between reason and understanding will from this point on replace the former opposition. Yet the original issue will not be resolved as long as God remains unintelligible: 'according to Kant, the supersensible is incapable of being known by reason'.[37]

Philosophy as Protestantism's 'poetry of grief'

Reason can know God only as something unknowable. In the feeling that 'God himself is dead', consciousness is crying over the pain of being thus abandoned by God: a God who can no longer be present in the world. Such an emotion reflects 'the atheism of the modern age' expressed in 'the metaphysics of subjectivity' or, in another sense, 'the nihilism of transcendental philosophy'.[38]

In the Hegelian analysis of *Faith and Knowledge*, a primary axis is formed by the demonstration that this 'nihilism' is in fact a radicalization of 'the poetry of grief'[39] of Protestantism and the outcome of its 'infinite nostalgia'.[40] Critical philosophy, at the very moment when it believed itself definitively emancipated from its relation to theology, emerges in fact as the translation of a certain moment in religious consciousness:

> The great form of the world spirit that has come to cognition of itself in these philosophies (of Kant, Jacobi and Fichte), is the principle of the North, and from the religious point of view, of Protestantism. This principle is subjectivity for which beauty and truth present themselves in feelings and persuasions, in love and intellect.[41]

Both metaphysics and 'the religion of the modern epoch'[42] depend on the same state of feeling. But how can it be that religion is based on the very principle which destroys it?

For Hegel, the Reformation's insistence on 'faith alone' is linked to the spread of modern subjectivity. In faith, man has immediate access to God. There is no need for Him to reveal himself through any sort of finite reality, whether that be an institution (the people, the family, the church), or a human act or artefact. Only faith, in the Lutheran view, prevents God from being made finite through intellection or intuition:

> Religion [Protestantism] builds its temples and altars in the heart of the individual. His sighs and prayers seek for the God whom he denies to himself in intuition because of the danger that the intellect will cognize what is intuited as a mere Thing, reducing the sacred grove to mere timber.[43]

Protestantism thus excludes any intuition of God through the institutions of finitude.

But paradoxically, in so doing, Protestant religion has built a rigid and insurmountable opposition between subjectivity in its urge towards the eternal, and the eternal itself. Lacking finite mediation, infinity remains immediate and abstract. The very foundation of Lutheranism – its disdain for all identification between God and empirical reality as such – turns back against itself. It is threatened with the prospect of ineffectuality, because the scorn it expresses makes any reconciliation between the finite and the infinite impossible. The culture that arose from Protestantism allowed the anti-religious and anti-theological attitude to gain its own place in history, but without thereby resolving its own problem, the problem of subjectivity gripped by absolute solitude and loneliness. If that finitude which had claimed validity as a manifestation of the infinite is scorned, the consequence seemed to be that only the finite on its own, in the form of the human self, can be considered infinite.

Within the culture of the *Aufklärung* we find repeated the situation of faith: detached from any kind of tangible and sensory effectiveness, living a pain it creates for itself, changing inevitably into an unhappy consciousness. If 'the infinite can only be believed' via a negative relation to the finite reality of experience, there is no escaping the feeling that God can neither be present nor alive in this world. The phrase 'Death of God' thus begins to acquire a further connotation, meaning that faith henceforth exists in separation from all worldly experience: this state of feeling will become, as it is said, 'historical in the formative process of culture (*Bildung*)'.

The 'vacuum' of philosophy

At the very moment when subjectivity affirms itself as the ground of certainty, when it acquires its full autonomy and freedom, it alienates itself. The 'I = I' finds itself deprived of its own content. The *Encyclopedia*'s allusion to 'these modern assertions that man cannot ascertain God',[44] can now be grasped in its full force. The conclusions of 1827 and 1830 are an exact repetition of the conclusion of 1802: critical philosophy spawned by the *Aufklärung*, lacking the standpoint of the speculative concept, posits its own negativity within itself as an interior *vacuum*.

On this account it must be evident that the old opposition between faith and knowledge, when transposed into philosophy, continues and completes the significance of *kenosis*. From being an act of the divine, this becomes a philosophical process. The truth of *kenosis* is philosophically realized by subjectivity's *self-dispossession* when it confronts the limits it cannot cross. Thus there is an essential and indissoluble rapport between the *kenosis* of the divine and the emptiness of the transcendental. Working his way from one emptiness to another, Hegel brings to light the essence of modern subjectivity as *kenosis*.

The unity of divine alienation and the alienation of the modern subject

Representation

By analysing the Death of God in its two meanings, religious and philosophical, it becomes clear that both aspects, divine *kenosis* and the *kenosis* of the transcendental subject, are mutually informing and constructing. Indeed, the divine sacrifice finds its ultimate conceptual expression in the *Aufklärung*'s philosophical categories. Reciprocally, modern philosophy would not have its own *subject* if God's sacrifice had not occurred. The exposé of such a structural solidarity between the speculative content of *Revealed Religion* and the philosophical categories apparently excluded from such a content represents an aspect of Hegel's thought at its most original and most difficult.

One and the same process operates in both instances of the kenotic movement, thus allowing their mutual self-fashioning. This is the process of *representation* or *Vorstellung*. Representation is defined as a dynamic that is at once an exteriorization (*Ent-Äußerung*) and an interiorization

(*Erinnerung*) of the content of thought.[45] On the one hand, as Bernard Bourgeois puts it, '*representation* is . . . intelligence's positing as its *own* of content delivered by intuition'; on the other hand, 'representation in itself is to be seen always as the representation of an *Other*'.[46]

Vorstellung, in its economy, unites itself to the movement of *kenosis*: pure thought is driven out into the space of the empirically given; alienated thought returns to itself.[47] Representation is the process through which individual subjectivity repeats the movements of the divine alienation. To the degree that it posits its object outside itself and thus alienates itself in it, representation is the kenotic ordeal of thought. Its double and agonistic play, its incessant struggle between an inside and an outside, condemns it to a painful oscillation. The process of representational thinking translates the sacrifice of the self into the material of thought.

If subjectivity restores to itself the kenotic movement, it is because representation is a movement actually inscribed in the very being of God and not an arbitrary projection of consciousness. In the *Lectures on the Philosophy of Religion*, Hegel writes:

> God is this: not merely to be *in* himself, but to be just as essentially *for* himself. That God is spirit consists in this: that he is not only the essence that maintains itself in thought but also the essence that appears, the essence that endows itself with revelation and objectivity (*Gegenständlichkeit*). Although we consider the idea of God this way in the philosophy of religion, we at the same time also have before us the mode of God's representation. God represents only himself and does so only to himself (*er stellt sich nur vor und stellt sich selber vor sich*). This is the aspect of the being-there (*Dasein*) of the absolute.[48]

What appears from this passage is that consciousness only represents God because *God re-presents himself*; consciousness is only at a distance from God because God distances himself from himself.

Yet why should we insist on the fact that the process of representation seals into one the divine *kenosis* and the *kenosis* of the transcendental subject? The reason is obvious. Without such an explanation, it is impossible to understand why representation should give its form (that of 'separate spheres') to the content of religion. Although theologians and philosophers have interpreted the role of representation in Hegel in a number of different ways, they seem to have evaded the question of its origin and its necessity, the fact that it initially translates a process internal to God Himself into the terms of individual thought.

Representation is all too often understood as a figurative procedure unique to consciousness. Thus the fact that consciousness posits God as a beyond, something inaccessibly distant, is taken to be a function of the way consciousness renders God figuratively without God having anything to do with it.[49]

Yet what reasons can we give for the claim that it is impossible to identify representation as Hegel understands that with the simple idea of 'figurative thought'? First of all because the realm of the imaginary, whether symbolic or mythical, only constitutes for Hegel one moment of representation, representation at its most indeterminate, immediate and natural. Hence it is illegitimate – at the risk of remaining stuck in the operations of the 'religion of art' – to think that God's originary distancing, by virtue of which the religious consciousness constitutes itself as representational, is a function of consciousness's rendering the divine in images. Furthermore, representation, for Hegel, is not a form of consciousness. The exposition of representational processes in the *Encyclopedia* doesn't belong to the *Phenomenology of Spirit* but to *Psychology*. That is to say that representation is not a faculty, but a psychological act defined as the combined work of interiorization and exteriorization. In Hegel, representation is not a figurative process but an act whereby the speculative content is given form.[50]

Towards the plasticity of God

In the last instance, how are we to understand such a giving of form that is not figurative? The detailed exposition of *Revealed Religion* in the *Encyclopedia* has allowed us to see that representation is a process of temporal formation.[51] Thus, if representation does entertain a relationship with images, this is not a matter of the empirical image, but the image understood as a schema, as will become clear in the next chapter.

To insist on the fact that the representational process is not only a moment in individual spirit but also and in the first place a movement in God, allows us to conceive the divine alienation not as evidence of something uncompleted, but as the manifestation of a *temporalization*. For Hegel, the Trinity in its internal movement is not structured by a dynamic of lack – a primordial insatiability calling to be filled – but by the appearance of a new ontological guise of time. By alienating himself, God manifests to humanity a temporal mode of being for which, in retrospect, the philosophies of the *Aufklärung*, notably the Kantian, have supplied the conceptual form.

The concept of *Entäußerung* never appears when Hegel is analysing the thought of the Greeks. For the Greek mind, God is not posed as an unattainable beyond, nor is the relation to God conceived as a split between two 'sides'. Equally, a Greek god who distanced himself from himself in an 'appearance for himself' would be something unimaginable. Alienation is an idea which belongs unquestionably to modern times, and its temporality is that of the finite phenomenal subject. The divine *kenosis* and philosophical *kenosis* are for Hegel fundamentally interdependent to the degree that they share one another's mode of time.

Consequently, God's inner negativity can no longer be interpreted as 'passivity', unless we are to understand by this passivity the passivity of time itself. But since the passivity of time also is a *gift* of form, *plasticity* is demonstrably the right word. Invoking this name brings into play the future of God – God as the one 'who sees (himself) coming'.

8

DIVINE PLASTICITY

or, the *turn* of events

Time is not what it is.[1] It *turns*, and by its very concept is susceptible to revolution. Negativity is its turning point (*Wendungspunkt*).

Christianity brings about time's great 'volte face': 'This new principle is the axis (*Die Angel*) around which the history of the world turns.'[2] Christianity is not one moment among many but the *pivot* which brings all into motion, as we can see from the old distinction *ante natum*, *post natum*. 'History ends from that point (*bis hierher*) and begins from that point (*von daher geht*).'[3]

Revealed Religion enables the goal of a speculative world to be reached, completing 'the great day of spirit' that passed through universal history from East to West, since 'Europe is definitely the end and Asia the beginning of this history.'[4]

'When the time was fulfilled, God sent his Son (Galatians 4, 4).'[5] The turning point of time is also its plenitude, its fulfilment. This is the moment when man, as self-consciousness, raises himself to the standpoint of the trinitarian God. 'The identity of the subject with God appears in the world *when the time is fulfilled* (*als die Zeit erfüllt war*); the consciousness of this identity is the knowledge of God in his truth.'[6]

Christ appears at the religious *crossroads* represented by Israel. His arrival cuts across the oriental and occidental dimensions of spirit, and at that very moment he reconciles current oppositions (between the Orient's infinite divine abstraction and the absolutized finitude of the Roman world).

Further, the very fact of the Death of Christ is itself a *turning*: 'With the Death of Christ begins the conversion (*Umkehrung*) of consciousness . . . (It) is the central point (*Mittelpunkt*) around which everything turns (*um den es sich dreht*).'[7]

According to the theologians studied in Chapter 6, when God's being is reduced to the form of the speculative proposition – God determines himself and the Son appears as the predicate of the paternal substance – this represents the ruin of transcendence. Yet such a condemnation remains blind to the *temporal dimension* of this self-determination, demonstrated by the vocabulary of 'turning' and 'revolution' used constantly by Hegel in his discussion of revealed religion. By speaking of a 'plasticity' in God, I want to insist precisely on the very factor of the *time* or temporality of Christianity. Through this aspect, a *new* conception of self-determination becomes visible. This new modality of the donation and reception of form discovers its fundamental concept in *alienation* (*Entäußerung*): subjectivity determines itself by distancing itself from itself, becoming other than it is. Its form is *representation* (*Vorstellung*). And the phenomenon that performs the role of hypotyposis – the translation of the spiritual into the sensory – is the *Incarnation.*

What is divine plasticity?

The legitimacy of this concept

At first glance, referring to the God of Revelation as 'plastic' may strike us as odd or even illegitimate. How are we to justify using this concept in a context which *a priori* doesn't require it?

In fact, Hegel explicitly states that Christ, considered in the exceptional character of his subjectivity, cannot and should not be considered as a 'plastic individual' of the type represented by the 'substantial individuals' of Greece. For example, he should not be identified with Socrates. Against the plurality of Greek examples, there is only one absolute Example:

> If we consider Christ only in reference to his talents, his character and his morality, as a teacher, etc., we are putting him on the same plane as Socrates and others, even if we place him higher from the moral point of view. . . . If Christ is only taken as an exceptionally fine individual, even as one without sin, then we are ignoring the representation of the speculative idea, its absolute truth.[8]

The great revolution in time effected by Christianity is the paradoxical inauguration of a non-recurring time. The time which makes history *turn* is the time which itself does not turn or return: a linear time radically distinct from teleological time. The essential reason for this is that the Incarnation only happens *once*, and in a *unique individual.* God 'manifests himself to other men as an individual man, exclusive and single . . . like a man excluding all others (*ein ausschließender Mensch*).'[9]

The union of the divine and human natures can only be made manifest in *one* singular form:

> The appearance of God in the flesh occurs in a particular time and in this individual. Because it is a phenomenal appearance (*Erscheinung*), it is transitory and passes over into the history that is gone by (*wird zur vergangenen Geschichte*). This sensory mode must vanish and be raised up into the space of representation. . . .

> Only in the form of an individual is this intuition given; it does not constitute an inheritance and cannot be renovated.[10]

Christ is thus the figure of a pure event, the exact opposite of the habitual. To this extent, its artistic representation cannot fit that required by the classical ideal. For the 'representation of the absolute Idea', 'the forms of classical beauty will not suffice', Hegel writes in the *Aesthetics*.[11] The birth of modernity as registered in a self-regarding interiority, an individuality ruptured and self-absorbed, atomized and strange even to itself: these phenomena demand a form of art other than sculpture. 'Plastic individuality' presents to the world the perfect translation of the interior into the exterior and vice versa; its serenity arises from the individual's harmony with the objective conditions of the world. But within the Roman world, disharmony and rupture led to a different and modern conception of individuality, an individuality that tore itself away from a world grown ineffectual through brutality, that discovered its freedom wholly within itself, dependent only on the power of thought and the infinite value of the ego.

According to Hegel, sculpture cannot respond to this state of discord. Classical Greece presents the manifest and tangible forms of free individuality in all its serene and unbroken harmony; Greek art remains alien to the experience of heartbreak. The Christian God, on the other hand, is not only an individual gifted with a human *form*, but a human in *actuality* and *act*, exposed to all the vicissitudes of our existence.

It is only *painting*, launching the epoch of 'romantic art', that can give a face to an individual of this kind:

> What we called the ideal beauty of sculpture, is something that we would not require of painting to the same extent, nor may we make it the chief thing, because what is central now is the deep feeling of the soul and its living subjective character.[12]

Painting concerns itself with the subjectivity of the inner self and with an interiority that is *particular*.

> Painting, on the other hand, does not confine particularity of character to the ideal but develops precisely the whole variety of even accidental particulars, so that now we see confronting us not those plastic ideals of gods and men but particular persons in all the accidents of their particular character.[13]

No longer will the subjects of painting be ideal divinities, or even the idealized gods, but 'ideal men as they actually live and exist'.[14] The 'plastic individuals' of the Greeks owe the principle of their being to polytheism. When human beings can be seen as incarnating the divine, when they can invest both their psychic and physical beings with the free form of the ideal and exist at once as universal and individual, this will happen only in a world of many gods, in the presence of a plurality unconfined by limitation.

Plastic art in the service of plasticity: the becoming essential of the accident

Yet, under these conditions, can the concept of plasticity retain its relevance? Can it be asked to characterize the exclusive and singular subjectivity of the God who is revealed? Let us recall that the radical application of 'plasticity' proposed in this work does not simply characterize a type of individuality. It is meant to contribute to the way we can understand the substance-subject: as something that develops in a temporal fashion, or, so to speak, contains self-differentiation in its very concept. Such a role, far from invalidating the usefulness of plasticity for the analysis of modernity, in fact provides its justification. It is precisely because the substance-subject is plastic – that it is at once the giver and recipient of its own form – that we can establish the evolution of the concept of plasticity.

If this concept performed a central but different role in the epoch of classical Greece, as we have already noted, it is again active and powerful in modern times. 'Plasticity' still characterizes a process in which the substance-subject – God himself – 'sees (itself) coming'.

Although the *Aesthetics* seems at first glance to preclude the use of plasticity in characterizing the romantic ideal, its relevance is in fact decisively affirmed. Essential to the romantic ideal are those very elements that give the formula 'to see (what is) coming' its quasi-literal meaning:

> The inner being (of the Greek gods) does not look out of them as self-knowing inwardness in this spiritual concentration which the eye discloses. This light of the soul falls outside them and belongs to the spectator alone; when he looks at these shapes, soul cannot meet soul nor eye. But the God of romantic art appears seeing, self-knowing, inwardly subjective, and disclosing his inner being to man's inner being.[15]

The Christian God is for Hegel the primal instance of the speculative. In the Christian God the gaze is born, for he is the very exemplar of the reflecting eye. Here the formula 'to see (what is) coming' truly comes into its own, its structure expressing the self-movement of the divine hypotyposis. As God manifests himself to his own gaze, the specular presentation divides the divine self from itself, offering the divine the perspectival vision of its own self-presence.

The idea that God *must* see himself as/in a moment is, in Hegel's view, *the* speculative principle of Christianity. However, this expression can be read in several different ways. God sees himself only once, in one moment.

This moment is singular and unique, occurring only once, and in this uniqueness acquiring its absolute and exemplary value. God exemplifies himself, calling on humans to imitate this very unrepeatability. God envisages himself as a *moment*. Through his incarnation he is able to see himself in this momentary form, where 'moment' is understood as an adverb of time (as if answering to the question 'for how long?' 'A moment'). God 'transplants (*versetzt*) himself into the world of time', in the words of the *Encyclopedia*, and thus appears in time before himself. He sees himself *as* a moment, where 'moment' simply figures in apposition to 'himself' or '*ipse*'. (This is the speculative apposition because here God sees his '*ipse*' – his reflection – as a moment.) He sees himself as a moment in the sense that 'moment' functions as an attribute of himself (he sees his own moment as himself). Finally, the 'moment' of the Incarnation (an *Augenblick*, a moment of time) is a necessary *moment* (*Moment*, in the logical sense) of the development of the absolute Idea. Within God is revealed a speculative play of the divine with itself that translates his being into a multiplicity of moments, moments of time.

If God and man came together in an experience that turned history around, severing the world from itself in the twinkling of an eye, they are now united by a common fate: they see themselves pass by.

But how can this specular structure be understood in logical terms? Divine self-presence is interrupted, or rather opened up, by an inner distance. We can interpret this through the concept of the substance-subject and its movement, a movement in which God negates himself as immediate and substantial power, positing himself as other in the Incarnation which sees his birth as 'subject', before returning in the form of singularity to absolute substance.

The Greek concept of 'form-creation' (*Formtätigkeit*) assumes that self-determination is to be thought in terms of the becoming essential of the accident which finds sensuous representation in the 'exemplary individual'. On the other hand, the modern concept of plasticity seems to join itself with a concept of self-determination conceived as the becoming accidental of essence, the very development in which the fundamental significance of the Incarnation is expressed. *Kenosis* is the movement through which God, by positing Himself in exteriority and becoming alien to Himself, achieves the fulfilment of His being and becomes at once predicate and accident. Here we find the modern meaning of subjectivity, characterized by the relation the subject forms with itself through the mediation of its other.

Time Revealed/Revealed Time

The 'stages of life'

When such a relationship appears in the domain of the speculative, it does so as tributary to a more fundamental temporal determination, which we will henceforth call 'time which lies ahead' (*le temps que l'on a devant soi*). This definition will govern the alteration which occurs to the concepts of *finitude*, *phenomenon*, and *world*.

Hegel differentiates Revealed Religion from the previous figures of religion because it awakens in us the intuitive perception of the *necessity of coming-to-be* (*la nécessité du devenir*), the evolution or development (*devenir*) through which substance raises itself to the form of self-consciousness. Now this necessity could not be produced; it can only be something that 'offers itself' to intuition.[16]

> The self of existent spirit has . . . the form of complete immediacy; it is posited neither as something thought or imagined, nor as something produced, as is the case with the immediate Self in natural religion, and also in the religion of art; on the contrary, this God is sensuously and directly beheld as a Self, as an actual individual man. . . .[17]

The coming-to-be-human of the divine being is 'the simple content of absolute religion', a content sought by the previous configurations of religion but never achieved. What was missing was the manifest nature of this being, perhaps even the *time* of Revelation was missing: for isn't this another name for 'intuitively perceived necessity'? God revealing himself reveals a new modality of coming-to-be. A fundamental temporality, in its very concept irreducible to no other, arrives with the Incarnation.

In the *Lectures on the Philosophy of Religion*, Hegel speaks of 'the divine being in the stages of its life (its *Lebensverlauf*, or life-process)'.[18] It is not uncommon for commentators to translate *Lebensverlauf* as *curriculum vitae*. The temporality introduced in this *curriculum vitae* is none other than the temporality *posited* by the subject as *ahead of itself* (*vor-stellt*).

Now if Christ, as is claimed in the *Encyclopedia*, 'involves himself in time', this does not mean that he enters into a temporality which is already given, already there. The temporality he is involved with is a temporality whose very concept God has introduced. Indeed, He *creates* it. Without this correlative dimension of time, Revelation would not be a revelation. Without it, there would be no way of distinguishing the life of Christ from that of any other exemplary individual. By dying, Christ reveals to the Western world a new relation between spirit and finitude, in which death is the *limitation* (*borne*), the end of a linear series of moments linked one to the other.[19]

Finitude

At a number of points, Hegel will insist on the fundamental relation that holds between representational thought and the idea of this *limitation*, this negation inherent in determinate existence. In the *Science of Logic*, the philosopher distinguishes between 'limit' (*Grenze*) and 'limitation' (*Schranke*):

> In order that the limit which is in something as such should be a limitation (*Schranke*), something must at the same time in its own self transcend the limit. It must in its own self *be related to the limit as to something which is not.*[20]

Limitation establishes a relation between everything that falls within it and everything that is outside. What falls within the limitation is finite, but to the extent that the limitation is by definition other than itself, this constitutes at the same time 'the transcendence (*Hinausgehen*) of the finite, infinity'.[21] Limitation springs from the articulation of the same and the other, an articulation which representational thought is unable to understand as it really is, conceiving it only as a separation of two alien instances: the finite and the infinite, the sensible and the supersensible, time and eternity, and so on. Failing to understand that the negation of being is inherent in being as such, representational thinking conceives negation as something which comes upon being from somewhere else, as if it were something that *happens*, that is just found in front of oneself. It is in response to these considerations that Hegel, in the *Science of Logic*, connects his analysis of limitation to the analysis of the 'ought-to-be' (*das Sollen*). The 'ought-to-be' is a result of that operation of thinking which persists in dissociating the essential simultaneity of being and non-being, consigning them to a relation of succession: first being, then non-being, and so on unto infinity.

Christian revelation requires of thought that it tests out that time which is promise itself, that future which is 'pro-tension'. Representational thought is the result of this putting of time to the test. If the speculative meaning of Christianity surpasses this *limited* time and the metaphysics of subjectivity which follows from it, this is something we can only perceive after a *certain time*, after having finally achieved the extreme moment of *kenosis*. Only speculative philosophy has the potential to conceptualize the truth of time tested in the dimension of the limit. Without speculative thought this truth would never have been brought to light.

This 'test of time' consists in the act of divine alienation, an absolute negativity which exposes itself within a finite negativity. Thus the *curriculum vitae* of the divine appears as the articulation of two worlds, the sensible and the supersensible, the finite and the infinite. Christ is their living hypotyposis:

> The absolute content becomes manifest (something that to a certain degree happens through the symbolic or allegorical exposition of the content); this is presented as a sensible intuition (*Anschauung*), as the history of a particular individual, who lives within the forms

> of finitude, and this is the history of spirit made possible by an *mediating term* [emphasis ours], via a human existence which is common and external.[22]

This passage highlights the schematizing power of the divine subjectivity. Christ's life translates the union of the sensuous and the supersensuous into a sensible form, here making homogeneous two instances which seem at first heterogeneous. *Entäußerung*, the divine externalization, is the hypotyposis of the modern age, the translation of the senses as conceived by the era which looks ahead to time.

The phenomenon and the world

From the moment that this specific temporality appears, a new understanding of the concept of the *phenomenon* arises. If the sensible appearance of Christ 'does not constitute an inheritance and cannot be renovated' (*sie is kein Erbstück und ist keiner Erneuerung fähig*),[23] this is because 'sensible phenomena are by nature momentary'.[24] Henceforth, sensible presence can only be conceived as a sequential existence, the articulation of successive moments within a linear continuum. The Hegelian concept of 'interconnection' (*Zusammenhang*), which implies a certain understanding of *continuation*, is the Greek συμβαίνειν, *dialectical continuation* in its double sense, as 'logically following' and 'happening'.

From this point on, the play of appearing and disappearing is not guided teleologically by the move between act and potentiality. Instead it follows the linear movement of presence from sequence to sequence. It is as if an alternating current changing from one sensory moment to another has replaced the mode of appearing controlled by the different intensities of light frequencies.

'Appearance', declares Hegel in the *Lectures*, 'is being for the other'.[25] The phenomenon, *qua* moment, is always the manifestation of something other than itself. And this relation to alterity is a twofold one. The phenomenon, like the 'now' that passes by, implies a relation to a new 'now', to another instant. In so far as it designates an other, the phenomenon is immediacy which is at the same time mediated: it points towards the supersensible world just as it points to truth, the truth into which it is taken up. Hence, the phenomenon relates to alterity in both the sense of the 'other' moment and the 'other' world. This dual signification derives from the definition of phenomenal appearing, a movement that at once suddenly arises (*surgit*) and just as suddenly disappears (*disparaît*).

In the *Phenomenology of Spirit*, Hegel discovers a meaning of the concept 'dialectic' which no one before him had used, namely, the action of at once arising and disappearing. In his book *Die Enstehung der Hegelschen Dialektik*, Manfred Baum explains this innovation:

> When Hegel speaks of the 'dialectic of sense certainty' . . . he is thinking of the dialectic as a movement within which a determination establishes itself (*Zustandekommt*) and then again vanishes (*wieder vergeht*); . . . no one before him had associated this connotation with the term 'dialectic'.[26]

The concept of 'world', as it appears in §568 of the *Encyclopedia*, is continuous with this dialectical meaning of the phenomenon. In order to understand it, one must return to the exposition of the category of 'existence' in the *Encyclopedia Science of Logic*:

> Existence is the immediate unity of inward reflection and reflection-into-another. Therefore, it is the indeterminate multitude of existents as inwardly reflected, which are at the same time, and just as much, shining-into-another, or *relational*; and they form a *world* of interdependence and of an infinite connectedness of grounds with what is grounded.[27]

The phenomenal world appears as a totality of reciprocal relations which maintain among themselves all the determinations of existence. There is no substantial unity here as there was for the 'Greek world', rather a 'connectedness' (*Zusammenhang*) of atomistic particulars. In this we discern the logical form whose historical correspondence is the Roman world, the world where Christ first appeared.

The world is a necessary moment of the *appearance* of essence.[28] It is made up of existents and of phenomena which are immediately negated, since as finite things they carry their negation in themselves. The structure of the world which deploys and re-deploys this negativity, as a sequential procession of the appearing and the disappearing, is *the form of time.* Starting with this form and this structure it is possible to understand the Hegelian claim that representational thought gives to the elements of the speculative content the form of a 'series of *events* according to finite reflective categories'.[29]

Conclusion: the speculative conversation of theology and philosophy

The concepts which, for Hegel, structure the discussion of *Revealed Religion* – finitude, phenomenon, world – belong not to the vocabulary of theology but to philosophy. The indissoluble unity of a Christological and a critical vocabulary, so striking in Hegel, restores the two extreme and initially contradictory terms of the modern concept of subjectivity to each other, and by so doing, explains both: the emergence of Christianity and the emergence of a 'metaphysics of subjectivity'.

From the event of its origin to the advent of its philosophemes, from the suffering of God to the vacancy in the sphere of the transcendental, the subject *takes its time*. The subject extends, stretches out, and unwinds the linear continuum whose source and starting point is the subject as Ego, as 'I'. God gives to philosophic subjectivity its temporal form and, in his turn, receives from philosophy the melancholy echo and prolongation of his *kenosis*.

CONCLUSION

God and the transcendental imagination

The time of Revelation is a *specific* time. For Hegel it is Kantian philosophy that gives this time its most complete conceptual expression. Hegel characterizes divine subjectivity as a schematizing faculty, and in so doing he applies in his own way the Kantian problematic of *transcendental imagination*.

Feuerbach was not mistaken when he claimed, in *The Essence of Christianity*, that Christ 'is the unity of feeling and imagination',[1] and concluded: 'Only Christ is the *plastic personality* (*die plastische Persönlichkeit ist nur Christus*). Figure (*Gestalt*) belongs to personality. Figure is the effective reality of personality. Only Christ is the *personal* God (*Christus allein ist der persönliche Gott*).'[2]

Within speculative philosophy, the Hegelian interpretation of the transcendental imagination, which makes such affirmations possible, forms an unusually difficult crux. At once setting himself *for* and *against* Kant, Hegel in *Faith and Knowledge* identifies the transcendental imagination with the intuitive understanding, in other words, with the divine understanding, an identification that Kant rejects but which he makes possible. In this early text Hegel hails the great speculative scope of the Kantian discovery. We must

> reckon it to Kant's credit that . . . he assigned the idea of authentic apriority (*die Idee wahrhafter Apriorität*) to the form of the transcendental imagination and in so doing also established a beginning of the Idea of reason (*der Anfang der Idee der Vernunft*) within the understanding itself.[3]

Imagination is a 'truly speculative idea' when Kant is able to conceive it as originary and not as a 'middle term squeezed in between an existing absolute subject and an absolute existing world'.[4] Thought in this way, the imagination is a synthesis of the opposites, of subject and object, of *a priori–a posteriori*.

The difficulty arises from the fact that understanding (*Verstand*), 'the unity of a possible experience', and reason (*Vernunft*), 'resting on the understanding and its judgements', seem to be two separate instances. Because of this, reason does not enter into any constitutive relations with experience, nor with *a posteriori* knowledge. While Kant did posit the principle of the understanding, he retreated from 'the still purer Idea of an understanding (*Verstand*) which would be at the same time *a posteriori*, the idea of an absolute middle term formed by intuitive understanding'.[5] Even as he emphasized how intrinsically different this kind of understanding is from ours,

> Kant recognized that we are necessarily driven towards this Idea; and the Idea of an archetypal (*urbildlichen*), intuitive understanding (*Verstand*) is at bottom nothing else than this same *Idea of transcendental imagination*, which we have discussed above. For it is the activity of intuiting; and at the same time its inner unity is nothing else than the unity of the understanding itself, a category still immersed in the field of extension but which will become understanding and category to the extent that it separates itself out of extension. Transcendental imagination is itself intuitive understanding (*anschauender Verstand*).[6]

The radical thrust of Hegel's argument is at first sight a shock. How can we avoid seeing here a violent gesture aiming to conceal the Kantian restriction of thought to finitude? To assimilate transcendental imagination to intuitive understanding, isn't this a serious misunderstanding, the fruit of a systematic drive to invert oppositions and reverse their meaning?

Perhaps we could orient this interpretation differently. If God is conceptualized as transcendental imagination, this amounts to positing him as a *temporalizing instance*. Hegel never again puts into question the definition of transcendental imagination as an originary synthetic faculty which *a priori* makes possible the subject's relation to the sensuous entities encountered in experience. Indeed, quite to the contrary, he always stresses the importance and the speculative value of this discovery. Now could it be that this possibility of *seeing in advance* (*voir d'avance*) is exactly what opens up for the subject the horizon of a pure and absolute future? Could this be the very perspective inherent in the movement of 'to see (what is) coming'?

Imagination, which in Kant's famous definition is what permits 'something to be represented in its absence', initiates a determinate relation between being and non-being. The entity imagined is neither present nor absent. Transcendental imagination, presupposing the co-implication of being and non-being which governs every determination of presence, is specifically the modern modality of the originary unity of opposites. The concept of *ens imaginarium* supplies to the modern moment of plasticity that very category of a *relative non-being* which is its correlative.

Transcendental imagination is the *a priori* instance permitting the opening of a pure vision *of* and *in* the temporal. From this fact, Hegel, by conceiving the identity of God and transcendental imagination, inscribes time, and not lack, within God. The identification of divine subjectivity with the process of 'to see (what is) coming' is the very insurance, or even guarantee, of any future for God.

Heidegger's reading of the *Aufhebung* of Time

From the preceding analyses we can draw certain conclusions that give 'divine plasticity' its true meaning and force. The concept of plasticity is articulated in three ways: as process of self-determination, as sensuous translation of the spiritual or hypotyposis, and as one form of the relation consciousness enjoys with the speculative content. In the modern epoch, the subject 'sees itself coming' in the form of an 'other', and this encounter appears as an alienation (*Entäußerung*). Further, and in a different context, it is the Incarnation which represents in a modern mode spirit's translation into the sensuous. Ultimately, the relation between consciousness and the speculative content adopts the form of representation.

The modern moment of plasticity has thus exhaustively completed its route. Thought has passed all the way to the point of self-sacrifice,[7] and thus bestows on the divine *kenosis* its ultimate meaning. It is at this moment that the speculative content can and must 'ascend (*auferstehen*) to the most serene freedom of its shape'.[8] It is this moment which the *Encyclopedia* defines: 'it is only in proportion as the pure infinite form, the self-centered manifestation, throws off the one-sidedness of subjectivity . . . that it is the free thought which has the infinite characteristic at the same time as essential and actual content.'[9]

This event of the arrival of free thought is the advent of absolute knowledge and, accordingly, the transition from *Revealed Religion* to *Philosophy*. The last episode of the *Encyclopedia* corresponds to the chapter on 'Absolute Knowledge' in the *Phenomenology of Spirit*, and also to the chapter 'The Absolute Idea' in the *Science of Logic*.

Now is the moment to interrogate these conclusions. Does Absolute Knowledge mark the *end*, in the twofold sense of the term, of all events and any possible event? Must it be interpreted as the reduction of all temporality and the advent of the *parousia* of spirit?

These questions bring us to the crucial point of the analysis: the interpretation of the famous passage of the *Phenomenology* in the chapter on 'Absolute Knowledge':

> spirit necessarily appears in time, and it appears in time just as long as it has not *grasped* its pure concept, i.e. has not annulled time. It is the *outer*, intuited pure self which is *not grasped* by the Self, the merely intuited concept; when this latter grasps itself it sublates its

> time-form, comprehends this intuiting, and is a comprehended and comprehending intuiting. Time, therefore, appears as the destiny and necessity of spirit that is not yet complete within itself.[10]

Given our preceding analyses, it is impossible for us to accept without qualification Heidegger's interpretation of this passage, an interpretation that has become canonical. For Heidegger, the *Aufhebung* of time constitutes the Self's mastery of itself in its *parousia*, a mastery which implies the final banishment of all temporality and the advent of spirit's unchanging and indifferent present.

In opposition to this, by examining the modern concept of subjectivity, we can argue that the *Aufhebung* here does not apply to time in general but only to a *certain time*: the time that has just been characterized as 'time which lies ahead'. The claim that: 'In consciousness . . . the whole, though uncomprehended, is prior to the moments. Time is the concept itself that is *there* and which presents itself to consciousness as empty intuition',[11] would have made absolutely no sense in the Greek context. To understand it, one must presuppose the definition of time as a pure form of intuition, positing a certain relation the spirit bears both to the void (*vide*) and to alienation as the dispossession of the Self.[12] In its innermost possibility, this relation is tied to the emergence of Christianity.

Clearly, in the chapter on 'Absolute Knowledge', the time Hegel is talking about is the time of alienation: even more precisely, this time is *Entäußerung* itself.[13] As a form of temporality, the time analysed here represents a determinate epoch in the translation from spirit to the sensuous. It is, specifically, the moment in which the concept gives itself the shape of an existent thing, becoming in its turn the object of sensory intuition, of a momentary phenomenal presence. In the chapter on 'Absolute Knowledge' Hegel is not considering time in general but linear time, the time in which the subject 'sees itself as a passing moment'.

Furthermore, the *Entäußerung* is disclosed as linear time itself:

> The goal [of this succession] is the revelation of the depth (*die Offenbarung der Tiefe*) of spirit, and this is the *absolute concept*. This revelation is, therefore, the raising up (sublation, *Aufhebung*) of its depth, or its *extension* (*Ausdehnung*), the negativity of this withdrawn *'I'*, a negativity which is its externalization of its substance; and this revelation is also the concept's time, in that this externalization (*Entäußerung*) is in its own self externalized (*diese Entäußerung an ihr selbst entäußert*), and just as it is in its extension, so it is equally in its depth, in the self.[14]

Time is, therefore, imagined here simply as linear succession, and this is confirmed by another passage:

> The realm of spirits which is formed in this way in the outer world constitutes a succession in time (*eine Aufeinanderfolge*) in which one spirit relieved another of its charge and each took over the empire of the world (*Reich der Welt*) from its predecessor.[15]

The time of this 'gallery of images' (*Galerie von Bilden*) is that of a sequence understood as a *connection* (*Zusammenhang*), no longer as συμβαίνειν.

Although it cannot be ignored, the reading of Hegel proposed by Heidegger at the end of *Being and Time* leaves us perplexed on one essential point: when asserting that Hegel brings to its ultimate conclusion the 'ordinary (or vulgar) understanding of time' which has dominated the fate of Western metaphysics, doesn't Heidegger come to practise just what he denounces? Is he not led to level down the time of the dialectic in order to prove that dialectical time is a levelled down time? On the Hegelian conception of time, Heidegger writes:

> The most empty, formal-ontological and formal-apophantical abstraction into which space and time are externalized (*in die Geist und Zeit entäußert werden*) makes possible a kinship of the two. But since, at the same time, time is yet conceived in the sense of world time that has been absolutely levelled down, so that its provenance thus remains completely covered over, it simply confronts spirit as something objectively present. For this reason spirit *must first* fall 'into time'. It remains obscure what indeed is signified ontologically by this 'falling' and the 'actualization' of spirit that has power over time and really 'exists' outside of it.[16]

The problem posed by this way of reading is that it fails to make explicit the temporality of alienation. Alienation is allowed to operate as an atemporal category, while it is clear that Hegel only uses the concept of *Entäußerung* to characterize a process intrinsic and unique to the modern epoch of subjectivity. If there is no place in Hegel for the idea of a 'time *in* the world', there is, on the other hand, an idea of the *time of the world*, a concept that is specifically Christian. One may well complain of Heidegger that he inquires into neither the provenance nor the exact ontological significance of the Hegelian *Entäußerung*.

God at the crossroads of antiquity and modernity

To give sustenance to these claims, we must show how, for Hegel, the same question is posed in two different and separate times. Whether the issue is the idea of *kenosis*, or the interpretation of the Aristotelian Prime Mover, one and the same project is preoccupying Hegel, that of *plasticity*, or, to put it another way, the 'non-impassivity' of the subject. The philosopher's insistence on the unity of πάσχειν and ἐνεργεῖν in Aristotle, just like his analysis of the movement of *Entäußerung* in the case of the God of Revelation, turns on the same project: how to characterize the subject as a structure of anticipation, and, by the same token, a structure of temporalization.

In its very structure, the *Encyclopedia Philosophy of Spirit* explicitly demonstrates that God moves in a twofold way towards himself, *both* because it is in him that the movement of the substance-subject is accomplished, *and* to the extent that θεός constitutes the final term of this development, as confirmed in the final citation of the *Encyclopedia*. Hegel's God, a synthesis of the Christian God and the Aristotelian God, is situated at *the crossroads of time*.

The dialectical sublation of a specific temporal form, as presented in the chapter on Absolute Knowledge, would not be possible (who would decide and why?) if teleological time – the circular unrolling of δύναμις and ἐνέργεια – did not lie behind it. The criterion of completion assumed by modernity must come, in fact, from a time which is not modernity – from the time of teleological fulfilment, within which the end is identical with the beginning. For this is a time which can dismiss that other time, the one which does not lie ahead. At the very moment when we believed time had been dismissed, the two times meet and unite.

Part III

HEGEL ON THE PHILOSOPHER OR, TWO FORMS OF THE FALL

INTRODUCTION

Absolute Knowledge and the donation of form

For Hegel, the unfolding of the substance-subject in its logical and chronological modes is now complete. The *substance*-subject, in which the accident becomes essential, and the substance-*subject*, in which essence becomes accidental, merge as one in the unity of absolute knowledge. On the level of history, the advent of Absolute Knowledge corresponds to the *end of history*. As Bernard Bourgeois asserts,

> In substance, Hegel is saying: '*History, in principle, is over*.' Of course things will continue to happen, but they will not relate to the universal meaning of human life: in this area, nothing new or fundamentally important will be said.[1]

Now the end of history – whatever may be its ultimate meaning (it is not our intention to clear this up once and for all) – does not mark the end of all sudden and new appearances. The moment of Absolute Knowledge only causes the dialectical suppression of one *certain time*, one specific temporality. From this moment on, far from closing all horizons, Absolute Knowledge announces in fact a new temporality, one born from the synthesis of two temporalities, the Greek and the Christian. The moment which dialectically gives rise to the two temporalities marks the emergence of a new era of *plasticity* in which subjectivity gives itself the form which at the same time it receives. This event is presented in the last section of the *Philosophy of Spirit*, 'Philosophy'.

The exposition of the religious moment of spirit ended with a Remark announcing the movement whereby 'the pure infinite form (*die reine unendliche Form*) . . . throws off the one-sidedness of subjectivity (*die Einseitigkeit des Subjektiven . . . ablegt*)'.[2] Philosophy is the movement taken by this form. In the beginning of the new section, *Philosophy*, the same theme is repeated, and philosophy is presented as 'the liberation (*Befreiung*) from the one-sidedness of the forms and elevation of them into the absolute form'.[3]

This 'absolute form', essentially the form of the System itself, has not lost its plastic power as if it could, henceforth, no longer *form* anything. On the contrary: this 'elevation' and 'liberation' of philosophy from the representational form constitutes an original and unprecedented process of temporalization. It is not *stasis* but *metamorphosis* that characterizes Absolute Knowledge. Consequently it forms and transforms individuals, fashioning their ways of waiting for and expecting the future.

The transition from the predicative to the speculative

Such a knowledge has a transformative power akin to the *transition* which, in Hegel's terms, changes the *predicative proposition* into a *speculative proposition.* Paradoxically, this transition emerges from a retrospective movement in which the achieved substance-subject is reflected. Now the task falls to subjectivity to produce the form of its self-knowledge, once the movement of its self-determination has been completed.

The form in question grows out of subjectivity's reflexive return to the very form of determination, the form of predication, this being the act of attributing predicates to a substance.

In the Preface to the *Phenomenology of Spirit*, Hegel addresses this point: 'The sublation (*Aufhebung*) of the form of the proposition must not happen only in an *immediate* manner, through the mere content of the proposition. On the contrary, this opposite movement must find explicit expression (*muß ausgesprochen werden*).'[4]

But this leaves several questions that need to be asked: what is meant by the dialectical suppression of one form by another? why it is necessary for this suppression to be reversed as well? By the end of this inquiry, the production of a new type of discursivity will be revealed as the plastic operation *par excellence*, as powerful as the force of dynamite,[5] exploding whole centuries of discourse.

The itinerary

The meaning of this operation can be discovered in four successive stages. The first will involve a presentation of the section *Philosophy* as the context and framework in which the announcement of the 'absolute form' is situated. In the case of the second stage, what matters is the dialectical character as process, expressed through the reduplication of the negative and its capacity to transform itself. The meaning of the absolute synthesis, or the System itself, will be the object in the third stage. Finally, there remains the project of sketching the figure of the 'speculative thinker', of fashioning in some way this 'plastic individuality' for a new time and a new age.

9

PRESENTATION OF *PHILOSOPHY*

Philosophy, when it appears in its own moment, is presented as a conclusion. Philosophy, Hegel declares, 'seizes, at the close, its own concept', and '*looks back* (*Zurücksehen*) on its own knowledge'.[1]

The retroactive gaze, turning backward, brings about an inversion into the logical order of the exposition, here obeying the order of the triad: judgement, concept, syllogism. The two first paragraphs of the section of the *Encyclopedia Philosophy of Spirit*[2] recall that philosophy only differs from art and religion because of its *form*, and that 'the whole question turns entirely on the difference of the forms (*Formen*) of speculative thought from the forms of mental representation and reflecting intellect'.[3] Hegel begins the exposition of this section by examining this difference of form which philosophy has allowed to be its necessary split and defining division:

> it is the whole cycle of philosophy (*der ganze Verlauf der Philosophie*), and of logic in particular, which has not merely taught and made known this difference, but also criticized it, or rather has let its nature develop and judge itself by these very categories.[4]

The primacy and the necessity of the scission explains the fact that the logical moment of *judgement* appears first and governs the exposition.

Leaving behind the courtroom and the trial, philosophy returns to its own domain in the element of the *concept*: '(the) concept of philosophy is the self-thinking idea'.[5] It thus returns to its own beginning. Such a beginning, because it is the result of a return, is no longer immediate. The concept has returned to itself through the movement of its actual differentiation explicitly displayed in the three *syllogisms* which terminate this section.[6] These syllogisms retrospectively explain the entire speculative cycle of the *Encyclopedia* as a whole: Logic, Nature, Spirit. The retrospective look that philosophy gives itself allows it to become liberated from the 'one-sidedness of forms' and to establish the speculative content as a System, or 'absolute form'.

In order to grasp as precisely as possible the organic link which unifies these three moments of the exposition, conferring on the 'absolute form' its *plastic* force, we will keep, for the duration of this chapter, the traditional order: concept, judgement, syllogism.

The concept of Philosophy: Recovering its element[7]

The concept, 'universality approved and certified (*bewährte*) in concrete content as in actuality', occupies a mediating position between the judgement and the syllogism. Hegel adds: 'In this way science has gone back to its beginning: its *result* is the logical system. . . .'[8] The self-return of the concept completes what the *Science of Logic* calls its 'immanent deduction (*immanente Deduktion*)'.[9]

The identity of the abstract logical idea and the concrete knowledge of absolute spirit frees science of its immediate presuppositions and provides the proof for them.[10]

Philosophy's judgement: Form and the speculative content – art, religion, philosophy[11]

The moment of the judgement causes a split between form and speculative content, a split to which art and religion are still bound. Between the three moments of absolute spirit – art, religion and philosophy – the difference is not of content but of form, and this has two consequences. First, the spiritual in-formation, the labour in which speculative content gives itself its form, does not have the same nature or the same outcome in all three moments. To this extent, as a second consequence, the relationship enjoyed by spirit or by individual consciousness to these modalities of 'in-formation' is no longer uniform, and in its turn is differentiated into *figuration, representation*, and *conceptual thought*.[12]

Art, religion and philosophy, as Hegel puts it in the *Science of Logic*, are the three *modes* or *fashionings* of the absolute idea, or better, the hypotyposes of the spiritual:

> Nature and spirit are in general different modes (*Weisen*) of presenting its *existence*; art and religion its different modes of apprehending itself and giving itself an adequate existence; philosophy has the same content and the same end as art and religion.[13]

It is easy to understand the way art is able to confer a sensible form on the spiritual content: by imaging it and symbolizing it, art makes it accessible to immediate intuition. As for religion, we have seen that it is a *representation* of the spiritual content, which should not be confused with the figurative process proper to art. Religious art is the sensuous basis of religious representation. But the aim of representation is to elevate its sensuous content from a simple intuition to the form of *memory*. Representation is a *temporal* forming of the speculative content which renders it capable of being grasped, formally, in its *moments*. Further, this means that religion can be defined as a *sequential* comprehension of the speculative content. It introduces a break and a continuation into the undivided totality of intuition.[14]

Although the manner varies, the speculative element remains opposed to its form for both art and religion. In its extension, it is split between the exteriority of form (the material and sensuous presence of the work of art; the moment-by-moment and successive intuition that belongs to religion) and the interiority of its spiritual comprehension (reverence in front of the work, the interiorization of the death of Christ through the memory of the cultic community). Consequently, art and religion remain tributary to a partition between the inward, or 'subjective retreat into the self (*subjektives Insichgehen*)', and the outward, or 'subjective identification with the object (*subjektive Hinbewegung*)'.[15]

In respect of this moment critical to itself, what is philosophy's own way of proceeding?

> Philosophy thus characterizes itself as a cognition of the necessity in the *content* of the absolute representation (*absolute Vorstellung*), as also of the necessity in the two *forms* (*Formen*) – *on the one hand*, immediate intuition and its poetry, and the objective and external *revelation* presupposed by representation – *on the other hand*. . . . This cognition is thus the *recognition* of this content and its form; it is the *liberation* from the one-sidedness of the forms, elevation of them into the absolute form, which determines itself to content, remains identical to it, and is in that the cognition of that essential and actual necessity.[16]

Philosophical content is constructed out of thought determinations or 'forms of thought' (*Denkformen*).[17] Neither figuration nor representation can translate such a content: image or symbol have nothing to offer it. Nor can it be articulated sequentially, in 'separate spheres'. Hegel devotes a long Remark to the 'accusations of atheism' brought against philosophy, accusations based on two points. The first emphasizes the fact that philosophy never makes its content visible, failing to present anything at all in the way of material to intuition or representation. Moreover, philosophy claims to transcend the sphere which is intrinsically religious by virtue of the 'pure labor of the concept': it devotes itself to the concept alone and only here does it find its genuine deployment.[18]

Religion depends on the 'conviction that the phenomenal appearance has a *relation* to the essence, the finite to the infinite [God]'. Now 'this relation (is) called *incomprehensible* by the agnostic. The conclusion (*Am Schlusse*) of philosophy is not the place, even in a general exoteric discussion, to waste a word on what it means to "*conceptualize*".'[19]

To grasp the relation between appearance and essence we must do away with any *separation* between the terms: 'Philosophy has to do with unity in general'. Yet why is this power of synthesis, definitive of philosophy itself, so misunderstood? Why is it on this point that 'the whole difficulty of the matter lies'?[20]

Earlier in the section, Hegel had presented the points essential to answering this question:

> It is on the ground of form that philosophy has been reproached and accused by the religious party; just as, conversely, its speculative content has brought the same charges upon it from a self-styled philosophy – and from a pitiless orthodoxy. It had *too little* of God in it for the former; *too much* for the latter.[21]

This dual reproach collapses into one, despite the contradictory character of the grievances that motivate it. These come from a misunderstanding of the conceptual form intrinsic to philosophy. The 'religious party' sees in this philosophic form the result of an excessive faith in reason which simply and utterly dismisses faith in God: God is made intelligible, and theology expires in philosophy. The 'philosophical party', a branch of Kantian critique, reproaches speculative thought for its excessive faith in reason which, denying any limits to reason, challenges the separation between the sensuous and the supersensuous, and thus spells the ruin of philosophy: God is made intelligible, and philosophy expires as theology. In both examples, the concept is more or less worshipped on its own account; paradoxically, the charges of atheism and pantheism reunite: 'The charge of *atheism*, which used often to be brought against philosophy (that it has *too little* of God), has grown rare: the more widespread grows the charge of *pantheism*, that it has *too much* of Him.'[22]

All the 'difficulty of the matter' comes from this: philosophy does not have its own object. It is on this account that it can neither exist in its own domain, nor in the form of artistic intuition, nor in the form of representation. Philosophy is unable to put its own content *in front* of itself, to bring itself face to face with its own content.

Nevertheless, in so far as it is a dialectical reconciliation of content and form, philosophy remains an activity of 'form-donation': it is, moreover, the 'Dasein adequate to' spirit. To say this is to say that philosophy is a *form* which, while it is neither intuitable nor representable, remains all the same something that can be sensed. 'Absolute form' enjoys a fundamental relationship to sensibility. For how could one be a philosopher without being *affected* by the philosophical content? Yet there is still the problem of understanding this *conceptual sensibility*. At this difficult juncture we are led to the elucidation of philosophy's own plasticity, the sensuous translation of the labour of the concept, its material and its temporality.

The philosophical syllogism: reflecting nature[23]

As Hegel will show in the syllogistic moment of philosophy, this plastic activity sets into motion the three following moments: logic (pure thought), nature (sensuous existence), and spirit (the synthesis of both).

In the *Science of Logic*, during the exposition of the absolute Idea, Hegel writes:

> The *logical aspect* of the absolute Idea may also be called a *mode* of it; but whereas *mode* signifies a *particular* kind, a *determination* of form, the logical aspect, on the contrary, is the universal mode in which all particular modes are sublated and enfolded. The logical Idea is the Idea itself in its pure essence, the Idea enclosed in simple identity within its concept prior to its *immediate reflection* in a form-determination.[24]

The logical element is the primal environment of thought, its *genre*. Genre, like animal genus or race, is also a process of individuation. Thought, like life, possesses the power of determining and embodying itself. Here nature has its moment in the economy of the absolute Idea. The Idea leaves itself behind and is 'projected into the *externality* of existence'.[25] This 'projection' into externality is its test by contingency, the idea's encounter with absolute alterity and finitude.

Spirit is the syllogistic instance that gathers together logical abstraction and natural contingency, categorial and sensuous forms. The syllogisms making up absolute spirit in its philosophical moment demonstrate how spirit's life takes on different positions in relation to two other lives, logical life and natural life.

The first syllogism: Logic–Nature–Spirit. Apprenticeship

The first syllogism

> is based on the *logical* system as starting-point, with nature for the middle term which couples (*zusammenschließt*) *spirit* with it. Logic becomes nature, and nature spirit.[26]

The first syllogism corresponds to the philosophical education of spirit: that is, the passage from the pure idealities of abstract thought to real spiritual life. Initially, spirit 'confronts life as its other'; contingency and the pure externality of existence immediately contradict the necessity that marks thought-determinations. A philosophical education is a matter of overcoming this split and understanding that, for the speculative to be effective, the spiritual must be incorporated into a sensuous existence. Without this incorporation, logical life remains an abstraction. It is a requirement of the philosophical apprenticeship that logical categories be translated into the contingent determinations of 'there-being (*l'être-là*)', and vice versa.

Second syllogism: Nature–Spirit–Logic. Science appears

The 'standpoint' of the second syllogism is

> spirit itself, which – as the mediating agent in the process – *presupposes nature* and couples it with the logical principle. It is the syllogism where spirit *reflects* on itself in the Idea; philosophy appears as a subjective *cognition*, of which liberty is the aim, and which is itself the way to produce it.[27]

Spirit, in this second of the syllogisms, finds itself midway between nature and logic. It thus assumes a role of mediator between the domain of sensory contingency and the pure essentialities of thought: 'It is the syllogism where spirit reflects on itself in the Idea.'[28] In the syllogism of reflection, universality is the 'negative of the beginning, or what was first, now posited in its *determinacy*; it is . . . the *relation* of distinct terms, or *the moment of reflection*.'[29]

For Hegel, this syllogism marks the appearance (*Erscheinung*) of science as a 'subjective *cognition* (*connaissance*) of which liberty is the aim, and which is itself the way to produce it'.[30] Its correlative is the intellectual position reached by the philosopher who, having arrived at the end of his process of formation, now experiences the sheer liberty of thinking for himself.

In the case of this syllogism, how are we to understand the way in which the starting point (where thought assumes sensuous and determinate being) is connected to the middle-term (this appearance of a subjective cognition)? When we turn to the second chapter of the section 'Idea' in the *Science of Logic*, 'The Idea of Cognition', philosophy is specifically envisaged as 'cognition' (*Erkennen*). The 'reality of the concept', at this point in its development,

> is the *form* of its determinate being, and the point of interest is the determination of this form; on this determination rests the difference between what the concept is *in itself* or as *subjective*, and what it is when submerged in objectivity. . . .[31]

On the basis of this passage, we can respond to the previous question. Spirit emerged in the second syllogism as thought that has become particularized, active in its own material and determinate being, its individuality. Hence it is able to reflect its own schematizing operation. Occupying the intermediate position between nature (or objectivity) and logic (or subjectivity), spirit appears as the originary synthetic unity of apperception, the liberty of the 'I think': '*Thinking*, *spirit*, *self-consciousness*, are determinations of the Idea where it has itself for object, and its determinate being (*Dasein*), that is, the determinateness of its being, is its own difference from itself.'[32]

The movement of spirit rendered sensuous, as conceived historically before the time of Hegel, is set forth in the second syllogism of *Philosophy*. If 'incarnation' – the embodying of the spiritual – can be said to have a fate (*destin*), this fate was formed by the two temporal regimes of plasticity discussed earlier. 'Fashioning a second nature' and the 'turn of the double nature' defined two different modalities of mediation between category and sensibility, between logic and nature, one in the classical and one in the modern age. The first epoch borrowed its concept of 'hypotyposis' from the world of art: for it, spiritual individuality was created as a statue is made. The second epoch is the heir of a Christological category – the alienation of God – which it draws on to conceptualize the relation between subjectivity and its other term, the phenomenal world.

For Hegel, then, these two modalities of spirit's sensuous expression, as they have been known in the history of philosophy, have still failed to give spirit its 'own and proper determinate being'. Pure thought remains 'over against' its world, confronting the 'object' it is supposed to figure or represent.

Third syllogism: Spirit–Logic–Nature. The detachment of the ideal

The dialectical sublation of this division is completed in the third syllogism. Its presupposition is nature; its extreme term, spirit. Logic occupies the medial position between these two terms:

> The third syllogism is the Idea of philosophy, which has *self-knowing reason*, the absolutely universal, for its *middle term*: a middle, which divides itself into spirit and nature, making the former its presupposition, as process of the Idea's subjective activity, and the latter its universal extreme, as process of the objectively and implicitly existing Idea.[33]

The moment of 'logic' is the concept as a return to Self out of the judgement, a judgement formed by the division between the subjectivity of the

'I think' (spirit) and objectivity (nature). While for the moment we will defer a proper analysis of this syllogism,[34] it marks the emergence of speculative philosophy itself. In the form of speculation, thought will renounce the rigidity of its position; it will reconcile the fixed terms of that division which it had not been able to overcome. Returning to itself after the ordeal of its judicative partition, the concept freely opens itself to nature and to natural existence.

10

THE DIALECTICAL SIMPLIFICATION

Towards a plastic conception of the *Aufhebung*

Absolute Knowledge: coup de force or bad infinite?

Even during Hegel's lifetime, the aridity of these three syllogisms of *Philosophy* was sharply criticized. In the 1827 edition of the *Encyclopedia* they were suppressed by Hegel, yet he reintroduced them in the final edition of 1830. Even if we cannot know why he made those decisions, it is possible to imagine that, for once, Hegel was overwhelmed by the attacks on his work.

'The publication of the second edition of the *Encyclopedia*', Bernard Bourgeois explains, 'provoked criticisms which, as Hegel himself said, "were indeed all too base".'[1] During his lifetime, Hegel came up against a great deal of incomprehension from readers who rejected 'the allover *quietism* of the system, which disowns the very mobility of the method at work in its position'.[2] Already, then, the question had been raised of how the mobility and the dynamism of the dialectical processuality could be so brutally suspended and put to rest by this final intervention of Absolute Knowledge.

On this point, one of Hegel's readers, C. H. Weiße, responded in a particularly eloquent letter. If, Weiße puts it,

> the dialectical transition from a concept to its negation – not to any kind of negation but rather to the very negation of itself – is at the same time a positing, or rather more precisely, a deepening into itself of the concept in transition,

then the concept of philosophy must itself be dialectically sublated by a higher instance. Weiße continues his criticism in these terms:

> This demand for a growth by dialectical negativity always and ever occurs to me. It has seemed to me that it could in no way be

> put aside by the supposition of a closed circle in which what is most elevated returns to the beginning *without* growing by this fact.[3]

Of course one can unceremoniously dismiss Weiße's objections by pointing out that the claim that the speculative development undergoes a gradual 'growth' confuses dialectic with the bad infinite progression. However, if we take this tack, it would only lead to a second question, of central importance to any reader of Hegel: Isn't a bad infinite the outcome of the process of dialectical sublation? Isn't the *Aufhebung* subject to an incessant activity that cancels itself at every instant it posits itself? If it is true that Absolute Knowledge does necessarily mark a stopping point in the speculative development, why couldn't this *pause* be the unjustifiable but real result of a forceful intervention?

Heidegger raises these same problems in his own distinctive manner:

> The question which immediately comes to mind is . . . to know if and how the dialectical movement itself can be prevented from falling back under the domination of finitude – finitude in the shape of false infinity, or endlessness (*Endlosigkeit*). Several responses, in particular the suggestion of circularity, simply stumble into this difficulty rather than resolving it. In addition, it is futile to invoke from the outside the sheer grandeur of the Absolute. Nor is the point to look around for some stopper which the false infinite might chance to run across.[4]

If we cannot establish exactly how the *conclusive* role of Absolute Knowledge is neither a question of chance nor an arbitrary decision, then the very credibility of Hegel's philosophy – its *future* – will immediately be put into question.

Preservations and suppressions

The clarification we need requires in the first instance that we examine how the *Aufhebung* functions. Everyone is familiar with the debates over how to find a French equivalent for the substantive *Aufhebung* and the verb *aufheben*. Readers will have noted that Derrida's suggestion of 'relève' and 'relever' (sublation and sublate) have been adopted here.[5] We will not spend any more time defending this choice as the questions of translation are not (or have ceased to be) the most urgent. Every translator tries to convey the twofold sense of *aufheben*: to suppress and to preserve. But – and this in our opinion is the most important question – why has no translator or interpreter of Hegel dreamt of applying to the terms *aufheben* and *Aufhebung* the very meanings for which they stand?

The efficacy of the dialectical logic assumes that the *Aufhebung* must be itself susceptible to a dual suppression–preservation; it must be itself susceptible to transformation. The *Aufhebung* evolves, as a term, within the same process which it regulates and measures. If one considers this process as a logical movement for which Hegel has already fixed and determined the direction, then there is no way to escape from the vicious circle. Indeed, if 'sublation' is always the sublation of something other than itself, then it would remain always something *relative*: then we would have to admit that absolute knowledge is an intervention by force which arbitrarily suspends the bad infinity of relation.

In actual fact, and in the entire course of spirit's development, there is no perfect identity between preservation and suppression; they are neither unchangeable nor undifferentiated. What must be demonstrated is the fact that Hegel does indeed restore the essential dialectical performativity of the *aufheben* and *Aufhebung*, that he in effect 'sublates' *aufheben* into *aufheben*, *Aufhebung* into *Aufhebung*. The possibility of a new reading of Absolute Knowledge emerges from this truly plastic operation.

Past and Future of the Aufhebung

In the earlier discussions concerning the temporalizing synthesis in Hegel, with its two moments, the Greek and the modern, we offered an interpretation that relies on this plastic interpretation of the *Aufhebung*. The purpose of these discussions – of Aristotle on the originary unity of πάσχειν and ἐνεργεῖν, of Kant on the *a priori* unity of opposites in the transcendental imagination – was to present these two synthetic instances as themselves structures that already co-imply presence and nothingness: in other words, as already structurally the forms of the *Aufhebung*.

Coexisting in ἕξις are στέρησις (privation) and σωτηρία (preservation). Aren't these two terms a match in all possible respects for the terms of the *Aufhebung*? And, in another context, if transcendental imagination creates the possibility for 'any relation between being and non-being', isn't this capacity also a power akin to 'sublation' (*Aufhebung*)? The imaginary entity, because of its negativity, is neither present nor absent, and it can be considered a being in which presence is at once suppressed and preserved.

If we are always to stigmatize the *Aufhebung* as an idiosyncrasy – the 'tic' in Hegel's thought – aren't we forgetting that this structure has always been at work in the history of philosophy? Aren't we forgetting that the *Aufhebung* itself has a *history*, brought together and elaborated by Hegel? In its movement, the dialectical sublation is not a frozen process whose modalities are fixed once and for all, remaining detached and separate from everything it sets into motion. Quite the contrary: reintegrated and synthesized in this process are the two synthetic instances already mentioned, the two instances of 'sublation' (*instances relevantes*). These represent, on the one hand, the Aristotelian originary unity of πάσχειν and ἐνεϱγεῖν – where ἕξις plays the mediating role – and, on the other hand, the Kantian originary synthetic unity of apperception, where the transcendental imagination plays the role of mediator. The power of the dialectical process presupposes the combined operation of two factors conditioned by negativity, these being the two modalities of suppression and preservation: they are the *virtual* and the *imaginary*, both together forming the *energy of the negative*.

In the philosophy of Hegel, the dual meaning of *Aufhebung* as suppression and preservation must itself be understood as having a double meaning, one that mobilizes not only the two meanings of *suppression* but also the two meanings of *preservation*. Dialectical sublation proceeds through a movement whereby, at one and the same time, it *contracts* and *alienates* the material on which it acts. There are two movements here which our analysis must take the time to distinguish in their specific features, as the dynamic of the *Aufhebung* consists in its power to synthesize and to relate these same two movements.

Each moment of the development of spirit is itself an ἕξις. On their own, the figures of spirit's past history constitute a *habitus*, a way of being or permanent disposition whose virtual existence remains always ready to be reactualized. Consequently, it can be argued that dialectical processuality behaves in the manner of speculative habit: permitting spirit to possess its own past moments, granting spirit's development a pedagogical dimension.

Spirit's bygone moments, which form its *habitus*, present themselves by the same token as its 'exteriorizations' (*Äußerungen*).[6] Out of necessity, spirit projects itself into the outside, an alienation which enables the opposite movement by which each of its moments become interiorized, and this 'interiorization' is also seen to be an essential process of the speculative pedagogy. Hence, every one of spirit's shapes will appear retroactively, as an exteriorization which is reinteriorized, making each a kind of imaginary presence, a spectral mode of being their past selves. In this sense, the *Aufhebung* can be interpreted as the labour of speculative mourning.[7]

The tendencies of simplification

But how are we to prove the definition just given of the *Aufhebung*'s synthetic operation? As Hegel would argue, to find the process manifesting the dual implication – sublation via contraction and sublation via alienation – we should look to the process of *simplification* (*Vereinfachung*). Simplification is at work throughout the development of spirit. For as the speculative content is unfolded, it moves towards simplifying itself, which is to say, it abbreviates and accelerates itself. Of prime importance to Hegel in his logic and ontology, simplification is the essence and aim of speculative teleology. The simplifying speculative *telos* requires as its precondition that cooperative play of habit and alienation.

Conceptual abbreviation

In a passage from the Preface to the *Phenomenology of Spirit*, Hegel, trying to define philosophical education as it exists in his day, declares:

> The manner of study in ancient times differed from that of the modern age in that the former was the proper and complete formation (*Durchbildung*) of the natural consciousness. Putting itself to the test at every point of its determinate being, and philosophizing about everything it came across, the individual made itself into a universality that was active through and through. In modern times, however, the individual finds the abstract form ready-made (*vorbereitet*); the effort to grasp and appropriate it is more . . . the truncated (*abgeschnitetne*) generation of the universal than it is the emergence of the latter from the concrete variety of determinate being.[8]

Simplification operates through this 'abstract form' which the individual finds 'ready made' and 'truncated'. The verb *abschneiden* means on the one hand to cut, to slice, to segment; on the other hand, to reduce or shorten. As a process simplification is the result of an activity of self-abbreviation.

Each moment of spirit emerges as an original and concrete configuration, a world and a substantial totality: in these, the life of thought is not separable from a life that is more elemental and simple. The 'actual (*wirklich*) life' of spirit's moments is constituted by 'the earth and the elements which constituted their substance, the climate which gave them their peculiar character'.[9] In each particular moment, the different forms of representation or conceptions appropriate to it – whether religious, philosophical or aesthetic – get their meaning and strength from this original soil. The life that is elemental and primal is necessarily doomed to decline: the substantial wealth of an epoch, as it inscribes itself in memory's register, will vanish, contracting into an abstract determination. Thus, the substantial atmosphere of ancient Greece is lost for all time; thus we read Plato and Aristotle, or gaze at the statues and works of art of Greece, under the final shadow of a vanished sun. Hegel writes to this effect in a celebrated passage:

> The statues are now only stones from which the living soul has flown, just as the hymns are words from which belief has gone. The tables of the gods provide no spiritual food and drink, and in his games and festivals man no longer recovers the joyous consciousness of his unity with the divine. The works of the Muse now lack the power of the spirit, for the spirit has gained its certainty of self from the crushing of gods and men. They have become what they are to us now – beautiful fruit already picked from the tree, which a friendly Fate (*ein freundliches Schicksal*) has offered us, as a young girl might set the fruit before us.[10]

The 'young girl', the 'spirit of the Fate that presents us with these works of art',[11] is an allegory of the principle of spiritual simplification. It is a principle which can appear simultaneously as a power of *thanatos*, effacing primal life, and as a power of assemblage, abbreviating what it collects, giving it the form of a logical essence.

In the *Lectures on the Philosophy of History*, Hegel argues that 'Thought ... is the most trenchant epitomist (*der mächigste Epitomator*).'[12] Events that traverse 'long periods of time' end up 'foreshortened in abstractions (*mit Abstraktionen abkürzen*)': in other words, as pure *thought-determinations.*[13] At the level of generality, everything essential to thought is an abbreviation:

> For what a host of particulars of outer existence and actions is embraced by a conception – battle, war, nation, ocean, or animal, for example. And in the conception of God or of love there is epitomized in the *simplicity* of such idealizing an infinite host of ideas, actions, states, etc.![14]

From all this, an initial definition of the principle of simplification can be extracted: it merges with the labour of the concept itself in the way it brings about 'the immeasurable abbreviation of the multitudes of particular things (*die unermeßliche Abbreviatur gegen die Einzelheit der Dinge*)'.[15]

The blunt tip of meaning

It is understanding which abstracts the universal meaning from the rich variety of the sensuous. Yet despite the initial impression it gives, abstraction does not unambiguously mean that something is dying, for it can appear just as strongly as a force of animation, of life. As the *Science of Logic* argues:

> The understanding, through the form of abstract universality, does give them, so to speak, a *rigidity* (*Härte*) of being such as they do not possess in the qualitative sphere and in the sphere of reflection; but at the same time through this simplification (*durch diese Vereinfachung*) it *spiritually animates* (*begeistert*) them and so sharpens them.[16]

Henceforth the determinations of thought will be 'points'.[17]

Yet what does this 'rigidity' mean for Hegel? 'Rigidity of being' could simply mean 'consistency of being' (*Halt*), at once something firm, consequential, resistant (as, for example, in 'resistance to time', as time is more resistant than any and all phenomena). Rigidity represents the dialectical emergence of a quality that has absorbed its phenomenal quality. In thought's determination a hardness of heart follows, for the concept's effect will not be as 'sensitive' as that produced by the phenomenon. Indeed the subject is much less implicated in its relation to the 'point' – the determination – than it was in its relation to the innumerable sensuous 'traits' of the phenomenon. Paradoxically, the 'sting' of that 'point' can leave the living thing insensible. But, at another level, it is the point which makes it possible to follow the phenomenon *until the very end*, to bring it to completion at least in some sense, and that may well mean for it to die in becoming its concept. Moreover, the terms rigidity and point also evoke a 'steep slope' (*l'abrupt*), a 'point' in the logical sense reached when a decision is reversed, as when we say 'from this point on . . .'.

Of course, 'rigidity' and 'point' suggest nothing less than the absence of soul, if not a complete loss of spirit or even heart. What then can be made of the concept of 'animation' or dynamism [Trans: or as the English translators have it, the 'spiritually impregnated' (*begeistert*)] in reference to these ideas of rigidity and points? Animation in this connection is nothing but the 'soul' of the relation epitomized by the concept. At one and the same time the concept abstracts, collects, links together, and unifies all the animated ways of being from the sphere of the phenomenal. On the part of the speculative content, this represents a formalizing reduction, indeed a *logical writing* or inscription, which paradoxically gives back to the entity that has lost its singular features a new form of singularity, a singularity *par excellence*, its own, exclusive and 'characteristic' (*Eigentümlichkeit*).[18]

In the development of spirit each stage progresses towards its reduced form, its single, dominant characteristic, its epitomization and logical *sign*. 'Spirit has embodied in each shape . . . its entire content'. *A posteriori*, this form is revealed to be simply 'incomplete spirit, a concrete shape in whose existence *one* determination (*Einer Bestimmtheit*) predominates, the others being present only in blurred outline (*nur in verwischten Zügen vorhanden sind*)'.[19]

We find in this text a second definition of the principle of simplification: to take the entire physiognomic constellation of a being, a thing, or a moment of thought, and reduce it to its singular distinctive feature or trait.

However, one should note that this power to sharpen meaning has another, corollary side, where it becomes a process of *levelling* and *blunting*. For the individual who appropriates spirit's history

> the content is already the actuality reduced to a possibility (*zur Möglichkeit getilgte Wirklichkeit*), its immediacy overcome (*bezwungene*), the embodied shape reduced to abbreviated, simple determinations of thought (*die Gestaltung bereits auf ihre Abbreviatur, auf die einfache Gedankenbestimmung, herabgebracht ist*).[20]

Or, to put it another way, in the work of *sharpening* meaning, the result is to reduce the path of spirit to a stamp that rubs out the rough edges.

> In a spirit that is more advanced than another, the lower concrete existence has been reduced to an inconspicuous moment (*zu einem unscheinbaren Momente herabgesunken*): what used to be the important thing is now but a trace (*nur noch ein Spur*); its pattern is shrouded to become a mere shadowy outline (*eine einfache Schattierung geworden*). . . . The single individual must also pass through the formative stages of universal spirit so far as their content is concerned, but as shapes which spirit has already left behind (*schon abgelegte Gestalten*), as stages on a way that has been made level with toil (*als Stufen eines Wegs, der ausgearbeitet und geebnet ist*). Thus, as far as knowledge is concerned, we find that what in former ages engaged the attention of men of mature mind, has been reduced (*herabgesunken*) to the level of facts, exercises, and even games for children. . . .[21]

Since the accumulation of spirit's content has been reduced to its 'point', the path to its acquisition has accordingly become shorter. Hence the effort required of the individual is less. As the point digs its own furrow, it erodes what it has already dug. It is true that the individual must patiently endure the journey in all its pain; he cannot 'by the nature of the case comprehend his own substance more easily'. However, 'he does have less trouble (*hat er zugleich geringere Mühe*), since all this has already been *implicitly* accomplished (*vollbracht*)'.[22] The *reduction*, which is a reduction of effort – a reduced effort – evidently does not cheat on the length of the path.

These texts have brought to light a third definition of the principle of simplification, supplementing the second: spirit's facilitation (*le frayage spirituel*) is the combined result of the two operations of the point, the act of sharpening and the act of effacing.

The acceleration 'abridged'

Outline: the German word is *der Grundriß*, i.e. the 'précis' or the abridgement. In Hegel's opinion the outline is the best and most appropriate format for a work of philosophy. '*Grundriß*' also means plan or sketch. Yet, oddly enough, such a 'cull' (*coupe*) represents for Hegel not a propaedeutic but the definitive form of speculative presentation. In the Preface to the first edition of the *Encyclopedia Science of Logic*, Hegel alludes to the ordinary conception of 'outline':

> Where the content is one that is already presupposed and familiar and has to be presented in a short space already decided upon, what is aimed at is that the order and arrangements of the topics should be *externally suitable*. The present exposition is not like that: on the contrary, it sets out a new elaboration of philosophy, according

> to a method that will, I hope, be recognized eventually as the only genuine one.[23]

The Hegelian Outline presupposes only itself. Rather than being the summary of a fuller development that will follow, it represents the original and genuine form of philosophical exposition. The 'cramping' of the 'systematic derivation' of ideas, i.e. their 'proof'[24] as formerly understood, must not be an arbitrary amputation, but must respect the intrinsic movement of speculative unfolding. If Hegel can insist that this method is not one applied externally to the content, it is because it embraces the same rhythm: hence its movement is simply to *accelerate* its own course, decreasing the effort involved and shortening the time taken to complete it. 'The nature of an encyclopedia is to abbreviate.'[25]

From these considerations, a fourth definition of the principle of simplification can be derived: the originary tendency of knowledge to pursue its own condensation.

Modalities of form, in brief

Simplification is form playing with form: as such, it engages all the distinctively Hegelian differentiations of form's modalities. Simplification takes the *sensuous configuration* of existence and reduces it. It shapes the figure (*Gestalt*) into an abbreviated form-determination (*Formbestimmung*), which is a mode of logical essentiality. The two 'forms' open the path of *Bildung* – formation or cultivation – either of the individual or of spirit in general, in so far as spirit is 'educated by its concept'. Moreover, 'form' as Hegel uses it relates explicitly to the tradition's three modalities of form.

Through the act of simplification, each figure of spirit is reduced to its dominant characteristic. On this account, it can be compared to the understanding of form suggested by the Aristotelian term μορφή, meaning form in the sense of *trait*, a form acquired at the cost of the absence and loss it delineates. When a *Gestalt* banishes itself as figure, it is not on that account annihilated but rather displaced; in its place, as its summary, we find an inscription.

In another context, a synonymy between 'form-determination' and the Greek ὅρος is explicitly attested in the Preface to the *Phenomenology*. In Hegel's thought, ὅρος – limit, frontier, stop – signifies the singular and individuating break: the 'for oneself' which establishes determinate meaning. Only what is limited is intelligible: 'Only what is completely determined is at once exoteric, comprehensible, and capable of being learned and appropriated by all.'[26]

Last of all, Hegelian 'form' is essentially and fundamentally related to εἶδος. Εἶδος or ἰδέα is defined by Hegel as 'determinate universality, species or kind'.[27] Εἶδος is a thing's ideal image. Reducing anything to its characteristic trait grants it a greater degree of ideality. Simplification, then, is an *eidetic*. Through its abbreviating power, it reveals the style of the singular. In the process of self-simplification, each determinate moment clarifies itself, rubbing up against its own reflection, polishing itself, one might say. Because the original sheen has been tarnished, this new illumination replaces it. Consequently, simplification is also responsible for determining the conditions under which presence becomes visible.

Simplification – a matter of habit and of *kenosis*

Just as the soul, thanks to habit, 'penetrates' the body in 'forming' it, so spirit pervades its own sensuous existence and the corporeal reality of all its moments. When spirit renders its own substantial being fluid, the result is, again, simplification. Indeed, at first 'spirit is at war with itself: it has to overcome itself as its most formidable obstacle. That development which in the sphere of nature is a peaceful growth, is, in that of spirit, a severe, mighty conflict with itself.'[28]

Through simplification, spirit reduces its own resistance, becomes more supple, flexible, malleable, hence converting itself into an instrument. Simplification produces spirit's second nature, reducing the first nature into the form of logical determinations which, henceforth, are contractions of potential energy, hence *possessions* (ἕξεις).[29] This engages a mechanism which familiarises spirit with its own development just, as it brings the individual into familiarity with its own spirit. This mechanism, constituted through the gathering together and reanimation of traces 'long since absorbed',[30] is that of habit.

Putting this mechanism into place elicits from spirit an alienation we could call *sacrificial*. Just as spirit reduces the distance from itself to itself with the help of habit, spirit is also shedding its own self. The effect of simplification is to transform the speculative narrative into 'a row of closed and labelled boxes in a grocer's stall'.[31] Spirit submits to its self-sacrifice and is transformed into a lifeless, skeletal thing, a thing 'without flesh and blood'.[32]

Yet, all the while this life-destroying formalization is a guarantee of *survival*:

> The excellent, however, not only cannot escape the fate of being thus deprived of life and spirit, of being flayed and then seeing its skin wrapped round a lifeless knowledge and its conceit. Rather we recognize even in this fate the power that the excellent exercises over the hearts, if not over the minds, of men; also the constructive unfolding into universality and determinateness of form in which its perfection consists, and which alone makes it possible for the universality to be used in a superficial way.[33]

Immanent in the development of the Hegelian concept is this process of formalization, a future it cannot avoid. If spirit sacrifices its own flesh in reducing concrete there-being to a simplified determination, this has nonetheless allowed spirit to appropriate the speculative content. The individual 'devours' culture as if it were his 'inorganic nature', and then reproduces in his own being that very destruction innate to simplification. This is the only way the individual can *interiorize* culture.

Conclusion: the System as the dwelling place of spirit

At the same moment, the determination thus simplified exists as a type, an exemplar – mourning its individuality – and a particular essence – mourning its universality. To produce this ontological residue involves a *double suppression* and a *double preservation*. Suppression occurs through the work of habit, with its blunting and flattening effects, and through sacrifice, or alienation. Preservation has involved two forms of permanence: the virtuality created by reactualizing, and the singularity which, in its disappearance, has left itself behind as an interiorized trace:

> Even 'to preserve' includes a negative element, namely, that something is removed from its immediacy and so from an existence which is open to external influences, in order to preserve it. Thus what is sublated is at the same time preserved; it has only lost its immediacy but is not on that account annihilated.[34]

At once the result of habit and the act of *kenosis*, the *Aufhebung* suppresses, but what it suppresses it saves and shelters. To achieve this safekeeping requires the process of simplification. Generally speaking, all preservation involves an economy of loss. Maintenance always demands distress (*perdition*): without that, how can there be a threat of loss (*déperdition*) to counteract? For Hegel, this relation between maintenance, distress, and loss functions in the same way as the relationship between reduction and abbreviation. Foreshortening, paradoxically, is the precondition of longevity.

By breaking the determinations of spirit into 'points', simplification gives each the status of absolute particulars: thus they enjoy their own distinctive characteristic, and can maintain the 'rigidity' of their singular being. By becoming *moments*[35] – which, by definition, means something whose meaning depends on its place within the totality to which it belongs – these determinations remain connected in a fundamental way to the whole:

> The richest is therefore the most concrete and most *subjective*, and that which withdraws itself into the simplest depth is the mightiest and most all-embracing. The highest, most concentrated point is

> the *pure personality* which, solely through the absolute dialectic which is its nature, no less *embraces and holds everything within itself. . . .*[36]

Within the totality of place, each determination finds its own unique and appropriate position. In this way, the 'customary-sacrificial' economy determines the resting place of spirit, and that is nothing other than the *System*, or 'absolute form'.

11

'ON THE SELF'

If dialectical sublation is not a process whose terms and operation are fixed in advance, frozen and immutable, the *Aufhebung* still needs to be shown as responding to its own law, the law that requires it to transform and simplify itself. Far from enforcing a violent stoppage of the dialectical progress, the advent of Absolute Knowledge will imply instead the exact opposite: its *metamorphosis*. Dialectical sublation will become absolute sublation – its own absolution.

Such a metamorphosis can only be revealed at the moment when philosophy 'looks back onto its own knowledge', when it reflects upon its own *systematization*. But, in this connection, what becomes of the 'Self' (*Selbst*), now the fulfilled substance-subject? From this moment on, what form will be taken by the process of self-determination?

Contrary to all expectations, these inquiries into the subject of the System lead us to the very place where the Hegelian theory of the *event* is to be discovered.

The 'release of the Self'

Revisiting the third syllogism of 'Philosophy'

Spirit–Logic–Nature, the third syllogism of philosophy, is the idea of philosophy

> which has *self-knowing reason*, the absolutely universal, for its *middle term*: a middle, which divides itself into spirit and nature, making the former its presupposition, as process of the idea's *subjective* activity, and the latter its universal extreme, as process of the objectively and in itself existing idea.[1]

In this syllogism the idea has returned to itself after the ordeal of the judgement, and now opens itself up to an existence in nature. The very last paragraph of the *Doctrine of the Notion* [*Concept*], gives a more exact description of this 'opening'. Here Hegel is depicting the final passage between the idea and nature, in the following terms: 'The idea', in its 'resolve' (*Entschluß*), *'freely releases itself (sich selbst frei entläßt). . . .'*[2] The idea's self-detachment or self-release, through which it posits itself as free and independent existence, is the critical point for understanding Absolute Knowledge.

In the sequence of the syllogism, self-certainty ('self-knowing reason') occupies the mediating position between subjectivity and objectivity. Consequently, in the realm of subjectivity, the 'I think', or *cogito*, loses its place as the point of origin, a position normally allotted to it; instead it is simply one term of a larger order. The 'self', therefore, is a form of subjectivity that transcends and goes beyond the 'I'.

Aufhebung and abrogation

In the logical economy of spirit's unfolding, the idea's 'free release of itself' is by no means an isolated movement. Indeed, if we look at Hegel's philosophical lexicon, there are many words that designate such a 'self-release'. Thus we can thematize in Hegel's work a motif of *speculative abrogation or letting-go* (*dessaisissement*). Given that 'abrogation' (*dessaisissement*) suggests renunciation and dispossession, or, in legal language, the action whereby one gives up one's property to another, this seems at first to present a term opposite in meaning to 'sublation', that movement which apparently gives up nothing and lets nothing escape.

However, contrary to what one would initially imagine, these two processes of sublation and abrogation are completely interdependent. Considering the last moment of absolute spirit (*Philosophy*), one readily notes the synonymy between the verbs *aufheben*[3] and *befreien* (' to liberate'), as well as *ablegen* ('to discard', 'to remove', 'to take away').[4] Speculative abrogation, in no way alien to the process of the *Aufhebung*, is indeed its fulfilment. Abrogation is a *sublation of sublation* (*relève de la relève*), the result of the *Aufhebung*'s work on itself and, as such, its transformation. The movement of suppression and preservation produces this transformation at a certain moment in history, the moment of Absolute Knowledge. Speculative abrogation is the *absolute sublation*, if by 'absolute' we mean a relief or sublation (*relève*) that frees from a certain type of attachment.

Synthesis without the 'I'

In *Philosophy*'s third syllogism, 'self-knowing reason', or self-certainty, occupies the mediating position. This momentanization of the 'I think' was already given its own characteristic elaboration in the Preface to the *Phenomenology of Spirit*. There Hegel had formulated a claim critical to the understanding of his philosophy:

> Thoughts become fluid (*die Gedanken werden flüssig*) when pure thinking, this inner immediacy, recognizes itself as a moment, or when the pure certainty of self abstracts from itself – not by leaving itself out, or setting itself aside (*auf die Seite setzen*), but by giving up (*aufgeben*) the fixity of its self-positing, by giving up not only the fixity of the pure concrete, which the 'I' itself is, in contrast with its differentiated content, but also the fixity of the differentiated moments which, posited in the element of pure thought, share the unconditional nature of the 'I'.[5]

The theme of abrogation appears here explicitly, as we see from the use of the verb *aufgeben*, 'to give up', to 'let go'. By 'letting go' the fixity of its self-positing, thought *lets go its hold*, just like a hand which opens up and relinquishes what it has been holding. From this comes a relaxing of the tension that had separated thought from its object and preserved their encounter only by maintaining them in this divide. Speculative abrogation is first of all an act whereby the 'I' renounces itself, renounces its power of preservation and mastery. Yet the difference between thinking and what is thought is not in fact reduced because of this letting-go. Rather the relationship between them becomes supple or fluid: they are no longer two 'sides' frozen or fixed in their opposition, as an 'I' or 'pure certainty of self', opposing all that is objective and determinate, the 'differentiated content'.

The consequences of this fluidification are considerable, marking the end of the 'confrontation' which traditionally underlies the idea of the subject–object relation. By 'giving up' this relation, thought frees itself from the rigidity of a confrontation that has nothing left to show us. For Hegel, this relationship in its traditional form corresponded to a certain historical state, a certain perspectival epoch or way of seeing which, logically and chronologically, has had its day (*fait leur temps*).

Absolute Knowledge, confirming the identity of substance and subject, introduces a relation between knowing and the known unlike any that has gone before. For this knowledge does not emerge from a new formation of this subject–object gap; instead it arrives in the suspension of that gap. Hence that gap, emerging when the subject separates itself from all its determinations in order to 'see them coming' (*les voir venir*), is neither definitive nor fundamental. Consequently, the end of the gap obviously does not mean the closure of all perspective. On the contrary: this end reveals, in the process of becoming-fluid, a more fundamental mode of occurrence (*structure de l'advenir plus originaire*) than the rigid and fixed way in which the subject distanced itself from its own determinations, its own accidents. The 'I think' – the pure certainty of self – is simply one moment, lasting only for a certain period of time in the deployment of subjectivity itself. In the third syllogism, the very sequence followed makes this clear. The originary synthetic unity, or the *a priori* concordance of opposites, was not always a unity of apperception, nor will it always be so, if by 'apperception' we mean exclusively that absolute identity of a subject, a subject defined as an 'I = I'. From now on, there will be a synthesis but without an I.

On cause

The Self and its automatism

But how can this abandonment of self and free abrogation be possible? In so far as they also arise from a 'decision', a 'resolution' (*Entschluß*), isn't this a case, again, of an assertion of mastery? If we abandon the 'fixity of the self-position', isn't this tantamount to adopting, yet again, another position? The motif of coercion, of *coup de force*, reappears: *who* decides on the abrogation?

To this question Hegel does have an answer: it is the 'Self' (*Selbst*). Yet do we know what this 'Self' is in this case? It is a primordial subjectivity, a synthetic instance earlier than the 'I-self': I is the *System* itself, the System as a Self. The System collects and is made up of all the determinations or aspects. Yet how does such a 'Self' have the power to decide? And how will the 'I-Self', in its detachment from self, be able to renounce itself in favour of this later 'Self'?

Abrogation, or letting-go, works by itself (*aus sich selbst*), but through an *automatic* and not an *autocratic* movement. The terms 'Self', and 'itself' are translations of the Greek αὐτοῦ. αὐτόματος means the self-moving, that which goes, comes, and acts propelled by its own motion. Self, or *Selbst*, appears in Hegel's concepts of *Selbstbewegung*, self-motion, *Selbstbestimmung*, self-determination. By employing these terms, Hegel draws attention to a law of composition and a process of synthesis which are self-initiating and self-causing. For this automatism to function it requires the principle of *self-distribution* and *self-classification*. The Preface to the *Phenomenology of Spirit* explains it in these terms:

> The content shows that its determinateness (*Bestimmtheit*) is not received from something else, nor externally attached to it (*aufgeheftet*), but that it determines itself, and ranges itself as a moment having its own place in the whole (*rangiert sich aus sich zum Momente und zu einer Stelle des Ganzen*).[6]

The sharpening of the 'point', which is inherent in the process of dialectical simplification, does not emerge from the activity of the 'I think' as if this were something that would take its simple form and 'attach' it onto the content (or, more precisely, as the German word *heften* suggests, 'hook', 'afix', or 'pin' it). Rather, the sharpening to a 'point' also, like the others, results from a process of release or letting-go immanent in the objective determinations themselves. As Hegel writes in the chapter on Absolute Knowledge:

> Each in relation to the other lets go (*läßt . . . ab*) of the independent determinateness with which it comes forth against it. This letting-go (*dies Ablassen*) is the same renunciation (*dasselbe Verzichttun*) of the one-sidedness of the concept that in itself constituted the beginning.[7]

The principle of simplification, taken as a tendency or inclination, is actually the potential on which the automatism of the System draws. At the moment of Absolute Knowledge, the System emerges as a movement, reassembling that presence which is not present to itself. Here again, this is not something done by the 'I'. Rather, it is because being, on its own account, tends to form itself into a System, that the self-determination of substance – totality's differentiation into individual and determinate forms – appears at the end of the day as a movement of ontological taxonomy.

Let us return to the relation between abrogation and *Aufhebung*. The verbs *ablegen* ('to remove', 'to discard'), *aufgehen* ('to disappear'), *ablassen* ('to leave off'), *weglassen* ('to let go'), also contain this double meaning of suppressing and preserving. *Ablegen* means 'to take off', 'to lift off', 'to get rid of', 'to cast off', but also 'to file away'. The moments of the System are at once 'left behind' and used ('preserved') in the very space they convert for their own use. *Aufgeben* means on the one hand to abandon, to leave, to mourn; on the other hand to register, to put in, to send off (as one would send something by the post). Each moment mourns (*fait le deuil*) its uniqueness and renounces its separate and distinct autonomy, thereby both integrating and preserving itself in the totality.

If these verbs characterize what we are calling abrogation, how can we distinguish that from sublation? To the degree that it acts as a sublation which has been absolved and made absolute, abrogation describes the dual process of suppression/preservation. Yet the process of suppression/preservation it describes is one that has been *detached* from the subject–object relation, one that has been liberated from the instance which had traditionally claimed to be its master while in reality being its subordinate, its derivative. The verbs *ablassen* and *weglassen*, meaning at the same time 'to empty', 'to send off', 'to let go', 'to let be', help to confirm this dynamic meaning of the absolute as at once a liberation and an absolution.

Speculative simplification is a movement which dismisses the very intellectual faculties – consciousness, intellect, reason – it had originally made possible. In the course of the *Phenomenology of Spirit* these faculties are recorded in their progressive deployment, in their work of abstracting their content, aiming always towards the abbreviated form. Yet in this process, the faculties find themselves 'reduced' by the very orientation of their project. The System lacks an author.

Unless we take into account this automatism, which functions as the condition of auto-determination and auto-momentum, we will never grasp what happens at the stage of Absolute Knowledge. Without this same *force of detachment*, present everywhere in the Hegelian text and everywhere freeing spirit from its attachment to maintenance, it would be impossible to distinguish the process of the *Aufhebung* from that of the bad infinite.

Contingency, necessity, freedom

To invoke an automatism does not mean that we are falling into the common practice of attaching to the Hegelian System the image of a mechanism pure and simple: as if there is a machine, indeed a dialectical machine, in which everything finds its place without the slightest intervention of free choice.

If we consider its Greek etymology, the concept of automatism immediately reveals its speculative character. In fact what ὁ αὐτοματισμός means is: 'that which happens on its own'. And this can be understood in two ways: (i) what happens by itself out of necessity, its own internal necessity; (ii) what happens by itself, yet by accident or chance. Aristotle uses τὸ αὐτόματον with this sense of chance, occurrence, when he opposes it to τέχνη. And the verb αὐτοματίζειν expresses both meanings: it means to do something oneself – i.e. autonomously – and to act unreflectively, by chance, where contingency is a kind of heteronomy. If automatism has a conceptual significance it is the one deployed here, at the intersection of the essential and the accidental.

Speculative automatism is an economy. It economizes for Hegel by incorporating both tendencies immanent to the process of auto-determination: the becoming essential of the accident, and the becoming accidental of essence.

Contradiction in all its forms arises originally out of the tension between substance as a *totality* – the synthesis of all the predicates – and substance as *particularity* – as separate or absolved existence, as accident. 'External reflection', writes Hegel in the *Science of Logic*, posits on the one side 'formless substance', and, on the other 'the flux of accidents (*Wechsel der Akzidenten*)'.[8] On the one 'side', indeed, totality tends to negate its determinate being only to feel its simple self-identity: 'Spirit is . . . formally speaking, *liberty*, the concept's absolute negativity or self-identity. Considered as this formal aspect, it *may* withdraw itself by abstracting from everything exterior and from its own externality, its very existence.'[9]

On the other 'side', particularity tends to take itself for the whole, without considering the other aspects:

> The circle that remains self-enclosed and, like substance, holds its moments together, is an immediate relationship, one therefore which has nothing astonishing about it. But that an accident as such (*das Akzidentelle als solches*), detached from what circumscribes it, what is bound and is actual only in its context with others, should attain an existence of its own and a separate freedom – this is the tremendous power of the negative.[10]

In the 'immediate concept', he writes, 'this is the relation of *substance and accidents*', which is a relation (*Verhältnis*) between necessity (*Notwendigkeit*) and contingency (*Zufälligkeit*) .[11] Substance is at once 'the totality of the whole (*Totalität des Ganzen*)'[12] which 'embraces *accidentality* within it', the tranquil relation of self-identity, and 'totality in the form of illusory (*scheinende*) being, *accidentality*',[13] or 'the sphere of coming-to-be and ceasing-to-be' of the accidents (*prédicats*). Substantial necessity is experienced as *necessity* within the *chance* (*Zufall*) and *contingency* (*Zufälligkeit*) of the accidents. This relationship of substance to non-substance (to the accidents) is the 'actuosity' (*Aktuosität*) of substance. By and as actuosity, substance manifests itself at one and the same time as 'creative power' and 'destructive power'. However, 'the two are identical; the creation is destructive and the destruction creative; for the negative and the positive, possibility and actuality, are absolutely united in substantial necessity.'[14]

Speculative automatism is the principle of this self-regulation of contingency and necessity. As such, it appears to be a particular regime of causality, of, so to speak, the processing of the event.

As a rule, Hegel's theory of the relation between necessity and contingency – the 'relation of causality (*Kausalitätverhältnis*)'[15] – is interpreted as showing a simple or mechanical inversion: this seems obvious when we line up phrases like 'necessity determines itself as contingency', or 'contingency is . . . absolute necessity',[16] or even 'the unity of necessity and contingency . . . is to be called absolute actuality'.[17] One can deduce from this that everything which is possible is to become actual, that every accident has a meaning and thus that, for Hegel, there is no such thing as a pure accident.

But such a reading is wrong. Necessary being is being which is *causa sui*, and for that reason, cannot be other than it is. As Hegel puts it: 'Necessity is being, *because* it is – the unity of being with itself that has itself for ground.'[18] But he adds immediately: 'But conversely, because it has a ground it is not being, it is an altogether illusory being (*nur Schein*), *relation (Beziehung*) or *mediation*.'

Hegel is showing here that there is a contradiction inherent in every ground in so far as that ground is 'relative' (i.e. in relation, in *Beziehung*) to what it grounds. To ground or to cause oneself creates a relation in which one element *repels* the other, causing one to be an active self and one a passive. Hegel speaks of 'a passivity posited by its own activity' and demonstrates that, in a prior moment, absolute substance 'repels itself as necessity from itself'.[19] There is one *fact* which makes this necessity what it is: grounding itself, necessity is never its own ground, but conversely experiences itself as radically passive in relation to itself. Although it has its source within itself it feels this to be independent of itself. Necessity forgets its own origin.

A point of sheer randomness dwells within essential being, within the 'original substance'. This is the perspective we need to understand the claim that the essence of necessity is contingency. The becoming accidental of essence originally stemmed from the process whereby necessity sets itself up as an event.

At this point what can we say about contingency? Contingent being is that which can be other than it is. Those determinations appearing as 'indifferent, self-external substances' are contingent.[20] Now that 'violence (*Gewalt*)'[21] through which contingency arises even out of the heart of necessity ensures in the same move that contingency has its own and full autonomy. To the degree that it is the origin of violence, contingency acquires the status of a cause, and becomes the power of necessity.

The dialectical result of this 'mutual support (*entretien*)' of necessity and contingency is freedom:

> Necessity does not become *freedom* by vanishing, but only because its still *inner* identity is *manifested*, . . . Conversely, at the same time, *contingency* becomes *freedom*, for the sides of necessity, which have the shape of independent, free actualities . . . are now *posited* as *self-identical*, so that these totalities of reflection-into-self in their difference are now also reflected as *identical*, or are posited as only one and the same reflection.[22]

Essence and accident in mutual support

What conclusion should be drawn from the dialectical identity of necessity and contingency? In the passage just cited, we see how each term, necessity and contingency, is freed through the help of the other, and how both free themselves from one another. The process is the same as that of the generation of meaning: meaning is never original but always produced, engendered when its passivity is made manifest. 'It is because it is': the necessity of meaning, or necessity as meaning, at the same time sharply reveals meaning's absolute passivity – its contingency. Conversely, contingency here determines meaning as being a power of eruption, a pure event, imposing itself absolutely and hence of necessity.

Contrary to the widespread view, Hegel does not deny contingency, nor does he deny that any specific thing can happen. But he does claim that, in the face of what occurs, it is useless to place necessity and contingency within *an order of occurrence* (*un ordre d'arrivée*). What occurs does not arise out of a pre-existing foundation, nor is the accident itself the foundation. Contingency and necessity support one another in such a way that spirit is free from their division and can simply let go its two-sided claim: it could have been otherwise, it could not have been otherwise. It would be futile to want to determine some ontological priority of essence over accident, or accident over essence, for their co-implication is primary.

This fundamental truth of Hegelianism reverberates within the System, and echoes throughout its logical and historical aspects. With this truth, we can better understand the concept of *tradition* as that figures as a central question for contemporary philosophy (most prominently, indeed, for Heidegger). In his continual concern to prove that philosophy can be nothing outside its own history, that philosophical truth is indistinguishable from the movement of its evolution, Hegel shows that a philosophical tradition refers to two things at once: to the movement through which a particular accident (for example, something that arises in its own place and time, like the birth of philosophy in Greece) becomes essential (i.e. it becomes *fate*), and to the way a destiny, standing for the essential, then actualizes itself in its accidents, i.e. in its epochs and stages. Whether one is prior to the other is not something that can be known. This is what Absolute Knowledge *knows*. Hegelian philosophy assumes as an absolute fact the emergence of the random in the very bosom of necessity and the fact that the random, the aleatory, becomes necessary.[23]

Dialectically sublating the 'time form', spirit cancels all tendency to question whether a wholly different origin might have been possible, whether there could have been a wholly different destination from the one that actually came to pass. At the stage of Absolute Knowledge, the time which is sublated – that empty time posted outside itself by consciousness, giving the unfolding of spirit the appearance of a 'free contingent event' – leaves us always time to think what might otherwise have been. In this fact, Hegel believes, there remains the possibility of *alienation* which, in principle, depends on the feeling of lost necessity.

To know the *provenance* of the speculative is a question beyond any possible scope; thus, by itself, spirit abandons it. More than a century later, Heidegger would assert that it is impossible and futile to ask about the possibility of a wholly different 'way (*Weise*)' of Being from the one which occurred in the metaphysical tradition as a 'forgetfulness of Being'. But for him to say that, Hegel's entire work on the essence of history and tradition was necessary.[24]

The question of the *wholly other* – something that cannot be thought without a feeling of vertigo – is always in fact a question about an origin that could have been wholly otherwise. A vertigo of thought, this is still a solicitation which thought finds inevitable. Yet it is a solicitation which does not come from a real outside but, rather, from the Same. 'It is because it is' – the formal and immediate tautology of necessity – and 'it could be otherwise' – the heterology of contingency: in Hegel's thought these reveal their original and inherent complicity, shown in the two meanings of the phrase: 'what arrives from itself/what happens on its own (*ce qui arrive de soi-même*)'.

Everything begins in the same moment, where the becoming essential of the accident and the becoming accidental of essence mutually imply one another. There is nothing beforehand. The dialectic is primordial, indeed it is the origin. When we note the first appearance of the idea of dialectic in the Greek world, something strikes us: the contradiction that marked its definition was already there. Indeed there was barely a generation that had passed, hardly any time at all, before the understanding of the word 'dialectic' showed the full extent of its contradictory connotations. For Plato, who invented the concept, dialectic signifies the way Ideas become known. In his sense, dialectic is an *essential* discourse. Yet in the hands of Aristotle it became a method for deriving syllogisms from plausible propositions. Dialectic, the appropriate form for presenting contingent truths, thus became a discourse of the *accidental*.

In the *Science of Logic*, Hegel alludes to the tormented history of the dialectic which, starting from its Platonic esteem as 'the highest discourse', came in the course of time to mean an utterly contingent discourse, hardly distinguishable from sophistry:

> Besides the fact that dialectic is generally regarded as contingent, it usually takes the following more precise form. It is shown that there belongs to some subject matter or other, for example the world, motion, point, and so on, some determination or other, for example (taking the objects in the order named), finitude in space and time, presence in *this* place, absolute negation of space; but further, that with equal necessity the opposite determination also belongs to the subject matter. . . . Now the conclusion drawn from dialectic of this kind is in general the *contradiction* and *nullity* of the assertions made.[25]

Throughout its history, dialectic continually oscillates between its status as essential – Kant once again recognized it as 'necessary to reason'[26] – and accidental discourse. For Hegel, this proves its high speculative content. The basic tension constituting it is the very pulse and vital spark of thought. The dialectic of the origin is inscribed within the very origin of dialectic as a concept.

Conclusion: the liberation of energy

Simplification is finally complete in the stage of Absolute Knowledge, when from a distance spirit looks on at the determinatenesses in their self-movement, as they take on the form of essential accidents, in other words, of *singularities* (*singularités*). At the end of the *Doctrine of Essence* Hegel shows how the dialectic of necessity and contingency results in a movement in which 'the self-identical determinateness is likewise posited as the whole'.[27] This determinateness is then posited as the '*self-identical negativity*: the *singular* (*das Einzelne*)'.[28]

To understand this crucial point, we must return to a dual movement of letting-go that transpires when, on both sides, the 'I think' and the objective determinatenesses renounce the fixity and independence of their positions. From this they pass into a stage of fluidification, and this fluidification should be recognized as a liberation of energy. Force, previously contained within the strict limits imposed by a transcendental perspective, which the gap between subject and object particularly sustains, now breaks away from these bonds and becomes free for other combinations and other syntheses.

Hegel's philosophy makes it possible to see clearly the transition from one mode of ontological gathering to another: from the transcendental operation of consciousness to the mechanism of singularities in their automatic distribution. According to Hegel, there is an energy produced when the determinatenesses – the forms of what occurs – come into being, and that energy has always remained imprisoned. In the chapter on 'Absolute Knowledge' he shows that the moments shown are not to be conceived as static but rather as 'pure motions', which 'impel themselves forward.'[29] The space laid out by this dynamic does not require the intervention of an Ego: it is the work of *no one*.

Under the heading of 'singularities' – or, negatively self-identical determinatenesses – must be included all the *styles* and *versions* of spirit, everything left behind by the past, its residue, works, monuments, doctrines. These appear to be *cases* in the double sense of the word.[30] They are the determinate moments that have 'happened', erupting into the light of day as events or, as it were, pure accidents, but also as exemplary individualities, revealing their necessity and its force. Once simplified, these determinate moments arrange themselves in new relationships with respect to one another. In relation to the other, each lets go of its independence, as they engage themselves in a relationship of reciprocal tension that creates a 'space' between them, a space not of confrontation but of difference-within-continuity. What is crucial is not the extreme positions held by the confronting terms, but the distance that separates them, the totality of the space-between.

This structure of competing tensions creates a multiple and mobile perspective, a reciprocal mirroring (i.e. a reflection) that is no longer the work of individual consciousness and no longer depends on a single centre. It is a composition of perspectives, allowing the determinate moments to be connected to each other even while they are in opposition, rather than simply being opposed. Each determinate moment brings the other into view through a new angle, as part of a systematic structure sparked by the establishment of contact points.

As Hegel shows us, the teleological structure ends by reversing its course, in that the forms already actualized discharge their potential energy and consequently liberate future possibilities of actualization. Distributed in this way, the individuals are ready to engage again, in new constructions, new readings, new thoughts.

12

THE PHILOSOPHER, THE READER AND THE SPECULATIVE PROPOSITION

Can we *read* (with) Hegel?

Towards a speculative hermeneutics

Judging from the conclusions we have reached so far, the 'backward look' which philosophy 'directs' onto 'its own knowledge' could not be a look of passive contemplation, but rather an *act of reading*. In lieu of an author, the System necessarily has interpreters. Absolute Knowledge engages thought in the movement of speculative hermeneutics, in modalities unknown and unforeseen. According to Hegel, there is no such thing as an immediate grasping of the absolute, neither, it follows, will there be any such thing as an immediate transparency of meaning. For Absolute Knowledge to come on the scene, it is assumed that the discursive conditions both for its announcement and for its reception must have been produced.

The responsibility for this final and definitive formulation (*mise en forme*) – requiring as it does an idiom, a form of utterance, a discipline of reading – falls to the philosopher. Philosophy's Self, or absolute subject, would indeed remain formless unless shaped into a style by a particular philosophical subjectivity. In return, it is only Absolute Knowledge which gives philosophical subjectivity its rightful form. Thus speculative hermeneutics must consist of a mutual gift of form, from the Self to the self.

The project of such a hermeneutic appears from the outset of the Preface to the *Phenomenology of Spirit*, from the moment when Hegel announces specifically what the future of philosophy will be. As he says, it will consist of the passage from the predicative to the speculative proposition: 'Only a philosophical exposition (*philosophische Exposition*) that rigidly excludes (*strenge . . . ausschlöße*) the usual way of relating the parts of a proposition could achieve the goal of plasticity (*würde es erreichen, plastisch zu sein*).'[1]

Now this 'exclusion' explicitly requires the proposition's *reading subject*. For Hegel pursues his analysis of the speculative proposition by placing himself in the perspective of its addressee, namely the reader. Indeed it is the latter who experiences the conflict between the form and the content of the proposition. It is the reader who has the responsibility of 'setting forth (*darstellen*)' the 'return of the concept into itself (*das Zurückgehen des Begriffs in sich*)'.[2] Consequently, the plasticity of meaning is inseparable from a plasticity of reading, a reading which gives form to the utterance it receives. The philosophical decision finds itself in a new modality determined by the transition from the predicative to the speculative. This is the freedom and the responsibility of *interpretation*.

Objections

Yet we may find ourselves objecting: what kind of status can be enjoyed by this interpreting subjectivity if, as our analysis has shown, the Ego has been dismissed? Doesn't the 'Self', because of its anonymity and its automatism, threaten to annihilate all individual exegetical initiative? We could go on: it is hard to see how the philosopher could survive the speculative precipitation of philosophy (precipitation understood here in two senses, of 'haste' and the chemical phenomenon of the precipitate). What could be the task of the philosopher when the unfolding of the speculative content abbreviates before his eyes into simplified determinate moments? At first glance, Absolute Knowledge would confine the philosopher to a restricted economy which, in its turn, is imposed on thinking as a principle narrowing its scope to the absolute limits. Isn't philosophy thereby reduced to the simplest of tools?

'An idiom', we were saying before. According to Hegel, the philosopher must think in his or her own, that is, native, idiom, the sole material for the work of philosophy, and must strip off all the ornaments that come from a technical or artificial language (*Kunstsprache*):

> Philosophy therefore stands in no need of a special terminology; true, some words have to be taken from foreign languages but these have already acquired through usage the right of citizenship in it (i.e., in the philosophical realm) – and an affected purism would be most out of place where it was the distinctive meaning which was of decisive importance.[3]

But what after all can we make of a hermeneutic that lacks all potential for conceptual invention?

'A form of utterance', we went on to say. In Hegel's view, the dialectical sublation of the predicative proposition can only occur *within* the arena of the proposition itself. It happens 'at the level of the form (*an der Form*)', as he says in the *Encyclopedia Science of Logic*.[4] Hence to pass from one form – the predicative – to another – the speculative – requires no other form than that of the proposition.

But what can a hermeneutic be if it is not in a position to produce any forms at all?

'A discipline of reading'. At last. Hegel, particularly in the Preface to the *Phenomenology of Spirit*, insists on the need for philosophy to 'renounce its personal intrusions into the immanent rhythm of the concept'.[5]

But what can we say about an unenterprising hermeneutic? Can reading be nothing but simple repetition, with no invention at all? Our initial objection crops up again.

At first sight, then, there is nothing much left for the philosopher to do, constrained as he or she is to exploit only the resources of a knowledge possessed already. The natural languages and the proposition make up philosophy's ordinary fare, and it is hard to see what new booty it will be allowed to receive.

Hegel's reply

Declaring that 'the forms of thought are, in the first instance, displayed (*herausgesetzt*) and stored (*niedergelegt*) in human *language*',[6] Hegel instances this natural deposit as if it were a consignment coming from nowhere, as if it fell from the sky, like a gift to be kept. *Niederlegen* in German means ' to lay down', 'to deposit', 'to write onto a piece of paper', but also 'to resign', 'to give up'. Hence when the philosopher works on natural language, he or she is working on a new space and time: stored by spirit in the idiom itself.

The speculative is not only stored lexically. Syntax is equally fundamental, marking the consignment in language of the elementary forms of logic. In the Nuremberg *Propädeutik*, Hegel asserts that the logical categories are, in their immediate form, 'the content of grammar'. These categories are 'the singular letters, and even the vowels, of the spiritual realm, and it is with them that we begin to speak, then to read'. In a certain sense grammar makes up the alphabet of the spiritual realm. To the extent that it contains 'the categories and unique creations of the intellect', it inaugurates 'our logical culture (*Bildung*)'.[7] In consequence, for the philosopher, to work on the relation of subject and predicate amounts to an exploration of the *temporal* connections between the philosophical proposition and its grammatical origins.

Language and philosophy: the space and time of the idiom

In the *Nuremberg Propädeutik* Hegel states:

> No people can be regarded as cultivated (*gebildet*) that cannot express all the richness of science in their own language, or cannot

> move smoothly within that language in its full extent. The inwardness which we enjoy with our own language is lacking with knowledges which we have access to only in foreign languages. It is as if they are separated from us by a wall which doesn't let spirit be truly at home.[8]

Ordinarily this type of statement would be considered a call for intellectual nationalism, indeed philosophical xenophobia. This seems all the more plausible because Hegel does frequently extol the speculative virtues of the German language, notably in the Preface to the second edition of the *Science of Logic*, where he asserts that 'German has many advantages (*viele Vorzüge*) over other modern languages.'[9] Thought finds itself forced to stay within the borders of a language, forbidden to leave.

Yet we must notice that by 'foreign language' Hegel means, in this particular case, foreign *philosophical* language. Above all, what he has in mind is the traditional philosophical terminology, that formal and technical language made up of artificial terms borrowed from ancient languages: 'transcendental', 'noumenal', 'ectype', 'archetype', and so on. A distinctively philosophical language would claim to be free of all equivocity, the flaw that afflicts ordinary language. Technical language seems on the face of it to be perfect in its univocity and, in this sense, universally intelligible.

Yet when philosophy resorts to foreign terminology, on the grounds of its international and universal character, this leads to nothing less than an erasure of language's naturalness. If Hegel shows that philosophical language, in its true form, implies the rejection of any ready-made philosophical idiom, it is not because he wants to retain the purity of a national origin, but because, contrary to expectation, he wants to preserve the strange and alien character of any and all language, that is, to preserve the irreducibility of its place and time.

The material which speculative thought starts from is the apparently non-speculative nature of language. This is by no means to be banished. Indeed it must be welcomed unconditionally. The equivocity imported into speculation as its non-speculative ancestry is primordial and innate. The philosopher must accept it, think it and think in it. The non-speculative origin of the speculative is formed by a 'naïveté' – a nativity – which the concept can neither suppress nor erase. To speak a language is always to experience a *fall*. One *falls* into a language; this straight away returns us to the chance that is *birth*. Jacques Derrida evokes this 'wound and finitude of birth (of *the* birth) without which one cannot even open language, one would not even have a true or false exteriority to speak of'.[10]

Hegel remarks that a number of German words:

> have the further peculiarity of having not only different (*verschiedene*) but opposite (*entgegengesetzte*) meanings so that

> one cannot fail to recognize a speculative spirit of the language in them: it can delight a thinker to come across (*stoßen*) such words and to find (*vorfinden*) the union of opposites naïvely (*auf naïve Weise*) shown in the dictionary as one word with opposite meanings, although this result of speculative thinking is nonsensical to the understanding.[11]

Stoßen means 'to bump against', 'to stumble across', 'to fall upon something' in a metaphorical sense. One stumbles onto language, onto that part of it which falls to one's share (*qui vous échoit*) and which is 'found there' as something to be picked up. Language is a stamped and hallmarked material (*gestempelt*), that sends us back to an original, authorless formation, an original *plasticity*. The naturalness of language allows us to experience an immemorial past.

The stress on such 'speculative words' seems to confirm the privilege Hegel accords to the German language.[12] Nonetheless, for him all languages are speculative. When, on an invitation from Peter van Ghert, Hegel believed he would leave Germany for the Netherlands, he wrote to his friend:

> As for the language in which lectures at Dutch universities are usually delivered, at least in the beginning this would have to be Latin. If custom permitted a departure from this, I would soon seek to express myself in the language of the country. For I hold it essential to the genuine mastery of a science for one to do it in one's mother tongue.[13]

There is no such thing as a superior language or benchmark idiom. Every language is an instance of the speculative. Philosophy's role is to show how, in each language, the essential is said and exhibited through the idiom's accidents. By working only on the natural language and shunning all artificial and foreign terminology, philosophy establishes the spiritual character of the linguistic examples. Far from imprisoning thought within a circle, the labour of philosophy ushers into language, as into philosophy, the unexpected event of language *and* of philosophy.

The speculative proposition

The downward slope of predication

By working on the proposition, the philosopher reveals the becoming essential of the accident and the becoming accidental of essence. For philosophy, the historical task is to elaborate the speculative significance of a grammatical structure, a structure which, by determining a certain relation between the subject, the copula, and the predicate, opens the way to the comprehension of substance.

In so far as syntax inaugurates order and creates relations between its elements, it shows philosophy how to proceed. The relation subject–copula–predicate is a sequence, an order of events, a way things are to happen, and to the speaking subject who makes use of it, it gives a direction. The order in which the elements of the proposition occur, both in the logical and chronological sense, indicates what is the precedent and what the consequence. If philosophy has a horizon already constituted by grammar, its task will be to raise this order of preceding cause and succeeding consequence to its higher form of truth, in other words, to its 'necessity'. Philosophy must show that the difference carved out by the copula between subject and predicate does not represent a simple and random juxtaposition of terms (where the relation is something external and indifferent to the terms), but derives from a partition intrinsic to the subject itself. The coming of the event takes place in the proposition, revealed as the scene of the advent (*lieu d'avènement*). This is something we could recall from the Greek verb συμβαίνειν (from which comes συμβεβηκός, accident, contingency, predicate), meaning at once to follow logically and to happen, to come to pass. Hence the proposition, in which the subject develops its own self-differentiation, is the very place that promises the future.

How can we speak of language as being the place of a primal 'fall' of meaning? As a metaphor, this is not out of bounds inasmuch as grammar is, in an exact sense, a certain way of conceptualizing falling. In the *Introduction to Metaphysics* Heidegger recalls that

> What the Roman grammarians designate with the bland expression *modus* the Greeks call ἔγκλισις, an inclining to the side. This word moves in the same direction of meaning as another Greek word meaning grammatical form or rubric. We know this word, πτῶσις better in its Latin translation: *casus*, case, in the sense of the inflection of the noun. But to begin with, πτῶσις designates any kind of inflection of the fundamental form (deviation, declension), not only in substantives but also in verbs. Only after the difference between these word forms had been more clearly worked out were the inflections that belong to them also designated with separate terms. The inflection of the noun is called πτῶσις (*casus*); that of the verb is called ἔγκλισις (*declinatio*).[14]

The very spirit of grammar manifests the original property of presence, its primordial capacity to bend and incline. Within the space of the proposition is inscribed this movement – of the ἔγκλισις (inclination, slope) and the ἐξοχή (relief, projection) of the subject. Substance (οὐσία) is only expressing its own 'right' when it falls towards itself. The predicate does not add itself to substance; it comes from it (*il en vient*). Its coming-from is a coming-to-pass. Jean Beaufret comments

> According to [Aristotle] we have a proposition when the λόγος focuses on an internal distinction between subject and predicate and for the most part when the 'slope' of such a λόγος takes the indicative mode: what is said this way, and only this way, is said 'as if we were coming from it' (*comme si on en venait*).[15]

For example: 'the statue is made of bronze'. It is easy to see that bronze is no more being added or attached to the statue than the statue is being added to the bronze. Rather, the statue is defined *on the basis* of its bronze just as the bronze takes on a particular form *in* the statue. The two aspects mutually imply one another; they are essential to each other, they mutually impose themselves on each other (*s'imposent . . . l'un à l'autre*), and are not superimposed. They are a matter for sublation (*relève*), where '*relever*' in French does not just mean 'to be the concern of', or 'be under the jurisdiction of', but also 'to rise', ' to bring out the *true* relief'.[16] Consequently, every proposition can be understood as a sublation in this sense, for within it appears the overhanging relief (*surplomb*) that completes it.

The missed synthesis

When the predicative proposition, the traditional subject and source for philosophy, becomes a speculative proposition, it confers on the λόγος its real incline, thus successfully bringing the idea of συμβαίνειν into the context of predication. As long as it remains within the tradition, philosophy cannot, in Hegel's view, get past basic grammar. It fails to see the constitutive incline of the proposition, because no matter what philosophy says, it still sees the proposition as a straight course protecting itself from a fall to which it claims to be exposed. Captive to a linear conception which keeps subject, copula and predicate within a relation but alien to one another, traditional philosophy fails to forge a necessary foundation for the relation between the subject and its accidents. Normally,

> The Self is a *Subject* to which the content is related as accident and predicate. This subject constitutes the basis to which the content is attached (*geknüpft wird*) and upon which the movement runs back and forth (*auf der die Bewegung hin und wieder läuft*).[17]

On this sort of representation rests the understanding of the proposition as a kind of *passage* (*Übergehen*) from subject to copula and then to predicate, even though the idea of passage lacks the power to exhibit its own necessity.

The Greek moment of synthesis

Although the absolute synthesis has overwhelmingly preoccupied philosophy, it has never properly or effectively been conceptualized.

In the *Lectures on the History of Philosophy*, Hegel shows how Aristotle, at the very moment when he draws attention to the genuinely speculative principle of subjective self-differentiation (the predicative synthesis), nonetheless posits this difference as something *outside* the subject, as a sensory multiplicity which cannot be successfully conjoined.[18] The Aristotelian method defines absolute substance as self-differentiating negativity, yet the work of individuation, as it is pursued here, expands until it touches the very limits of indeterminacy and of nothingness. Aristotelian empiricism, celebrated by Hegel for its high speculative content, in fact falls apart into a kind of disorder for which, paradoxically, its acribolic scruples are responsible:

> The deficiency (*Mangel*) in the Aristotelian philosophy rests in the fact, that after the manifold of phenomena was through its offices raised into the concept, the latter (i.e. the concept), however, again fell asunder into a succession of determinate concepts, and the unity, the absolute concept which unites them, was not emphasized.[19]

Hence, the reciprocal determination of subject and predicate, their solid and substantial connection, remains unestablished. The subject extends the sensory manifold towards infinity without ever drawing it together as a whole. Aristotle was unable to think what Hegel would call the 'adequacy' of subject and predicate, which demands that 'the subject that fills its own content ceases to go beyond it, and cannot have any further predicates or accidental properties'.[20]

The modern moment of synthesis

Later in the *Lectures on the History of Philosophy*, after stating that Aristotle's method has failed to produce 'the unity of the concept', Hegel declares:

> this was the task which succeeding eras had to accomplish. At the present time it appears in this fashion: the unity of the concept is what is needed. This unity is absolute essence (*Wesen*). At first it presents itself as the unity of self-consciousness and consciousness, as pure thought, . . . and so we see it come to pass that pure self-consciousness makes itself essence.[21]

Modern philosophy, to which Hegel alludes when he speaks of 'the present time', responds to this 'need' for unity or synthesis by positing self-consciousness as a unity of subject and object, of certainty and truth. Critical philosophy confers on self-consciousness, understood as the originary synthetic unity of apperception, the faculty of combination (*rassemblement*).

In respect to the understanding of the proposition, this idea of unity marks an incontestable advance. Indeed, to imagine a unity of this type means that we have already gone beyond considering the connection between subject and predicate as if it were simply a *binary* relation. If the proposition is a result of the self-differentiation of the subject, the *mediation* responsible for the relationship between the two terms constituting the proposition must still be brought into view. Now Kant, in the *Transcendental Logic*, has done precisely this: he has illuminated the ternary structure of the proposition by insisting on the importance of a *medium*, a middle term between two concepts. This *medium*, 'the principle of the combination of subject and predicate in the judgement', is self-consciousness.[22]

The 'absolute synthesis' is not an 'aggregate of manifolds after they have been gathered together (*zusammengelesenen*)';[23] the predicate is not added afterwards to the subject as its very possibility is there *a priori*. With Kant,

> Idealism does make an infinite gain, for thereby the emptiness of *percipere* (*Perzipierens*), or of an *a priori* spontaneity is filled with content absolutely: the determinateness of form is nothing but the identity of opposites. As a result, the *a priori* intellect becomes, at least in principle, *a posteriori* as well; for *a posteriority* is nothing but the positing of the opposite. Thus the formal concept of reason is obtained: Reason has to be *a priori* and *a posteriori*, identical and non-identical, in absolute unity.[24]

Accordingly, the originary synthetic unity assumes, by its very concept, the *a priori* solidarity of the *a priori* and the *a posteriori*. However, for Hegel, the unity presupposed by this Kantian synthesis is ineffectual. The 'identity of the I and the manifold' remains purely formal. The aftermath, acting as the originary condition of possibility, is the possibility of something it never encounters:

> The manifold of sensibility, empirical consciousness as intuition and sensation, is itself something unintegrated (*Unverbundenes*), . . . the world is in itself falling to pieces (*in sich Zerfallendes*), and only gets objective coherence support, substantiality, multiplicity, and even actuality and possibility, through the good offices (*Wohltat*) of the self-consciousness of the human being endowed with intellect.[25]

Since it remains fundamentally something 'other' to the empirically given, self-consciousness – the mediating principle – cannot be a mediating principle. The phenomenal world surges up over against the Ego. Hence, the Kantian synthesis is only an 'ought-to-be' for, in Hegel's view, when we examine the relation consciousness adopts towards the world, we find that this relation in fact derives only from an analytic unity: consciousness and the world exist merely in a relation of juxtaposition. In other words, there would be no *a priori* synthesis in Kant, since he 'makes the true *a priori* into a pure unity again, a unity that is not in origin a synthetic unity'.[26]

Philosophy, Hegel argues, will have had no other effect but that of precipitating the coming-to-be analytic of the synthesis (*le devenir analytique de la synthèse*). The principle of the prior unity of opposites has certainly always played a part in philosophy. But both the Aristotelian pair, δύναμις–ἐνέργεια and the Kantian couple of *a priori–a posteriori* lack the moment of mutual recognition: where identity is retained within difference and difference preserved within identity. Synthesis remains an idea 'which succeeding eras have to accomplish'.

From the predicative to the speculative: the relevance of reading

Ordinary reading and predication

In the Preface to the *Phenomenology of Spirit*, Hegel contrasts two 'methods' of conceiving the proposition: the 'ratiocinative method' (*räsonnierende Weise*) and the 'speculative method' (*spekulative Weise*), stating that the 'mixture' of these two 'methods' constitutes a 'difficulty which should be avoided'.[27] What is original about the analysis here is that it presents the transition from one 'method' to another, whether that be from the predicative proposition to the speculative or the other way around, as something which is experienced through the practice of reading.

Hegel begins with the ordinary practice of reading and understanding philosophical writing. He reminds us of one 'particular complaint often made against philosophical writings, that so much has to be read over and over again before it can be understood'.[28] Now, as he interprets this, if the reader of a philosophical text generally does not understand what he or she has read, this is not the fault of an inadequate education. The work remains incomprehensible even for an individual 'who otherwise possesses the intellectual and cultural conditions required to understand it'.[29] The problem lies instead in the way the reader's ordinary habits of reading and understanding have been constructed.

Reading can be defined in a very simple fashion, as the linear action of connecting one utterance to another. This linkage is made possible by the syntax of the utterances, which is in turn a function of the linear organization of the constitutive elements. Grammatical and logical structure are responsible for the ductility of reading. Guided by this structure, the reader can absorb the utterance without playing any role whatsoever in producing the reading's content or form. Indeed, the ordinary or ratiocinative interpretation of reading practice assumes that it is not the reader who decides what is said, the subject or how it is said. The reader simply takes note of it. Subjected to the statement, the reading subject does not know how to be its subject.

The reader is found in the same position as the subject of the proposition that, according to the 'ratiocinative method', takes note of the predicates that have been attributed. Referring the accidents to the substance that accepts them without having produced them, the reader simply reiterates the attribution already contained in the proposition:

> Usually the subject is first made the basis, as the *objective*, fixed self (*als das gegenständliche fixe Selbst*); thence the necessary movement proceeds to the multiplicity (*Mannigfaltigkeit*) of determinations or predicates. Here, that subject is replaced by the knowing 'I' itself (*das wissende Ich*), which links the predicates to the subject holding them.[30]

The reader thinks he or she has understood the proposition when the attribution expressed in it can be accounted for. After having 'reported', the reader is in a position to enter into a relationship. The reader's 'I' replaces the subject of the proposition and turns that into a 'second subject (*ein zweites Subjekt*)' which duplicates the action – or rather the inaction – of the 'first'.[31] The 'knowing I' replaces the subject of the proposition in so far as the latter cannot sustain the relation on its own. By this talk of 'replacement', Hegel is thinking of the way in which, throughout the history of philosophy, the 'I', understood as consciousness, has become the synthetic instance, the condition of possibility for all predication whatsoever, the origin of all attribution and all judgement.

Yet why has the philosophical proposition not been understood? Because the linear *transition* between subject and predicate, although it is immediately suggested both by the philosophical statement and by its own form, encounters resistance. Faced with a proposition such as 'God is being', the reader discovers that 'being', as much as 'God', is the subject of the proposition:

> since the predicate itself has been expressed as a subject, as *the* being or *essence* which exhausts the nature of the subject, thinking finds the subject immediately in the predicate; and now, instead of being in a position where it has freedom for argument (*ratiocination*), having returned into itself in the predicate, it is still absorbed in the content, or at least is faced with the demand that it should be.[32]

It is the same situation when the proposition is: 'the *actual* is the *universal*':

> The actual as subject disappears in the predicate. The universal is not meant to have merely the significance of a predicate, as if the proposition asserted only that the actual is universal; on the contrary, the universal is meant to express the essence of the actual.[33]

The passive subject – be it the subject of the proposition or the reading subject – 'wavers' (*schwankt*). *Schwanken* means 'to vacillate', 'to swing in the balance', 'to oscillate'. The proposition strains like a wire pulled down suddenly, condemning thought to a strange game of backwards tightrope-walking: 'Thinking, instead of making progress in the transition from subject to predicate, feels itself checked in by the loss of the subject and thrown back onto the thought of the subject, because it misses it. . . .'[34]

Conversely,

> Thinking, when in the predicate, is thrown back onto the subject; it loses the firm objective basis it had at the level of the subject, and when in the predicate, it does not return into itself but into the subject of the content.[35]

Sometimes the statements made about the subject signify its concept, but at other times they signify its predicate or its accident. Hegel insists:

> Speculative (*begreifenden*) thinking behaves in a different way. Since the concept is the object's own self, which presents itself as the *coming-to-be of the object* (*als sein Werden darstellt*), it is not a passive subject (*ruhendes Subjekt*) motionlessly (*unbewegt*) supporting the accidents; it is rather the self-moving concept which takes its determinations back into itself.[36]

At the first attempt, the reader, trying to pass from subject to predicate, suffers a 'counter-thrust' (*ein Gegenstoß*).[37] Literally, the word *Gegenstoß* ('counter-attack', 'counter-thrust') indicates the opposite action of a *Stoß*, a 'thrust', a 'shock', an 'impact'. *Gegenstoß* is a shock with repercussions, the reverse of the original movement where meaning 'fell' into the lexicon and into grammar. Thus, by falling the wrong way, the subject takes in reverse the contingent path taken in the original fall, and finds itself caught up in the very necessity of something which, at first glance, had seemed a simple case: the order of a phrase, the syntax of an attribution. As she advances towards a possible understanding of this necessity, the reader is helped by the speculative oscillation which tosses her onto the subject when she arrives at the predicate, and onto the predicate just when she thought she could return to the subject.

Sinking into the content, the reader experiences a loss of ground and foundation. Thinking cannot get away from the proposition which it intended to do no more than pass through. Thinking remains sunk (*versenkt*) in its content. Now this state of being bogged down in the matter and this weight which holds the subject fast and impedes it are, paradoxically, the conditions of a genuine fall of predication. And this last formula should be understood in the double sense of a fall which predication itself causes and the decline which predication suffers.

How to re-read (with) Hegel?

The reader cannot go on, and must therefore read again:

> This attitude and this opinion are destroyed by the philosophical content (of the proposition): opinion (*die Meinung*) comes to experience the fact that it means something other than it intended to mean (*anders gemeint ist, als sie meinte*); and this correction of its opinion compels knowing to go back to the proposition and understand it in some other way.[38]

But how is the reading to be repeated? We have seen that the specific nature of the philosophical proposition lies in something which could not be available to the first reading. What seems obvious at the first grasp of the proposition is in reality its fundamental unreadability, because the propositional form is in conflict with 'the unity of the concept [the dialectical identity of the terms] which destroys the form [of the proposition]'. To transform this first chaotic encounter with the objectivity of the text into a structure adequate to the philosophical proposition, to change it 'right at the level of the form' (*an der Form*), we cannot do this just by duplicating this experience of unreadability.

At the moment when the reader suffers the 'counter-thrust', 'instead of being for itself, the reader has to remain associated (*zusammensein*) with the content itself' of the proposition, in other words to join its backward movement.[39] In so doing, the origin comes closer, the reader approaches the absolute origin which always retreats towards itself.

But at this place of return, the reader finds *nothing*. As the origin was never there the first time, the reader cannot discover any substantial presence or substratum waiting to be identified. The only thing that can be followed is the sheer movement of retrocession itself, a return that moves on, finding at its own back the drive to advance. Turning back to the original point at which all the forms had been presented, the reader is at the same time projected in advance: required to give form. Plunged into the void of the proposition, the reader is brought to formulate new propositions in return. It is in this sense that the following statement is to be understood: 'The return of the concept into itself must find explicit expression.' The return of the concept into itself would amount to nothing if it didn't involve its own enunciation, the new era of its saying, the grammaticality of its appearance.

The reader escapes confusion, we recall, when 'coming back to the proposition (*auf den Satz zurück zu kommen*)', that proposition can now 'be understood differently'. Because this understanding was not derived from itself (a first reading has never happened), the reader must have produced it, which means that the reader must also be a *philosopher*, and not just a subject, an 'I', who tries to become familiar with a philosophical text. Similarly, a statement, even if already written, is only speculative in the true sense when it cannot be read without being rewritten.

For Hegel, the movement from the ordinary to the philosophical proposition doesn't mean that the propositional form is abandoned, but that *new statements* must be created. Each time, the dialectical movement of the proposition must manifest three aspects of each and every philosophical statement: a shared form, the suppression of that form, and the presentation in return of the cancelled form.

What the dialectical movement demands is not a passivity, but a *plasticity*, from the reader. As we recall from the 1831 Preface to the *Science of Logic*:

> A plastic discourse demands, too, a plastic receptivity and understanding [on the part of the listener]; but such plastic youths and men, possessing a temper that calmly suppresses their *own* reflections and opinions, in which *personal* thought is so impatient to manifest itself, listeners such as Plato imagined (*wie sie Platon dichtet*) who would attend only to the matter at hand, these would be impossible to put on the stage of a modern dialogue: still less could one count on having such readers.[40]

Only a reader who is already 'formed' could recognize the cancellation of form and 'inform' this very cancellation. In the first stage, the reader definitely lets go every and all form, like the wax one has been modelling: the reader loses the form of the 'knowing I', which had represented the self 'relating to the content as to an accident or a predicate'. At the same time the reader, as a 'particular Self', disappears. But this ordeal, in which the 'Self' 'sinks' into the content, is only the first phase of the speculative fall. Plasticity is not polymorphism. In the second stage, the reader must recover from (*se relever de*) this decline so that the efficacy of its advent can be manifest, in the assumption of the meaning of the proposition.

The reader is led to articulate another proposition; and from this one the reading of the first, which never took place, is recovered but at the price of a new expenditure. Far from basing itself purely and simply on the content of what is read, this new reading must in return express the content; and to do so, to form new propositions, all it can do is to *transform* the content of its reading, that is to *interpret* it.

Interpretation

Yet does the theory of 'plastic reading' legitimate arbitrary exegesis? Clearly it is a conception of reading that will invalidate any idea of readerly 'objectivity' if by 'objectivity' we mean the attempt to bring to light, once and for all, what the text 'means'. Now isn't Hegel often reproached for indulging in such interpretative violence?

The question of arbitrariness comes up because the concept of plastic reading accords a determinative and decisive role to the subjectivity of the reader, the reader having become the author of the enunciation. The reader rewrites what he or she reads. Yet it is incumbent on no one but the reader to present, in return, the movement which, paradoxically enough, led to the collapse of the 'knowing I', hence to individuality itself. If this is the case, what differentiates an 'I' in this sense from the practice of interpretative subjectivity?

Let us recall the definition of plasticity put forward in the *Aesthetics*: the 'plastic' is at once universal and individual (*allgemein und doch individuell*). While clearly unique, at the same time it expresses the universal. Unquestionably, plastic reading does engage the 'Self' of the reader, and, by the same token, is always subjective. But, taking into account the definition of plasticity, we can maintain that the subjectivity required is a matter of singularity. Hence it is not just a matter of that simple and contingent particularity which always characterized the 'knowing I' and was manifestly and genuinely arbitrary. Singularity is the ostensive, open portion of subjectivity, and particularity is its occulting and concealing side: enclosed within itself, it reveals nothing but its own solipsistic being.[41]

By being guided through the ordeal of the speculative proposition and its proof to a letting-go of the particular 'I' and its rigid form, the reader no longer has a place for the interpretation that the 'I' had proposed. To sustain that particularity, the Self had worked hard to fashion itself, to become what it was not: namely a *style*. Now style, as we saw in the first part of this book, is its own necessity.

However, don't we always claim that, in principle, the validity of an interpretation relies on the effacement of *all* subjectivity? Hegel's great originality is that he shows exactly how an interpretation that aims at nothing more than universality, that disallows any role for the singularity of the exegete, an interpretation, indeed, that refuses to be plastic, in the sense of both 'universal and individual', would be in reality particular and arbitrary. Isn't the 'knowing I' fundamentally and paradoxically an 'I' that effaces itself? We have seen that, in order to understand the proposition, the reader must first put to work the attribution expressed in it: hence, the reader will be identified with the subject of the statement, and his or her own difference will be effaced. Nonetheless, such a reading, even though envisaged as a model of exemplary 'fidelity to the text', is absolutely nonphilosophical, and remains confined, as Hegel says, in 'ratiocination'.

The grammatical structure of the predicative proposition represents substance as if a passive subject were receiving its predicates from outside. From the perspective of ratiocinative thinking, the proposition reproduces an ontological model, a model which functions as referent for that particular proposition. The reader, by becoming a transparent stand-in for the subject of the statement, expects that the subject has thereby become transparent to its referent, and that the elocutionary dimension of the proposition will volatilize into something else of which it is only the sign and the index. The syntactical structure of the proposition, in so far as it reproduces an ontological order independent of language, necessarily determines for the reader what the exegetical procedure will be: one should look outside the text, for a non-textual meaning.

Against this, the absolute never occupies the place of a referent. It could never be '*what* we are talking about'. Yet, as soon as one says that the absolute has no referential status, one has placed it in a referential position. Representational thinking confines itself to this immediate understanding of the absolute. For it, the proposition is an instrument of ontological capture modelled, to adopt a metaphor from the Introduction to the *Phenomenology of Spirit*, on those lime-twigs with which birds are caught. The ratiocinative concept of interpretation, for which interpretation is an explication that traces the text, considered as a collection of indices, to an extra-textual referent, could qualify as 'physiognomic' in the sense we have developed in the first part of this book.

In this way, it is the 'knowing I', prisoner of the 'referential illusion', who occults true reading. In *The Space of Literature*, Maurice Blanchot remarks: 'What most threatens reading is this: the reader's reality, his personality, his immodesty, his stubborn insistence upon remaining himself in the face of what he reads – a man who knows in general how to read.'[42] This immodesty can even be the result of the very operation that ostensibly abolishes it. Its consequence is that the reader, instead of sticking to the text, looks for its intention.

A conception of reading like this one, for which reading turns out to be elucidating the 'hidden meaning' of the proposition, in fact dismisses the whole speculative way of working. With this in mind, we can understand the assertion in the Preface to the *Phenomenology of Spirit*, namely that philosophy should relinquish 'any personal intrusions (*eigenen Einfallens*) into the immanent rhythm of the concept, and not intervene in it either arbitrarily or with wisdom obtained elsewhere'.[43] But to renounce intervening as a 'knowing I' does not by any means suggest that all subjectivity is to be renounced. The letting-go of the Self in the act of reading does not suspend all power of decision; on the contrary, it produces the condition of the possibility of decision. The speculative proposition checks our confidence in 'knowing how to read', thus training the reader in an illiteracy of the second power which will make the reader write what he or she reads.

The way the reader balances between the two sides of the proposition, pushed into the transfer from one to the other, allows the reader to feel the very movement of the Self as a tension – at once a conflict and a unity – between two tendencies: the accident's tendency to account for the whole and substance's tendency to detach itself from its accidents. Indeed, by following this movement exactly (indeed, by adopting it), the reading subject enters on the scene at once as an accident (in the form of particularity, of the 'knowing I'), and as substance (substitution of this 'I' for the subject of the proposition). Progressively, in the course of reading, the reader's subjectivity is formed into a substantial accident, a style, a plasticity.

If philosophy must 'rigidly exclude the usual way of relating the parts of a proposition', this is because its task is to think the indissoluble dialectical relation between the movement of the becoming essential of contingency ('what seems to be the predicate becomes the whole independent mass'[44]) and that of the becoming aleatory of essence (the predicate fades away in the pure universality of the subject). Plasticity, informing the self-determining movement of substance and establishing the identity of contingency and necessity, is experienced in the act of reading. This is precisely what Absolute Knowledge knows.

CONCLUSION

The event of reading

Why, at the end of this work, do we invoke the concept of reading? The reason is clear. The Hegelian idea of plastic reading confers on the notion of 'to see (what is) coming' its real meaning. 'To see (what is) coming' denotes at once the visibility and the invisibility of whatever comes. The future is not the absolutely invisible, a subject of pure transcendence objecting to any anticipation at all, to any knowledge, to any speech. Nor is the future the absolutely visible, an object clearly and absolutely foreseen. It frustrates any anticipation by its precipitation, its power to surprise. 'To see (what is) coming' thus means to see without seeing – await without awaiting – a future which is neither present to the gaze nor hidden from it. Now isn't this situation of 'in-between' *par excellence* the situation of reading?

'I', the reader

First and above all, the reader of Hegel. More than any other philosopher, to read Hegel is to see and not to see. The text is in front of our eyes, yet its systematicity initially conceals its meaning because the speculative content at once is something yet to come and already arrived. The tremendous difficulty of reading Hegel's work is caused by the seeming impossibility of making any headway since from the outset we would need to carve out a beginning allowing us both to foresee and not to see what follows. How then are we to escape from the sheer tautology offered by a paraphrase, and at the same time from the absolute heterology posed by an arbitrary commentary?

Between ratiocinative repetition and delirious intrusion, between an excess of prevision and an excessive obliviousness to what comes, the reader ends by finding her way. This happens at the moment when the reader enters into the speculative ordeal constituted by the relationship between the difference of the reader and the identity of the text. Understanding Hegel is the necessary result of a readerly decision to be diverted from an initial confusion while accepting the release from the rigid form of the 'I'. The continuity found in the Hegelian philosophy, its systematic expository movement whose ultimate expression is the *Encyclopedia*, allows interruption, that is to say, the eruption of the interpreter, but only because it forms it. Hegel's absolute, writes Bernard Bourgeois:

> Is neither the absolute spirit present in the reading of the *Encyclopedia*, nor the absolute objective spirit present in the encyclopedia as a book. It is actualized in the final, concrete identity of this book's reading. . . . This concrete identity of the subjectivity of the speculative reader and the objectivity of the speculative text forbids us to consider their relation in the guise of a 'having', a possession . . . , a form of *repetition*. . . . A comprehensive reading of the *Encyclopedia* thus demands a personal engagement with its content; it is literally an adventure calling on the reader's own self. . . . If the self of the reader must create the content of the *Encyclopedia*, in return the substance of its content must be at one with the reader, which means that to bring the *Encyclopedia* back to life means to create it again for and in oneself: to re-read the *Encyclopedia* is to rewrite it.[1]

One never learns Hegel once and for all. He is not to be possessed like a body of doctrine to be known by heart in all its operations and concepts. Hegel may well be the first philosopher to think that the author is not a 'fixed and solid subject' but an instance of writing, conceived in the joint play and speaking of two subjects of enunciation: a speculative reader, and the one who wrote because he was, first and above all, a speculative reader. Interpretation is a *production* that presupposes the accident which gave it birth, which by the same token accepts that it cannot be definitive but promised to other readers. 'Plastic' reading has its place in an exegetical economy which, because there is nothing 'outside the text (*hors texte*)', places the text absolutely outside itself.

Having become experienced through the speculative ordeal of a shared speech, the reader is from now on able to *respond* to the reading. Hence it is now this reader who can finally speak in their own voice. I will now say what event of reading it was that allowed me to see coming (*voir venir*) Hegel's *Encyclopedia*.

Everything began, or began again, when, 'falling' one day onto the term 'plastic', I was brought to a stop, at once intrigued and grateful. Intrigued by its discreet presence in the Hegelian corpus, by that whole realm of the unknown which gestured through it. Grateful for something essential which was suddenly recognizable. Attempting to understand it more carefully, I started to study the way it functioned in the Hegelian text, focusing my attention onto everything in it which referred back to a dynamism of the reception and donation of form, hence to subjectivity itself in a process of self-determination. It was an 'accident' – the term 'plastic' could at first sight be considered something accidental in Hegel's text – that brought me to the essential.

Plasticity is essentially astonishing. To demonstrate that, it must be constituted in a schema which is at once verbal and conceptual. To understand plasticity as a concept required the launching of a reading programme in two stages. First of all, I had to establish an enumeration and an index of all the lexical usages of 'plastic' (*Plastik, Plaztizität, plastisch*) in Hegel's text, so that I could then uncover which could philosophically be at stake and propose an interpretation of it.

Yet have I, coming on stage with such a programme, taken on the method of the 'knowing I', the ratiocinative reader whose vanity Hegel denounces? To me it seems rather that plasticity was imposed on me at the very moment – but when was that moment? – when the 'I' was broken in the ordeal of its discovery, which is to say, at the moment of the discovery of plasticity which, by definition, doesn't need an 'I' to be deployed.

The two powers

Doubtless, it is by 'my' intervention, but outside the realm of the 'I', that an event of reading gave birth to a reading of the event in Hegel's philosophy. It is clear to me that the living grammar of the notion of plasticity was deeply at work in the speculative content, at once as its structure and as its rhythm. An integrating and informing power, an originary synthetic power, plasticity also requires a contrary power of dissociation and rupture. These two powers characterize perfectly the gait of the Hegelian text: gathering and splitting, both at work in the System's own formation. They are two inseparable powers, allowing an idea of temporalizing synthesis and an idea of factual eruption to be articulated together. My whole work is invested here, as it tries to show that the Hegelian notion of temporality is located nowhere else but in the economy opened up by this articulation.

Plasticity is a name for the originary unity of acting and being acted upon, of spontaneity and receptivity. A medium for the differentiation of opposites, plasticity holds the extremes together in their reciprocal action, enabling the function of a structure of anticipation where the three terms of the temporal process are articulated: the originary synthesis, the hypotyposis or embodiment of the spiritual, the relation of the moments of time. The meaning of the notion of plasticity is the same as its way of being. Plasticity is what it is, plastic. Indeed, the originary operation of receiving and giving form is not a rigid and fixed structure but an instance which can evolve, which means that it can give itself new forms. The temporal differentiation of plasticity makes possible the historical deployment of the substance-subject.

In the case of plasticity, because of the identity of its meaning and its way of being – its content and its form – we can say that the originary synthetic medium of opposites, as a reservoir of energy, itself obeys the law of its own power. It explodes its own reserves. Hegel's idea of the arising, the event, belongs in this place of contrasts where form forms itself and at the same time deforms itself, where it acquires consistency and bursts out like a bomb. A passage in the *Phenomenology of Spirit* describes the arising of the new as an overspill of energy coming in a sudden leap, like that of a detonator which strikes the organization of the vital forces:

> Spirit is never at rest but always engaged in moving forward (*in immer fortschreitender Bewegung*). But just as when the child after its long, silent nourishment takes a first breath, breaking (*abbricht*) the gradualness of merely quantitative growth – there is a qualitative leap – and then the child is born; so likewise spirit in its self-formation matures slowly and quietly into its new shape, dissolving bit by bit the structure of its previous world, whose tottering state is only indicated by scattered symptoms; the frivolity and the boredom which unsettle the established order, the vague foreboding of something unknown, are the heralds giving the signs that something other is in the offing (*im Anzuge ist*). The gradual crumbling (*Zerbröckeln*) that left unchanged the physiognomy of the whole, is broken through by the sunrise which, in its flash (*ein Blitz*), illumines the features of the new world in one moment (*in einem Male*).[2]

Presented, in the Introduction to the same work, as the 'pure act of looking on (*das reine Zusehen*)',[3] philosophy, for Hegel, can in a certain sense be defined as this attention brought to the newborn, who is the most vivid and sensuous image of the future. Birth combines blossoming (*éclosion*) and explosion. A process of formation and of the dissolution of form, plasticity, where all birth takes place, should be imagined fundamentally as an ontological combustion (*déflagration*) which liberates the twofold possibility of the appearance and the annihilation of presence. It is a process which functions on its own, automatically. As such, it comes out of nothing; as such, it is the bearer of the future, if it is true that the future, by definition, comes from nowhere. I have tried to bring into view the chance which, in Hegel's thought, constitutes the explosive side of subjectivity, forgotten by recent readers.

Composition and recomposition

Remaining irreducible to self-presence, this chance is hard to grasp (*saisir*). Have I grasped it? To justify the subject's explosive nature, I have tried to show what constitutes its mechanism or its apparatus: the ontological seesaw of the substance-subject. The process of substance's self-determination leans from side to side. Of necessity, one of its slopes will become larger than the other: either the 'becoming essential of the accident' in the Greek moment of subjectivity, or the 'becoming accidental of essence' in the modern moment. In the first case I showed how the 'exemplary individuals' of Greece tended on their own to acquire the force and the ontological dignity of essence. And then I looked at how the essential being of a revealed God, who enters into his own *kenosis* and into the life of contingency, completes the process of its own accidentalization.

The exemplary individuals of Greece become works of art, individuals of 'a single cast'. The moment of the slope or decline, in the process of the essentializing of the accidental, appears as a relief or projection (ἐξοχή) of the divine in the human, fashioning individuality into the style that belongs to the divine. 'Plastic' individuality elevates itself – an ascending movement – to its own relief and acquires the constancy of essence. Habit enables the incarnation of the divine in the human, and the human in the divine, an incarnation which Greek sculpture presents to the senses.

In the modern moment, the slope of the subject corresponds to the sending of the Son, an inclination which is also the inclination of the Father towards the Son. Through his act of falling – the descending movement – God shows himself to himself and completes thereby the movement of his proposition. He proceeds and results from this slope, and is not God except through its foundation. Hegel gives the 'ex' of 'ecstasy' all the dynamic meaning it possesses, making *kenosis* truly appear as a movement of departure and abasement of the Self in its fall. Alienation or externalization, the possibility of being other than it is, exists always for substance, provoking this 'relief' of the human in the divine, the divine in the human.

Philosophers who see a diminishment of God (yet God, without his incline, would be no more than an abstract and impoverished concept) in the necessity of this decline (involved as much in the essence of the Aristotelian θεός as that of the God of Revelation) are missing the profound originality of Hegel's thought. To introduce a negativity in God which puts him into motion and makes possible his flexing, is undoubtedly the highest possible way of imagining his eminence, the condition and dimension of his fall. Hegel is a thinker for whom the movement of falling is not a degeneration in the ordinary sense of the word, but a term of expiration – something which falls due. It is a matter of taking the future into account, a future which erupts when it 'comes from' and explodes while falling.

But has this demonstration really been explosive? I have shown that reading Hegel amounts to experimenting with a hall of mutually reflecting mirrors where perspectives are opened up by the different modalities of the auto-determination of substance, modalities forming the stages of plasticity. Apprehending the speculative content in its simplified form destines thinking to traverse anew its own route, to test out the self-distribution of its moments and its history. To go all the way, to the end of Hegel and with Hegel, this means to follow all the way to its extreme point the encyclopedic development, and this destines reading to a very singular experience. To follow the movement of spirit's unfolding leads without any doubt to the very heart of the Western tradition, thus to the very heart of a certain Greco-Christian past.

To affirm the future within Hegel's philosophy has not necessarily brought me to emphasize his fidelity to the past. I am aware of the paradoxical aspect of an approach which, anxious to underline the originality of Hegel's reading of Aristotle, could not however avoid the trap of considering his reading as the best one, i.e. in a sense, as the most authentically traditional. In the same manner, by insisting on the singularity of Hegel's interpretation of Christianity, perhaps I have done no more, in reality, than prove that Hegel's God is the *good* God. Desiring to bring out the philosophical novelty and freshness of Hegelianism, I have perhaps only insisted on his conformity to the traditional and onto-theological forms of thought.

Opening the question of the future always comes back to the risk we must assume, the risk of immediately closing it. This would only be the case because the question is, properly speaking, not a wholly new question. Its philosophical antiquity, its tradition, its history, don't they threaten to cancel out its meaning? The ambiguity of 'to see (what is) coming': trying to grasp in advance, to understand surprise, isn't this purely and simply to cushion the shock?

But what applies to the slope of Hegelian thought applies also to the slope of all speculative determinateness and propositions: they reverse. The path opened up by the encyclopedic development reaches all the way to the extreme tip of the Western philosophical tradition; but, for the same reason, it also takes thinking above and beyond those forms. Surprise, even in a weakened form, can always surprise again. If Hegelian philosophy insistently attends to the philosophical tradition, and does so with all its force, that same force ends by inflecting the course of that tradition, by offering, for that tradition, an other perspective.

But what forms that perspective? By equal right, the encyclopedic circle can be interpreted both as the final form in which the tradition is reassembled in all its purity and as the result of a process of recycling of that same tradition. By analysing dialectical simplification we discover that the movement of the singularities, in their auto-distribution, in fact proceeds from the energy produced in redistribution, in reprocessing and reclassifying the forms of spirit. It is as if Hegel did in fact anticipate one of the current connotations of the word 'synthesis', meaning less something that is composed than something *recomposed*. Indeed, we now speak of material, fabrics, forms that have been reconstituted chemically, as 'synthetic'. Hegelianism, that fundamentally systematic business, brings thought to the point where the synthesis of all philosophy – its forms reassembled in the unity of the encyclopedic totality – proceeds, in its specular and speculative movement, to mirror its 'other' self, an other different as well as the same: namely, synthetic philosophy, engendered by an exegetical recomposition, by an interpretative audacity now released from its connection to the authenticity or the 'objective' validity of its referent.

By that double and slanting movement of the incline which ties together the subject and its accidents, a movement which summons the reader to lean from one moment of the history of subjectivity to the other, the speculative proposition brings back to life the sedimented depths of an ontological deployment and, by fluidifying them, releases their energy. In its role as 'fall', as ordeal and trial, philosophy sparks off a necessary anamnesis that undoes spirit from its alienated relation to the familiar and well-known, which drives it away from the customs of the *doxa*, thus involving it in the work of recomposing new habits, new hermeneutical habits.

Hegel places face to face the two epochs which constitute the history of subjectivity. On one side, the epoch marked by the repetitions and habits inherent to the teleological process. On the other, the epoch dominated by the singular 'once and only', by the non-habitual, inseparable from the concept of time as external. This confrontation also presents the outline of the future which, henceforth, exists in the play of the habitual and the unusual, but no longer to be understood as two eras of philosophical thought, rather as the two faces, identical in a speculative sense, of one reality: completion. Hegel's philosophy announces that the future, from now on, depends on the way the shapes and figures already present can be put back into play, on the way the extraordinary and unexpected can only arise out of the prose of the well-known and familiar. Plasticity fulfils its promise for the future with its treatment of a past that has become rigid: if it *plasticizes* that past – by solidifying or laminating it – it also explodes that past, through what the French call *plasticage* or bombing.

From now on we can no longer have anything to do with things other than our own habits, in which we find ourselves immediately alienated. Thought's very life depends on its power to awaken that vital energy which always tends to 'mortify' itself, to become sedimented into fixed and rigid positions. The outcome that will follow depends on this awakening: thought has nothing to do but wait for the habitués to look at their habits. The projects whose aim is the reduction of the Western philosophical tradition, in particular that represented by Heidegger, all emerge from such a reflective look.

Hegel reads Heidegger

This gaze, which Hegel's philosophy uncovers, allows us to foresee the readings of his philosophy which came after it: readings which his philosophy didn't know but which it did, in a certain way, anticipate. It is by no means certain that Hegel would be unprepared to parry the attacks aimed at him by recent philosophy. We could begin with that assertion addressed to him by Heidegger, that there is no future *in* and *of* his philosophy.

Isn't the plasticity of the Hegelian concept of time itself the source of a clandestine resistance, ready and waiting to respond to the accusation of vulgarity which Heidegger raised against that same concept?

I have attempted to show that this temporalizing plasticity protects the Hegelian analysis of temporality from being instantly slotted into the cosmological framework of 'levelled-down time', the frame which a 'paraphrase' of Aristotle would have allowed Hegel to adopt without even putting it into question. On this account I decided to take as my starting point for this study not Hegel's *Philosophy of Nature*, but the *Philosophy of Spirit.*

To bring out the openness to the future, the openness to the event which is part and parcel of Hegel's philosophy, means that we will make explicit the existence of several times, as well as several stages of time: a plurality above and beyond the simple distinction between time in the vulgar, ordinary understanding and originary temporality. Perhaps what the notion of plasticity makes possible is a way to conceive the characteristics of authentic temporality which Heidegger himself brought out.

It is true that Heidegger, in a seminar on Aristotle's *Metaphysics* VIII, did devote a few remarks to the notion of plasticity. He stresses the meaning of the adjective 'plastic' in its connotation of 'strong', 'resistant'. Something plastic 'does not refuse itself . . . it can uphold'.[4] He continues: 'The lump of clay tolerates something; it allows the formation, that is, it is malleable (*bildsam, plastique*): plasticity[5] as a way of being for force.'[6]

The 'suffering' (*erleidet, pâtir*) described by Heidegger is also an active straining towards the future. We call 'plastic' only that 'to which, generally speaking, something can happen'.[7] Thus its orientation is towards the event and it is capable of withstanding the violence that comes with it.[8]

In any case, these remarks on plasticity are isolated occurrences in Heidegger's writings. For example, the term 'plasticity' never appears even once in *Kant and the Problem of Metaphysics*,[9] a work in which Heidegger never ceases to recall the decisive importance of Kant's definition of time as an originary power of formation. 'Time as pure intuition is the forming intuition of what it intuits *in one*'.[10] 'Time is only pure intuition to the extent that it prepares the *look* of the succession from out of itself and it *clutches* this as such *to itself* as the formative taking-in-stride.'[11] Time is not only the name given to a pre-formed form, i.e. to the sequence of nows. Rather, it *forms* that succession. For this reason, Heidegger argues, 'it is in no way permissible to think of time, above all in the case of the Kantian conception of time, as an arbitrary field, which the power of imagination just gets into for purposes of its own activity, so to speak.'[12] Imagination is on its own an 'original formative activity', a 'looking-at, a looking-ahead and a looking-back'.[13]

Heidegger never thematized Kant's 'breakthrough' in terms of plasticity, a notion which he did not invest with ontological significance. Thus it is as if Hegel retrospectively has offered to him an instrument indispensable to the intelligibility of his ideas. The times of Hegel's philosophy, with a generosity Heidegger consistently denies, were perhaps generous enough to offer him a name for his own time of ontological difference.

'To see (what is) coming'

Once the *resistance* of the dialectic is properly felt, we can appreciate its capacity to enter into dialogue with whatever is other than itself, to welcome its posterity and to let itself be surprised by that. It is not only in the workings of philosophical debate that this resistance is detected. A certain condition of modernity also reveals it. Hegel puts into perspective two temporal modes: teleology, corresponding to the Greek form of 'to see (what is) coming', and alienation, corresponding to the modern form of 'to see (what is) coming'. The arrangement of these two times determines the future of those creatures who no longer have time ahead of themselves, who live out a teleology which is shattered because already accomplished. Such a future is both beautiful and terrible. Beautiful because everything can still happen. Terrible, because everything has already happened.

This situation creates the contradictory couple of *saturation* and *vacancy*. Saturation to the extent that the future can, in our time, no longer represent the promise of far-off worlds to conquer. The philosophical tradition, reaching its completion, has as its double the exhaustion of the outside world. The 'new world order' means the impossibility of any exotic, isolated or geopolitically marginal event. Paradoxically, this saturation of theoretical and natural space is felt as a vacuum. The major problem of our time is in fact the arrival of *free time*. Technological simplification, the shortening of distances – all heralded by Hegel with his notion of simplification (*Vereinfachung*) – bring about a state where we must acknowledge that there is nothing more to do. The most sterile aspect of the future lies in the unemployment, both economic and metaphysical, which it promises. But this promise is also a promise of novelty, a promise that there are forms of life which must be invented.

If saturation follows from a closure of the horizon, vacancy, for its part, opens up perspectives. This contradictory unity of saturation and vacancy is exactly what appears in the very form of the Hegelian System, which integrates while it dissociates, which unifies everything while letting what comes come. Plasticity designates the future understood as future within closure, the possibility of a structural transformation: a transformation of structure within structure, a mutation 'right at the level of the form'.

It is not by chance that the notion of plasticity today operates in the domain of cell biology and neurobiology.[14] For example, the 'plasticity' of the nervous system or the immune system means their ability to tolerate modifications, transformations of their particular components which affect their structural closure, or modifications and transformations caused by perturbations from the environment.[15] Thus, the possibility of a closed system to welcome new phenomena, all the while transforming itself, is what appears as plasticity. Here again we find the process by which a contingent event, or accident, touches at the heart of the system, and, in the same breath, changes itself into one of the system's essential elements.

Hegel already shows how the twofold tendency of the becoming essential of the accident and the becoming accidental of essence is constitutive for all life, in other words, for all the 'three lives', identified by him as logical life, natural life, and spiritual life. As the principle of the attributive synthesis, this twofold tendency grounds the relation which connects substance and its accidents, and constitutes the development of 'Science' (*Wissenschaft*). On the other hand, it governs the momentalization of the life of spirit, a momentalization as much logical as structural, historical or chronological in nature. Ultimately it is a tendency which operates at the level of living. It is automatically inscribed 'right at the level' of life. Without doubt, Hegel is the only philosopher of the tradition to overcome the traditional opposition of the natural and the artificial. Accordingly, the automatism stressed throughout the entire system is definitely and simultaneously logical, natural and spiritual.

Thus it is Hegel who will have discovered before its discovery the plastic materiality of being: that free energy, whether organic or synthetic, which circulates throughout in each and every life. From now on the philosopher lives in the tension created by the existence of pure 'possibility' inherent in such an energy, and bears the responsibility of protecting and preserving the rudimentary being of subjectivity: its fragile and finite kernel.

Plasticity is the place where Hegel's idea of finitude is constituted. Between the emergence and the annihilation of form, plasticity carries, as its own possibility, self-engendering and self-destruction. If plasticity means what is vital and supple, it is nonetheless always susceptible to petrifaction. If it expresses what is most essential and primal in life itself, it is no less in alliance with the atomic bomb (*Plastikbombe*). A living and vital notion, plasticity is also a mortal notion. Sheltering, as long as it is possible, the space liberated by the interplay of the extremes between a living kernel and the nuclear nucleus, existing on the plane of saturation and vacancy, this is what the future requires.

The philosophy of Hegel invites us to enter into the serenity and the peril of the Sunday of life.

NOTES

PREFACE BY JACQUES DERRIDA

1 This text was originally published as 'Le temps des adieux: Heidegger (lu par) Hegel (lu par) Malabou' in *La Revue Philosophique* (Paris: PUF, no. 1, 1998, pp. 3–47).

2 The French word 'adieu' can mean at the same time 'hello', 'good day', 'salutations', 'greetings', and, 'farewell', 'go in peace', 'be saved', 'be with God'. The double meaning and almost contradictory signification of this word, torn between greeting someone, seeing someone arrive or return *and* taking from someone an indeterminate leave (often used in the Midi region of France) marks a particularly *aporetic* structure which Derrida analyses and 'sees coming' in the *promise*. 'Adieu' is here translated by 'farewell'. (Translator's note.)

3 It is Catherine Malabou's fundamental proposition which allows us to forge this odd expression 'history of the future', an expression that is justified for it relates to nothing less than a history of time. It is a history of *subjectiveness* as 'to see (what is) coming'. Such an extraordinary and necessary contortion of the concept: if history presupposes the existence of time, how can time be thought of as having a history? How may this be thought more radically than in the manner of a history of history (which is also a necessary reflection but which is also a much more common way of thought)? After having recalled the *plasticity* of time, that is its synchronic and diachronic capacity to auto-differentiate itself, Malabou stresses:

> to say that time is not always what it is also means that it temporally differentiates itself from itself, that it has, to put in another way, a *history*. In the *Encyclopedia* paragraphs on space and time, the implicit references to Aristotle and Kant make it possible to clarify a fundamental characteristic of Hegel's thought. 'To see (what is) coming', which is the originary possibility of all encounter, the structure of subjective anticipation, is *not the same in every moment of its history*, it doesn't 'see (what is) coming' in the same way, *it doesn't have the same future*. Subjectivity comes to itself in two fundamental moments: *the Greek moment and the modern moment*, which prove to be, both in their logical unity and in their chronological succession, 'subject as substance' and 'substance as subject'.
>
> (p. 16)

4 The French expression 'Voir venir' has been translated by the formula 'to see (what is) coming'. The parentheses in this translation mark the *waiting* or the

reserve implicit and inherent in the *coming* and in the modality of *sight*. See also the *Preliminary remarks* of *The Future of Hegel*. (Translator's note.)

5 *The Future of Hegel*, p. 13.

6 See in particular, Chapter III ('On the Self') of Part III.

7 At the risk of shocking linguists or lexicologists, I will proceed here as if there are no differences between language, idiom or dialect. Doesn't language's authority or status depend on some *external* legitimation? Isn't language the consecration of some kind of dialectical idiom? Doesn't its dignity rely on historical and political powers conferred on it and which are, for the main part, intrinsically linguistic? A dialect is accepted as a language, it seems, when its subjects demand it and most of all when these same subjects have the power to recognize and the force to urge others to acknowledge their very demand on a sociopolitical scene. Didn't some Englishman say that language is a dialect 'with a navy'?

8 Malabou emphasizes this expression 'works on and within the body', in a passage which can be read with one we will cite later, a passage which discusses plasticity as a *hypotyposis*, as a symbolic or schematic sensible figure in the Kantian sense, p. 18.

9 Hegel, *Phenomenology of Spirit*, translated by A. V. Miller (Oxford: Oxford University Press, 1977), p. 143.

10 *The Future of Hegel*, p. 18.

11 The book begins with a profound and dense semantic exposition of the word and of the concept of plasticity. Combining admirably the genealogical filiation with a taxonomic concern, Malabou organizes this presentation around a motif which is itself plastic, in other words, double and apparently contradictory, and which extends throughout the book: to give – to receive. If the substantive *plasticity* (*Plastizität*), implying that the term is always to be promoted to the dignity of a philosophical notion or concept, has been written in the French language since before the Revolution (1785) and entered the German language in the 'Age of Goethe' (according to the Brockhaus dictionary), it is an adjectival form, *plastisch*, which found in the Grimm dictionary its most plastic definition, a definition which deserves and preserves that alternation of giving and receiving, including it and thus at the same time sublating it, and includes also the alternation between passive and active applied either to a form or to a figure (*körperlich . . . gestaltend oder gestaltet*) (p. 8). This will thus be the guiding principle of *The Future of Hegel*. We could here imagine a question that would in fact obsess this guiding principle: what must be these elements (a body or a figure, the exemplary sensibility of a form, the example of whatever may be or could be . . .) in order for giving and receiving, and hence, giving and taking, etc. to be crossed in a sort of equivalence? What could 'sensuous' possibly mean, if we were to translate, as philosophy has always done, 'sensuous' by 'receptivity'? This is truly the question of the *schema*.

12 *The Future of Hegel*, p. 7.

13 It is the French translation of *Sein und Zeit* by F. Vezin which Malabou refers to here. We are entitled to ask what is the justification of this reference. Should Malabou have refrained from using the word 'vulgar' which is strong and marked in so many ways? Nonetheless, the word 'current' offers me here the chance and the possibility of the cursive and of the 'current-course' which permits us to join this conception to the course or flux of time here incriminated (*Lauf der Zeit*). I will not refuse this chance or possibility here for the time being and for my own personal use, even though I understand the problems of translating the German 'vulgar' by 'current'.

14 *Being and Time*, translated by J. Stambaugh (Albany: State University of New York Press, 1996), p. 390. Quoted by Malabou, p. 2.
15 Heidegger, *Hegel's Phenomenology of Spirit*, translated by K. Maly and P. Emad Indiana University Press, 1994), p. 82. Quoted by Malabou, p. 3.
16 *The Future of Hegel*, p. 18.
17 *The Future of Hegel*, p. 12.
18 That all living beings are not endowed with the faculty of seeing, does not stop Hegel from interpreting the appropriation of the organic through the inorganic as *theorein* (in the Aristotelian sense of contemplation and exercise, of informative reception and appropriating transformation of the middle point). This *theorein* would at once be, if I may say so, an act of seeing without seeing and an act of seeing *before* all sight, the *telos* of sight here at work. I can only here refer to the decisive pages on the *plasticity of life*, and more precisely, to the subchapter devoted to Aristotle, Hegel, Bergson and Deleuze ('Contraction and Theory'). Decisive meditations on meditation itself (between and schema by excellence), these pages and their implications would be such in the manner where the question of the living does not here belong to an ontological field amongst others. Even more so, it is not contained in some kind of anthropology or within that which in anthropology would refer to a simple living organism. Plasticity of life is a sort of pleonasm. And this is why we will not escape a certain confrontation with death (and with the farewell as adieu) in which the very experience (impossible experience of the impossible) of plasticity, of some sort of equivocal or contradictory plasticity, is present in all 'to see (what is) coming': what we see coming without ever seeing it come. And that the question of life-and-death is not here contained in a zoology or in an anthropology, we shall see confirmed at the very centre of the second part of Malabou's book (Hegel on God): 'The Death of God', 'The Divine Plasticity', etc.
19 *The Future of Hegel*, p. 184.
20 Very near its conclusion, *The Future of Hegel* multiplies the necessary and precious indications of the operative actuality of the concept and of the word 'plasticity' in cellular biology and neurobiology. In particular, as we are speaking of reading, for the study of 'neuronal mechanisms implied in the memory process' (pp. 192–3).
21 *The Future of Hegel*, p. 76.
22 Ibid., pp. 6–7.
23 Koyré, 'Time [for Hegel] . . . is constructed by and from the future', *Etudes d'histoire de la pensée philosophique* (Paris: Gallimard; 1971, p. 189; Kojève, 'Time which Hegel has in view . . . is characterized by the primacy of the future', *Introduction à la lecture de Hegel* Paris: Gallimard, 1947), p. 367.
24 *The Future of Hegel*, p. 7.
25 Ibid., p. 7.
26 There is an excellent special issue of the English journal *Parallax* entirely devoted to Kojève's heritage. Shortly after arriving in Paris in 1928, Kojève became Koyré's assistant at the École Pratique des Hautes Études. See *Parallax* 4 (London, 1997).
27 *The Future of Hegel*, p. 60.
28 Heidegger, *Hegel's Phenomelogy of Spirit*, p. 147. Translation slightly modified, p. 147.
29 See *La Phénoménologie de l'esprit de Hegel* (Cours du semestre d'hiver 1930–1931), by E. Martineau (Paris : Gallimard, 1984), p. 224. French translation of Heidegger's *Hegel's Phenomenology of Spirit.*
30 *The Future of Hegel*, p. 4.

31 'These preliminary remarks indicate that my work will not follow the path set out by Koyré and Kojève, although both pursue this question of the "future" *in* Hegel's philosophy' (p. 6).

32 *Beyond Good and Evil*, Part 1, '*On the philosopher's prejudices*'. On the 'perhaps' or the 'maybe' between Hegel and Heidegger, see Rodolphe Gasché, 'Perhaps – a modality? On the way with Heidegger to language', *Graduate Faculty Philosophy Journal*, vol. 16, no. 2 (1993), p. 469, and also the chapters which I have devoted to this question in *The Politics of Friendship*, translated by George Collins (London and New York: Verso, 1997).

33 *The Future of Hegel*, p.161. In an important passage concerning contingency, necessity and freedom, the 'speculative automatism' as the essential becoming (or the becoming essential) of the accident and, *at the same time*, the accidental becoming (or the becoming accidental) of essence, Malabou recalls the conventional reading: 'One can deduce from this that everything which is possible is to become actual, that every accident has a meaning, and thus that, for Hegel, there is no such thing as a pure accident.' But it is in order to confront it with a strong refutation: 'Such a reading is erroneous.' We should naturally follow in all of its folds, something which we could not do here, the deployment of this counter-reading.

34 *The Future of Hegel*, p. 162.

35 Ibid., p. 163.

36 Ibid., p. 163. I ask myself what is the subtle difference which distinguishes this interpretation, that of Malabou (as to what remains foreign to knowledge, 'cannot be an object of knowledge', even if this limit, *its* limit is 'what Absolute Knowledge knows'), from the one proposed by so many 'different authors', theologians and thinkers of the Lutheran or Catholic faith, authors whom Malabou confronts. For she recognizes at one point that they do not 'deny any implication of unintelligibility'.

> They concentrate on what, in God, cannot be comprehended, what cannot be seized, possessed, or assimilated. Not because Spirit – by some flaw, by some fallibility – is impotent to constitute the divine as object of knowledge, but because, he is not simply *a matter for* knowledge. God is not a concept.
>
> (p. 101)

What difference still subsists, in the end, between these two limits of Absolute Knowledge as knowledge? Between the exposed and assumed logic (p. 163) and the logic we are exposing while confronting (p. 101)?

37 Ibid., p. 163.

38 On folly, on fantasy, on hallucination, on fearfulness or on haunting, ('subjectivity does not reside itself in itself, it haunts itself', p. 35), the 'derangement of Spirit', see particularly pp. 31–6.

39 Ibid., pp. 17–18.

40 These words and concepts are at the centre of the Hegelian interpretation of the Trinity, see p. 96.

41 Ibid., p. 41 and following.

42 Ibid., p. 83.

43 Ibid., p. 97.

44 Ibid., p. 101, and following.

45 'God is dead in order for me to die in regard to the entire world and in the face of all created realities.' Meister Eckhart, quoted by Malabou, *The Future of Hegel*, p. 104.

46 Ibid., p. 104.
47 Hegel, translated and quoted by Malabou, p. 107.
48 Hegel, translated and quoted by Malabou, p. 107.
49 'The charge of atheism, which used often to be brought against philosophy (that it has *too little* of God), has grown rare: the more widespread grows the charge of pantheism, that it has *too much* of Him.' Quoted by Malabou, p. 138.
50 Ibid., p. 130 Malabou underlines.
51 Ibid., p. 114.

INTRODUCTION

1 Hegel, *The Phenomenology of Spirit,* translated by A. V. Miller, with analysis of the text and foreword by J. N. Findlay (Oxford: Oxford University Press, 1977), p. 487; G. W. F. Hegel, *Werke in zwanzig Bänden* (all future references to this text will be designated by 'Suhrkamp' with the volume number), edited by E. Moldenhauer and K. M. Michel (Frankfurt: Suhrkamp Verlag, 1969–), vol. 3, pp. 584–5. Translation modified.
2 *Being and Time* (translated by Joan Stambaugh from the seventh edition, Albany: State University of New York Press, 1996) p. 390. The original is on p. 428 of *Sein und Zeit, Gesamtausgabe* (Tübingen: Max Niemeyer Verlag, 1976), Bd 2.
3 Ibid., p. 422.
4 *Stigmē*, Greek for 'point'. [Trans.]
5 Hegel, *Philosophy of Nature*, Part II of the *Encyclopedia of the Philosophical Sciences*, §257, edited and translated with an introduction and explanatory notes by M. J. Petry, 3 vols (London and New York: George Allen and Unwin, 1970); henceforth *Encyclopedia Philosophy of Nature*; Suhrkamp, *Enzyklopädie der philosophischen Wissenschaften* II, Bd 9.
6 Compare Heidegger's formula in *Sein und Zeit*: 'a right-away that is no longer'. [Trans.]
7 *Hegel's Phenomenology of Spirit*, translated by Parvis Emad and Kenneth Maly (Bloomington and Indianapolis: Indiana University Press, 1988), p. 82. G. A., Bd 32. The English translation of this passage reads: 'Hegel occasionally speaks about having been, but never about the future. This accords with his view of the past as the decisive character of time. It is a fading away, something transitory and always bygone.' (French translation by Emmanuel Martineau, *La* 'Phénoménologie de l'esprit' *de Hegel* (Paris: NRF Gallimard, 1984, p. 135). Heidegger declares in the same lecture series that 'Hegel develops a fundamental view of being according to which what is a genuine being is what has returned to itself' (p. 46).
8 'The German language has preserved essence in the past participle (*gewesen*) of the verb 'to be' (*sein*); for essence is past – but timelessly past – being' (*Science of Logic, Doctrine of Essence,* translated by A. V. Miller, foreword by J. N. Findlay (Atlantic Islands, NJ: Humanities Press International, 1989), p. 389; Suhrkamp, *Wissenschaft der Logik*, II, Bd 6.
9 *Philosophy of Spirit*, Part 3 of the *Encyclopedia of Philosophical Sciences*, translated by W. Wallace, together with the *Zusätze* in Boumann's text (1845), translated by A. V. Miller, with foreword by J. N. Findlay (Oxford: Clarendon Press, 1971), §396, Addition; Suhrkamp 10.
10 Ibid.
11 §377, Addition.
12 Alexandre Kojève, *Introduction à la lecture de Hegel. Leçons sur la Phénoménologie de l'Esprit, professées de 1933 à 1939 à l'École des Hautes Études, réunies et publiées par Raymond Queneau* (Paris: Gallimard, 1947),

p. 531. [Trans.: The English translation, *An Introduction to the Reading of Hegel*, ed. A. Bloom, translated by J. H. Nichols Jr. (New York and London: Cornell University Press, 1969), unfortunately does not include the lectures of 1933–4, in which this passage appears.]

13 Heidegger, *Hegel's Phenomenology of Spirit*, p. 147. Translation modified. [Trans.: Emad and Maly give: 'Hegel's explication of the genuine concept of being – in the passage just indicated, where time is mentioned – is nothing less than leaving time behind on the road to spirit, which is eternal.' Malabou cites the French translation, *La Phénoménologie de l'esprit de Hegel (Cours du semestre d'hiver 1930–1931)*, trans. Emmanuel Martineau (Paris: NRF Gallimard, 1984), p. 224.]

14 Heidegger, *Being and Time*, English, p. 302; German, p. 329.

15 The versions of Jena (1804–5 and 1805–6) and that of the *Encyclopedia of Philosophical Sciences* in its three editions (1817, 1827, 1830).

16 Alexandre Koyré, 'Hegel à Iéna', *Études d'histoire de la pensée philosophique* (Paris: NRF Gallimard, 1971), pp. 148–9.

17 Kojève, *An Introduction to the Reading of Hegel*, p. 367.

18 Koyré, 'Hegel à Iéna', p. 89.

19 *Science of Logic, Doctrine of the Notion [Concept],* translated by A. V. Miller (London and New York: Humanities Press, 1976), p. 841; Suhrkamp 6, p. 571.

20 Kojève, *Introduction*, p. 367.

21 Ibid., p. 387.

22 Bernard Bourgeois, *Eternité et historicité de l'esprit selon Hegel* (Paris: Vrin, 1991); Pierre-Jean Labarrière, 'Histoire et liberté', *Archives de Philosophie*, 33, 1970, pp. 701–18; 'Le Statut logique de l'altérité chez Hegel', *Philosophie*, 13, winter 1986, pp. 68–81. Gérard Lebrun, *La Patience du concept* (Paris: NRF Gallimard, 1972); Denise Souche-Dagues, *Recherches hégéliennes, Infini et dialectique* (Paris: Vrin, 1994).

23 Georges Canguilhem, 'Dialectique et Philosophie du Non chez Gaston Bachelard', in *Études d'histoire et de philosophie des sciences*, 2nd edition (Paris: Vrin, 1970), p. 206.

24 The word appears in the French language in 1785 (Robert dictionary). The Brockhaus dictionary attests that *Plastizität* appears in German 'at the time of Goethe (dead in 1832)'. 'Plastisch' is also an adverb which means 'plastically', 'in a plastic manner'.

25 I reproduce here what is written in Grimm's dictionary under the heading 'Plastik', 'Plastiker', and 'Plastisch'.

PLASTIK, f., *auf franz. plastique vom griech, πλαστική (nämlich τέχνη) die bildende kunst, welche die organischen formen selbst körperlich (durch formen, schnitzen, meiszeln, gieszen) hinstellt, im engern sinne die form-, modelliertkunst*: der hauptzweck aller plastik, welches wortes wir künftighin zu ehren der Griechen bedienen, ist, dasz die würde des menschen innerhalb der menschlichen gestalt dargestellt werde. GÖTHE 44, 34; plastik wirkt eigentlich nur auf ihrer höchsten stufe. 22, 229 ; die malerei hat ein viel weiteres reich, eine freiere natur als die plastik. H. MEYER *kl. schriften, 48, 35 neudruck.*

PLASTIKER, m, bildender kunstler: Dädalus der erste plastiker. GÖTHE 44, 250. wer sie zu dichten erkühnt, und die sprache verschmäh und den Rythmus, gliche dem plastiker, der bilder gehau'n die luft (PLATEN 2, 295). Ein plastischer dichter: unsere zwei gröszten romantiker, Göthe und A. W. von Schlegel sind zu gleicher zeit auch unsere gröszten plastiker. H. HEINE 13, 18.

PLASTISCH, adj. und adv. *körperlich bildend, gestaltend oder getstaltet, der plastik gemäsz, dienend: glaube, liebe, hoffnung fühlten eins . . . einen plastischen trieb in ihrer natur, sie befleiszigten sich zusammen und schufen ein liebliches gebilde . . ., die geduld.* GÖTHE, 56, 129; *plastische anatomie* 44, 60, ff; *die plastische Natur des menschen,* SCHILLER, 10, 80; *plastische darstellungen.* A. W. SCHLEGEL *Vorles.* 1, 128, 10 ; *plastischer künstler* Gervinus 5, 213, *auch plastischer dichter* (H. HEINE suppl 157), *dessen gestalten gleichsam körperlich hervortreten, danach plastische poesie* H. HEINE 13, 18; *plastisch darstellen, malen (mit stark abgegrundeten formen), schildern u. s.* w., *plastische schärfe* LENAU (1880) 2, 243, *ruhe* AUERBACH, *Ges.Sschriften* 19, 168, *anschauung* 176; *plastische gewaltsamkeiten (raub plastischer kunstschätze)* KLOPSTOCK 5, 533 Hempel; *plastischer thon, modellierthon.*

26 Hegel, *Aesthetics. Lectures on Fine Art*, translated by T. M. Knox, with an interpretative essay by C. Karelis (Oxford: Clarendon Press, 1975), vol. II, p. 709; Suhrkamp 14, p. 355.

27 Ibid., p. 719; Suhrkamp 14, p. 374.

28 Ibid. In the *Lectures on the Philosophy of History* (translated by J. Sibree with an introduction by C. J. Friedrich (New York: Dover Publications, 1956) [*Vorlesungen über die Philosophie der Geschichte*, Suhrkamp 12], Pericles is described as the very model of a 'plastic individual': 'Pericles was a statesman of plastic antique character (*Perikles war ein Staatsmann von plastischem antikem Charakter*)', p. 259; Suhrkamp 12, p. 317). At his instigation there began 'the production of those eternal monuments of sculpture'; his orations were addressed to a 'band of men whose genius has become classical for all centuries' (ibid., Suhrkamp 12, p. 318). Here again we meet the same examples: Thucydides, Socrates, Plato, and Aristophanes. Further, Alexander himself is characterized as a 'plastic spirit':

> [He] had been educated by the deepest and also the most comprehensive thinker of antiquity, by Aristotle, and the education was worthy of the man who had undertaken it. Alexander was initiated into the most profound metaphysics: therefore his nature was thoroughly refined and liberated from the customary bonds of mere opinion, crudities and empty fantasies (*dadurch wurde sein Naturell vollkommen gereinigt und von den sonstigen Banden der Meinung, der Roheit, des leeren Vorstellens befreit*). Aristotle left this grand nature as unconstrained as it was already, but impressed on it a deep consciousness of what Truth is, and formed the spirit so endowed with genius into a plastic character moving freely like a sphere roams through its own aether.
>
> (Ibid., p. 272; Suhrkamp 12, p. 332. Translation modified)

In all these instances 'plastic' clearly stands for that which 'has the character of mobility'. In comparing Athens to Sparta, Hegel describes the former as the cradle of 'plastic individuality', the exemplary home of 'great industry, excitation and stimulus, intense development of individuality within the sphere of a moral spirit (*eine große Betriebsamkeit, Regsamkeit, Ausbildung der Individualität innerhalb des Kreises eines sittlichen Geistes*)'. But in Sparta, 'we see on the other hand a rigid, abstract virtue (*die starre abstrakte Tugend*), a life devoted to the State. But in which the mobility and freedom of individuality are repressed (*aber so, daß die Regsamkeit, die Freiheit der Individualität zurückgesetzt ist*)', (p. 262, translation modified; Suhrkamp 12, p. 319).

In the *Lectures on the History of Philosophy*, Hegel says of Greek philosophy that it is 'plastic'. Later in this volume we find the description of Socrates as 'plastic individual' (English translation by E. S. Haldane, London, Routledge and Kegan Paul, 1955, vol. 1, p. 393; Suhrkamp 18, p. 452).

29 For these individuals are in fact called 'plastic' with direct reference to sculpture:

> All of them are out and out artists by nature, ideal artists shaping themselves (*ideale Künstler ihrer Selbst*), individuals of a single cast, works of art standing there, like immortal and deathless images of the gods, in which there is nothing temporal and doomed. The same plasticity is characteristic of the works of art which victors in the Olympics made of their bodies, and indeed even of the appearance of Phryne, the most beautiful of women, who rose from the sea naked in the eyes of all Greece.
>
> (*Aesthetics*, vol. II, pp. 719–20; Suhrkamp 14, p. 374)

30 *Science of Logic*, p. 40 (translation modified to reflect the French); Suhrkamp 5, p. 31.

31 In the *Lectures on the History of Philosophy*, Hegel says of Socrates' interlocutors: 'Such personages are, as we already saw in connection with Socrates (vol. I, 402), plastic personages as regards the conversations: no one is put there to state his own views, or, as the French express it, *pour placer un mot*' (vol. II, p. 17). [Trans.: Also in the *History of Philosophy*, Hegel sees fit to remind us that Socrates, the son of a sculptor, was brought up to practise this art (ibid., vol. I, p. 389; Suhrkamp 18, pp. 19–20.)]

32 In one of its synonyms, plasticity signifies 'malleability' (*Bildsamkeit*), meaning 'flexibility', 'docility'. Its second meaning – 'the power to give form' – finds illustration in the Hegelian vocabulary of in-formation; one can think in particular of the substantives '*Ein- und Durchbildung*'.

33 Hegel's *Phenomenology of Spirit*, p. 39; Suhrkamp 3, p. 60.

34 Bernard Bourgeois, from the Introduction to his translation of the *Encyclopedia Philosophy of Spirit* (Paris: Vrin, 1988), p. 201, note 3.

35 *The Encyclopedia Logic,* Part 1 of the *Encyclopedia of the Philosophical Sciences* with the *Zusätzte* [1830], translated by W. Wallace, with a foreword by J. N. Findlay (Oxford : Clarendon Press, 1975), §150; Suhrkamp 8, p. 294.

36 *Science of Logic*, p. 833; Suhrkamp 6, p. 561.

37 *Phenomenology of Spirit*, p. 34; Suhrkamp 3, p. 54.

38 In the conclusion of his essay on Natural Law, Hegel shows that spiritual development in its different moments (still characterized in this epoch with the Schellingian term Potenzen) emerges at once from an appearance and an explosion of form:

> The absolute totality restricts itself as necessity in each of its spheres, produces itself out of them as a totality, and recapitulates there the preceding spheres just as it anticipates the succeeding ones. But one of these is the greater power. . . . It is necessary for individuality to advance through metamorphoses, and for all that belongs to the dominant stage to weaken and die, so that all stages of necessity appear as such stages in this individuality; but the misfortune of this period of transition (i.e. that this strengthening of the new formation has not yet cleansed itself absolutely of the past) is where the positive resides. And although nature, within a specific form, advances with a uniform (not mechanically uniform but uniformly accelerated) movement, it still enjoys a new form which it acquires. As nature enters that form, so it remains in it, just as a shell starts suddenly towards its zenith and then rests for a moment in it; metal when heated does not turn soft

> like wax, but all at once becomes liquid and remains so – for this phenomenon is the transition into the absolute opposite and so is infinite, and this emergence of the opposite out of infinity or out of its nothingness is a leap (*ein Sprung*). The shape, in its new-born strength, at first exists for itself alone, before it becomes conscious of its relation to an other. Just so, the growing individuality has both the delight of the leap in entering a new form and also an enduring pleasure in its new form, until it gradually opens up to the negative; and in its decline too it is sudden and brittle (*und auch in ihrem Untergange auf einmal und brechend ist*).
>
> (*Natural Law*, translated by T. M. Knox, introduction by H. B. Acton (Philadelphia: University of Pennsylvania Press, 1975), pp. 131–2; Felix Meiner edition (PhB), 319b, p. 484)

39 'Sie ist das Sein, das, indem es ist, nicht ist, and indem es nicht ist, ist' (*Philosophy of Nature*, §258; Suhrkamp 9).

40 Derrida adds that it is 'well known that Heidegger considered Hegel to have covered over and erased Kant's audaciousness in many respects (*on sait qu'[aux yeux de Heidegger], Hegel aurait à bien des égards recouvert et efface l'audace kantienne*)' ('Ousia et Grammè', *Marges de la philosophie* (Paris: Minuit, 1972), p. 49). English translation: 'Ousia and Grammè', *Margins of Philosophy*, translated by Alan Bass (New York and London: Harvester, 1982), p. 44.

41 Ibid., p. 45.

42 Ibid., p. 54.

43 Ibid., p. 55.

44 Ibid., p. 56.

45 *Encyclopedia Philosophy of Nature*, §254, Remark.

46 [Trans.: Hegel uses *Auseinandersetzen* in the sense of juxtaposition as well as separation.]

47 *Encyclopedia Philosophy of Nature,* §254.

48 *Lectures on the Philosophy of History*, p. 319.

49 Bernard Bourgeois, 'Sur le Droit Naturel de Hegel 1802–03', in *Études hégéliennes* (Paris: PUF, 1992), p. 68.

50 *Lectures on the History of Philosophy*, vol. II, p. 138. Cf. Hegel on Aristotle: 'the δύναμις' is the disposition, the 'in itself', the objective element: also the abstract universal in general, the Idea, in so far as merely *potentia*'. '"For itself" means "in act": ἐνέργεια is the actualising element, negativity which relates itself to itself'.

51 'All *hypotyposis* consists in making a concept sensuous, and is either schematic or symbolic' (Kant, *Critique of Judgment,* translated by W. Pluhar (Indianapolis: Hackett, 1987), p. 226).

52 *Phenomenology of Spirit*, p. 143 (trans. modified); Suhrkamp 3, p. 183.

53 *Encyclopedia Philosophy of Spirit*, §552, Remark.

54 Ibid., §552, Remark.

55 Ibid., §387, Remark.

56 Ibid., §389, Remark.

57 Aristotle, *Metaphysics,* Λ, 7, 1072b, 18–30.

58 *Philosophy of Spirit*, §565.

59 [Trans.: The concept is never, as we say now, 'history'.]

PART I
HEGEL ON MAN: FASHIONING A SECOND NATURE

INTRODUCTION

1 Jan van der Meulen offers a complete commentary on the section in his article 'Hegels Lehre von Leib, Seele und Geist', *Hegel-Studien*, vol. 2, 1963, pp. 251–280. See also: Alain, *Idées,* chapter on 'Hegel' (Paris: Flammarion, 1983); Jacques Derrida, 'The Ends of Man', in *Margins of Philosophy*, pp. 129–164; and, more recently, Bernard Bourgeois, 'Les deux âmes: de la nature à l'esprit' in *De saint Thomas à Hegel* (Paris: PUF, 1994), pp. 117–151.
2 *Encyclopedia Philosophy of Spirit*, §377.
3 Ibid., §411, Addition.
4 Ibid., §396, Addition; Suhrkamp 10, p. 430.
5 Ibid., §396, p. 62; Suhrkamp 10, p. 438.
6 Ibid.
7 Ibid., pp. 63–64; Suhrkamp 10, p. 439.
8 Ibid., p. 57; Suhrkamp 10, p. 432. Translation modified.
9 Ibid., p. 62; Suhrkamp 10, p. 438.
10 Ibid., §396, Addition, p. 63; Suhrkamp 10, p. 439.
11 Ibid., p. 63; Suhrkamp 10, p. 438.
12 When read in this way, does not the Anthropology lead to the traditional crossroads of the two 'Ends of Man' as Jacques Derrida described them in his article of the same name, 'end as finitude' and 'end as telos' ? *Margins of Philosophy*, note 54, p. 144.
13 §410, Addition, p. 141.
14 Ibid., p. 142.
15 §§409–410.
16 The Hegelian speculative Anthropology does not have the aim Kant assigned to this science – that of suggesting a 'knowledge of man as citizen of the world'. See Kant, *Anthropology from a Pragmatic Point of View*, translated by V. Lyle Downdell (Carbondale: Southern Illinois University Press, 1978), p. 4. The French translation is by Michel Foucault, A*nthropologie du point de vue pragmatique* (Paris: Vrin, 1979), p. 11.
17 *Philosophy of Spirit*, §411.
18 Ibid., §378.
19 Ibid.
20 See Bourgeois's article, '(Les deux âmes . . .)', note 54.
21 *De Anima, or On the soul,* Book II. English translation edited by Jonathan Barnes, *The Complete Works of Aristotle* (Princeton: Princeton University Press, 1984), p. 656.
22 [Trans.: Malabou is alluding to Jacques Derrida's term 'le propre de l'homme', itself a reference to the Heideggerean family of terms, *Eigen, eignen, Eigentlichkeit, Aneignen*. See Derrida's essay, 'The ends of man', in *Margins of Philosophy*, trans. Alan Bass (Chicago, 1982), pp. 109–136: 'The near is the proper; the proper is the nearest (*prope, proprius*). Man is the proper of Being . . .; Being is the proper of man . . . the proper of man, here, is not an essential attribute, the predicate of a substance, a characteristic among others, however fundamental, of a being, object or subject, called man.'(133)]

1 INTRODUCTION TO THE *ANTHROPOLOGY*

1 *Encyclopedia Philosophy of Spirit*, §389.
2 §411.
3 Ibid., §391.
4 §§392–395.
5 §§396–398.
6 §§399–402.
7 §§403–404.
8 §§405–406.
9 §§407–408.
10 §§409–410.
11 §§411–412.
12 *Encyclopedia Science of Logic*, §163.
13 §§388–389. We create the third sub-moment at §391, 'Sensation'.
14 §§389–390.
15 §391.
16 §389.
17 [Trans.: *être-là* is the French for *Dasein,* the German word that means both existence and, as Hegel and later Heidegger will use it, 'Being there' or 'determinate being'. The most recent translation of the *Encyclopedia Logic* uses 'being there' as equivalent for *Dasein*, and has these remarks to make on the choice: The word *Dasein* presents 'one of the most vexing problems in Hegel's logical chain'. Earlier translators made 'a disastrous decision' based on Hegel's ostensible definition of 'Dasein' as 'determinate being'. But *Dasein*, as the new translators remind us, is far broader than 'determinate being' as is 'in fact, the most general and indeterminate form of finite being'. They recommend 'being-there' as most faithful to the place *Dasein* occupies in Hegel's logical progression (from 'becoming' to 'something'), and I agree with their choice, which has the added virtue of preserving the French construction. See the Translators' Introduction to *The Encyclopedia Logic*, trans. T. F. Geraets, W. A. Suchting, and H. S. Harris (Indianapolis and Cambridge, 1991, pp. xx–xxi]
18 *Encyclopedia Logic*, §90.
19 *Encyclopedia Philosophy of Spirit*, §392. Hegel uses also the expression 'das Mitleben mit der Natur'.
20 On the Hegelian notion of 'influence' see the work by François Roustang, *Influence* (Paris: Minuit, 1990), in particular pp. 14ff.
21 §392.
22 §393.
23 §394.
24 §394.
25 §395.
26 *Encyclopedia Science of Logic*, §163, Addition.
27 Ibid.
28 *Encyclopedia Philosophy of Spirit*, §397.
29 §398.
30 The German word *Urteil* means both 'judgement' and 'original division'. Hegel writes: 'The etymological derivation of judgment in our language is . . . profound and expresses the unity of the notion as the first moment, with its differentiation appearing as the original division (*als die ursprüngliche Teilung*), this is what the judgment truly is.' *Encyclopedia Science of Logic*, §166, Remark.
31 The presentation of this process is the task of §§399–408, from the end of the 'Natural soul' to 'Self-feeling' in its first two moments.

32 §395. Translation modified.
33 §408, Addition.
34 §405. Translation modified.
35 §399, Addition [translation modified].
36 Ibid. [translation modified].
37 §401 [translation modified].
38 Ibid.
39 Ibid., Addition.
40 Hegel says:

> The most interesting side of a psychical physiology would lie in studying not the mere sympathy, but more definitely the bodily form adopted by certain mental modifications, especially the passions or emotions (*Affekte*). We should have, for example, to explain the line of connection by which anger and courage are felt in the breast, the blood, the 'irritable' system, just as thinking and mental occupation are felt in the head, the centre of the 'sensuous' system.
>
> (§401)

41 §402.
42 §403. [Translation modified.] On the difference between *empfinden* and *fühlen* and the difficulties of translating them, see the remarks of Bernard Bourgeois, 'Les deux âmes', pp. 188 and 194.
43 §404.
44 Ibid.
45 §405, Addition.
46 §405.
47 Ibid.
48 §406.
49 Ibid.
50 §407.
51 §408.
52 §407.
53 §408. [Translation modified.]
54 Ibid.
55 §405, Addition.
56 Ibid.
57 *Encyclopedia Philosophy of Nature*, §371.
58 In the Remark to §408, Hegel emphasizes the achievement of Pinel, who understood this problem and advocated a humane, benevolent treatment of the mad.
59 Alain, *Idées*, p. 200.
60 *Encyclopedia Philosophy of Spirit*, §410, Remark.
61 §410. [Translation modified.]
62 See *Encyclopedia Science of Logic*, §181.
63 *Encyclopedia Philosophy of Spirit,* §410. [Translation modified.]
64 §410.
65 §410, Addition. Jan Van der Meulen sees in the Hegelian treatment of the mutual relations between soul and body an anticipation of the work of Merleau-Ponty (on the body as 'flesh') and Sartre (on the body as 'for itself'). See 'Hegels Lehre von Leib, Seele und Geist', especially pp. 259f.
66 §409, Addition.

2 ON NOETIC PLASTICITY: HEGEL'S READING OF *DE ANIMA*

1 The main appearances of the term 'man' in *De Anima*, aside from those connected to the development of the notion of ἕξις are the following: 'the nutritive soul belongs to other animate beings beside man' (II, 4, 415a). At II, 9, 421a, Aristotle argues that man is superior to all the other animals because of the 'refinement of his sense of touch'; characteristic of man is that he cannot 'feel without breathing', which leads to the claim: 'it seems clear that in man the olfactory organ is different from that of the other animals'. On the question of intelligence (III, 3, 427b), Aristotle recalls the fragment of Empedocles: 'For it is in respect of what is present that man's wit is increased'. He continues: 'In the animals other than man, there is neither intellection nor reasoning, but only imagination' (III, 10, 433a). But it has already been established that imagination 'is a type of intellection'. The motor faculties, appetite and intellect are, to different degrees, present in all animals.

2 There is indeed in the *Lectures* a more complex treatment of the notion of 'man', but it confirms rather than refutes our thesis: 'When (the soul) is at once intuitive, sensitive and intelligent, it is the spirit of man'.

> In man we see vegetative nature as developed as sensitive nature: – this is an idea expressed clearly when the modern Philosophy of Nature claims that *man is both plant and animal, and this is directed against the sharp separation between these forms.*
>
> (*Lectures on the History of Philosophy*, vol. II, p. 184, translation modified. Malabou's italics)

3 *Encyclopedia Philosophy of Spirit*, §389.

4 It is not possible to follow the whole trajectory of Hegel's interpretation of passive νοῦς from its appearance in the Jena Lecture series (1805–6) to the *Berlin Lectures on the History of Philosophy* (1819–20 and 1829–30), not to mention the Heidelberg versions of these lectures (1816–17 and 1817–18). What is clear is that Hegel thinks the Aristotelian inquiry into νοῦς, and above all passive νοῦς, is the leading philosophical idea of *De Anima*. In this connection we must mention a translation Hegel produced in Jena, probably in 1805, of a passage from *De Anima* devoted to the passive νοῦς' (II, 4–5, 429b22, 430a25). The manuscript is titled *Aristotle. De Anima* III. 4 – Απορησειε- *5*. Walter Kern reproduces this translation with a commentary in his article 'Eine Übersetzung Hegels zu *De Anima*, III, 4–5, mitgeteilt und erläutert', *Hegel-Studien*, 1, 1961, pp. 49–88. We should also mention another article by this same author which collates all the discussions of the passive νοῦς in Hegel's writings: 'Die Aristotelesdeutung Hegels. Die Aufhebung des Aristotelischen "Nous" in Hegels "Geist"', *Philosophisches Jahrbuch* 78, 1971, pp. 237–259.

5 §389.

6 Book III, 4, 430a10–15, (*The Complete Works of Aristotle,* II, p. 684). The translation cited by Malabou is Barbotin's *Traité de l'âme* (Paris: Budé, Belles Lettres, 3rd edition, 1989, 82), more faithful on this point than Tricot's. The translation Hegel proposes for this passage in his Jena manuscripts is the following:

> So nun ist der Nus beschaffen einerseits dadurch, daß er alles wird, anderseits daß er alles macht, als ein thätiges Wesen, wie das Licht; denn auf eine gewisse Weise macht auch das Licht die nur der Potenz nach seyende Farben zu actu Farben.

('So on the one hand νοῦς is constituted as that through which everything becomes what it is, on the other hand as that which produces everything, as an active being like light: for in a certain way light makes the potential colors into actual colors.')

Cf. Kern, 'Eine Übersetzung Hegels zu De Anima . . .', p. 51.

7 νοῦς can 'think itself', *De Anima*, III, 4, 8.

8 In the Jena manuscript of 1805, Hegel translated ἕξις as 'active being (*thätiges Wesen*)'. In a footnote he remarks: '*ἕξις, Gewohnheit aber an und für sich ; Gew. Ein Thun bewußtlos (Wesen, Postwesen, Examinationswesen)*' ('Habit, but in the sense of in and for itself . . .').

9 'Passive intellect' and 'active intellect' are the headings given to sections 4 and 5 of *De Anima*, Book III. Tricot remarks: 'Aristotle, only using the term 'ὁ παθητικὸς νοῦς', never speaks of an 'ὁ ποιητικὸς νοῦς': it was the ancient commentators who added this distinction between the two forms of the intellect.' *De Anima*, French translation, p. 181, note 1.

10 One will notice that Kern, in the two articles mentioned above, never asks about the precise reasons that might have led Hegel to make passive νοῦς the true *foundation* of his 'Anthropology'. According to Kern, passive νοῦς is, in Hegel, assimilated purely and simply to 'human mind'. See, primarily, 'Die Aristotelesdeutung Hegels', p. 73).

11 *De Anima*, 429a10.

12 Ibid., 429a13–18.

13 Ibid., 417a13–18.

14 Ibid., 429b15–18.

15 II, 5, 418b2–3.

16 Pierre Aubenque, 'Hegel et Aristote', in *Hegel et la pensée grecque*, published under the direction of Jacques d'Hondt (Paris: PUF, 1974), pp. 103–104. The Hegel passages are in the *Lectures on the History of Philosophy*, vol. II, pp. 163–164.

17 *Lectures on the History of Philosophy*, II, pp. 145–146.

18 Ibid.

19 Ibid., II, p. 140.

20 'Hegel et Aristote', p. 105.

21 Ibid.

22 Ibid., p. 107.

23 Ibid.

24 Ibid.

25 Ibid., p. 105.

26 Dominique Janicaud, *Hegel et le destin de la Grèce* (Paris: Vrin, 1975), note 1, p. 301.

27 *De Anima,* II, 5, 416b35.

28 Ibid.

29 II, 5, 417b6–7.

30 II, 12, 424b18–25.

31 *Lectures on the History of Philosophy,* II, p. 191. Translation modified.

32 On this, see Aristotle's *On Generation and Corruption*, I, 7, 323b18, in the *Complete Works of Aristotle*, vol. I : 'They are alike generically and specifically unalike'.

33 *De Anima*, II, 4, 417b19–21.

34 *Lectures on the History of Philosophy*, II, p. 191.

35 *De Anima*, II, 5, 417b12–13.

36 III, 5, 417a24–26.
37 Ibid., II, 5, 417a26–30.
38 Ibid., pp. 31–33. [Translation modified.]
39 Ibid., 417b2–5.
40 Ibid., 417b15–16.
41 *Lectures on the History of Philosophy*, II, p. 187. Hegel generally translates 'energeia' as 'Wirklichkeit'. He sometimes uses *Wirksamkeit* (efficiency), or *Tätigkeit* (activity).
42 *De Anima*, II, 4, 417b30–34. Hegel quotes this passage in abbreviated form: 'Speaking generally, the difference is that potentiality is twofold; as we say a boy may become a soldier, and a grown man may also become so, for the latter has the effective power' (*Lectures on the History of Philosophy*, II, p. 189).
43 *De Anima* II, 5, 417b20–25.
44 *De Anima* III, 4, 429b30–34.
45 *Lectures on the History of Philosophy*, II, p. 197; Suhrkamp 19, p. 215.
46 *De Anima*, III, 4, 429b6–9.
47 *De Anima* III, 5, 430a20–22.
48 *Vorlesungen über die Geschichte der Philosophie*, Suhrkamp 19, p. 214 (this passage is not in the English edition).
49 Suhrkamp 19, p. 218. Kern notes that Hegel's interpetation of 'passive νοῦς' as 'in itself (*an sich*)' and of 'active νοῦς' as 'for itself (*für sich*)' comes later in the Berlin Lectures. Before those Lectures, he only speaks of *leidender und tätiger Verstand*. 'Eine Übersetzung Hegels . . .', p. 61.
50 *Lectures on the History of Philosophy*, II, pp. 143–144 ; Suhrkamp 19, pp. 158–159.
51 'Hegel et Aristote', p. 107.
52 *Hegel et le destin de la Grèce*, p. 293.
53 Suhrkamp 19, p. 218. [Trans.: This passage does not appear in the English translation.]
54 *Lectures on the History of Philosophy*, II, p. 140; Suhrkamp 19, p. 155.
55 In the *Sophist,* Plato draws attention to the philosophical significance of such a distinction: here he separates 'negation' proper, understood as the absolute contradiction of being, from the 'non-being' which is intertwined with Being, and is understood as a relative negation, characterizing Being through its relation to a determinate alterity. (*Sophist* 240a–c.)The difference between μὴ ὄν and οὐκ ὄν is discussed explicitly at 257b–c.
56 *Science of Logic*, Doctrine of Being, p. 104.
57 *Metaphysics, The Complete Works of Aristotle*, II, pp. 1614–1615. Aristotle explains that 'ἕξις (habit)', 'δίαθεσις (disposition)', and 'πάθος (pathos)' are three types of 'quality' (ποιόν). His work *The Categories* makes the same distinctions. (Barnes edition, I, pp. 14f.) On the other hand, in *Metaphysics*, Book V, Aristotle claims that habit:

> a kind of activity of the haver and the had; something like an action or movement. When one thing makes and the other is made, between them there is a making; so too between him who has a garment and the garment which he has there is a having. This sort of having, then, evidently we cannot have: for the process will go on to infinity, if we can have the having of what we have.
>
> (20, 1022b4–8)

It should not be surprising that ἕξις presented here as a 'kind of ἐνέργεια'. In so far as it is a reservoir of movement and action, habit is not rest, but a certain efficacy already at work within δύναμίς'. Ἕξις adapts δύναμις and ἐνέργεια to each other, just as the garment gets used to (*se faire à*) the wearer. This form of 'getting used to' is not use in the literal sense (there is no integral state which is worn down by this 'use'), but means a kind of familiarization, a becoming-supple and flexible. Ἕξις guides something through its own power to what it can achieve.

58 Hegel describes the circularity of θεωρεῖν in a famous passage of the *Phenomenology of Spirit*:

> The individual who is going to act seems, therefore, to find himself in a circle in which each moment already presupposes the other, and thus he seems unable to find a beginning, because he only gets to know his original nature, which must be his End, from the deed, while, in order to act, he must have that End beforehand. But for that very reason he has to start immediately, and, whatever the circumstances, without further scruples about beginning, means, or End, proceed to action (*zur Tätigkeit zu schreiten*); for his essence and intrinsic nature is beginning, means, and End, all in one.
>
> (*Phenomenology of Spirit*, 'The spiritual animal kingdom and deceit, or the 'matter in hand' itself', p. 240; Suhrkamp 3, p. 297)

3 HABIT AND ORGANIC LIFE

1 *Elements of the Philosophy of Right*, edited by A. Wood, translated by H. B. Nisbet (Cambridge: Cambridge University Press, 1991), §151, Addition, p. 195. *Philosophische Bibliothek, G. W. F. Hegels Gesammelte Werke, Studienausgaben auf der Grundlage der Akademieausgabe*, (Hamburg: Felix Meiner Verlag, 1967), Bd 124 a: *Grundlinien der Philosophie des Rechts.*

2 See note 81, (supra), on the Derridean term '*propre*'.

3 Félix Ravaisson, *De l'habitude, 'Corpus des œuvres de philosophie en langue française'* (Paris: Fayard, 1984), p. 9.

4 Aristotle, *Eudemian Ethics*, freely translated by Ravaisson, p. 10.

5 Ibid., p. 10.

6 *Lectures on the History of Philosophy*, II, p. 174, translation altered; Suhrkamp 19, 192. Quotations from Aristotle refer to *Physics* VII, 3, 245b3–9 and 246a11–246, b2.

7 Ibid.

8 *Phenomenology of Spirit,* p. 158; Suhrkamp 3, p. 201.

9 *Encyclopedia Philosophy of Nature*, §350.

10 *Phenomenology of Spirit,* p. 158; Suhrkamp 3, 201.

11 André Lalande, *Vocabulaire technique et critique de la philosophie* (Paris: PUF, 1931), p. 393.

12 Ravaisson, on the other hand, believes that:

> There is very little room for habit in vegetative life. However, the duration of change already leaves permanent traces, not only in the material constitution of the plant, but also in the higher forms of plant life. Even the wildest of plants lend themselves to cultivation.
>
> (*De l'habitude*, p. 15)

Ravaisson cites Vergil, *Georgics* II:

> Nonetheless, even the wild plants, if they are transplanted and grafted, or moved into well-prepared beds, will quickly lose their natural

> wildness and, as you will see, when treated with care they will before very long adapt themselves to the forms you prefer them to be in.

Lalande recalls: 'The "habits" of plants as discerned through experiments performed on them, for example by placing a flowering plant under direct light during the night, and hiding it in the dark during the day.' (*Vocabulaire*, p. 394).

13 *Encyclopedia Philosophy of Nature*, §345.

14 Ibid., §346, trans. modified.

15 François-Xavier Bichat, *Recherches physiologiques sur la vie et la mort*, facsimile reproduction of the edition of 1800 (Gauthier-Villars, Paris, 1955), p. 40 (*Physiological Researches on Life and Death*, edited by R. J. Kastenbaum, translated by F. Gold (Ayer Company Publishers 1977)). Bichat distinguishes between 'animal life' and 'organic life', reserving the acquisition of habits to the animal:

> The animal's functions constitute two distinct classes. One group includes the habitual succession of assimilation and excretion: here the molecules of contiguous bodies are constantly being transformed into the body of the organism, while the molecules that have become unnecessary are rejected and expelled. Through this class of functions, the organism only lives within itself. But through the other class, it lives outside itself: it is the citizen of the world, unlike the vegetable organism which is simple the place where the world is born. The animal organism feels and perceives everything that surrounds it, reflects upon its sensations, develops consciously in response to their influence, and in many instances can communicate its desires, fears, pleasures and pains through its own voice. Organic life is the group of functions belonging to the first class, because all organic beings, whether vegetable or animal, partake in these to a greater or lesser degree, and here it is organic material which supplies the sole condition necessary to exercise these functions. Animal life is composed of the united functions of the second class, and are called this because they alone possess them.

Hegel also refers to Bichat in the *Encyclopedia Philosophy of Spirit*, §398, Addition.

16 On the question of the elements and their synthesis in living beings, the relevant text is the beginning of Book II.1 of Aristotle's *Parts of Animals*, where Aristotle argues that 'there are three degrees of composition'. Of these there are, in the first place,

> composition out of what some call the elements, such as earth, air, water, and fire. . . . For wet and dry, hot and cold, form the material of all composite bodies. . . . The second degree of composition is that by which the homogeneous parts of animals, such as bone, flesh, and the like, are constituted out of the primary substances. The third and last stage is the composition which forms the heterogeneous parts, such as face, hand, and the rest.
>
> (*The Complete Works of Aristotle*, I, pp. 1005–1006)

17 *'Die animalische Organismus ist die Rekonstruktion der physischen Elemente zu Einzelnen'). Jenaer Systementwürfe III: Naturphilosophie und Philosophie des Geistes,* Felix Meiner Verlag, PhB Bd 333, p. 136.

18 *Philosophy of Nature*, §368, Remark (Suhrkamp 9, 501) [Trans.: The English translation of the *Philosophy of Nature* by Michael John Petry is based on the third edition and departs in many places both from the German and French editions which are ciited here. The passage quoted above is found in §370 of the Petry edition, vol. III (London: George Allen and Unwin, 1970), p. 178.] See Cuvier:

> The smallest face of a bone, the least apophysis has a determinate character, relative to its class, its order, its genus, and to the universal species to which it belongs; this is true even to the point that, given access to nothing more than the end of a bone, if that bone is well preserved and we apply some effort, we can, by drawing upon analogies and comparisons to other things, determine with confidence what other features belonged to the entire animal.
>
> (*Recherches sur les ossements fossiles de quadrupèdes, où l'on rétablit les caractères de plusieurs espèces d'animaux que les révolutions du globe paraissent avoir détruites* (Paris, 1812), Introduction, p. 65 (*Fossil Bones and Geological Catastrophes*, translated by M. J. S. Rudwick (Chicago: Chicago University Press, 1997)

19 Even though the plant is in itself a process of auto-differentiation, this does not go so far as to constitute a 'Self'. In this sense, the plant is not properly speaking a subject. As he continues the discussion of §346 in §347, Hegel asserts that for the plant, the 'return to Self' which 'brings assimilation to a conclusion does not lead to a sentiment of Self (*Selbstgefühl*)' (Suhrkamp 9, p. 412).
20 §358, Remark, Suhrkamp 9, p. 466.
21 The German verb closest in meaning to contraction is *zusammenziehen*: draw together, reduce, concentrate. Even if it is not possible to say in German 'contract a habit', the meaning of *zusammenziehen* (literally 'to contract', 'pull together') expresses precisely the economy of the process analysed here. Note that in German to say 'to take on a certain habit, to contract a habit', we would use the expression *die Gewohnheit zu annehmen*. The phrase *die Gewohnheit etwas zu tun* means to have a habit of doing something; *die Gewohnheit ablegen* means 'to give up the habit'.
22 §350, trans. modified (Suhrkamp 9, p. 430).
23 Gilles Deleuze, *Différence et répétition* (Paris: PUF, 1968) p. 101; *Difference and Repetition*, translated by P. Patton (New York: Columbia University Press, 1994), p. 74.
24 Ibid.
25 Ibid., p. 73.
26 Ibid., p. 96.
27 Bergson, *L'Évolution créatrice* (Paris: PUF, collection 'Quadrige', 1981), p. 116. *Creative Evolution*, translated by A. Mitchell (Lanham, MD: University Press of America, 1911), p. 115.
28 Ibid. Translation modified.
29 *Enclopedia Philosophy of Nature*, §345, Addition, Suhrkamp 9, p. 381: 'Es tritt ein Punkt ein, wo die Verfolgung der Vermittlung, es sei in chemischer Weise oder in mechanischer Allmählichkeit, abgebrochen und unmöglich wird. Dieser Punkt ist allenthalben und durchdringend. . . .' (Translation modified.)
30 §352.
31 As Hegel presents these in §354, Suhrkamp 9, pp. 439f.

32 *Encyclopedia Philosophy of Spirit*, §410, Addition. Bichat, analysing the same phenomenon, asks:

> From whence arises this ability of sensations to undergo so many and such contrary modifications? In order to understand this, we should note first that the central point of these circles of pleasure, pain and indifference, does not lie in the organs which receive or transmit sensation, but in the soul which perceives it. . . .
>
> (*Recherches* . . ., p. 41)

33 One could recall here Bergson's fine hypothesis that there is 'at the root of life, an effort to graft on to the necessity of physical forces the greatest possible amount of indetermination'. *Creative Evolution*, p. 114; *L'Évolution créatrice*, 116.
34 *Encyclopedia Philosophy of Nature*, §366, Addition; Suhrkamp 9, 494.
35 Augusto Vera, translation of Hegel's *Philosophie de la nature* (Paris: Ladrange, 1863), pp. 388–389; Suhrkamp 9, p. 495 (Addition to §365).
36 *Encyclopedia Philosophy of Nature*, §359.
37 §369.
38 §370. [Translation modified.] See also *Encyclopedia Philosophy of Spirit*, Addition to §381.

4 THE 'PROPER OF MAN' IN QUESTION: HUMAN SPECIFICITY AND PLASTIC INDIVIDUALITY

1 *Encyclopedia Philosophy of Spirit*, §411, Addition [Translation modified.]
2 §411.
3 §410, Addition. Translation modified.
4 *Philosophy of Nature*, §357: 'The animal organism, in this external relation, [is] immediately intro-reflected.'
5 *Phenomenology of Spirit*, p. 186; Suhrkamp 3, p. 234.
6 Ibid., p. 189; Suhrkamp 3, p. 238.
7 Ibid., p. 187; Suhrkamp 3, p. 235.
8 Ibid., p. 189; Suhrkamp 3, 238.
9 Ibid., p. 187; Suhrkamp 3, 235.
10 Ibid., p. 193; Suhrkamp 3, p. 242.
11 Ibid., p. 191; Suhrkamp 3, pp. 239–240.
12 Ibid., pp. 185–186; Suhrkamp 3, p. 233.
13 Ibid., p. 187; Suhrkamp 3, p. 235.
14 Ibid., p. 193; Suhrkamp 3, p. 242. Translation modified.
15 Ibid., p. 204; Suhrkamp 3, p. 255.
16 Ibid., p. 191; Suhrkamp 3, p. 240.
17 *Aesthetics*, II, p. 716. Translation modified.
18 In sculpture, the human form must be purified of all its 'superficial and alterable characteristics' (Ibid., II, p. 713).
19 'This externality, in other words, represents not itself, but the soul, of which it is the sign.' *Philosophy of Spirit*, §411.
20 *Aesthetics*, II, p. 738. Translation modified.
21 Ibid., p. 716. Translation modified.
22 *Philosophy of Spirit*, §410, Addition.
23 §411, Addition.
24 §410, Addition.

25 §412.
26 §410.
27 As that is described in §457.
28 §457.
29 §410, Addition, p. 143.
30 The role of habit in directing the will's struggle with itself helps to explain why Hegel gives habit such a central part in ethical life (*Sittlichkeit*). The *Philosophy of Right* argues that

> Education (*Pädagogik*) is the art of making human beings ethical: it considers them as natural beings and shows them how they can be reborn, and how their original nature can be transformed into a second, spiritual nature so that this spirituality becomes habitual to them . . . In habit, the opposition between the natural and the subjective will disappears, and the resistance of the subject is broken; to this extent, habit is part of ethical life, just as it is part of philosophical thought, since the latter requires that spirit should be trained to resist arbitrary ideas and that these ideas should be destroyed and overcome to clear the way for rational thought.
>
> (§151, Addition)

31 *Aesthetics*, II, p. 716.
32 Ibid., II, p. 717.
33 Ibid., II, p. 718.
34 Ibid., II, p. 719 [translation modified].
35 Ibid., II, pp. 719–720.
36 Ibid., I, p. 427. [Trans.: The standard translation has been modified to reflect Malabou's phrasing.]
37 Ibid., II, p. 751.
38 II, p. 701.
39 [Trans.: 'Mais s'agit-il encore d'un propre?'.]

CONCLUSION

1 *Encyclopedia Philosophy of Spirit,* §412.
2 *Elements of the Philosophy of Right,* §151, Addition.
3 *Encyclopedia Philosophy of Spirit*, §410.

PART II
HEGEL ON GOD: THE TURN OF THE DOUBLE NATURE

INTRODUCTION

1 [Trans.: the subtitle of this Part is 'le *tour* de la double nature'. 'Tour' can mean spin, turn, revolution, outline, measurement, all of which have some relevance to the portrayal of the Trinitarian and Incarnate God in Hegel.]
2 The principle of 'spiritual inwardness' could not arise in the Roman world except against a background of ethical and political chaos. It is the result of a new conception of citizenship, itself imposed by certain events (i.e. the tyranny of the emperors), and signalled the end of Greek political idealism, which had posited the substantial unity of state and individual within the ethical totality. Beginning in this epoch the individual experienced his relation to the state as something

separable and discontinuous, finding only in himself the sanctuary and security of his autonomy. See *Lectures on the Philosophy of History*, III, Section III, chapter 2: 'Christianity', pp. 334f.

3 Ibid., p. 334.

4 *Encyclopedia Philosophy of Spirit*, §552.

5 Eberhard Jüngel, *Gott als Geheimnis der Welt* (Tübingen: J. C. B. Mohr, 1978). *God as the Mystery of the World*, translated by D. L. Guder (Grand Rapids, MI: Eerdmans Publishing Company, 1983).

6 Ibid., p. 126.

7 Ibid.

8 *Lectures on the History of Philosophy*, III, p. 228 [translation altered]; Suhrkamp 20, pp. 130–131.

9 *Encyclopedia Philosophy of Spirit*, §424, Addition.

10 *Science of Logic, Doctrine of the Notion [Concept]*, Suhrkamp 6, p. 254. One discovers the same claim in the Addition to §42 of the *Encyclopedia Science of Logic*, where Hegel recalls the Kantian distinction between pure apperception and ordinary apperception. 'The latter takes up the manifold into itself, as a manifold, whereas pure apperception must be considered the activity of making (the object) "mine". Now this certainly expresses correctly the nature of all consciousness.'

11 On this point see the excellent analysis of Jean-Luc Marion, discussing the Cartesian rejection, in the *Regulae*, of the *habitus scientarum*, *L'Ontologie grise de Descartes*, (Paris: Vrin, 1981), ch. 1.

12

> This absolute religion is the *revelatory* (*offenbare*) religion, the religion that has itself as its content and fulfilment (*Erfüllung*). But it is also called the *revealed* (*geoffenbarte*) religion – which means, on the one hand, that it is revealed by God, that God has given himself for human beings to know what he is; and on the other hand, that it is a revealed, *positive* religion in the sense that it has come from without (*von Außen*), has been given to them.
>
> (*Lectures on the Philosophy of Religion*, edited by P. C. Hodgson, translated by R. F. Brown and J. M. Stewart, with the assistance of H. S. Harris (Berkeley: University of California Press, 1984–7), vol. III, p. 394. *Vorlesungen über die Philosophie der Religion*, ed. Georg Lasson, Felix Meiner Verlag, PhB 59–63, Bd 61–63, Dritter Teil, 'Die Absolute Religion', p. 19)

13 Bernard Bourgeois notes: 'the rejection of that Hegelian pretension which, for the theologians, is inadmissible . . .: the speculative suppression of the creative freedom in God himself' ('Le Dieu de Hegel: concept et creation', in *La Question de Dieu selon Aristote et Hegel*, edited by Thomas de Konninck and Guy Planty-Bonjour (Paris: PUF, 1991), p. 319).

14 Heidegger states:

> That the Hegelian concept is the sublated concept of traditional logic – which serves as the guideline for ontology – is shown, however, in the same way: The essence of God for Hegel is what presents itself finally in the specifically Christian consciousness of God, in the form in which it has passed through Christian theology and above all through the doctrine of the Trinity. . . .
>
> (*Hegel's Phenomenology of Spirit*, p. 99)

15 Ibid. With exemplary perspicacity, Otto Pöggeler differentiates the lines of force governing the Heideggerean interpretation of the *Phenomenology of Spirit*, reminding us of what Heidegger considered the onto-theological content and structure of this Hegelian work. See his article, 'Hölderlin, Schelling und Hegel bei Heidegger', *Hegel-Studien*, Bd 28, 1993, pp. 327–371, in particular pp. 359ff.
16 On this point, it is worth consulting a commentary by Abbé Leonard which brings out the 'unheard-of audacity' of this passage of Origen; see his article, 'The law of the absolute in Bruaire', in *La Question de Dieu selon Aristote et Hegel*, pp. 401–427.

5 PRESENTATION OF *REVEALED RELIGION*

1 My discussion here, in its details, relies on Adriaan Pepersack's exposition of 'Revealed Religion' in '*Selbsterkenntnis des Absoluten. Grundlinien der Hegelschen Philosophie des Geistes Absolute*', *Spekulation und Erfahrung, Texte und Untersuchungen zum Deutschen Idealismus*, II, Bd. 6 (Frommann-Holzboog: 1987). Pepersack divides the section into two main moments: 'Der Begriff der geoffenbarten Religion (§564–565)' and 'Die Entfaltung des Begriff der geoffenbarten Religion (§566–571)', ch. IV, pp. 93–97.
2 *Encyclopedia Philosophy of Spirit*, §564–566.
3 Ibid., §564.
4 Ibid., §565.
5 Ibid., §566.
6 Ibid., §567.
7 Ibid., §568.
8 First part of §570.
9 Second part of §570.
10 §571.
11 §564.
12 Ibid.
13 §564, Addition [translation modified].
14 §565. Translation modified.
15 Ibid. [translation modified].
16 §566.
17 §567. Translation modified.
18 §568.
19 §568.
20 Hegel designates these as (1), §569; (2) and (3), §570. U, S, P stand for 'Universal', 'Particular', 'Singular'.
21 *Encyclopedia Science of Logic*, §183.
22 Ibid., §569.
23 Ibid.
24 Ibid.
25 Ibid., §570, first part.
26 *Encyclopedia Science of Logic*, §189.
27 Ibid., §190.
28 *Encyclopedia Philosophy of Spirit*, §570. Translation modified.
29 Ibid.
30 *Encyclopedia Science of Logic*, §191.
31 §570. Translation modified.
32 §565. Translation modified.
33 §571.

6 GOD WITHOUT TRANSCENDENCE? THE THEOLOGIANS CONTRA HEGEL

1 Indeed we should recall that Luther uses the German *Entäußerung* to translate the Greek κένωσις.

2 Bernard Bourgeois, who adopts this term, explains: '*Entäußerung* expresses an exteriorization (*Äußerung*) which separates from the Self, or a separation from the Self by exteriorisation' (translation of the *Philosophy of Spirit* (Paris: Vrin, 1988), note 4, p. 98). Now 'alienation' can also at times translate *Entfremdung*. According to Bourgeois, *Entfremdung* signifies a movement of dispossession which alters both the form and content, while *Entäußerung* only alters the form. We share this opinion to the degree that *Entäußerung*, in the religious context, is the *representational* expression of the divine dispossession, its presentation in the *form* of a representation. The content and the spiritual significance of this dispossession remain the same for speculative philosophy.

We suggest that *Entfremdung* should be translated as 'making strange', *extranéisation* in French, referring back to the legal term in France that designates the juridical status of the foreigner. Because of its ambiguity (it is a distinctively Freudian notion) and the archaic word to which it refers (Old French 'estrangier'), we cannot retain the translation *étrangeté*, 'strangeness', suggested by Jean-Pierre Lefebvre. Nor do we want to adopt the option of Labarrière and Jarczyk: 'extériorisation' for *Entäußerung* and the neologism 'extérioration' for *Äußerung*.

3 *Lectures on the Philosophy of Religion*, III, p. 466.

4 §566.

5 §570.

6 *Lectures on the Philosophy of Religion*, III (German edition, Meiner 61–63), Dritter Teil, 'Die Absolute Religion', p. 4: 'In dem Bewußtsein Gottes also sind zwei Seiten, die eine ist Gott, die andre ist die, auf der das Bewußtsein und das Wesen im endlichen Verhältnisse. . . .'

7 Emilio Brito, *La Christologie de Hegel. Verbum Crucis*, translated from the Spanish by B. Pottier (Paris: Beauchesne, 1983), p. 639.

8 *Encyclopedia Philosophy of Spirit*, §567.

9 *La Christologie de Hegel*, p. 538.

10 Xavier Tilliette explains:

> The mystery of exinanition or of the *kenosis* of Christ is precisely the mystery of the Incarnation. It is solemnly announced in the *Letter to the Philippians*, using probably the words of a hymn. This rhythmical text, unique in its size, unfathomable in its daring, was clearly not unique among Paul's sermons. The Epistles constantly return to the affirmation of the paradox of Christ, the supreme expression of *kenosis*.
> ('L'Exinanition du Christ: théologies de la kénose', in *Le Christ visage de Dieu*, 'Les Quatre, Fleuves', *Cahiers de recherche et de réflexion religieuses*, no. 4 (Paris: Seuil, 1975), p. 50)

11 This is the traditional version. See Athanasius, *Against the Arians (Contra Arianos)*, I, 40–41.

12 Cited from the article '*Kenosis*' in the *Dictionnaire de théologie catholique*, volume VIII, 2nd part (Paris: Librarie Letouzey et Ana, 1925), p. 2343.

13 See Paul Althaus, *Die Theologie Martin Luthers* (Gütersloh: 1963), pp. 172f.

14 See the article '*Kenosis*' in the *Dictionnaire de théologie catholique*, p. 2339.

15 *Die Bekenntnisschriften der evangelisch-lutherischen Kirche* (Göttingen: Vandenhoeck and Ruprecht, 1979), p. 1030. We must forego here entering into

the details of this complicated theoretical history surrounding Lutheran kenoticism, in particular the polemic in the eighteenth century between the theologians of the School of Giessen and those of the Tübingen School, on the topic of God's renunciation of his own majesty.

16 *Lectures on the Philosophy of Religion*, III, Meiner 61–63, p. 135.

17 Ernst Jüngel, *God as the Mystery of the World*, pp. 96–97 [Translation modified] (*Gott als Geheimnis der Welt*, p. 127).

18 *Lectures on the Philosophy of Religion*, III, Meiner 61–63, p. 93.

19 The title of an article by Jean-Louis Chrétien ('Le Bien donne ce qu'il n'a pas', *Archives de philosophie*, vol. XLIII, 1980, 2, pp. 263–298). On the other hand we must allude here to the theological project attempted by Stanislas Breton, where superabundance is to be thought of outside the categories of the gift and generosity: 'It will never be in generosity, no matter how it shows its face, that we will discover the secret of superabundance and its own form of play' (*Être, monde, imaginaire* (Paris: Seuil, 1976), p. 169). Paul Ricœur, commenting on these theses in his *Lectures 3. Aux frontières de la philosophie* (Paris: Seuil, 1994, p. 145), writes:

> For the gift, there must always be a subject who is richly endowed, endowed in advance, a Self which gives because it has the wealth to give. Is it true that one must be a proprietor to be a giver?

Hegel could have formulated this last question in his own terms, which would be identical. Nonetheless, it is clear that Breton's discussion is faithful to the notion of superabundance, and this is a notion absent from the thought of Hegel.

20 However, it was Origen who chose the metaphysical expression '*hypostasis*'. See here Albert Chapelle: 'There is one essence and three divine hypostases, said the Greeks. There are three persons subsisting in the divine essence, said the Latin Fathers' (*Hegel et la Religion* (Paris: Éditions Universitaires, 1967), vol. 2, p. 84). See on the poverty of 'Person' in relation to the divine, the *Lectures on Philosophy of Religion*, III, p. 285, Meiner 61–63, pp. 210–211.

21 *Lectures on the Philosophy of Religion*, III, p. 84, Meiner p. 22. Trans. modified.

22 Ibid., pp. 84–85, Meiner pp. 22–23. Translation modified.

23 Ibid. Translation modified.

24 Lasson, editing the *Lectures*, thought he should amend Hegel's manuscript to 'ob der Geist vom Vater oder vom Vater und Sohn ausgeht . . .', indicating in the notes: 'Manuscript: *vom Sohne (ein seltsamer Irrtum Hegels)*' *G. W. F. Hegel: Sämtliche Werke*, Bd XIV (Leipzig: Felix Meiner Verlag, 1929), p. 64. The correction is found also in Gibelin's translation (*Leçons sur la philosophie de la religion* (Paris: Vrin, 1954–9), III, p. 68), but not in the English translation.

25 According to these experts, Hegel never made more than average progress in this discipline (at the Tübingen Seminary): 'mediocres in theologia commonstravit progressus'. Cf. G. Hoffmeister, *Dokumente zur Hegels Entwicklung*, p. 439.

26 *Encyclopedia Science of Logic*, §238–242.

27 Urs von Balthasar, *Prometheus. Studien zur Geschichte des deutschen Idealismus* (Heidelberg, 1947), p. 575.

28 *Lectures on the Philosophy of Religion*, III, p. 126, Meiner, p. 158.

29 Ibid., p. 127, Meiner, p. 159. Trans. modified.

30 These organs being the spiritual powers of intuition, imagination and memory.

31 *Encyclopedia Philosophy of Nature*, §345.

32 Ibid.

33 *Encyclopedia Philosophy of Spirit*, §552, Remark. Translation modified.

34 Marion, *Dieu sans l'être* (Paris: PUF, collection 'Quadrige', 1991), p. 238. *God without Being*, translated by T. A. Carlson (Chicago: University of Chicago Press, 1991), p. 169. Translation modified.
35 *Lectures on the Philosophy of History*, p. 377, cited in Marion, *God without Being*, p. 169.
36 Ibid.
37 Ibid., p. 170.
38 Ibid., p. 170. See also p. 170, note 16:

> Obviously it is not by chance that Hegel brings to light the metaphysical ('ordinary') conception of time *and* rejects the Catholic real presence: this presence, at a distance from consciousness (of Self and of time), disqualifies by its independence and its great perpetuity the two fundamental characteristics of 'the vulgar concept of time': the primacy of the *here and now* and the reduction of time to the perception of it that consciousness experiences.

39 Karl Barth, *Die protestantische Theologie in 19. Jahrhundert* (Zürich: Theologischer Verlag, 1947), *Protestant Theology from Rousseau to Ritschl*, translated by B. Cozens and H. H. Hartwell (New York: Harper & Row, 1959).
40 Ibid., p. 293; German, p. 366.
41 Ibid., p. 302; German, p. 374.
42 Ibid.
43 Ibid., p. 304, German p. 375.
44 Ibid., p. 304, German p. 377.
45 Ibid.
46 From Luther's '95 Theses' cited by Henri Strohl in *Luther jusqu'en 1520* (Paris: PUF, 1962), Thesis 47, p. 230.
47 *Encyclopedia Philosophy of Spirit*, §571.
48 Ibid., §564, Addition.
49 As Jean-Luc Marion insists, *God without Being*, p. 16.
50 'Order' is here understood in Pascal's sense.
51 *Protestant Theology from Rousseau to Ritschl*, p. 302, German, p. 375.
52 Marion, *God without Being*, p. 194.
53 In the terms used by Jean Beaufret in his *Introduction to Parmenides' Poème* (Paris: PUF, 1955), p. 48.
54 Jacques Derrida, *Glas*, 2 vols (Paris: Denoël-Gonthier, 1981), vol. 2, p. 309, translated by J. P. Leavey, Jr., and R. Rand (Lincoln: University of Nebraska Press, 1986), p. 221; translation modified.
55 Cf. on this point the reading of Hans Küng offered by Bernard Bourgeois in 'Hegel et l'Incarnation selon Hans Küng', in *Le Christ visage de Dieu*, 'Les Quatre Fleuves', pp. 81–84. For Küng as well, Hegel reduces transcendence to immanence 'sinking their unity into the immanence of *thought* to itself, which is brought to its conclusion in Absolute Knowledge. The Hegelian project will deny that the living God is transcendent to the Absolute Knowledge where history is fulfilled.' Bernard Bourgeois concludes: 'For Küng, refusal of the future and refusal of transcendence are intimately linked' (p. 84).

7 THE DEATH OF GOD AND THE DEATH OF PHILOSOPHY: ALIENATION AND ITS DOUBLE FATE

1 *Faith and Knowledge: An English Translation of 'Glauben und Wissen'*, translated and edited by W. Cerf and H. S. Harris (Albany, NY: SUNY Press, 1977),

p. 190; Hegel, PhB 319c: *Jenaer Kritische Schriften* (III): *Glauben und Wissen* (Hamburg: Felix Meiner Verlag, 1986).

2 Ibid.; Meiner, p. 134.

3 For the philosophers of the Enlightenment,

> God is something incomprehensible and unthinkable. Knowledge knows nothing save that it knows nothing; it must take refuge in faith. All of them agree that, as the old distinction puts it, the Absolute is no more against Reason than it is for it; it is beyond Reason.
>
> Ibid., p. 56; Meiner, p. 2

4 *Encyclopedia Philosophy of Spirit*, §569.

5 Ibid., 564, Addition.

6 *God as the Mystery of the World*, p. 64 [Translation modified]; *Gott als Geheimnis der Welt*, p. 84.

7 'This expresses an awareness that the human, the finite, the weak, the negative are themselves a moment of the divine, that they are within God himself, that finitude, negativity, otherness are not outside of God and do not, as otherness, hinder unity with God. Otherness, the negative, is known to be a moment of the divine nature itself. This involves the highest 'idea' of spirit.' *Lectures on the Philosophy of Religion*, III, p. 326; Meiner, p. 172.

8 See Hans Küng, *Menschwerdung Gottes: Eine Einführung in Hegels theologisches Denken als Prologomena zu einer künftigen Christologie* (Freiburg: Herder, 1970).

9 'O grosse Not, Gott selbst ist tot, am Kreuz ist er gestorben – hat dadurch das Himmelreich uns aus Lieb' erworben.'

10 *God as the Mystery of the World*, p. 64; *Gott als Geheimnis der Welt*, p. 85. See note 25 on the scholarly debates, p. 64 (85).

11 *Adv. Marc.* II, 27. *Deus pusillus inuentus est, ut homo maximus fieret. Qui talem deum dedignaris, nescio, an ex fide credas deum crucifixum.*

12 *Adv. Prax.* 29.

13 *Contra Arianos*, III, 34. This means that one 'does not attribute suffering to the Logos itself but to the flesh He possesses as proper to His nature.'

14 Cited by Jüngel in *God as the Mystery of the World*, p. 66.

15 *The Spirit of Christianity and its Fate*, in *Early Theological Writings*, translated by T. M. Knox, with an introduction, and fragments translated by R. Kroner (Chicago: University of Chicago Press, 1948), pp. 293–292. *Hegels theologische Jugendschriften* (Tübingen: Nohl edition, 1907), p. 325.

16 *Faith and Knowledge*, p. 190 [translation modified]; *Glauben und Wissen*, p. 134.

17 Ibid., p. 191; *Glauben und Wissen*, p. 134.

18 *Phenomenology of Spirit*, p. 416; Suhrkamp 3, p. 502.

19 The stages here are put into perspective by Richard Kroner in *Von Kant bis Hegel*, 2 vols (Tübingen: J. C. B. Mohr, 1921–1924), Bd 2, pp. 403–415.

20 *Phenomenology of Spirit*, p. 424; Suhrkamp 3, 511.

21 Ibid., p. 453; Suhrkamp 3, p. 545.

22 Ibid., p. 426; Suhrkamp 3, p. 514.

23 Ibid., p. 453; Suhrkamp 3, p. 545.

24 Ibid., p. 454; Suhrkamp 3, p. 547.

25 Ibid., p. 455; Suhrkamp 3, p. 547.

26 Ibid., p. 457; Suhrkamp 3, p. 550.

27 Ibid., p. 471; Suhrkamp 3, p. 565.

28 *Lectures on the Philosophy of Religion*, III, p. 321 [translation modified]; Meiner, pp. 169–170.

29 Ibid., p. 323; Meiner, p. 167.
30 Ibid. Translation modified.
31 *Faith and Knowledge*, p. 55 [translation modified]; *Glauben und Wissen* in Meiner edition, p. 1.
32 Ibid, p. 189; Meiner, p. 132.
33 By *Aufklärung* Hegel means the tradition of thought begun by Descartes and continued by Kant and his immediate successors.
34 *Faith and Knowledge*, p. 55; Meriner, p. 1.
35 Ibid., p. 56; Meiner, p. 2.
36 Ibid., p. 55–56; Meiner, pp. 1–2. Translation modified.
37 Ibid., p. 56; Meiner, p. 2.
38 Ibid., p. 170; Meiner, p. 115.
39 Ibid., p. 61; *Glauben und Wissen,* p. 7. [Trans.: On p. 9 of *Glauben und Wissen*, Hegel speaks of 'einer unendluchen Sehnsucht und eines unheilbaren Schmerzens' Harris and Cerf. translated the words as 'the poetry of Protestant grief'; the French, *Foi et savoir*, trans. Alexis Philonenko and Calude Lecouteux (Paris: Vrin, 1988), is more faithful to the German: Protestantism and its 'poetry of infinite grief'.]
40 Ibid., p. 58; *Glauben und Wissen*, p. 4.
41 Ibid., p. 57; *Glauben und Wissen*, p. 3.
42 [Trans.: Harris and Cerf: 'The religion of more recent times'.]
43 Ibid., p. 57; *Glauben und Wissen*, p. 3:

> Die Religion baut im Herzen des Individuums ihre Tempel und Altäre, und Seufzer und Gebete suchen den Gott, dessen Anschauung es sich versagt, weil die Gefahr des Verstandes vorhanden ist, welcher das Angeschaute als Ding, den Hain als Hölzer erkennen würde.

44 *Encyclopedia Philosophy of Spirit*, §564.
45 See on this §452 of the *Encyclopedia Philosophy of Spirit*.
46 Bourgeois, 'Translator's Introduction' to the *Philosophie de l'esprit*, pp. 68–69.
47 Ibid., pp. 68–69. This return is equivalent, in the exposition of speculative *Psychology*, to the transition from representation to speculative thought, a transition 'developed in three moments: recall in and of the Self, imagination, and memory (*Gedächtnis*)'.
48 *Lectures on the Philosophy of Religion*, I, p. 119 [translation modified]; Meiner, pp. 31–32.
49 Paul Ricœur interprets Hegelian representation as nothing but figurative thought:

> The term [*Vorstellung*] is clarified by the opposition *Vorstellung* and *Begriff* (representation and concept). This is why it must be translated not by 'representation' but by 'figurative thought'. The term 'representation' is only acceptable to the degree that it draws attention to the way *Vorstellung* is amplified in its Hegelian usage, applying not just to narratives and symbols, to 'images', if you like, but also to expressions as elaborated and in a certain fashion conceptualized, as the Trinity, Creation, the Fall, the Incarnation, Salvation, etc. In short, not just to a religious discourse but to a theological discourse. Hegel's argument is precisely that, no matter how rationalized this discourse may be, it is not yet conceptual in the strict sense of the word, but still and only figurative . . .
>
> ('Le statut de la *Vorstellung* dans la philosophie hégélienne de la religion', *Lectures 3. Aux frontières de la philosophie*, p. 41)

50 On the Hegelian definition of representation as 'form' see in particular the *Encyclopedia Philosophy of Spirit*, §573, Remark.
51 On this refer to the preceding discussion of §565.

8 DIVINE PLASTICITY: OR, THE *TURN* OF EVENTS

1 'Le temps n'est pas ce qu'il est.'
2 *Lectures on the Philosophy of History*, p. 319.
3 Ibid. Translation modified.
4 Ibid.
5 Ibid., p. 319.
6 Ibid., p. 323. Translation modified.
7 *Lectures on the Philosophy of Religion*, III, p. 321; Meiner, pp. 169–170.
8 *Lectures on the Philosophy of History*, III, p. 325. Translation modified.
9 *Lectures on the Philosophy of Religion*, III, Meiner, p. 142. [Not in English edition.] Repeatedly Hegel insists on the necessity of distinguishing this sort of Incarnation from the multiple incarnations of Brahma, and draws attention to the absolute distance separating Revealed Religion from all the forms of pantheism, for example those discussed in the Remark to the *Encyclopedia* §573: 'But so little concrete is the divine unity . . . that Hinduism, with a monstrous inconsistency, is also the maddest of polytheisms.' The *Lectures on the Philosophy of Religion* show further how the Christian Incarnation also differentiates itself from the solitary subjectivity of the One in Judaism as well as from the beautiful individuality of the Greek ideal.
10 *Lectures on the Philosophy of Religion*, III, Meiner, p. 168. [Not in English edition]
11 *Aesthetics*, II, p. 822.
12 Ibid., p. 864.
13 Ibid., pp. 863–864.
14 Ibid., p. 865. These are the individuals as created by Michelangelo, Raphael and Leonardo da Vinci. All attempts to represent Christ in an idealized and Greek manner are illegitimate and disappointing, as Hegel remarks when he considers the paintings of Van Eyck. The latter has indeed 'achieved the summit of perfection' in his picture of God the Father

> above the altar at the Cathedral of Ghent; this is a work which can be set beside the Olympian Zeus. Nevertheless, however perfect it may be in its expression of eternal peace, sublimity, power, and dignity, etc., it still has in it something deeply unsatisfying according to our ideas. For God the Father is presented here as at the same time a human individual, and this can only be Christ the Son. In him alone have we a vision of this factor of individuality and humanity as a factor in the Divine, and we see it in such a way that it is not a naïve imaginative shape, as in the case of the Greek gods, but proves to be an essential revelation, as what is most important and significant.
>
> (Ibid., p. 820)

15 Ibid., p. 521.
16 This is one of the central meanings of *kenosis* in Hegel's doctrine of the Incarnation.
17 *Phenomenology of Spirit*, p. 459. Translation modified.
18 *Lectures on the Philosophy of Religion*, III, p. 321; Meiner, p. 157.
19 'The Death of Christ, the Death of his 'initial existence'', is 'the highest limit, the finitisation' (*Verendlichung*). Ibid.

20 *Science of Logic, Doctrine of Being*, p. 132; *Wissenschaft der Logik*, I; Suhrkamp 5, p. 143.
21 *Science of Logic, Doctrine of Being*, p. 134. We should note here Hegel's inversion of the Kantian employment of the concepts of limitation (*borne*) and limit. As opposed to limitation, limit, in Kant, is a dynamic concept because it permits the two frontiers it divides to enter into relation (cf. his expression 'the limits of reason').
22 *Lectures on the Philosophy of Religion*, III, Meiner, p. 156.
23 Ibid., p. 168.
24 Ibid.
25 'Erscheinen ist Sein für anderes.' Ibid., p. 138.
26 Translated from Manfred Baum, *Die Enstehung der Hegelschen Dialektik* (Bonn: Bouvier Verlag, 1986), p. 4.
27 *Encyclopedia Science of Logic*, §123.
28 In this way the category of existence is developed 'into a *totality* and a *world* of appearance, or of reflected finitude'. Ibid., §132.
29 *Encyclopedia Philosophy of Spirit*, §565.

CONCLUSION

1 Ludwig Feuerbach, *Das Wesen des Christenthums* (Stuttgart: Frommann Verlag, 1903), 'Das Geheimnis des christlichen Christus oder der persönnlichen Gottes', p. 177. *The Essence of Christianity*, Introduction translated by Z. Hanti (1972), remainder translated by G. Eliot (1854), transcribed Andy Blunden (New York and London: Harper and Row, 1957). Part I, *The True or Anthropological Essence of Religion*, ch. XV, 'The Mystery of the Christian Christ, or the Personal God', p. 148.
2 Ibid.
3 *Faith and Knowledge*, p. 79. Translation modified, Meiner, p. 28.
4 Ibid., p. 73. Translation modified, Meiner, p. 20
5 Ibid., p. 80. Translation modified, Meiner, p. 28.
6 Ibid., p. 89. Translation modified, Meiner, p. 36.
7 A sacrifice which means that reason will not be able to recognize itself in its own productions:

> Theoretical reason . . . makes no claim to an autonomous dignity, no claim to beget the Son out of itself. We must leave it to its own emptiness and the unworthiness that comes from its being able to put up with this dualism of a pure unity of reason and a manifold of the intellect, and from its not feeling any need for the middle and for immanent cognition (*nach immanenter Erkenntnis zu sein*).
>
> (Ibid., pp. 81–82; Meiner, p. 30)

8 Ibid., p. 177; Meiner p. 134.
9 *Encyclopedia Philosophy of Spirit*, §571, Remark.
10 *Phenomenology of Spirit*, p. 487 [translation modified]; Suhrkamp 3, p. 384.
11 Ibid.
12 Cf. Deleuze: 'If the greatest initiative of transcendental philosophy lies in introducing the form of time into thought itself, then this pure and empty form in turn signifies indissolubly the death of God.' *Difference and repetition*, p. 87.
13 True sacrifice is always linked, in Hegel, to alienation, to the self-being transformed into an other, as we can see from this extract from the 'Absolute Knowledge' chapter of the *Phenomenology of Spirit*:

> To know one's limit is to know how to sacrifice oneself (*seine Grenze wissen, heißt sich aufzuopfern wissen*). This sacrifice is the alienation (*Entäußerung*) in which Spirit displays the process of its becoming Spirit in the form of *free contingent happening* (*in der Form des freien zufälligen Geschehens darstellt*) intuiting its pure Self as time outside of it (*als die Zeit außer ihm*), and equally its being as space.
>
> (Translation modified, p. 492; Suhrkamp 3, p. 590)

14 Ibid., pp. 492–493, translation modified; Suhrkamp 3, p. 591.
15 Ibid., pp. 492, 591.
16 *Being and Time*, p. 523.

PART III
HEGEL ON THE PHILOSOPHER OR, *TWO FORMS* OF THE FALL

INTRODUCTION

1 Bernard Bourgeois, 'Entretien avec Francis Fukuyama', in *Le Monde*, Tuesday, 25 February 1992, p. 2. Under 'end of history', Hegel places the period which extends from the Reformation to today. 'This formally absolute principle brings us to *the last stage of history, our world, our own time*.' *Lectures on the Philosophy of History*, p. 442. The principle articulated in the Reformation, the triumph of subjective liberty, is brought to perfection by the French Revolution. Hence 'the solution to the problem of history', as Bernard Bourgeois writes, 'has been found since the French Revolution'.
2 *Encyclopedia Philosophy of Spirit*, §571, Remark.
3 Ibid., §573.
4 *Phenomenology of Spirit*, p. 39; Suhrkamp 3, p. 61.
5 [Trans. 'L'operation plastique' could also be the explosion of a bomb.]

9 PRESENTATION OF *PHILOSOPHY*

1 *Encyclopedia*, §573.
2 Ibid., §§572–573.
3 §573.
4 §573.
5 §574.
6 §§575–577.
7 §574.
8 Ibid.
9 *Science of Logic, Doctrine of the Notion* [*Concept*], p. 582; Suhrkamp 6, p. 252.
10 Commenting on this movement, Pepersack insists on the fact that: 'The identity of the logical and abstract idea with the concrete knowledge of absolute spirit releases science from its unproven presuppositions and through that, from all immediacy.' *Selbsterkenntnis des Absoluten*, p. 125.
11 §§572–573.
12 §572 and beginning of §573.
13 *Science of Logic, Doctrine of the Notion* [*Concept*], p. 824; Suhrkamp 6, p. 549.
14 This same distinction between art and religion is clarified by Hegel already in the beginning of §572: 'Science is the unity of art and religion', in other words, the unity between 'the first, the intuition-method of art, external in point of form', and 'the subjective production by which the substantial content is shattered

(*versplittert*) into many separate shapes (*in viele selbständige Gestalten*)' and 'the totality of the second' (*Philosophy of Spirit*, §572; Suhrkamp 10, p. 378; translation modified)

15 Ibid., §573. Translation modified.
16 Ibid.
17 Ibid., §572.
18 Ibid., §573, Remark; Suhrkamp 10, p. 381. Translation modified.
19 Ibid., Suhrkamp 10, p. 389.
20 Ibid., Suhrkamp 10, p. 389.
21 Ibid., Suhrkamp 10, p. 380.
22 Ibid.
23 §§575–577.
24 *Science of Logic, Doctrine of the Notion* [*Concept*], p. 825.
25 Ibid., p. 763; cf. also *Encyclopedia Science of Logic*, §216.
26 *Encyclopedia Philosophy of Spirit*, §575; Suhrkamp 10, p. 393. Translation modified.
27 Ibid., §576.
28 §576.
29 *Encyclopedia Science of Logic*, §239.
30 §576.
31 *Science of Logic, Doctrine of the Notion* [*Concept*], p. 775; Suhrkamp 6, p. 487.
32 Ibid.
33 *Encyclopedia Philosophy of Spirit*, §577. Translation modified.
34 It will be the object of Chapter 11.

10 THE DIALECTICAL SIMPLIFICATION

1 'Es ist in der Tat in diesem Schriften vieles zu niederträchtig.' Letter to Daub, 27 September 1829. *Briefe von und an Hegel*, edited by Johannes Hoffmeister (Hamburg: Felix Meiner, 1961), vol. III, p. 274. Quoted by Bernard Bourgeois in the 'Introduction' to the *Philosophie de l'esprit*, note 34, pp. 82–83. *Hegel: The Letters*, translated by C. Butler and C. Seiler, commentary by C. Butler (Bloomington: Indiana University Press, 1984).
2 Bourgeois, 'Introduction', pp. 82–83.
3 Letter from C. H. Weiße to Hegel, 11 July 1829, in *Briefe* III, pp. 262–263, English pp. 539–540.
4 *Thor Seminar*, from the proceedings of the session of 6 September 1968 (Max Niemeyer Verlag, 1969). English translation in 'A Heidegger Seminar on Hegel's *Differenzschrift*', *Southwest Journal of Philosophy*, 11, pp. 9–45. Translation modified.
5 '"*Aufheben*", writes Derrida, is *relever*, in the sense in which *relever* can combine to relieve, to displace, to elevate, to replace and to promote, in one and the same movement'. *Marges de la philosophie*, (Paris: Minuit, 1972), p. 143. *Margins of Philosophy*, trans. A. Bass (Hemel Hempstead: Harvester Wheatsheaf, 1982), p. 121. On the pertinence of this translation of *Aufhebung* by 'relève', see also Jean-François Courtine, 'Relève-répétition', in *Heidegger et la phénoménologie* (Paris: Vrin, 1990), pp. 89–106 (96f.).
6 *Encyclopedia Philosophy of Spirit*, §387.
7 The 1805–6 *Philosophy of Spirit* presents this spectrality as *the night of the human gaze*:

> Man is this night, this empty nothingness, which contains everything in its simplicity: the wealth of an infinite number of representations, of

> images, not one of which comes precisely to mind – or which are not [there] in so far as they are not really present. It is the night, the interiority of Nature which exists here: [*the*] pure personal self (*reines Selbst*), – in phantasmagorical representations (*phantasmagorischen Vorstellungen*); . . . here suddenly surges up a blood-splattered head (*ein blütig Kopf*), – there another white apparition (*eine andere weisse Gestalt*), and they disappear just as abruptly (*verschwinden ebenso*). This is the night one perceives if one looks a man in the eyes: then one is delving into a night which becomes terrible (*furchtbar*); it is the night of the world presenting itself to each and every one of us.
>
> (*Jenaer Systementwürfe III: Naturphilosophie und Philosophie des Geistes* (Hamburg: Felix Meiner, 1987), PhB 333, p. 172)

8 *Phenomenology of Spirit*, p. 19, Suhrkamp 12, pp. 36–37. Translation modified.
9 Ibid., p. 455; Suhrkamp 3, p. 548.
10 Ibid.
11 Ibid., p. 456; Suhrkamp 3, p. 548.
12 *Lectures on the Philosophy of History*, p. 5; Suhrkamp 12, p. 16.
13 Ibid.
14 *Science of Logic*, Preface to the 1831 edition, p. 34; Suhrkamp 5, p. 24.
15 Ibid., p. 39; Suhrkamp, p. 29.
16 Ibid., *Doctrine of the Notion [Concept]*, p. 611; Suhrkamp 6, p. 287.
17 [Trans.: *pointes* means also 'tips', 'spikes'.]
18 *Phenomenology of Spirit*, p. 17; Suhrkamp 3, p. 33.
19 Ibid., p. 16, 17; p. 33.
20 Ibid., p. 17; p. 34.
21 Ibid., p. 16; p. 32. Translation modified.
22 Ibid., p. 17; p. 34.
23 Preface to the 1817 edition of the *Encyclopedia Science of Logic*, p. 1; Suhrkamp 8, p. 11.
24 Ibid.
25 Bernard Bourgeois, *Introduction* to the French translation of the *Encyclopedia Science of Logic*, pp. 11–12.
26 *Phenomenology of Spirit*, p. 7; Suhrkamp 3, p. 20. Hegel is scathing on the subject of his contemporaries' resistance to ὅρος. For them the absolute is indeterminate and unlimited, hence formless: 'This prophetic talk supposes that it is staying right in the centre and in the depths, looks disdainfully at determination (ὅρος), and deliberately holds aloof from concept and necessity.' Ibid., p. 6; Suhrkamp 3, p. 17.
27 Ibid., p. 34.
28 *Lectures on the Philosophy of History*, p. 55.
29 In the Preface to the *Phenomenology of Spirit,* Hegel writes: 'Already an *abstract thought* (*ein Gedachtes*), its content is now the *property* of substance.' Suhrkamp 3, p. 34.
30 Ibid, p. 16; Suhrkamp 3, p. 32.
31 Ibid., p. 31; Suhrkamp 3, pp. 50–51.
32 Ibid.
33 Ibid.
34 *Science of Logic*, *Doctrine of Being*, p. 107; Suhrkamp 5, p. 114.
35 'Something is sublated only in so far as it has entered into unity with its opposite; in this more particular signification as something reflected, it may fittingly be called a *moment*' (ibid.).
36 Ibid., p. 841; Suhrkamp 6, p. 570.

11 'ON THE SELF'

1 *Encyclopedia Philosophy of Spirit*, §577; Suhrkamp 10, p. 394. Translation modified.
2 *Science of Logic, Doctrine of the Notion [Concept]*, p. 843; Suhrkamp 6, p. 573.
3 See §573.
4 See the last part of §571.
5 *Phenomenology of Spirit*, p. 20; Suhrkamp 3, p. 37.
6 Ibid., p. 32; p. 52.
7 Ibid., p. 484; p. 581.
8 *Science of Logic, Doctrine of Essence*, p. 556; Suhrkamp 6, p. 220.
9 *Encyclopedia Philosophy of Spirit*, §382. Translation modified.
10 *Phenomenology of Spirit*, pp. 18–19; Suhrkamp 3, p. 36.
11 *Science of Logic, Doctrine of Essence*, p. 554; Suhrkamp 6, p. 218.
12 Ibid., p. 556; Suhrkamp 6, p. 220.
13 Ibid., p. 555; Suhrkamp 6, p. 219.
14 Ibid., p. 556; Suhrkamp 6, p. 220–1.
15 Ibid., p. 558; Suhrkamp 6, p. 222.
16 Ibid., pp. 551–553; Suhrkamp 6, pp. 214–216.
17 Ibid., p. 550; Suhrkamp 6, p. 213.
18 Ibid., p. 570; Suhrkamp 6, p. 239.
19 Ibid., pp. 570–571; Suhrkamp 6, pp. 238–240.
20 Ibid., p. 571; Suhrkamp 6, p. 240.
21 Ibid., p. 567; Suhrkamp 6, p. 235.
22 Ibid., p. 571; Suhrkamp 6, pp. 239–240.
23 At this point one should refer to the very valuable book of Gabriella Baptist, *Il Problema della modalità nelle logiche di Hegel. Un itinerario tra il possibile e il necessario* (Genoa: Pantograf, 1992).
24 Derrida is referring to Hegel when he speaks of a twofold impossibility for philosophy: it cannot both claim that Greece is simply a 'happy accident' and, on the contrary, argue that the Greek origin of the tradition is a necessity within the eschatological order. See 'Violence and Metaphysics', in *L'Ecriture et la différence* (Paris: Seuil, 1967), p. 227; *Writing and Difference*, translated by A. Bass, (London: Routledge and Kegan Paul, 1981), p. 153.
25 *Science of Logic, Doctrine of the Notion*, pp. 831–2; Suhrkamp 6, p. 558.
26 Ibid.
27 Ibid., *Doctrine of Essence*, p. 571; Suhrkamp 6, p. 250.
28 Ibid. Translation modified.
29 *Phenomenology of Spirit*, p. 487; Suhrkamp 3, p. 584.
30 [Trans.: *cas* means both occurrence and example.]

12 THE PHILOSOPHER, THE READER AND THE SPECULATIVE PROPOSITION

1 *Phenomenology of Spirit*, p. 39; Suhrkamp 3, p. 60.
2 Ibid., p. 39; Suhrkamp 3, p. 61.
3 *Science of Logic*, Preface to the 1831 edition, p. 32. Translation modified. Suhrkamp 5, p. 21.
4 *Encyclopedia Science of Logic*, §189. The paragraph itself displays the proposition unfolding syllogistically:

> With regard to the form a double result has now been established. (1) Since each of the moments has assumed the determination and the place

> of the *middle term*, and hence of the whole in general, it has *in-itself* lost the one-sidedness of its abstraction . . .; (2) *the mediation* . . . has been completed, but again *only in itself*, i.e. only as a *circle* of mediations that reciprocally presuppose one another.

5 *Phenomenology of Spirit*, p. 37. Translation modified; Suhrkamp 3, p. 56.
6 *Science of Logic*, Preface to the 1831 edition, p. 31; Suhrkamp 5, p. 20.
7 From the *Rede zum Schuljahrabschluß*, 29 September 1809, Suhrkamp 4, pp. 322–323.
8 Ibid., p. 315.
9 *Science of Logic*, Preface to the 1831 edition, p. 32; Suhrkamp 5, p. 20.
10 Derrida, 'Violence and Metaphysics', in *Writing and Difference*, p. 112.
11 *Science of Logic*, Preface to the 1831 edition, p. 32; Suhrkamp 5, pp. 20–21.
12 Some examples of German words with contradictory meanings: *Aufhebung*, *aufheben*; *Abgrund*: the ultimate foundation and the bottomless abyss; *Sinn*: sense and meaning; *Geschichte*: the events and the narration of events, history's objective as well as subjective side; *plastisch*: able to receive and to give form. Other words, while not in the strict sense words with opposing meanings, also exhibit just as much the speculative spirit of the language: *Urteil*: judgement and the original division; *meinen*: to have an opinion, to mean, and to make something 'mine'; *Sitten*: mores in the double sense of ethical determinations and general or universal customs.
13 From *Hegel: The Letters*, 16 December 1809, pp. 539–540. Translation modified. *Briefe von und an Hegel*, Bd. I, p. 299. Quoted in Jean-Luc Nancy, *The Speculative Remark*, translated by C. Suprenant (Stanford: Stanford University Press, 2001), p. 63.
14 Martin Heidegger, *Introduction to Metaphysics*, translated by G. Fried and R. Polk (New Haven and London: Yale University Press, 2000), p. 62.
15 Jean Beaufret, 'Hegel et la proposition spéculative', in *Dialogue avec Heidegger* (Paris: Minuit, 1973), p. 137.
16 [Trans.: Or perhaps they may also belong to the domain of the word *relève* – English: *relief* – as in the 'relief' forces, or shifts, which 'relieve' those who are exhausted.]
17 *Phenomenology of Spirit*, pp. 36–37; Suhrkamp 3, p. 57.
18 Aristotle acts like a 'natural historian' of the forms of thought, creating an 'inventory' of the logical categories as he had done with living creatures and composite substances:

> He has only presented thought as defined in its finite application and aspect, and he has described this thought in an exact way. He is the describer of the nature of these forms of thought as if he were a naturalist, and his logic is thus a natural history of finite thought.
>
> (*Lectures on the History of Philosophy*, II, p. 211; translation modified)

19 Ibid., pp. 227–228; Suhrkamp 19, p. 244. Translation modified.
20 *Phenomenology of Spirit*, p. 37; Suhrkamp 3, p. 58.
21 *Lectures on the History of Philosophy*, II, p. 228; Suhrkamp 19, p. 244. [Translation modified.]
22 See Kant, *Critique of Pure Reason*, 'Deduction of the Pure Conceptions of the Understanding', §19. *Kritik der reinen Vernunft*, edited by Wilhelm Weischedel, *Werkausgabe*, III (Frankfurt am Main: Suhrkamp, 1956), p. 142.

23 Hegel, *Faith and Knowledge*, p. 71; *Glauben und Wissen*, p. 19.
24 *Glauben und Wissen*, p. 26.
25 Ibid., p. 22.
26 Ibid. According to Hegel, there is no genuine synthetic *a priori* judgement in the entire Kantian philosophy. On this point, see André Stanguenne, *Hegel, critique de Kant* (Paris: PUF, 1985), covering every instance where the *a priori* judgement is discussed in Hegel (pp. 58–66).
27 *Phenomenology of Spirit*, p. 39; Suhrkamp 3, p. 60.
28 Ibid.
29 Ibid. Translation modified.
30 Ibid., p. 37; Suhrkamp 3, p. 58.
31 Ibid.
32 Ibid, p. 38; Suhrkamp 3, p. 59. Translation modified.
33 Ibid, pp. 38–39; Suhrkamp 3, pp. 59–60.
34 Ibid., p. 38; Suhrkamp 3, p. 59. Translation modified.
35 Ibid., p. 38; Suhrkamp 3, p. 60. Translation modified.
36 Ibid., p. 37; Suhrkamp 3, p. 57. Translation modified.
37 Ibid.; Suhrkamp 3, p. 58.
38 Ibid., p. 39; Suhrkamp 3, p. 60.
39 Ibid., p. 38; Suhrkamp 3, p. 59. Translation modified.
40 *Science of Logic*, Preface to the 1831 edition, p. 40; Suhrkamp 5, p. 31. Translation modified.
41 Hans-Georg Gadamer, in *Truth and Method*, distinguishes 'repetition' (*Wiederholung*) from 'bringing forth' (*Hervorholung*). The latter is a reflection which is not 'imitative (*nachahmend*)', but 'ostensive (*zeigend*)'. It is precisely this economy of bringing forth which we are calling interpretation: 'imitation is not itself a repetition, but a "bringing forth"'. *Wahrheit und Methode*, 4th edition (Tübingen: J.C.B. Mohr, 1975), p. 109; *Truth and Method*, translated by J. Weinsheimer and D.G. Marshall (Crossroads Publishing Company, 1989), p. 114.
42 *The Space of Literature*, translated by A. Smock (Lincoln: University of Nebraska Press, 1982), p. 198.
43 *Phenomenology of Spirit*, p. 36; Suhrkamp 3, p. 56. Translation modified.
44 Ibid., p. 37; p. 58.

CONCLUSION

1 Bernard Bourgeois, 'Translator's Introduction', in *Science de la logique de l'Encyclopédie des sciences philosophiques*, pp. 61–62.
2 *Phenomenology of Spirit*, pp. 6–7; Suhrkamp 3, pp. 18–19. Translation modified.
3 Ibid., p. 54; Suhrkamp 3, p. 77.
4 Heidegger, *Aristoteles, Metaphysik H 1–3, Von Wesen und Wirklichkeit der Kraft*, G. A. Bd 33, §8, p. 64: 'versagt nicht, vermag zu ertagen'). *Aristotle Metaphysics Theta 1–3, On the Essence and Reality of Force*, translated by W. Brogan and P. Warneck (Bloomington: Indiana University Press, 1995), p. 74.
5 [Trans.: The English translators have 'malleability' for the German *Bildsamkeit*; the French text uses *plasticité*.]
6 Ibid., English translation, p. 74; German, pp. 88–89.
7 Ibid.
8 Ibid. 'Der Lehmklumpen erleidet etwas, er läßt die Gestaltung zu, d. h. er ist bildsam; Bildsamkeit als eine Weise der Kraft.' GA, Bd 33, §10, p. 88.
9 Nor in *Being and Time*. On the question of the relation between the two works, see Jean-François Courtine, 'Kant et le temps', in *Heidegger et la Phénoménologie*, pp. 107–127.

10 *Kant and the Problem of Metaphysics*, G. A. Bd 3, translated from the fifth, enlarged edition, by R. Taft (Bloomington: Indiana University Press, 1997), p. 123.
11 Ibid., p. 132.
12 Ibid., p. 123. Translation modified.
13 Ibid., p. 122.
14 In the cell, plasticity designates the power to form or to help form. Other terms derived from πλάσσειν/πλάττειν are (a) 'plasma', one of matter's simplest states (the fourth state); (b) 'protoplasm' (in German *protoplasma*): 'an organized substance, a complex and variable chemical compound which constitutes the living cell; (c) 'plaste': said of particles such as grains or filaments contained in the protoplasm of vegetal cells and which form its synthesizing agents.
15 Francisco Varela, in his fascinating study *Autonomie et connaissance. Essai sur le vivant* (Paris: Seuil, 1989), talks in terms of a 'structural plasticity' of these systems. In another context, the concept of 'plasticity' has become an important concept for the study of neural mechanisms involved in the mnemonic processes. See also Varela and H. Maturana, *Autopoiesis and Cognition*, Boston Studies in Philosophy of Science, vol. 42 (Dordrecht: Reidel, 1980), pp. 79–80. The American psychologist Donald Olding Hebb (1904–1985), author of *The Organization of Behavior* (London: J. Wiley and Sons, 1949) was the first to postulate the efficacy of their transmission. Towards the end of the 1930s, several results observed in experiments brought him to abandon the idea of a rigid localization of the circuits of memory (the reflex circuits responsible for the stimulus/response associations proposed by Pavlov). Hebb formulated the hypothesis of neural circuits able to organize themselves, in other words to modify their own connections during the neural activity required to perceive or to learn. The synapse is the privileged location where neural activity leaves a trace that can be modified by the repetition of a past functioning.

Since Hebb, 'plasticity' continues to denote the capacity of the synapse to modify its efficiency in transmission. Indeed, the work of the last twenty years has culminated in the proof that the synapse is not something set: in this sense, the synapses are not simple transmitters of nervous information, but themselves act to *form* and *inform* that information. Their ability to transmit signals from neuron to neuron can increase ('a long-term potentialization') or decrease ('long term degeneration') under the influence of the individual's milieu or 'history'. A more far-reaching and detailed study of these scientific discoveries will allow us to show the sense in which it can be asserted that the synapses are the brain's reserves of the *future*. See Sue D. Healy, 'Plasticité du cerveau et du comportement', in *Plasticité*, edited by Catherine Malabou (Paris: Editions Léo Scheer, 2000), pp. 98–114.

BIBLIOGRAPHY

Hegel in German

(a) G. W. F. Hegel, *Gesammelte Werke (G.W.), Studienausgaben auf der Grundlage der Akademieausgabe. Philosophische Bibliothek* (Hamburg: Felix Meiner Verlag, 1968–) (Abbreviated 'Meiner'):

PhB 319b: Jenaer Kritische Schriften (II): *Wissenschaftliche Behandlungsarten des Naturrechts.*

PhB 319c: Jenaer Kritische Schriften (III): *Glauben und Wissen.*

PhB 333: Jenaer Systementwürfe (III): *Naturphilosophie und Philosophie des Geistes.*

PhB 59/60, PhB 61/63: *Vorlesungen über die Philosophie der Religion.*

PhB 124a: *Grundlinien der Philosophie des Rechts.*

PhB 235–238b: *Briefe von und an Hegel.*

(b) *G. W. F. Hegel. Werke in zwanzig Bänden*, edited by E. Moldenhauer and K. M. Michel, 20 vols and Index (Frankfurt: Suhrkamp Verlag, 1983) (Abbreviated 'Suhrkamp').

Bd 2 : *Berliner Schriften 1818–1831.*

Bd 3 : *Phänomenologie des Geistes.*

Bd 4 : *Nürnberger und Heidelberger Schriften 1808–1817.*

Bd 5–6 : *Wissenschaft der Logik.*

Bd 12 : *Vorlesungen über die Philosophie der Geschichte.*

Bd 13–15 : *Vorlesungen über Ästhetik* I, II, III.

Bd 18–20 : *Vorlesungen über die Geschichte der Philosophie* I, II, III.

Hegels theologische Jugendschriften, hrsg. von Nohl (Tübingen, 1907).

Hegel in English

G. W. F. Hegel, *Early Theological Writings*, translated by T. M. Knox, with an introduction, and fragments translated by R. Kroner (Chicago: University of Chicago Press, 1948).

—— *Faith and Knowledge: An English Translation of 'Glauben und Wissen'*, translated and edited by W. Cerf and H. S. Harris (Albany: SUNY Press, 1977).

—— *Natural Law*, translated by T. M. Knox, introduction by H. B. Acton (Philadelphia: University of Pennsylvania Press, 1975).

—— *Phenomenology of Spirit,* translated by A. V. Miller, with analysis of the text and foreword by J. N. Findlay (Oxford: Oxford University Press, 1977).

—— *Science of Logic* (*Doctrine of Being, Doctrine of Essence, Doctrine of the Notion [Concept]*), translated by A.V. Miller, foreword by J. N. Findlay (Atlantic Highlands, NJ: Humanities Press International, 1989).

—— *The Encyclopædia Logic. Part 1 of the Encyclopædia of the Philosophical Sciences withe the Zusätze* [1830], translated by T. F. Geraets, W. A. Suchting and H. S. Harris (Indianapolis: Hackett Publishing, 1991).

—— *Philosophy of Nature, Part 2 of the Encyclopædia of the Philosophical Sciences,* edited and translated with an introduction and explanatory notes by M. J. Petry, 3 vols (London: George Allen and Unwin, 1970).

—— *Philosophy of Mind [Spirit]. Part 3 of the Encyclopædia of the Philosophical Sciences* (1830), translated by W. Wallace, together with the *Zusätze* in Boulmann's text (1845), translated by A.V. Miller, with foreword by J. N. Findlay (Oxford: Clarendon Press, 1971).

—— *Philosophy of Right*, translated with notes by T. M. Knox (Oxford: Clarendon Press, 1952).

—— *Elements of the Philosophy of Right*, edited by A. Wood, translated by H. B. Nisbet (Cambridge: Cambridge University Press, 1991).

—— *Lectures on the History of Philosophy*, translated by E. S. Haldane and F. H. Simpson, 3 vols (London: Routledge and Kegan Paul, 1955).

—— *Aesthetics. Lectures on Fine Arts*, translated by T. M. Knox, with an interpretative essay by C. Karelis (Oxford: Clarendon Press, 1975).

—— *The Philosophy of History*, translated by J. Sibree, with an introduction by C. J. Friedrich (New York: Dover Publication, 1956).

—— *Lectures on the Philosophy of Religion*, edited by P. C. Hodgson, translated by R. F. Brown, P. C. Hodgson and J. M. Stewart, with the assistance of H. S. Harris, 3 vols (Berkeley: University of California Press, 1984–7).

Hegel: The Letters, translated by C. Butler and C. Seiler, commentary by C. Butler (Bloomington: Indiana University Press, 1984).

Secondary works on Hegel

ALAIN, *Idées* (Paris: 'Champs' Flammarion, 1983), ch. 'Hegel', pp. 165–238.

AUBENQUE, P., 'Hegel et Aristote', in *Hegel et la pensée grecque*, publié sous la direction de Jacques d'Hondt (Paris: PUF, 1974), pp. 97–120.

BAPTIST, G., *Il Problema della modalità nelle logiche di Hegel. Un itinerario tra il possibile e il necessario* (Genoa: Pantograf, 1992).

BARNETT, S., ed., *Hegel after Derrida* (London and New York: Routledge, 1998).

BAUM, M., *Die Enstehung der Hegelschen Dialektik* (Bonn: Bouvier Verlag, 1986).

BEAUFRET, J., 'Hegel et la proposition spéculative', in *Dialogue avec Heidegger* (Paris: Minuit, 1973), pp. 110–142.

BOURGEOIS, B., 'Les Deux Âmes: de la nature à l'esprit', dans *De saint-Thomas à Hegel*, publié sous la direction de Jean-Louis Vieillard-Baron (Paris: PUF, 1994), pp. 117–151.

—— 'Le Dieu de Hegel: concept et création ', dans *La Question de Dieu selon Aristote et Hegel*, publié sous la direction de Thomas de Konninck et Guy Planty-Bonjour (Paris: PUF, 1991), pp. 285–320.

—— *Le Droit naturel de Hegel. Commentaire* (Paris: Vrin, 1986).

—— *Études hegeliennes* (Paris: PUF, 1992).

—— 'Entretien avec Francis Fukuyama', *Le Monde* (25 Feb. 1992), p. 2.

—— *Éternité et historicité de l'esprit selon Hegel* (Paris: Vrin, 1991).

—— 'Hegel et l'Incarnation selon Hans Küng', dans *Le Christ visage de Dieu*, 'Les Quatre Fleuves', *Cahiers de recherche et de réflexion religieuses*, no.4 (Paris: Seuil, 1975), pp. 81–84.

—— Présentation de la *Science de la logique de l'Encyclopédie des sciences philosophiques* (Paris: Vrin, 1970), pp. 7–112.

—— Présentation de la *Philosophie de l'esprit de l'Encyclopédie des sciences philosophiques* (Paris: Vrin, 1988), pp. 7–93.

BRITO, E., *La Christologie de Hegel. Verbum Crucis*, translated from the Spanish by B. Pottier (Paris: Beauchesne, 1983).

BURBIDGE, J., *On Hegel's Logic. Fragments of a Commentary* (Atlantic Highlands, NJ: Humanities Press, 1981).

CHAPELLE, A., *Hegel et la religion*, 3 vols (Paris: Éditions Universitaires, 1963–1971).

DERRIDA, J., *Glas*, translated by J. P. Leavey, Jr. and R. Rand (Lincoln: University of Nebraska Press, 1986).

—— '*Ousia* and *Grammè*', in *Margins of Philosophy*, translated, with additional notes, by A. Bass (Brighton: The Harvester Press, 1982).

—— 'Violence and Metaphysics', in *Writing and Difference*, translated with an introduction and additional notes by A. Bass (London: Routledge and Kegan Paul, 1978).

Dokumente zur Hegels Entwicklung, hrsg. von J. Hoffmeister (Stuttgart, 1936).

HEIDEGGER, M., *Hegels Phänomenologie des Geistes*, G. A. Bd 32. *Hegel's Phenomenology of Spirit,* translated by P. Emad and K. Maly (Bloomington: Indiana Press, 1988).

HOULGATE, S. *Freedom, Truth and History. An Introduction to Hegel's Philosophy* (London: Routledge 1991).

—— *Hegel, Nietzsche and the Criticism of Metaphysics* (Cambridge: Cambridge University Press, 1986).

INWOOD, M., *A Hegel Dictionary* (Oxford: Blackwell Publishers, 1992).

JANICAUD, D., *Hegel et le destin de la Grèce* (Paris: Vrin, 1975).

KERN, W., 'Eine Übersetzung Hegels zu *De Anima*, III, 4–5, mitgeteilt und erläutert', *Hegel-Studien* 1, 1961, pp. 49–88.

—— 'Die Aristotelesdeutung Hegels. Die Aufhebung des Aristotelischen "Nous" in Hegel's "Geist"', *Philosophisches Jahrbuch* 78, 1971, pp. 237–259.

KOJÈVE, A., *An Introduction to the Reading of Hegel*: *Lectures on the 'Phenomenology of Spirit'*, edited by A. Bloom, translated by J. H. Nichols, Jr. (Ithaca: Cornell University Press, 1980).

KOLB, D., *The Critique of Pure Modernity: Hegel, Heidegger, and After* (Chicago: University of Chicago Press, 1987).

KOYRÉ, A., 'Hegel à Iéna', in *Études d'histoire de la pensée philosophique* (Paris: NRF Gallimard, 1971), pp. 148–189.

KRONER, R., *Von Kant bis Hegel*, 2 vols (Tübingen: J. C. B. Mohr, 1921–1924).

KÜNG, H., *Menschwerdung Gottes* (Freiburg: Herder, 1970).

LABARRIÈRE, P.J., 'Histoire et liberté', *Archives de philosophie*, 33, Oct.–Dec. 1970, pp. 701–718.

LEBRUN, G., *La Patience du concept, Essai sur le discours hégélien* (Paris: N.R.F. Gallimard, 1972).

LÉONARD, A., 'Le Droit de l'absolu chez Bruaire', dans *La Question de Dieu selon Aristote et Hegel*, publié sous la direction de Thomas de Konninck et Guy Planty-Bonjour (Paris: PUF, 1991), pp. 401–405.

NANCY, J.-L., *The Speculative Remark*, translated by C. Surprenant (Stanford: Stanford University Press, 2001).

PEPERSACK, A., 'Selbsterkenntnis des Absoluten. Grundlinien der Hegelschen Philosophie des Geistes', *Spekulation und Erfahrung. Texte und Untersuchungen zum Deutschen Idealismus*, II, Bd 6 (Frommann-Holzboog, 1987).

PIPPIN, R., *Hegel's Idealism. The Satisfactions of Self-consciousness* (Cambridge: Cambridge University Press, 1989).

PLOTNITSKY, A., *In the Shadow of Hegel: Complementarity, History and the Unconscious* (Gainesville: University of Florida Press, 1993).

PÖGGELER, O., 'Hölderlin, Schelling und Hegel bei Heidegger', *Hegel-Studien*, 28, 1993, pp. 327–371.

ROSE, G., *Hegel Contra Sociology* (London: Athlone Press, 1981).

SOUCHE-DAGUES, D., *Recherches hégéliennes. Infini et dialectique* (Paris: Vrin, 1984).

STANGUENNEC, A., *Hegel, critique de Kant* (Paris: PUF, 1985).

VAN DER MEULEN, J., 'Hegels Lehre von Leib, Seele und Geist', *Hegel-Studien* 2, 1963, pp. 251–280.

WARMINSKI, A., *Readings in Interpretation: Hölderlin, Hegel, Heidegger* (Minneapolis: University of Minnesota Press, 1987).

WESTPHAL, K. R., *Hegel's Epistemological Realism. A Study of the Aim and Method of Hegel's Phenomenology of Spirit* (Dordrecht: Kluwer, 1989).

Other references

ALTHAUS, P., *Die Theologie Martin Luthers* (Gütersloh, 1963).

ARISTOTLE, *The Complete Works of Aristotle*, English translation edited by Jonathan Barnes (Princeton: Princeton University Press, 1984):

—— *On Generation and Corruption*, vol. I.

—— *Metaphysics*, vol. II.

—— *Parts of Animals*, vol. I.

—— *On the Soul*, vol. II.

AUBENQUE, P., *Le Problème de l'être chez Aristote* (Paris: PUF, 1962).

BALTHASAR, U. von, *Prometheus. Studien zur Geschichte des deutschen Idealismus* (Heidelberg, 1947).

BARTH, K., *Die protestantische Theologie im 19. Jahrhundert, ihre Vorgeschichte und ihre Geschichte*, zweite verbesserte Ausgabe (Zürich: Evangelischer Verlag, Zollicon, 1952).

—— *Protestant Theology from Rousseau to Ritschl*, translated by B. Cozens and H. H. Hartwell (New York: Harper and Row, 1959).

BEAUFRET, J., Présentation à la traduction du *Poème* de Parménide (Paris: PUF, 1955).

BERGSON, H., L'Évolution créatrice, Collection 'Quadrige' (Paris: PUF, 1969); *Creative Evolution*, translated by A. Mitchell (Lanham, MD: University Press of America, 1911).

BICHAT, F. X., *Physiological Researches on Life and Death,* edited by R. J. Kastenbaum, translated by F. Gold (Ayer Company Publishers, 1977).

BLANCHOT, M., *The Space of Literature*, translated by A. Smock (Lincoln: University of Nebraska Press, 1982).

BRETON, S., *Être, monde, imaginaire* (Paris: Seuil, 1976).

CANGUILHEM, G., *Études d'histoire et de philosophie des sciences* (Paris: Vrin, 1970, 2nd edition).

CHRÉTIEN, J. L., 'Le Bien donne ce qu'il n'a pas', *Archives de philosophie*, vol. XXLIII, 1980, Cahier 2, pp. 263–298.

CUVIER, G., *Fossil Bones, and Geological Catastrophes*, translated by M. J. S. Rudwick (Chicago: Chicago University Press, 1997).

DELEUZE, G., *Difference and Repetition*, translated by P. Patton (New York: Columbia University Press, 1994).

DERRIDA, J., *L'Écriture et la difference* (Paris: Seuil, 1967); *Of Grammatology*, trans. by G.C. Spivak (Baltimore: Johns Hopkins University Press, 1976).

Dictionnaire de théologie catholique (Paris: Librairie Letouzey et Ana, 1925).

Die Bekenntnisschriften der evangelischer-lutherischen Kirche [BSLK], (Göttingen: Vandenhoeck und Ruprecht, 1979).

FEUERBACH, L., *Das Wesen des Christenthums* (Frommann Verlag: Stuttgart, 1903). *The Essence of Christianity*, Introduction translated by Z. Hanti (1972), remainder translated by G. Eliot (1854), transcribed by A. Blunden.

GADAMER, H. G., *Hermeneutik* I, *Wahrheit und Methode* (Tübingen: J.C.B. Mohr, G.W. 1). *Truth and Method*, 2nd revised edition; revised and translated by J. Weinsheimer and D. G. Marshall (Crossroad Publishing Company, 1989).

HEALY, S. D., 'Plasticité du cerveau et du comportement', *in Plasticité* edited by Catherine Malabou (Paris: Editions Léo Scheer, 2000), pp. 98–114.

HEBB, D. O., *The Organization of Behaviour* (London: J. Wiley and Sons, 1949).

HEIDEGGER, M., *Gesamtausgabe* (Frankfurt am Main: Vittorio Klostermann).

—— *Aristoteles Metaphysik*, G. A. Bd 9, *Aristotle's Metaphysics Theta 1–3. On the Essence and Actuality of Force,* translated by W. Brogan and P. Warnek (Bloomington: Indiana University Press, 1995).

—— *Sein und Zeit*, G. A. Bd 2. *Being and Time*, translated by Joan Stambaugh (Albany: State University of New York Press, 1996).

—— *Kant und das Problem der Metaphysik*, G. A. Bd 3. *Kant and the Problem of Metaphysics*, translated from the fifth, enlarged edition, by R. Taft (Bloomington: Indiana University Press, 1997).

—— *Einführung in die Metaphysik*, G. A. Bd 40. *Introduction to Metaphysics*, translated by G. Fried and R. Polk (New Haven and London: Yale University Press, 2000).

—— *Thor Seminar* (Max Niemeyer Verlag, 1969). 'A Heidegger Seminar on Hegel's *Differenzschrift', Southwest Journal of Philosophy*, 11: 9–45.

JÜNGEL, E., *Gott als Geheimnis der Welt* (Tübingen, J.C.B. Mohr, 1978). *God as the Mystery of the World*, translated by D. L. Guder (Grand Rapids, MI: Eerdmans Publishing Company, 1983).

KANT, I., *Werksausgabe*, Suhrkamp Verlag.

—— *Anthropology from a Pragmatic Point of View*, translated by V. Lyle Downdell (Carbondale: Southern Illinois University Press, 1978).

—— *Critique of Pure Reason*, translated by N. Kemp-Smith, 2nd edition (London and Basingstoke: Macmillan, 1933).

—— *Critique of Judgment*, translated by W. Pluhar (Indianapolis: Hackett, 1987).

LALANDE, A., *Vocabulaire technique et critique de la philosophie* (Paris: PUF, 1931).

MARION, J.L., *Sur l'ontologie grise de Descartes* (Paris: Vrin, 1981).

—— *God without Being,* translated by T. A. Carlson (Chicago: University of Chicago Press, 1991).

RAVAISSON, F., *De l'habitude*, 'Corpus des œuvres de philosophie en langue française' (Paris: Fayard, 1984).

RICŒUR, P., *Lectures 3. Aux frontières de la philosophie* (Paris: Seuil, 1994).

ROUSTANG, F., *Influence* (Paris: Minuit, 1990).

STROHL, H., *Luther jusqu'en 1520* (Paris: PUF, 1962).

TILLIETTE, X., 'L'Exinanition du Christ: théologies de la kénose', in *Le Christ visage de Dieu*, 'Les Quatre Fleuves', *Cahiers de recherche et de réflexion religieuses*, no. 4 (Paris: Seuil, 1975), pp. 48–59.

VARELA, F., *Autonomie et connaissance. Essai sur le vivant* (Paris: Seuil, 1989).

—— with H. Maturana: *Autopoiesis and Cognition*, Boston Studies in Philosophy of Science, vol. 42 (Dordrecht: Reidel, 1980).

INDEX

Made in the USA
San Bernardino, CA
05 April 2016